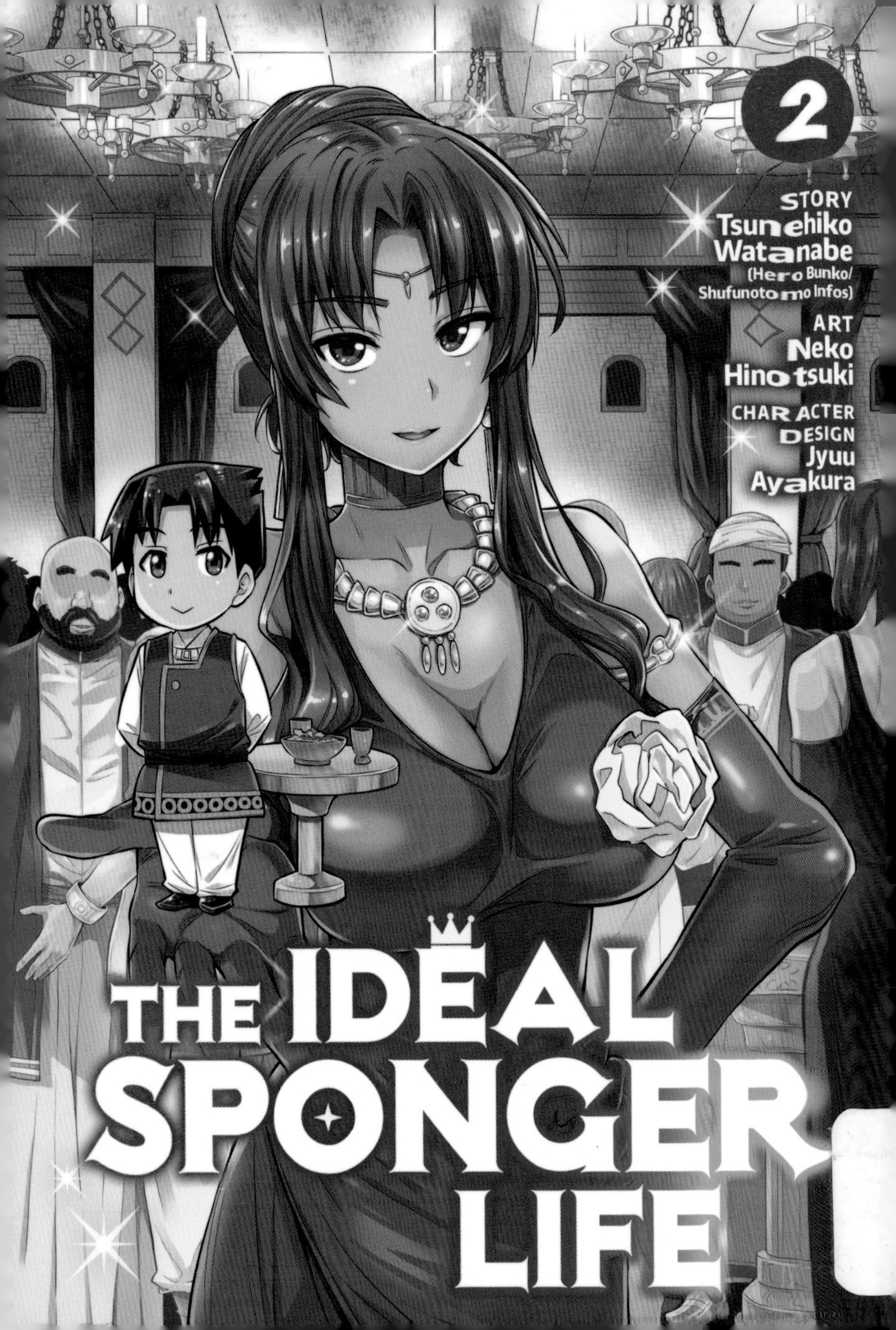
2
STORY
Tsunehiko Watanabe
(Hero Bunko/ Shufunotomo Infos)
ART
Neko Hinotsuki
CHARACTER DESIGN
Jyuu Ayakura
THE IDEAL SPONGER LIFE

CHAPTER 6

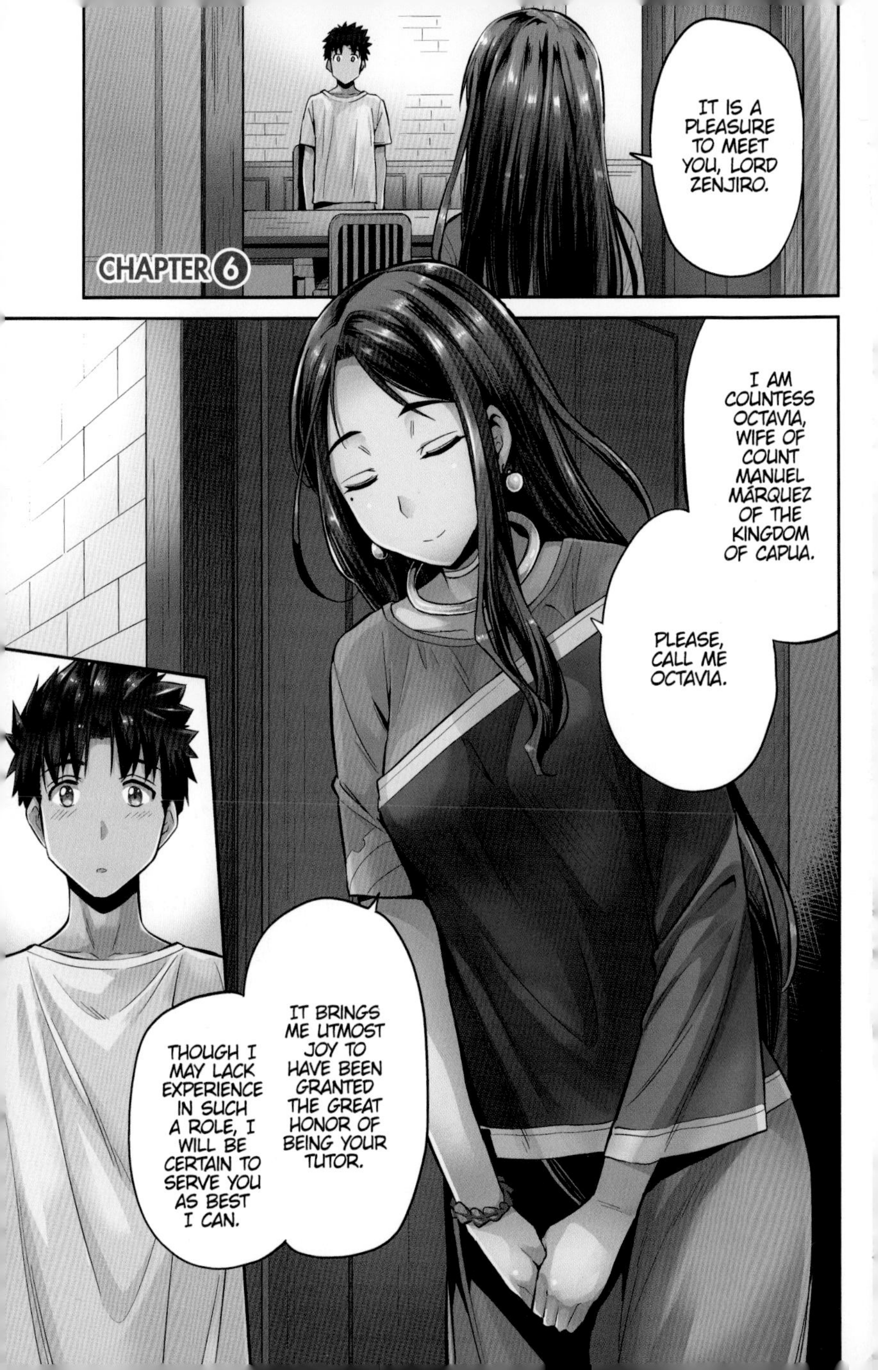
IT IS A PLEASURE TO MEET YOU, LORD ZENJIRO.
I AM COUNTESS OCTAVIA, WIFE OF COUNT MANUEL MÁRQUEZ OF THE KINGDOM OF CAPUA.
PLEASE, CALL ME OCTAVIA.
IT BRINGS ME UTMOST JOY TO HAVE BEEN GRANTED THE GREAT HONOR OF BEING YOUR TUTOR.
THOUGH I MAY LACK EXPERIENCE IN SUCH A ROLE, I WILL BE CERTAIN TO SERVE YOU AS BEST I CAN.

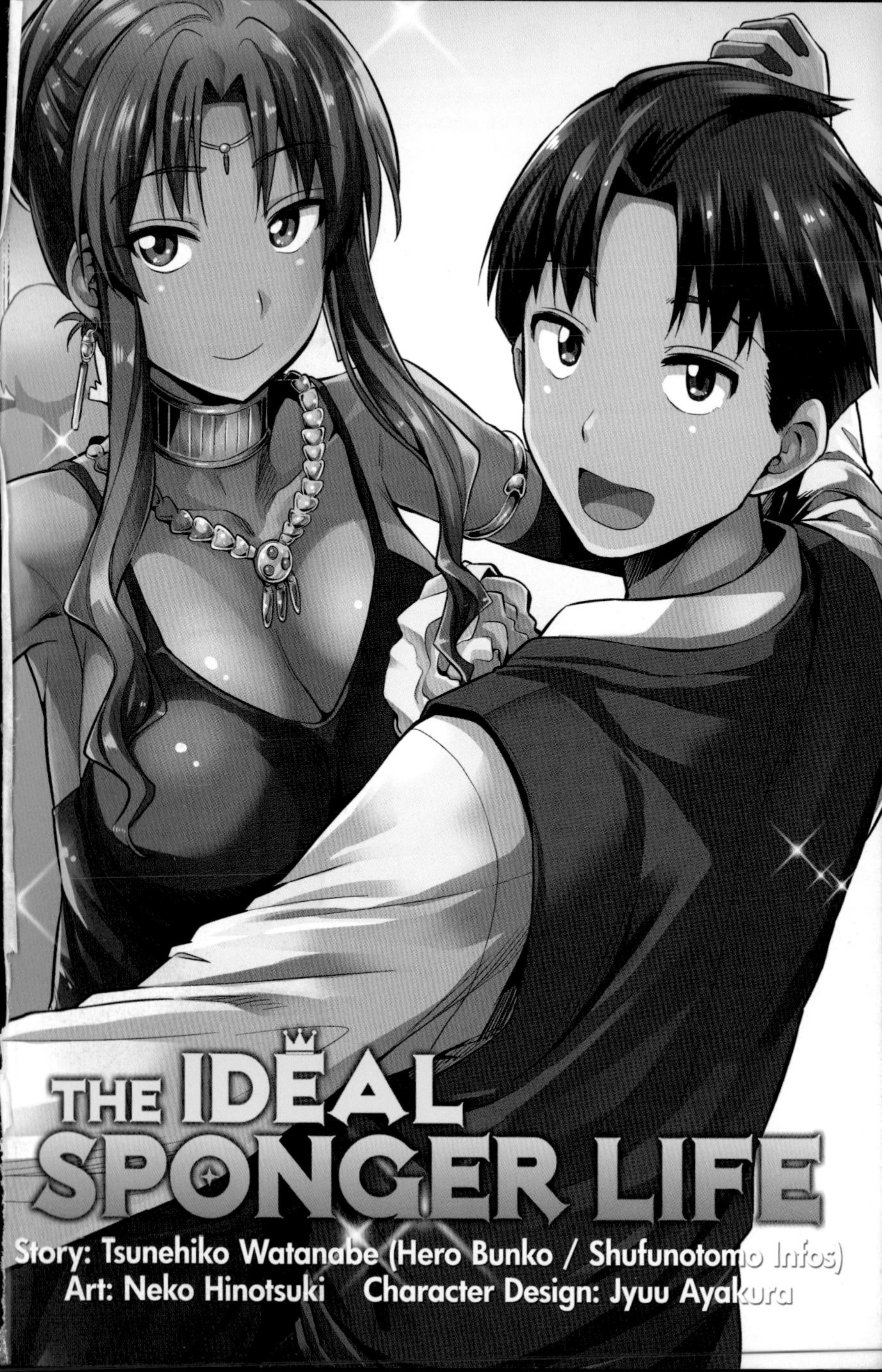
THE IDEAL SPONGER LIFE
Story: Tsunehiko Watanabe (Hero Bunko / Shufunotomo Infos)
Art: Neko Hinotsuki Character Design: Jyuu Ayakura

CHAPTER 6
A Lecture on Magic

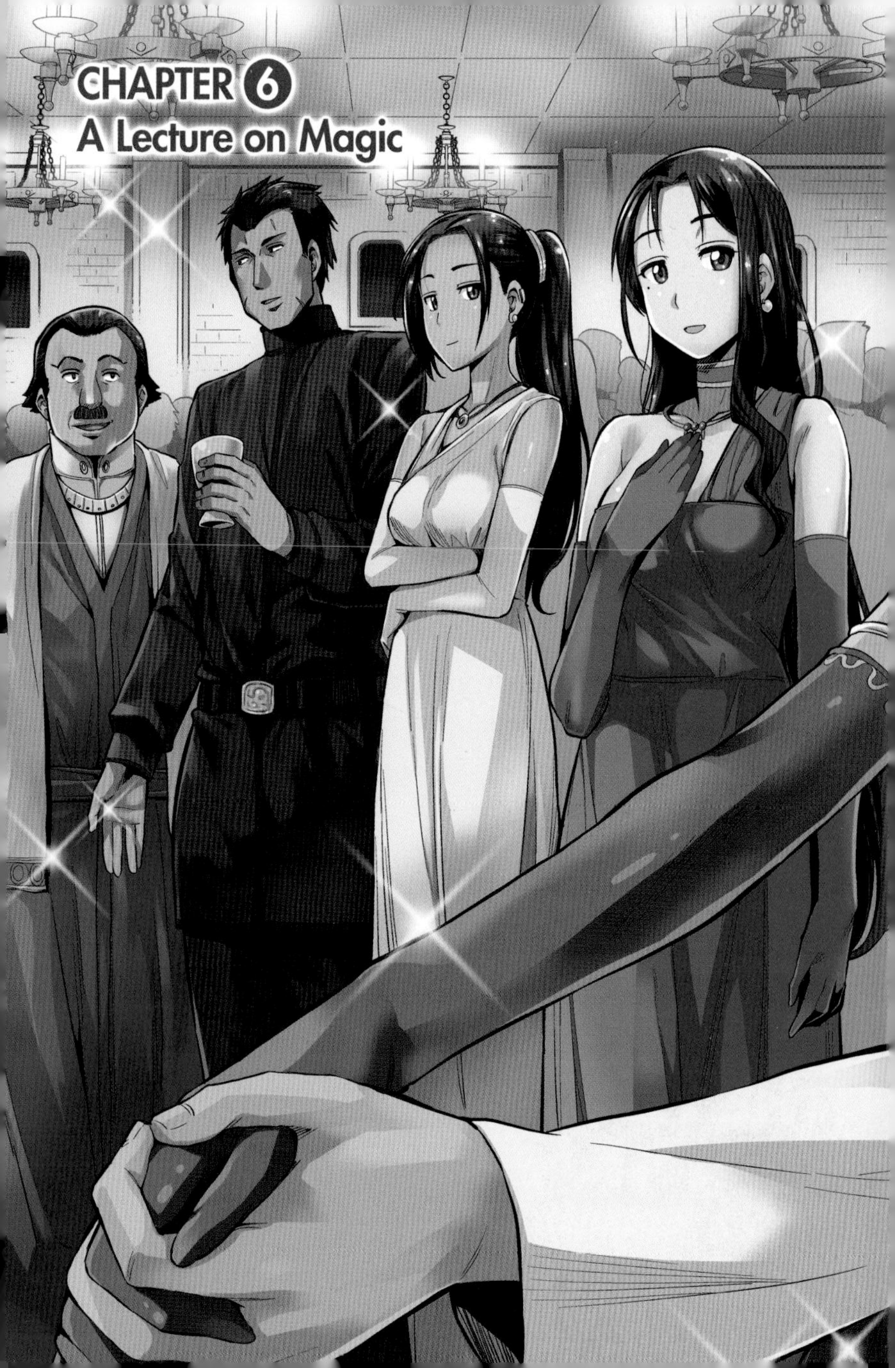

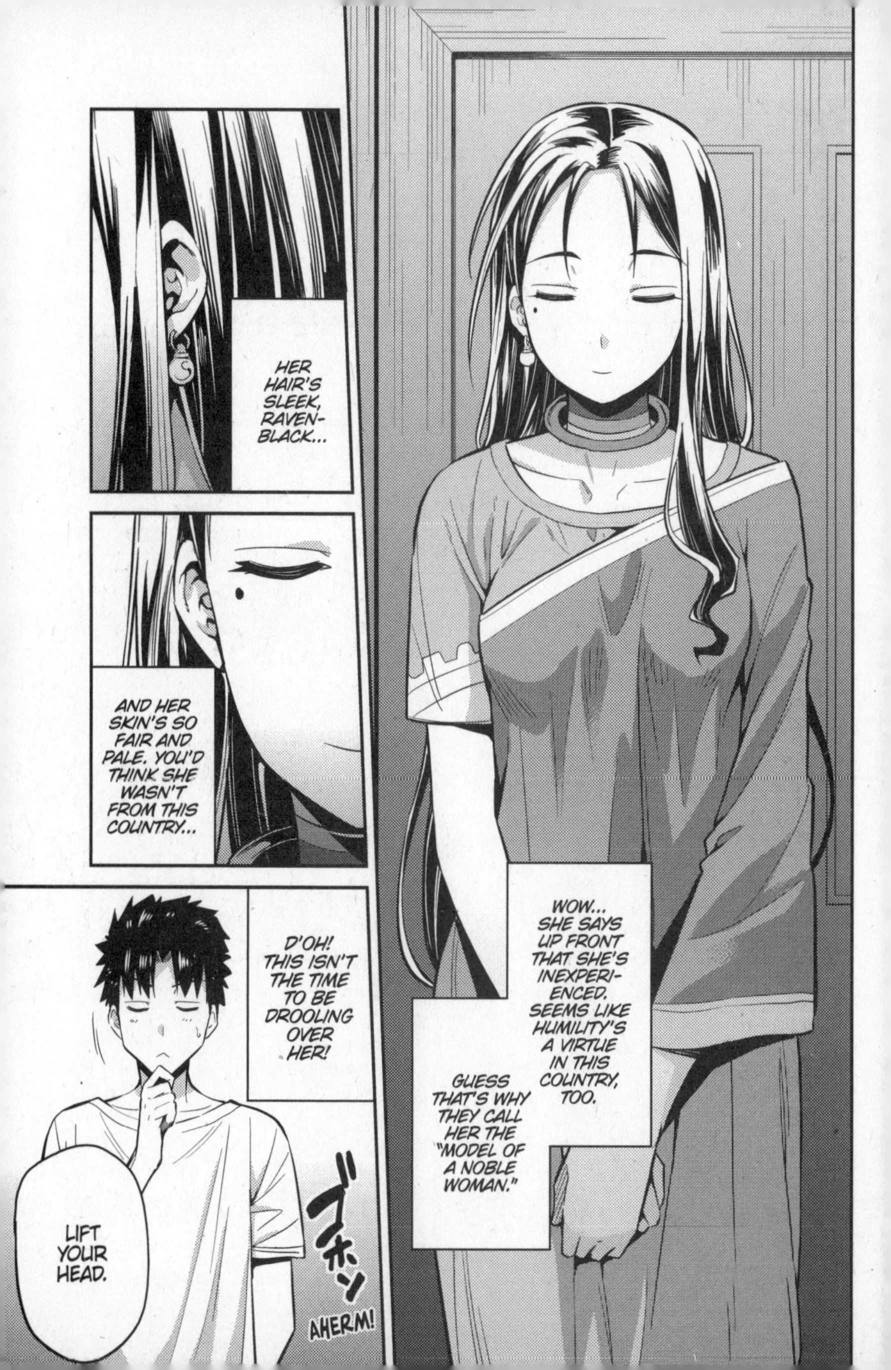
WOW... SHE SAYS UP FRONT THAT SHE'S INEXPERIENCED. SEEMS LIKE HUMILITY'S A VIRTUE IN THIS COUNTRY, TOO.
GUESS THAT'S WHY THEY CALL HER THE "MODEL OF A NOBLE WOMAN."
HER HAIR'S SLEEK, RAVEN-BLACK...
AND HER SKIN'S SO FAIR AND PALE. YOU'D THINK SHE WASN'T FROM THIS COUNTRY...
D'OH! THIS ISN'T THE TIME TO BE DROOLING OVER HER!
ゴホン
AHERM!
LIFT YOUR HEAD.

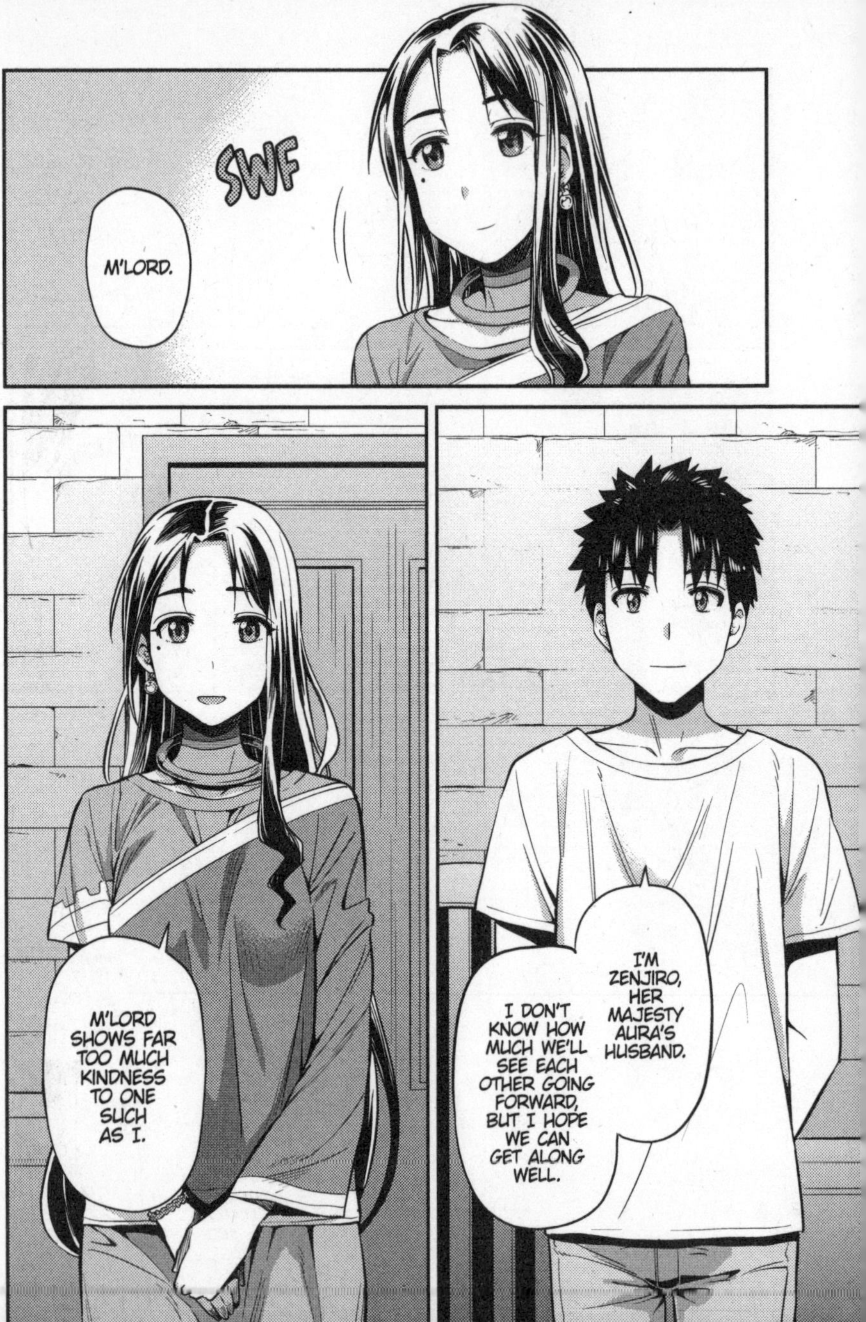
SWF
M'LORD.
I'M ZENJIRO, HER MAJESTY AURA'S HUSBAND.
I DON'T KNOW HOW MUCH WE'LL SEE EACH OTHER GOING FORWARD, BUT I HOPE WE CAN GET ALONG WELL.
M'LORD SHOWS FAR TOO MUCH KINDNESS TO ONE SUCH AS I.

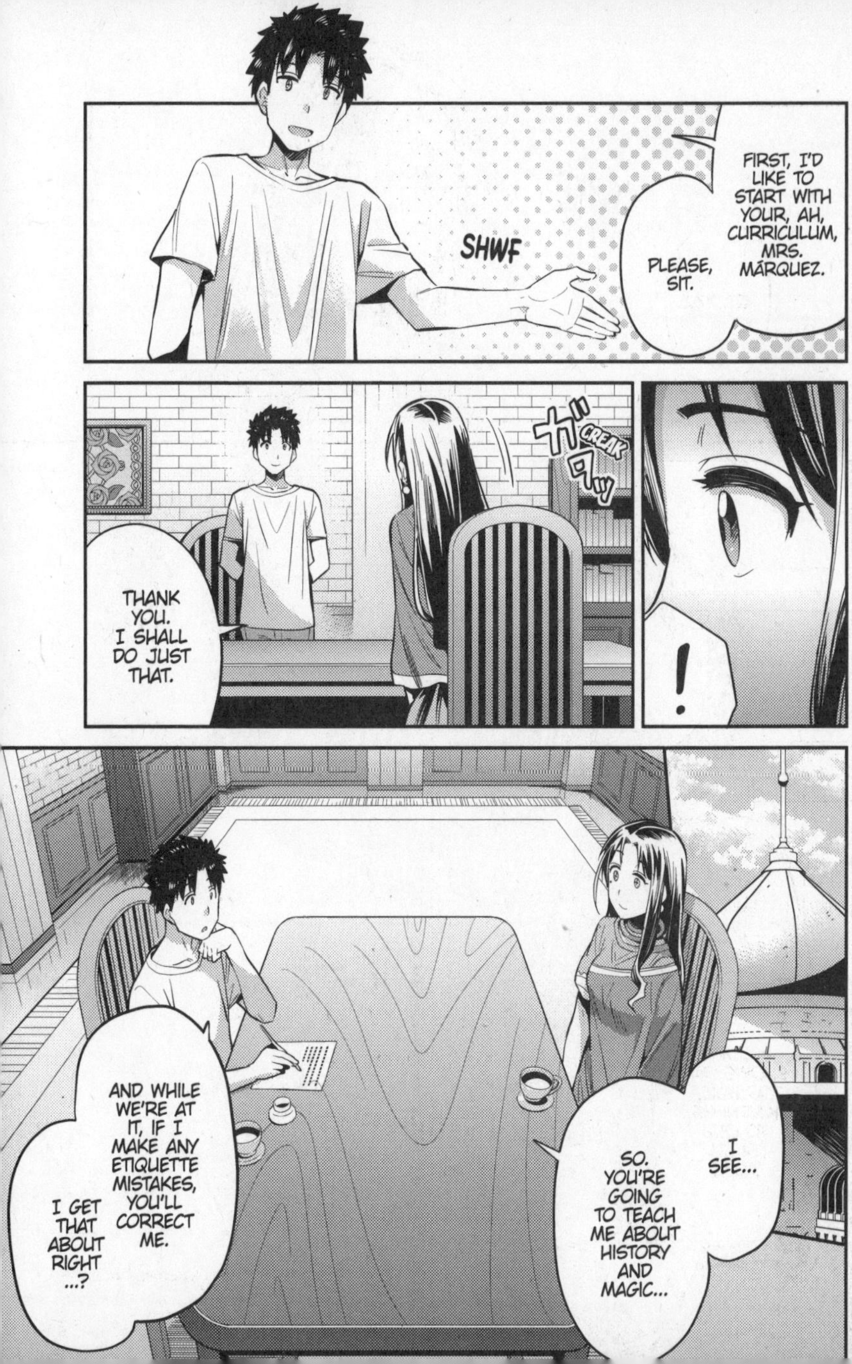
FIRST, I'D LIKE TO START WITH YOUR, AH, CURRICULUM, MRS. MÁRQUEZ.
PLEASE, SIT.
SHWF
!
ガタッ
CREAK
THANK YOU. I SHALL DO JUST THAT.
I SEE...
SO. YOU'RE GOING TO TEACH ME ABOUT HISTORY AND MAGIC...
AND WHILE WE'RE AT IT, IF I MAKE ANY ETIQUETTE MISTAKES, YOU'LL CORRECT ME.
I GET THAT ABOUT RIGHT ...?

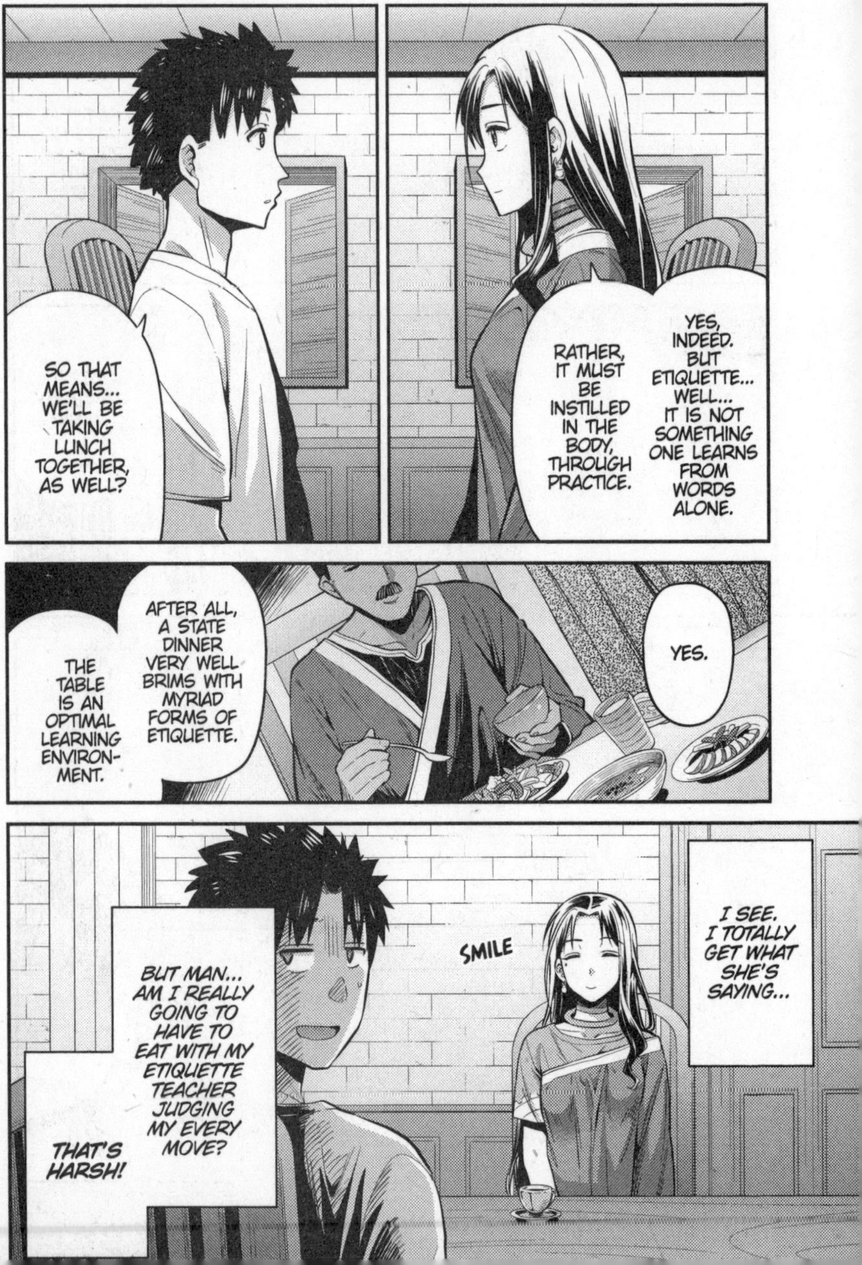
YES, INDEED. BUT ETIQUETTE... WELL... IT IS NOT SOMETHING ONE LEARNS FROM WORDS ALONE.
RATHER, IT MUST BE INSTILLED IN THE BODY, THROUGH PRACTICE.
SO THAT MEANS... WE'LL BE TAKING LUNCH TOGETHER, AS WELL?
YES.
AFTER ALL, A STATE DINNER VERY WELL BRIMS WITH MYRIAD FORMS OF ETIQUETTE.
THE TABLE IS AN OPTIMAL LEARNING ENVIRON-MENT.
I SEE. I TOTALLY GET WHAT SHE'S SAYING...
SMILE
BUT MAN... AM I REALLY GOING TO HAVE TO EAT WITH MY ETIQUETTE TEACHER JUDGING MY EVERY MOVE?
THAT'S HARSH!

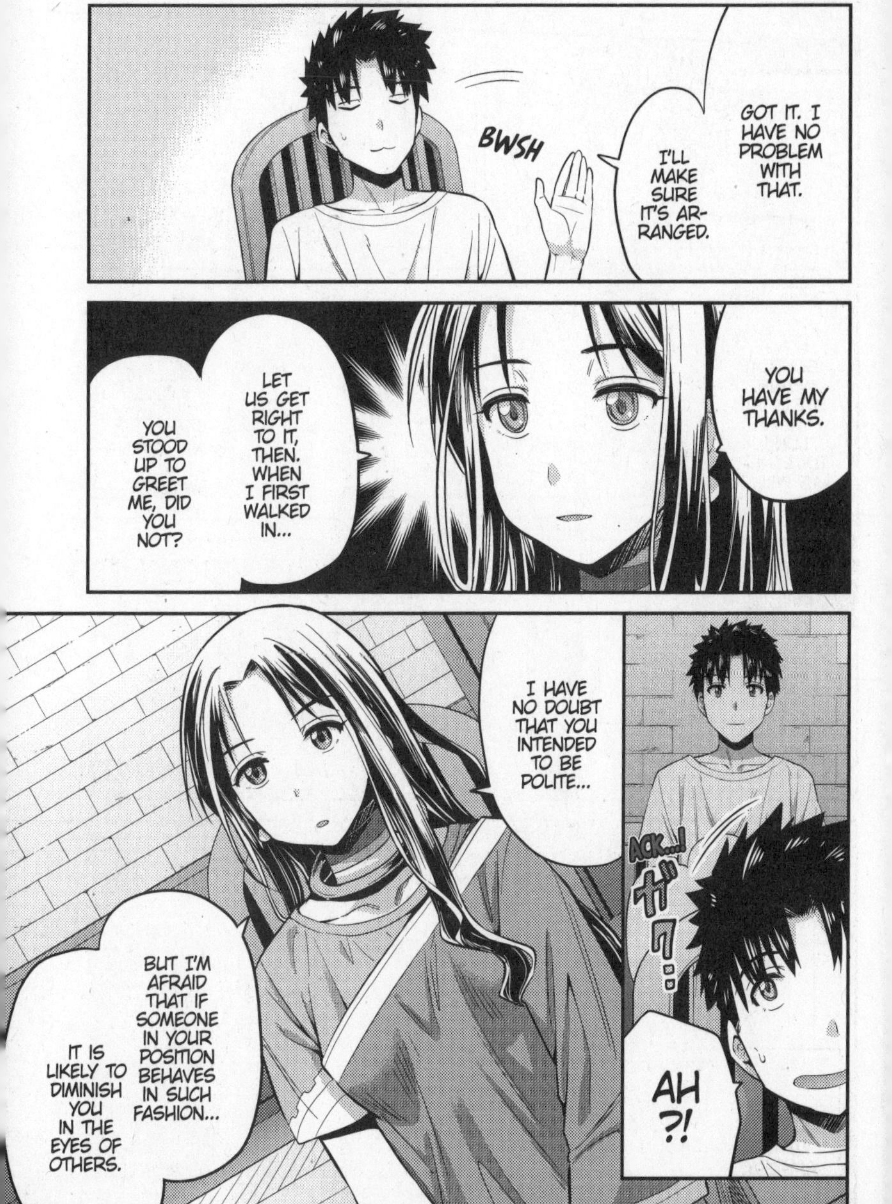
GOT IT. I HAVE NO PROBLEM WITH THAT.
I'LL MAKE SURE IT'S ARRANGED.
BWSH
YOU HAVE MY THANKS.
LET US GET RIGHT TO IT, THEN. WHEN I FIRST WALKED IN...
YOU STOOD UP TO GREET ME, DID YOU NOT?
ACK...!
AH ?!
I HAVE NO DOUBT THAT YOU INTENDED TO BE POLITE...
BUT I'M AFRAID THAT IF SOMEONE IN YOUR POSITION BEHAVES IN SUCH FASHION...
IT IS LIKELY TO DIMINISH YOU IN THE EYES OF OTHERS.

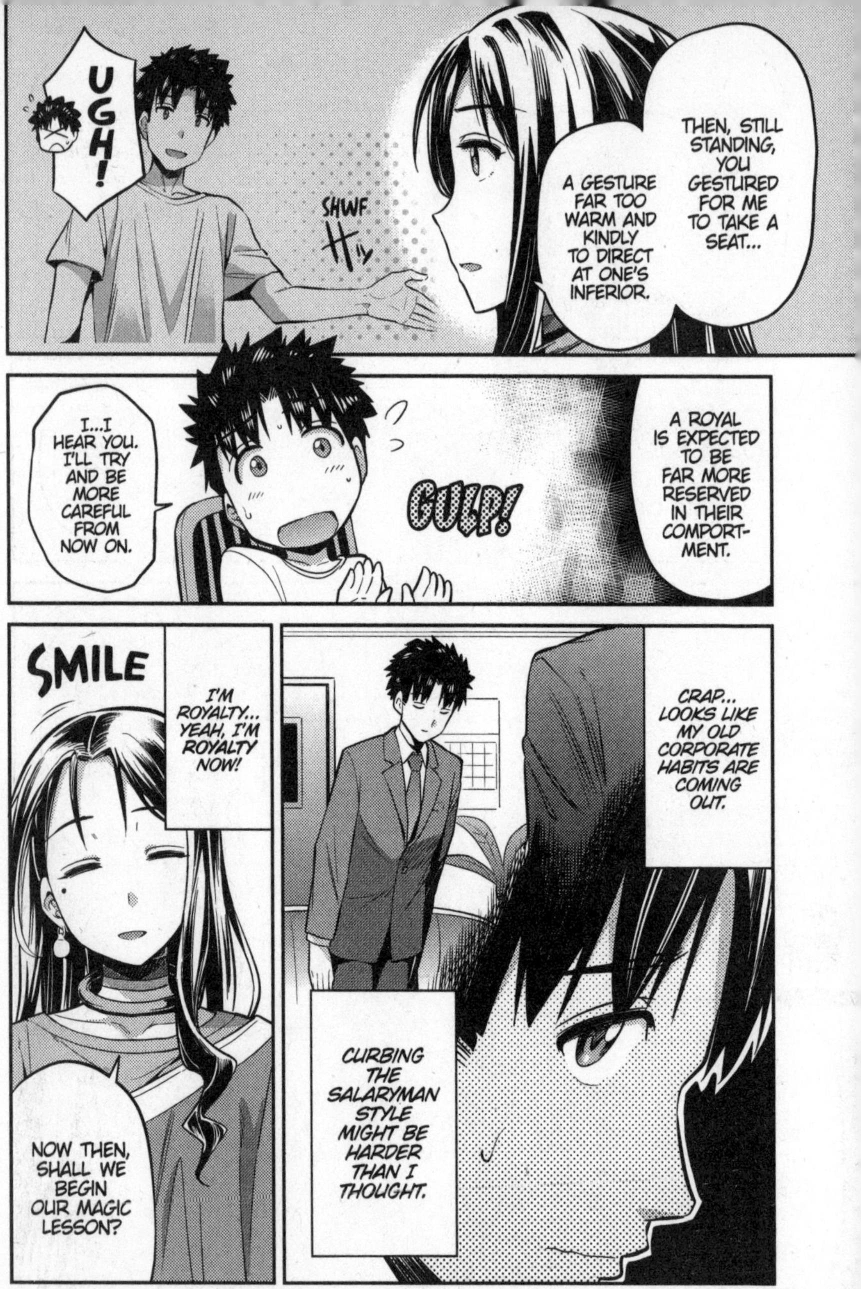
THEN, STILL STANDING, YOU GESTURED FOR ME TO TAKE A SEAT...
A GESTURE FAR TOO WARM AND KINDLY TO DIRECT AT ONE'S INFERIOR.
SHWF
UGH!
A ROYAL IS EXPECTED TO BE FAR MORE RESERVED IN THEIR COMPORT-MENT.
GULP!
I...I HEAR YOU. I'LL TRY AND BE MORE CAREFUL FROM NOW ON.
CRAP... LOOKS LIKE MY OLD CORPORATE HABITS ARE COMING OUT.
CURBING THE SALARYMAN STYLE MIGHT BE HARDER THAN I THOUGHT.
I'M ROYALTY... YEAH, I'M ROYALTY NOW!
SMILE
NOW THEN, SHALL WE BEGIN OUR MAGIC LESSON?

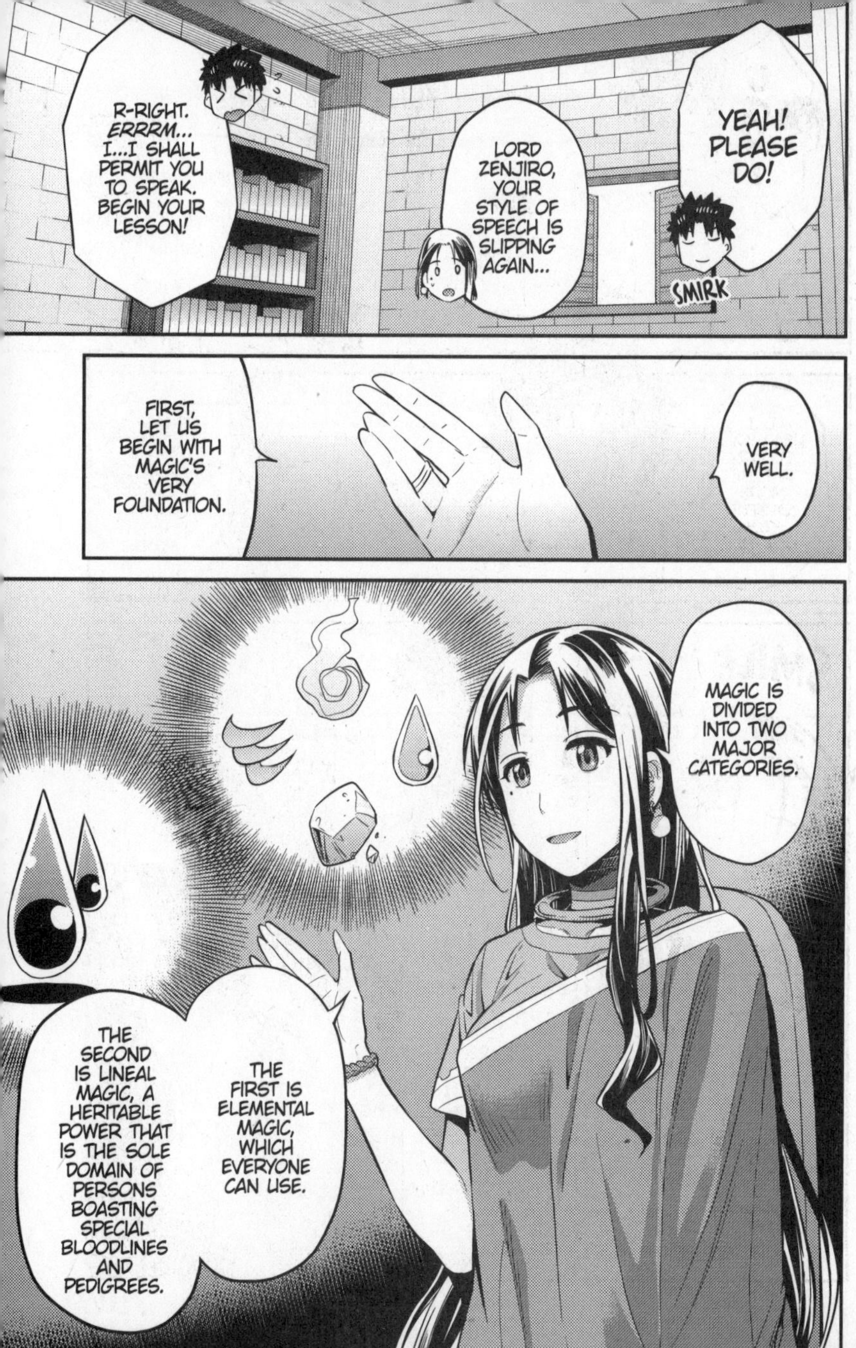
YEAH! PLEASE DO!
SMIRK
LORD ZENJIRO, YOUR STYLE OF SPEECH IS SLIPPING AGAIN...
R-RIGHT. *ERRRM...* I...I SHALL PERMIT YOU TO SPEAK. BEGIN YOUR LESSON!
VERY WELL.
FIRST, LET US BEGIN WITH MAGIC'S VERY FOUNDATION.
MAGIC IS DIVIDED INTO TWO MAJOR CATEGORIES.
THE FIRST IS ELEMENTAL MAGIC, WHICH EVERYONE CAN USE.
THE SECOND IS LINEAL MAGIC, A HERITABLE POWER THAT IS THE SOLE DOMAIN OF PERSONS BOASTING SPECIAL BLOODLINES AND PEDIGREES.

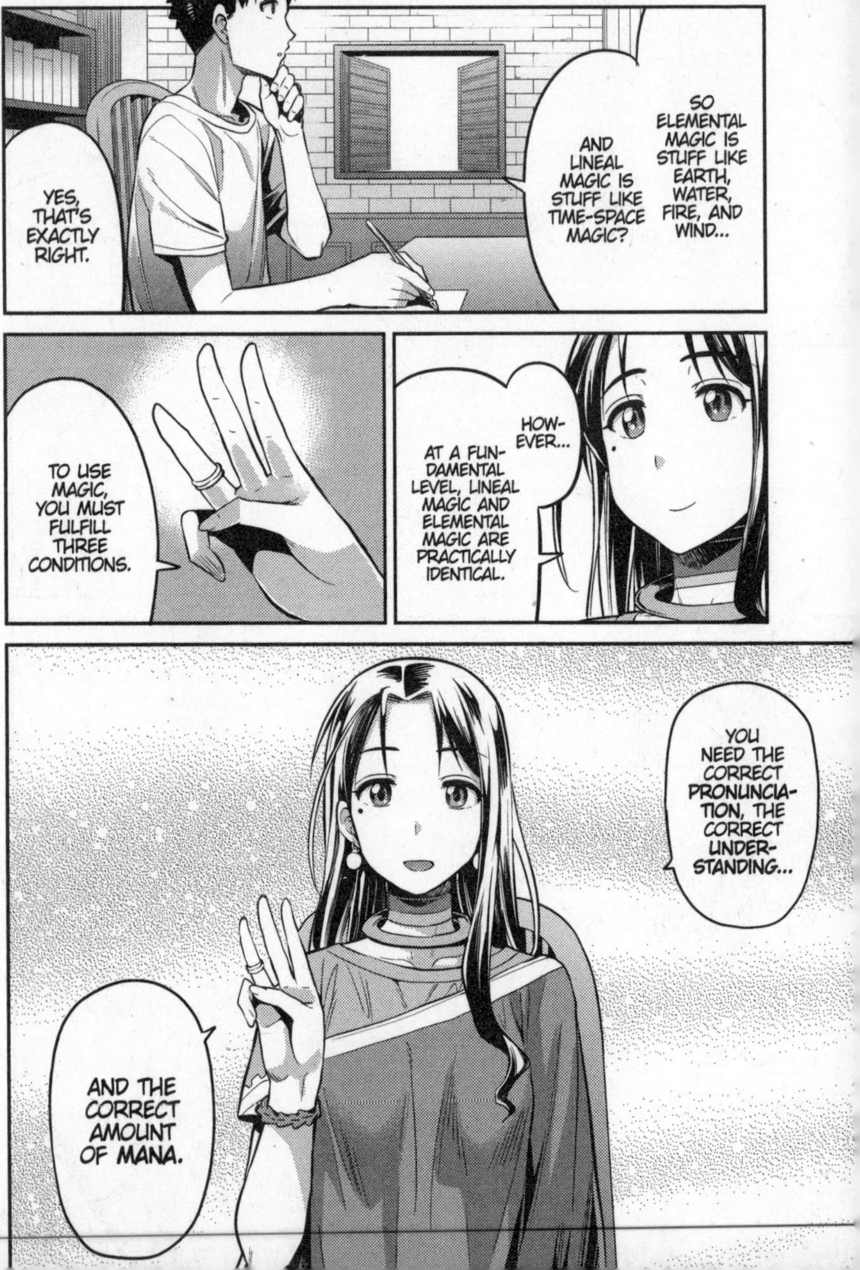
SO ELEMENTAL MAGIC IS STUFF LIKE EARTH, WATER, FIRE, AND WIND...
AND LINEAL MAGIC IS STUFF LIKE TIME-SPACE MAGIC?
YES, THAT'S EXACTLY RIGHT.
HOW-EVER...
AT A FUN-DAMENTAL LEVEL, LINEAL MAGIC AND ELEMENTAL MAGIC ARE PRACTICALLY IDENTICAL.
TO USE MAGIC, YOU MUST FULFILL THREE CONDITIONS.
YOU NEED THE CORRECT PRONUNCIA-TION, THE CORRECT UNDER-STANDING...
AND THE CORRECT AMOUNT OF MANA.

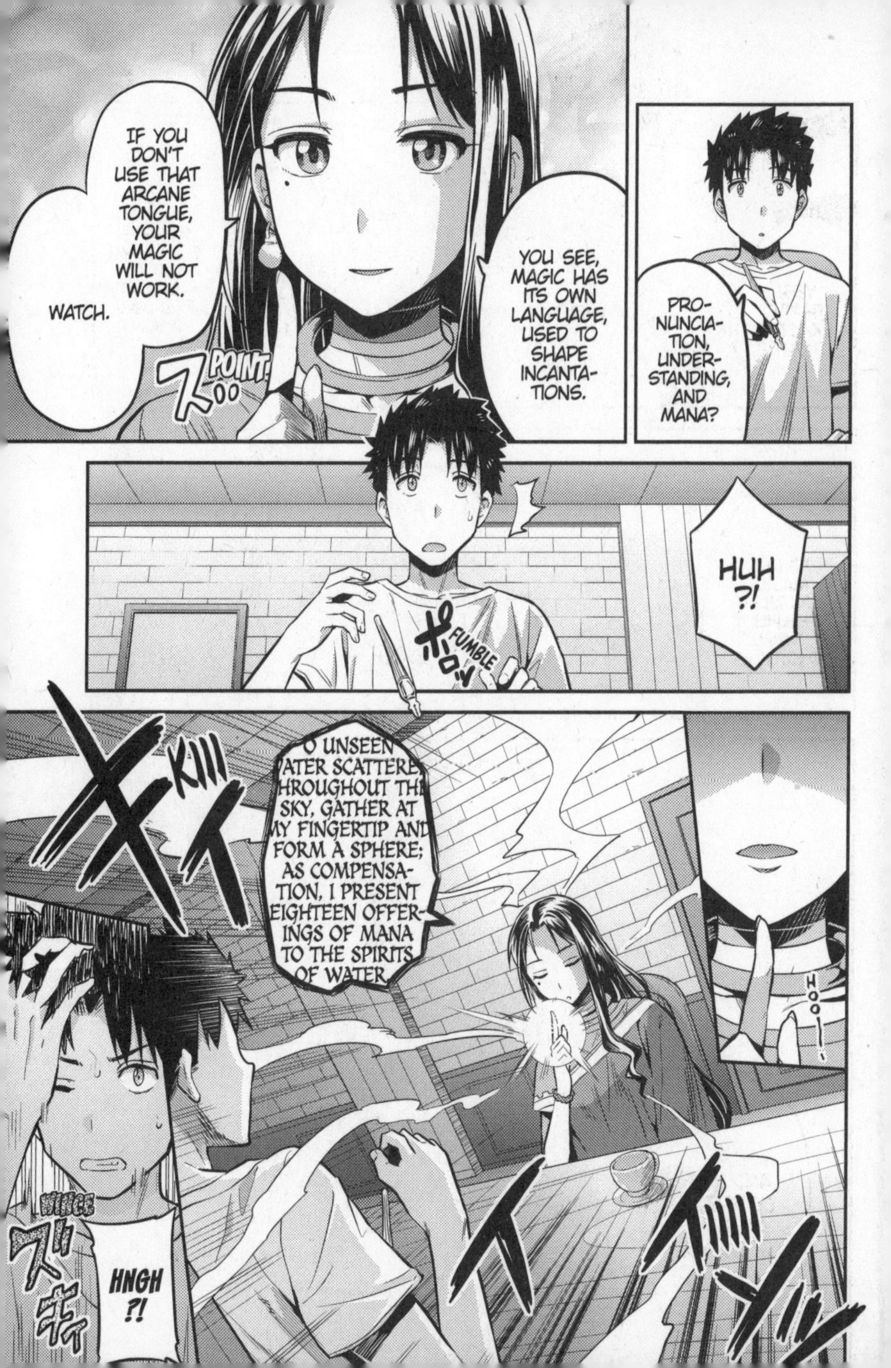
PRO-NUNCIATION, UNDER-STANDING, AND MANA?
YOU SEE, MAGIC HAS ITS OWN LANGUAGE, USED TO SHAPE INCANTA-TIONS.
IF YOU DON'T USE THAT ARCANE TONGUE, YOUR MAGIC WILL NOT WORK.
WATCH.
POINT
HUH ?!
FUMBLE
O UNSEEN WATER SCATTERED THROUGHOUT THE SKY, GATHER AT MY FINGERTIP AND FORM A SPHERE; AS COMPENSA-TION, I PRESENT EIGHTEEN OFFER-INGS OF MANA TO THE SPIRITS OF WATER.
KIII
HOO...
WINCE
HNGH ?!

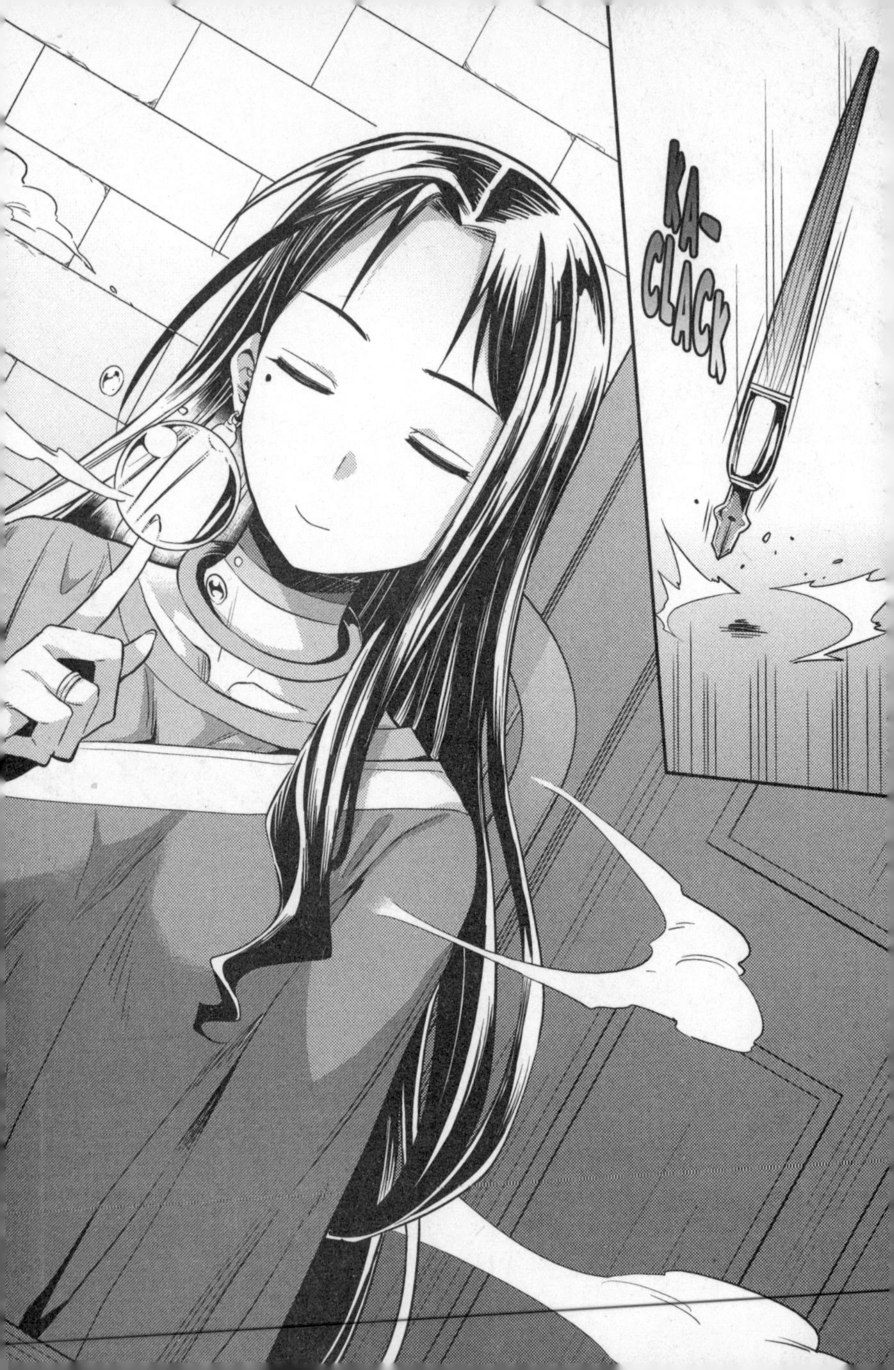
KA-CLACK

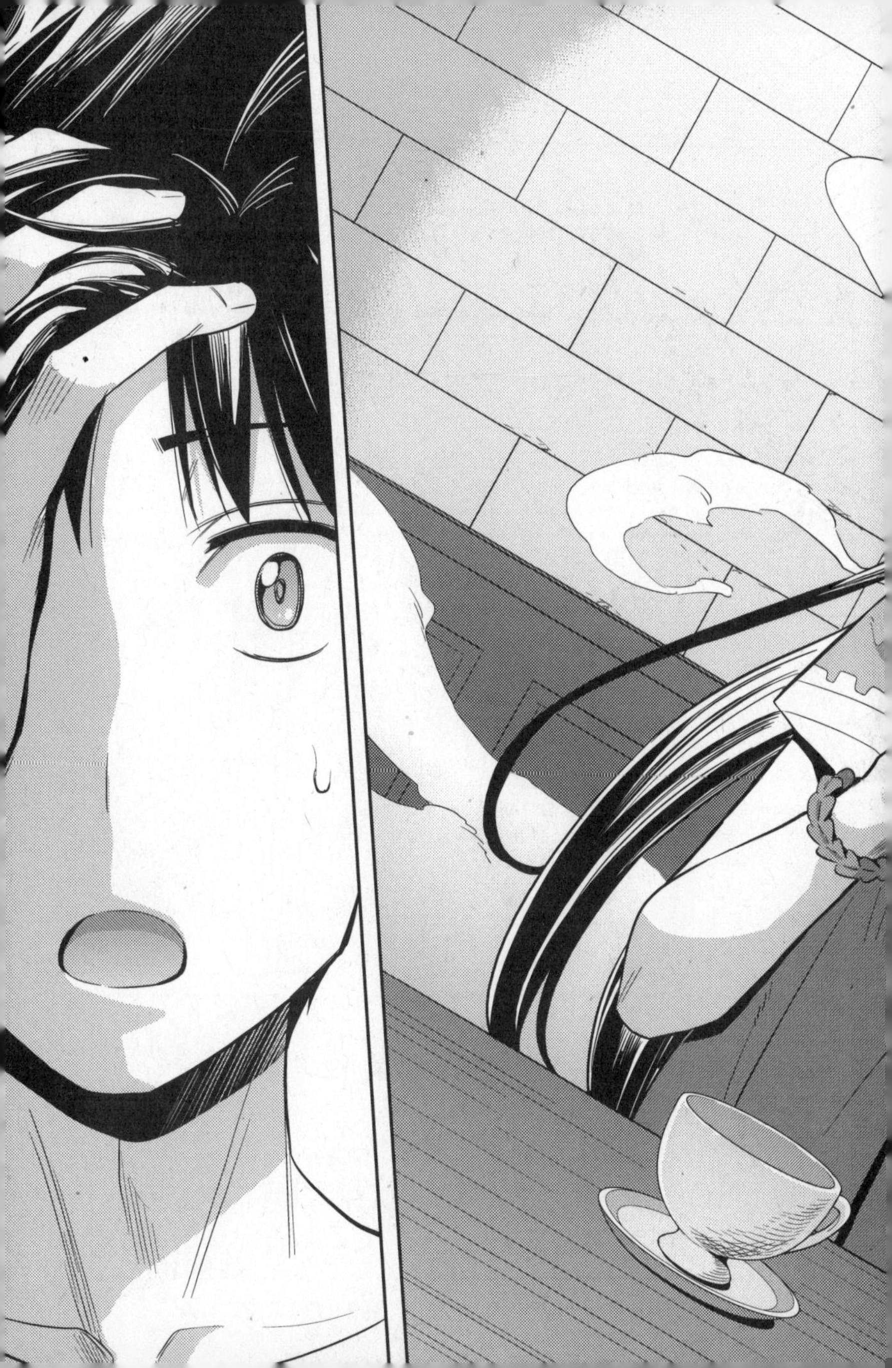

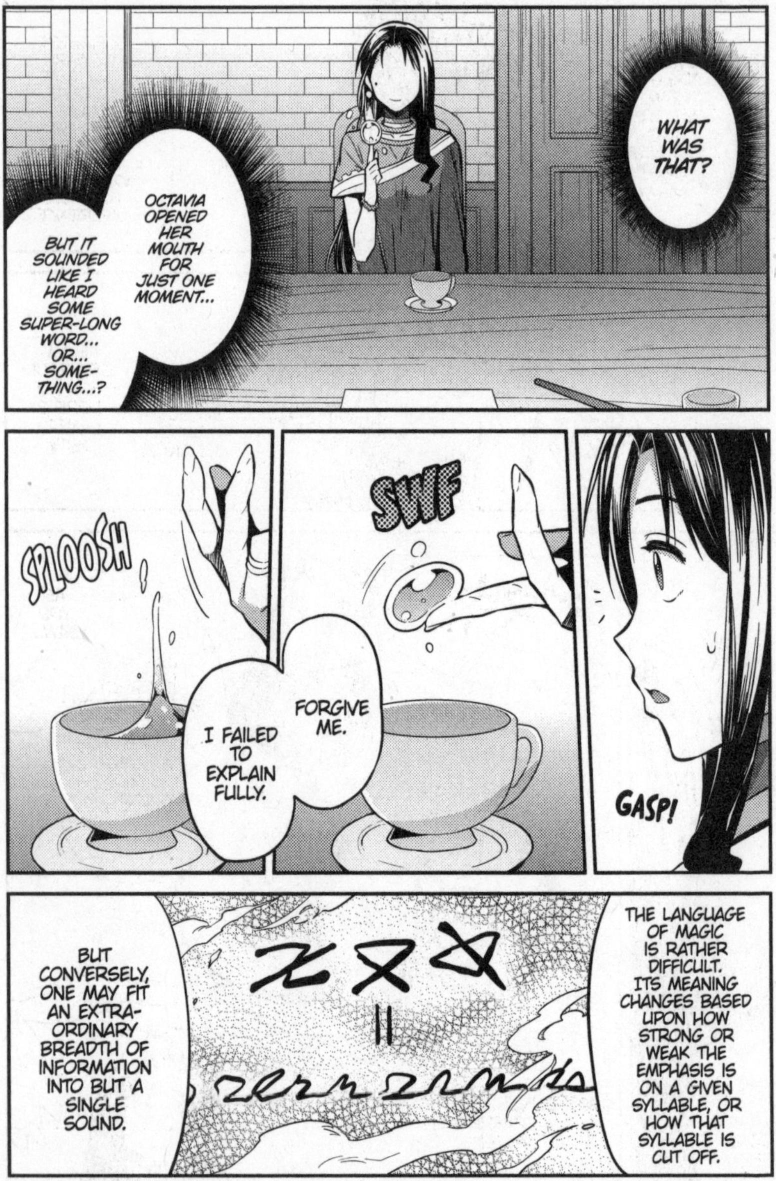
WHAT WAS THAT?
OCTAVIA OPENED HER MOUTH FOR JUST ONE MOMENT...
BUT IT SOUNDED LIKE I HEARD SOME SUPER-LONG WORD... OR... SOME-THING...?
GASP!
SWF
FORGIVE ME.
I FAILED TO EXPLAIN FULLY.
SPLOOSH
THE LANGUAGE OF MAGIC IS RATHER DIFFICULT. ITS MEANING CHANGES BASED UPON HOW STRONG OR WEAK THE EMPHASIS IS ON A GIVEN SYLLABLE, OR HOW THAT SYLLABLE IS CUT OFF.
BUT CONVERSELY, ONE MAY FIT AN EXTRA-ORDINARY BREADTH OF INFORMATION INTO BUT A SINGLE SOUND.

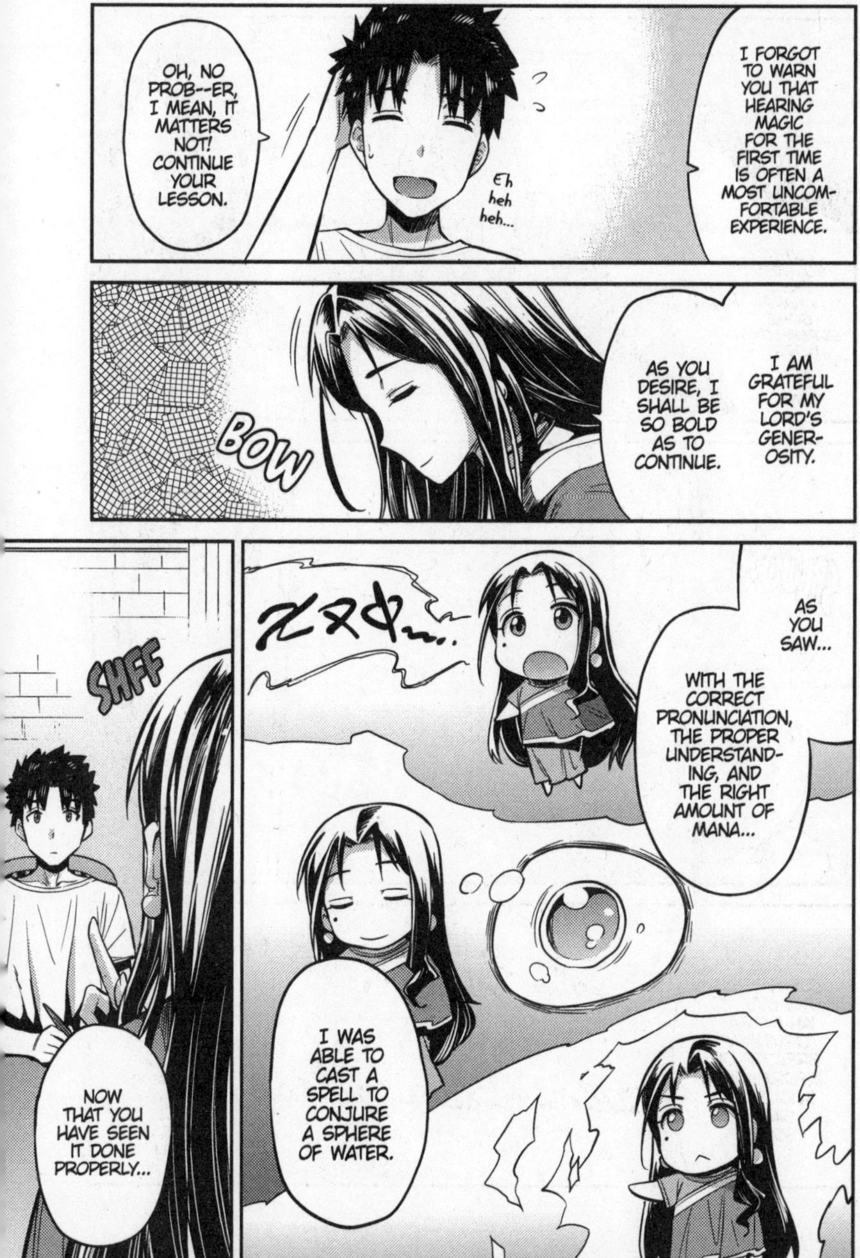
I FORGOT TO WARN YOU THAT HEARING MAGIC FOR THE FIRST TIME IS OFTEN A MOST UNCOMFORTABLE EXPERIENCE.
Eh heh heh...
OH, NO PROB--ER, I MEAN, IT MATTERS NOT! CONTINUE YOUR LESSON.
I AM GRATEFUL FOR MY LORD'S GENEROSITY.
AS YOU DESIRE, I SHALL BE SO BOLD AS TO CONTINUE.
BOW
AS YOU SAW...
WITH THE CORRECT PRONUNCIATION, THE PROPER UNDERSTANDING, AND THE RIGHT AMOUNT OF MANA...
I WAS ABLE TO CAST A SPELL TO CONJURE A SPHERE OF WATER.
SHFF
NOW THAT YOU HAVE SEEN IT DONE PROPERLY...

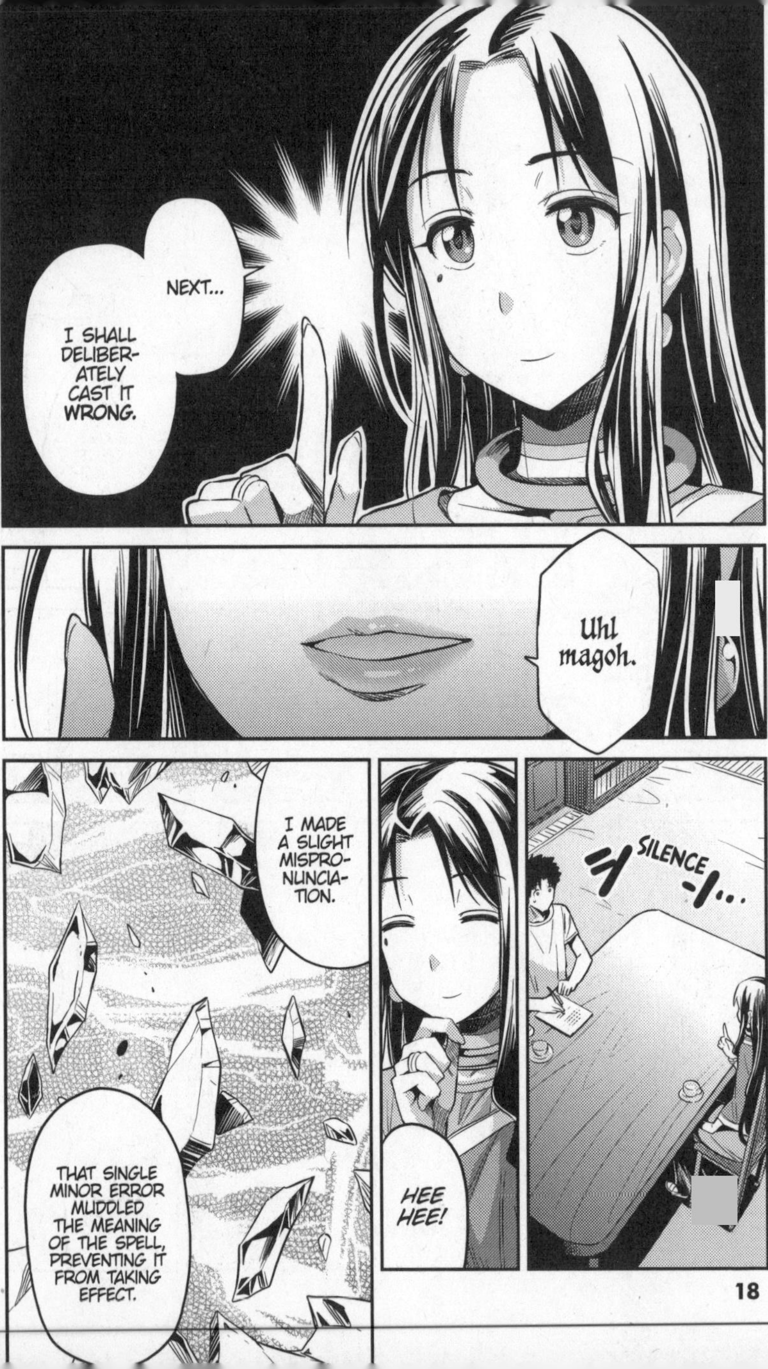
NEXT...
I SHALL DELIBERATELY CAST IT WRONG.
Uhl magoh.
SILENCE
HEE HEE!
I MADE A SLIGHT MISPRONUNCIATION.
THAT SINGLE MINOR ERROR MUDDLED THE MEANING OF THE SPELL, PREVENTING IT FROM TAKING EFFECT.

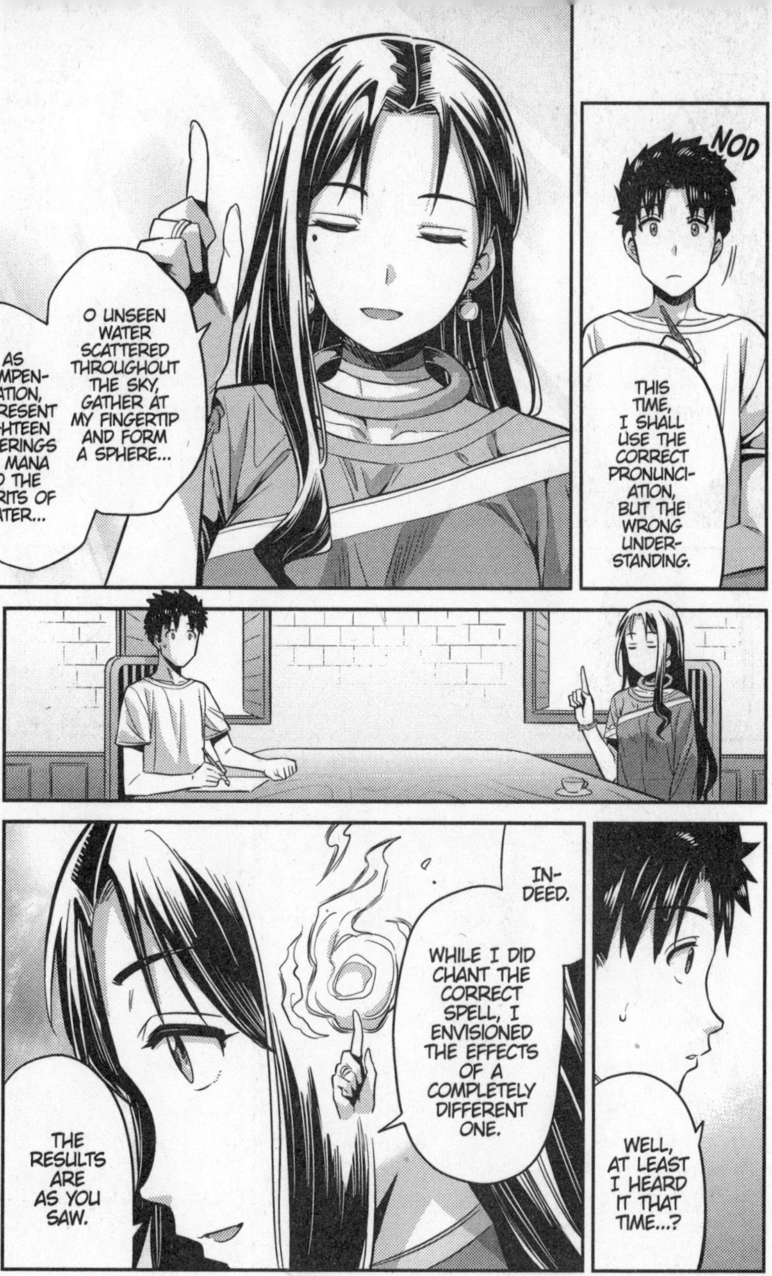
NOD
THIS TIME, I SHALL USE THE CORRECT PRONUNCIATION, BUT THE WRONG UNDERSTANDING.
O UNSEEN WATER SCATTERED THROUGHOUT THE SKY, GATHER AT MY FINGERTIP AND FORM A SPHERE...
AS COMPENSATION, I PRESENT EIGHTEEN OFFERINGS OF MANA TO THE SPIRITS OF WATER...
WELL, AT LEAST I HEARD IT THAT TIME...?
INDEED.
WHILE I DID CHANT THE CORRECT SPELL, I ENVISIONED THE EFFECTS OF A COMPLETELY DIFFERENT ONE.
THE RESULTS ARE AS YOU SAW.

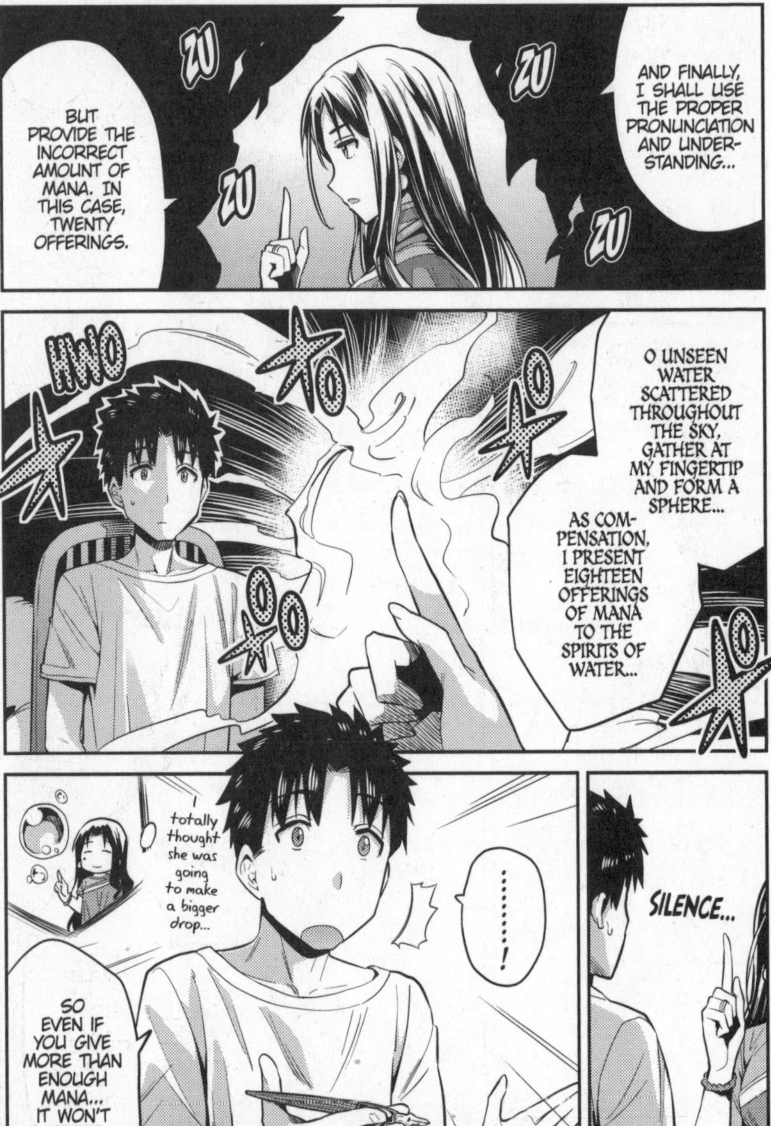
AND FINALLY, I SHALL USE THE PROPER PRONUNCIATION AND UNDER-STANDING...
ZU
ZU
ZU
ZU
BUT PROVIDE THE INCORRECT AMOUNT OF MANA. IN THIS CASE, TWENTY OFFERINGS.
O UNSEEN WATER SCATTERED THROUGHOUT THE SKY, GATHER AT MY FINGERTIP AND FORM A SPHERE...
AS COM-PENSATION, I PRESENT EIGHTEEN OFFERINGS OF MANA TO THE SPIRITS OF WATER...
HWO
SILENCE...
......!
I totally thought she was going to make a bigger drop...
SO EVEN IF YOU GIVE MORE THAN ENOUGH MANA... IT WON'T WORK?

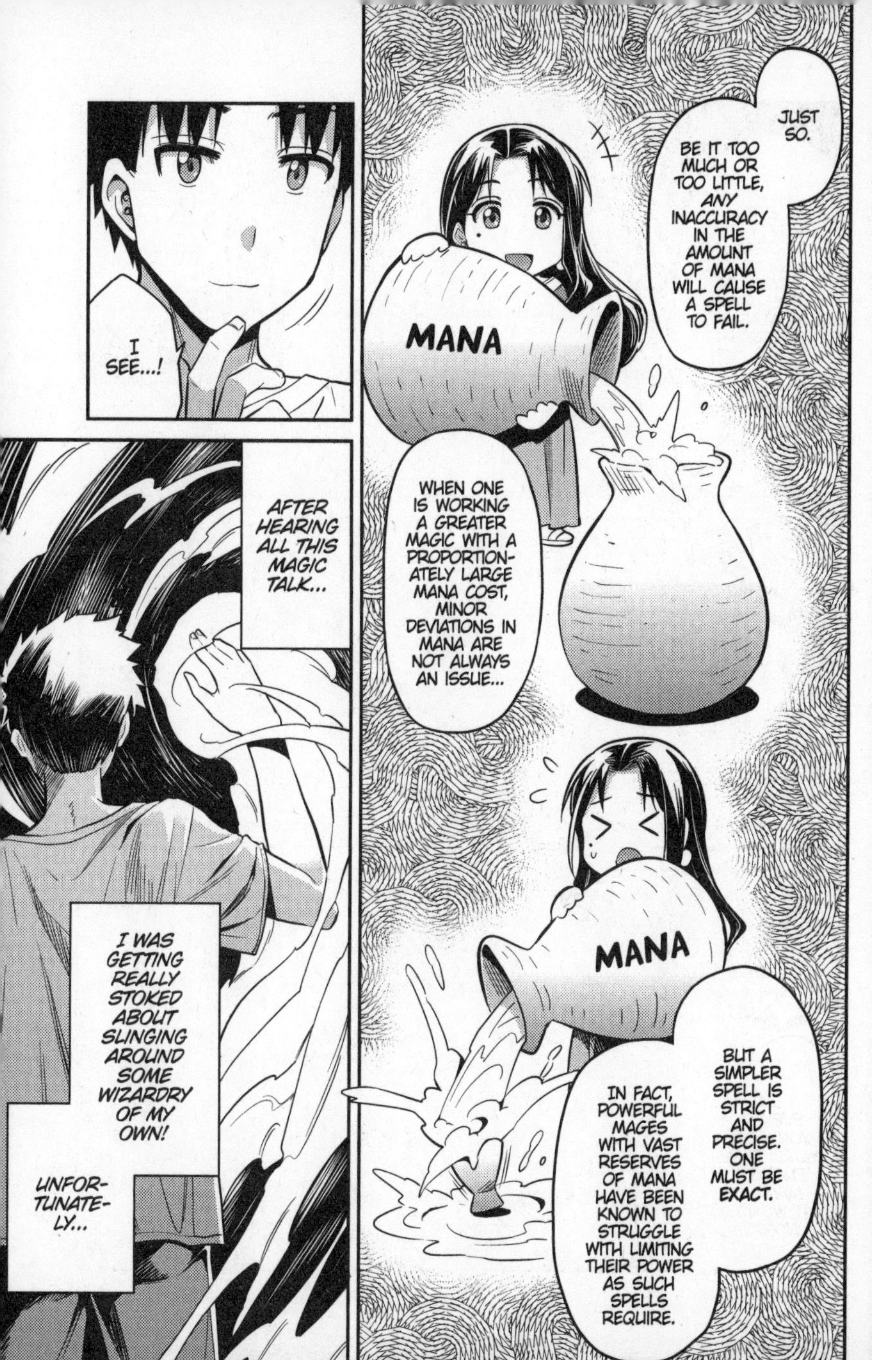
JUST SO.
BE IT TOO MUCH OR TOO LITTLE, ANY INACCURACY IN THE AMOUNT OF MANA WILL CAUSE A SPELL TO FAIL.
MANA
WHEN ONE IS WORKING A GREATER MAGIC WITH A PROPORTION-ATELY LARGE MANA COST, MINOR DEVIATIONS IN MANA ARE NOT ALWAYS AN ISSUE...
MANA
BUT A SIMPLER SPELL IS STRICT AND PRECISE. ONE MUST BE EXACT.
IN FACT, POWERFUL MAGES WITH VAST RESERVES OF MANA HAVE BEEN KNOWN TO STRUGGLE WITH LIMITING THEIR POWER AS SUCH SPELLS REQUIRE.
I SEE...!
AFTER HEARING ALL THIS MAGIC TALK...
I WAS GETTING REALLY STOKED ABOUT SLINGING AROUND SOME WIZARDRY OF MY OWN!
UNFOR-TUNATE-LY...

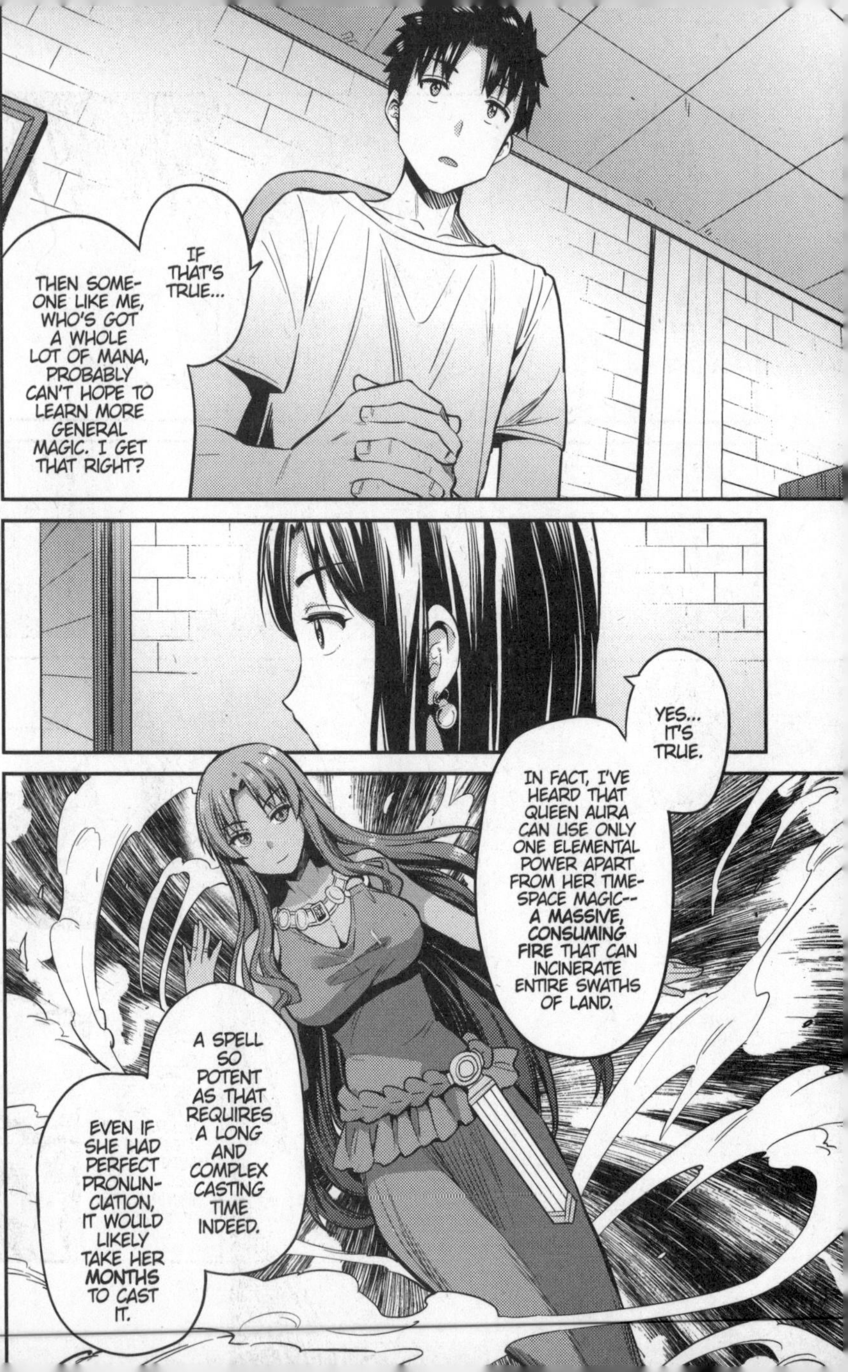
IF THAT'S TRUE...
THEN SOME-ONE LIKE ME, WHO'S GOT A WHOLE LOT OF MANA, PROBABLY CAN'T HOPE TO LEARN MORE GENERAL MAGIC. I GET THAT RIGHT?
YES... IT'S TRUE.
IN FACT, I'VE HEARD THAT QUEEN AURA CAN USE ONLY ONE ELEMENTAL POWER APART FROM HER TIME-SPACE MAGIC-- A MASSIVE, CONSUMING FIRE THAT CAN INCINERATE ENTIRE SWATHS OF LAND.
A SPELL SO POTENT AS THAT REQUIRES A LONG AND COMPLEX CASTING TIME INDEED.
EVEN IF SHE HAD PERFECT PRONUN-CIATION, IT WOULD LIKELY TAKE HER MONTHS TO CAST IT.

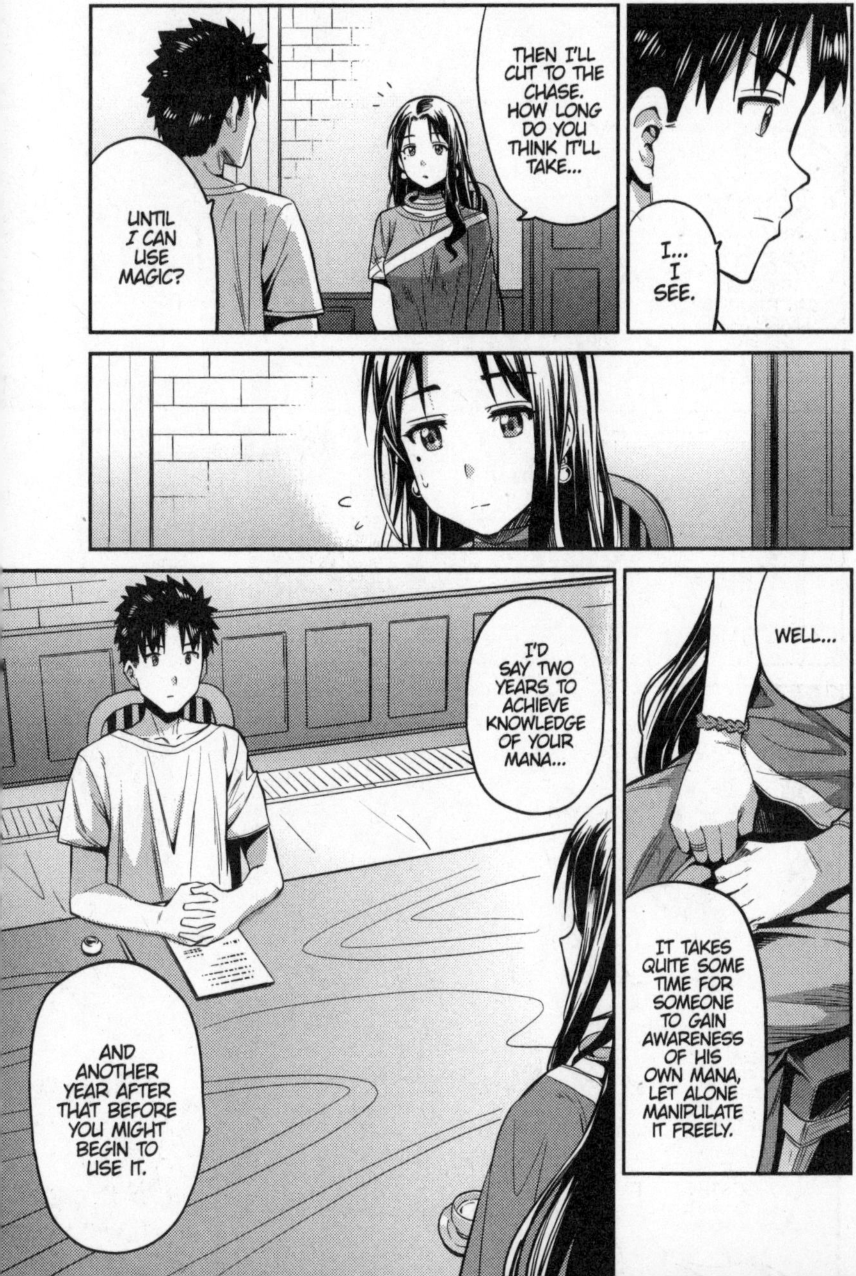
I... I SEE.
THEN I'LL CUT TO THE CHASE. HOW LONG DO YOU THINK IT'LL TAKE...
UNTIL I CAN USE MAGIC?
WELL...
IT TAKES QUITE SOME TIME FOR SOMEONE TO GAIN AWARENESS OF HIS OWN MANA, LET ALONE MANIPULATE IT FREELY.
I'D SAY TWO YEARS TO ACHIEVE KNOWLEDGE OF YOUR MANA...
AND ANOTHER YEAR AFTER THAT BEFORE YOU MIGHT BEGIN TO USE IT.

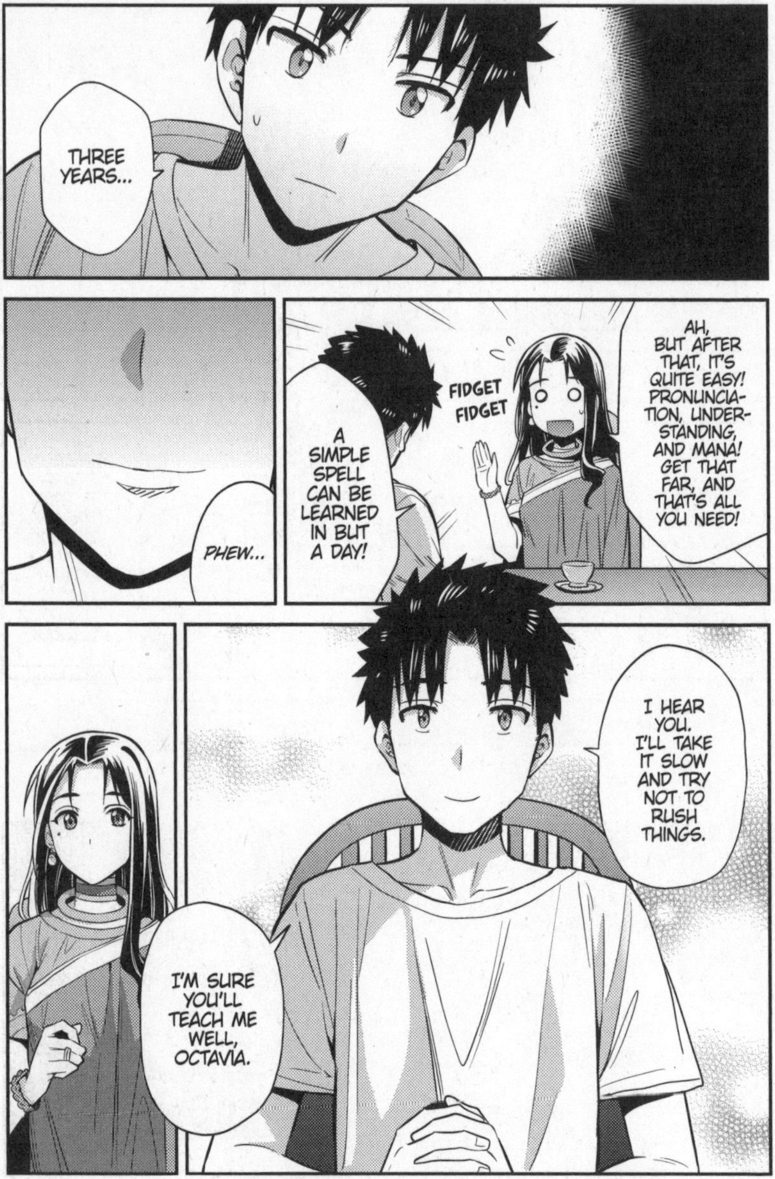
THREE YEARS...
AH, BUT AFTER THAT, IT'S QUITE EASY! PRONUNCIA-TION, UNDER-STANDING, AND MANA! GET THAT FAR, AND THAT'S ALL YOU NEED!
FIDGET FIDGET
A SIMPLE SPELL CAN BE LEARNED IN BUT A DAY!
PHEW...
I HEAR YOU. I'LL TAKE IT SLOW AND TRY NOT TO RUSH THINGS.
I'M SURE YOU'LL TEACH ME WELL, OCTAVIA.

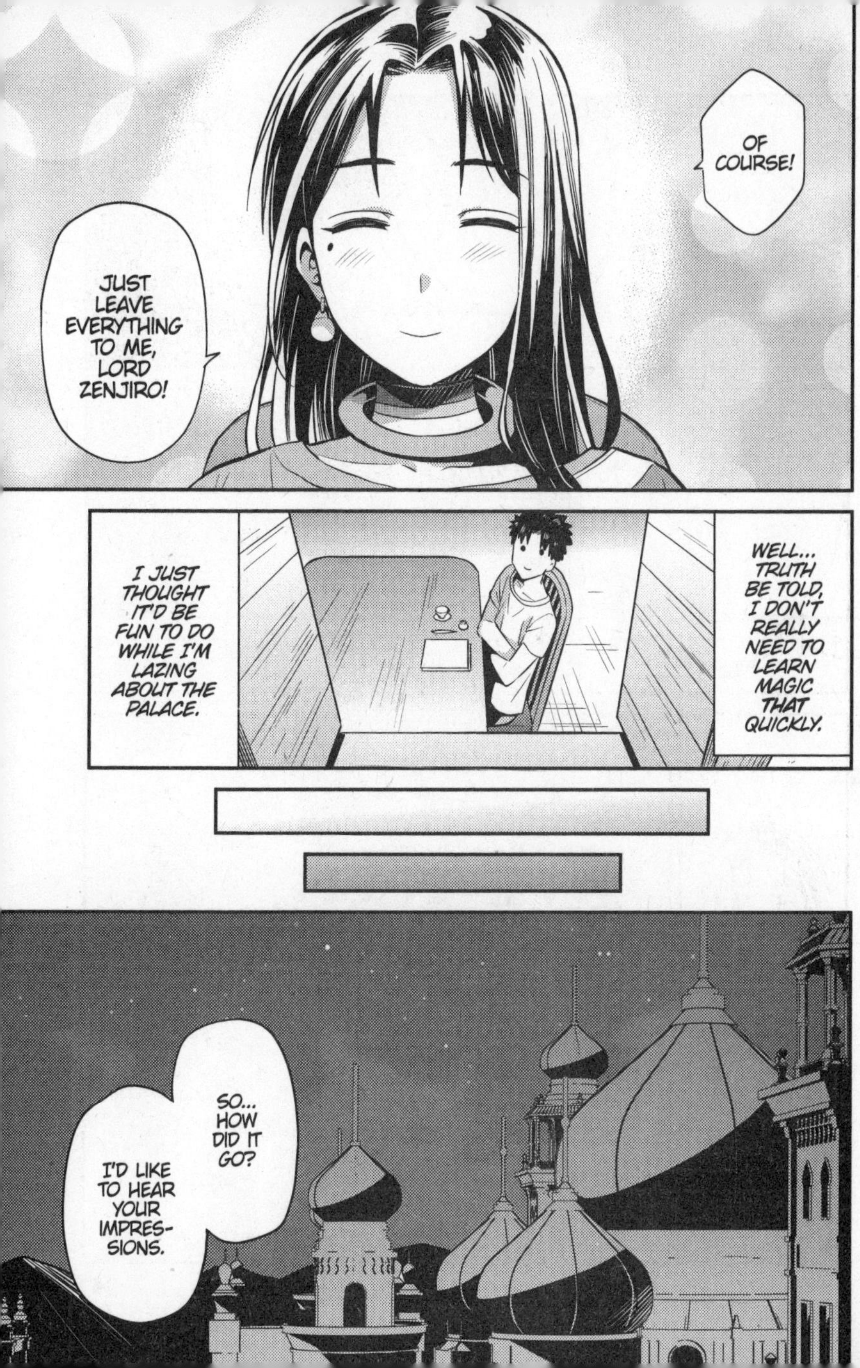
OF COURSE!
JUST LEAVE EVERYTHING TO ME, LORD ZENJIRO!
WELL... TRUTH BE TOLD, I DON'T REALLY NEED TO LEARN MAGIC THAT QUICKLY.
I JUST THOUGHT IT'D BE FUN TO DO WHILE I'M LAZING ABOUT THE PALACE.
SO... HOW DID IT GO?
I'D LIKE TO HEAR YOUR IMPRESSIONS.

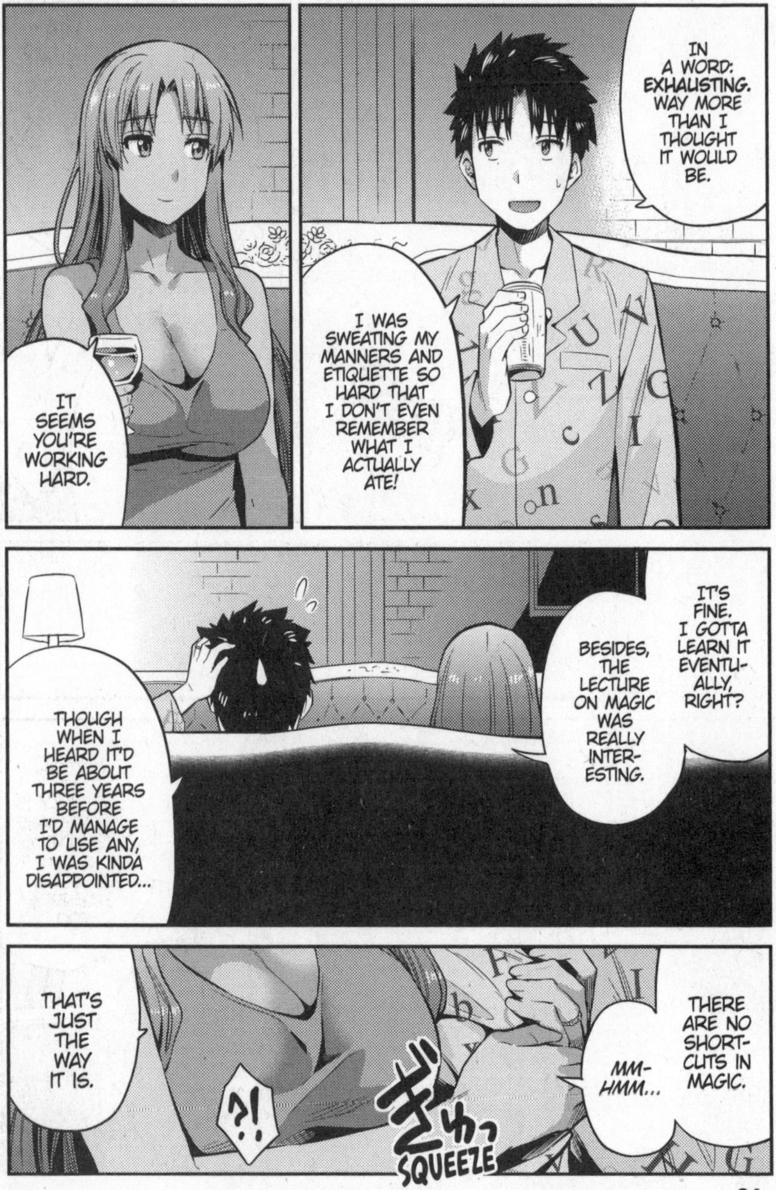
IN A WORD: EXHAUSTING. WAY MORE THAN I THOUGHT IT WOULD BE.
I WAS SWEATING MY MANNERS AND ETIQUETTE SO HARD THAT I DON'T EVEN REMEMBER WHAT I ACTUALLY ATE!
IT SEEMS YOU'RE WORKING HARD.
IT'S FINE. I GOTTA LEARN IT EVENTU-ALLY, RIGHT?
BESIDES, THE LECTURE ON MAGIC WAS REALLY INTER-ESTING.
THOUGH WHEN I HEARD IT'D BE ABOUT THREE YEARS BEFORE I'D MANAGE TO USE ANY, I WAS KINDA DISAPPOINTED...
THERE ARE NO SHORT-CUTS IN MAGIC.
MM-HMM...
ぎゅっ
SQUEEZE
?!
THAT'S JUST THE WAY IT IS.

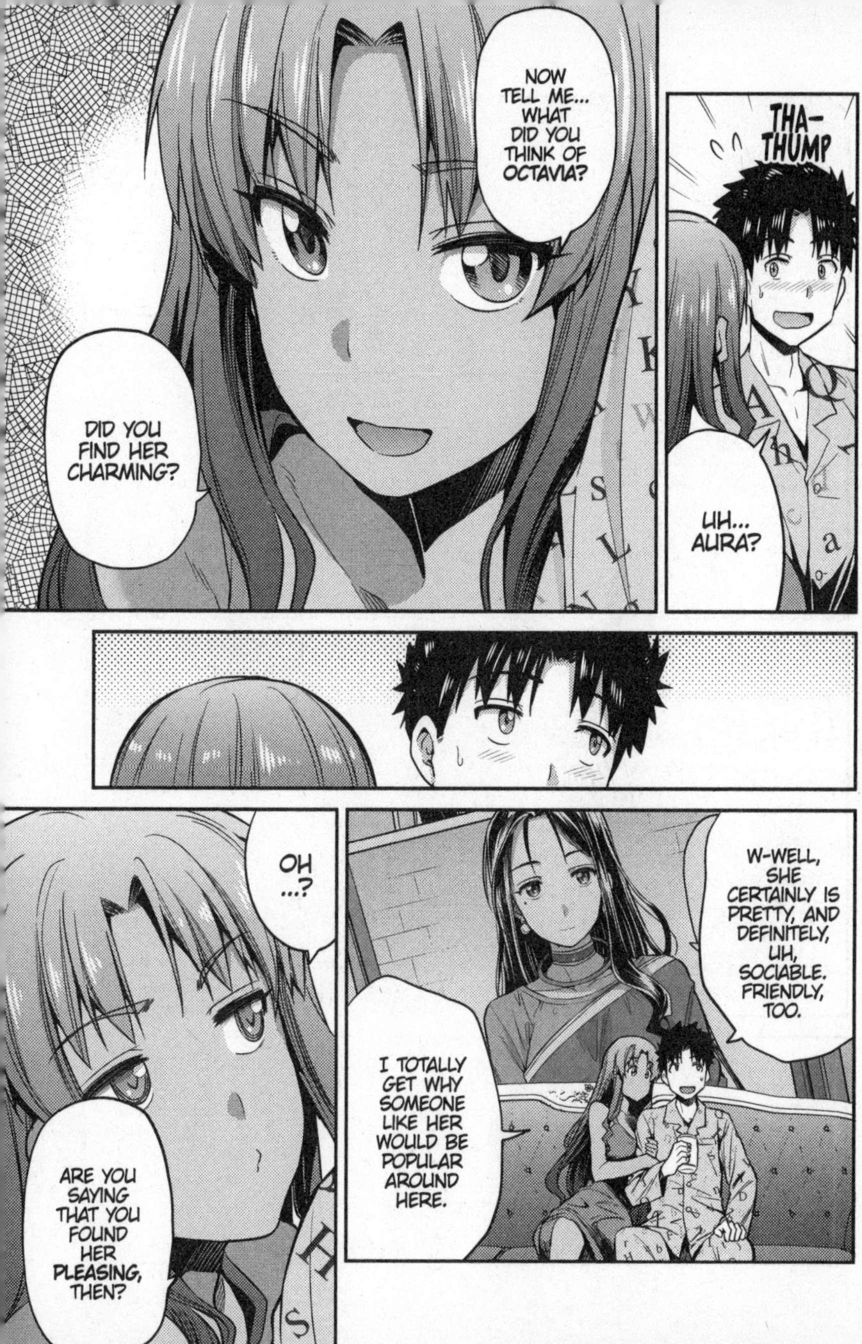
THA-THUMP
UH... AURA?
NOW TELL ME... WHAT DID YOU THINK OF OCTAVIA?
DID YOU FIND HER CHARMING?
W-WELL, SHE CERTAINLY IS PRETTY, AND DEFINITELY, UH, SOCIABLE. FRIENDLY, TOO.
I TOTALLY GET WHY SOMEONE LIKE HER WOULD BE POPULAR AROUND HERE.
OH ...?
ARE YOU SAYING THAT YOU FOUND HER PLEASING, THEN?

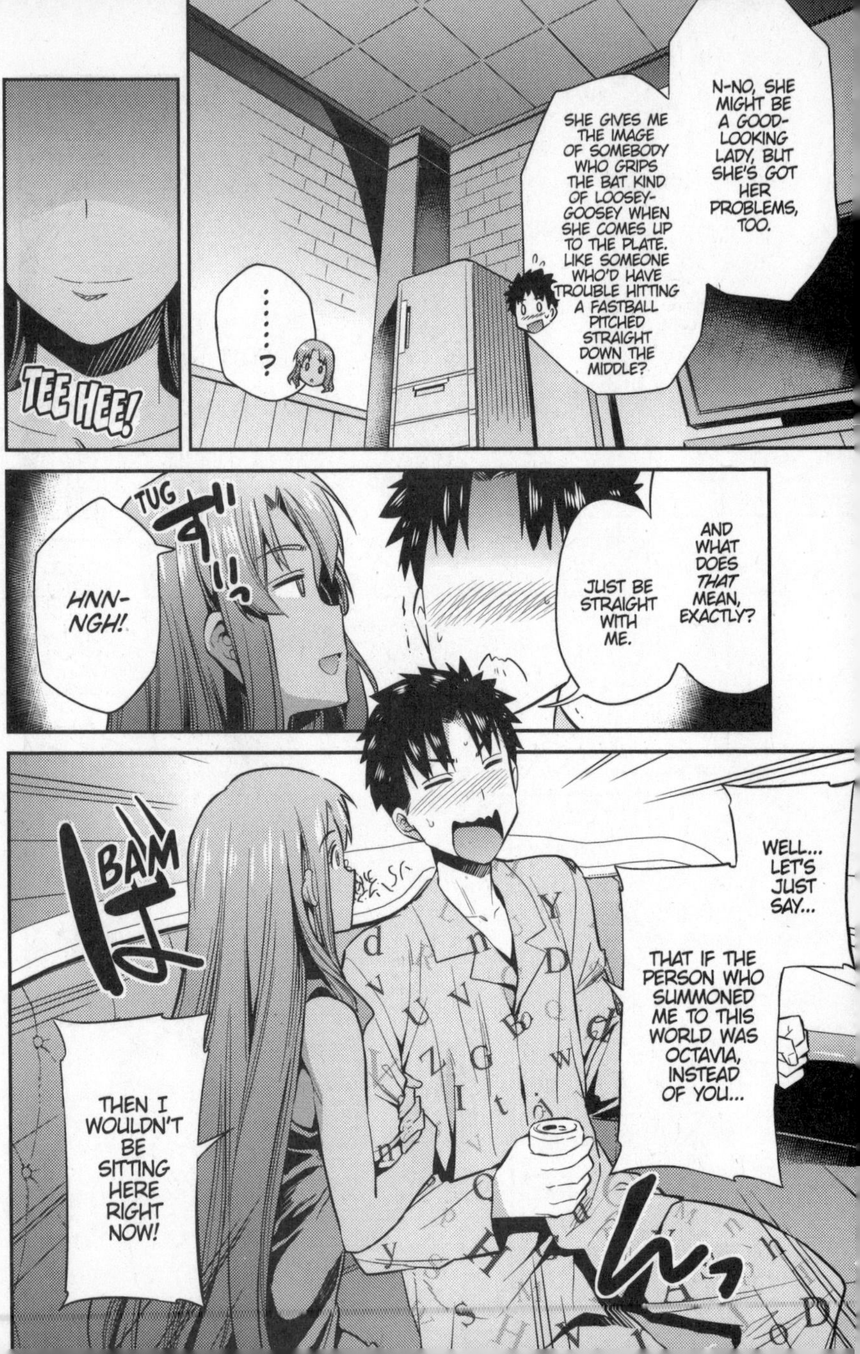
N-NO, SHE MIGHT BE A GOOD-LOOKING LADY, BUT SHE'S GOT HER PROBLEMS, TOO.
SHE GIVES ME THE IMAGE OF SOMEBODY WHO GRIPS THE BAT KIND OF LOOSEY-GOOSEY WHEN SHE COMES UP TO THE PLATE. LIKE SOMEONE WHO'D HAVE TROUBLE HITTING A FASTBALL PITCHED STRAIGHT DOWN THE MIDDLE?
......?
TEE HEE!
AND WHAT DOES *THAT* MEAN, EXACTLY?
JUST BE STRAIGHT WITH ME.
TUG
HNN-NGH!
WELL... LET'S JUST SAY...
THAT IF THE PERSON WHO SUMMONED ME TO THIS WORLD WAS OCTAVIA, INSTEAD OF YOU...
BAM
THEN I WOULDN'T BE SITTING HERE RIGHT NOW!

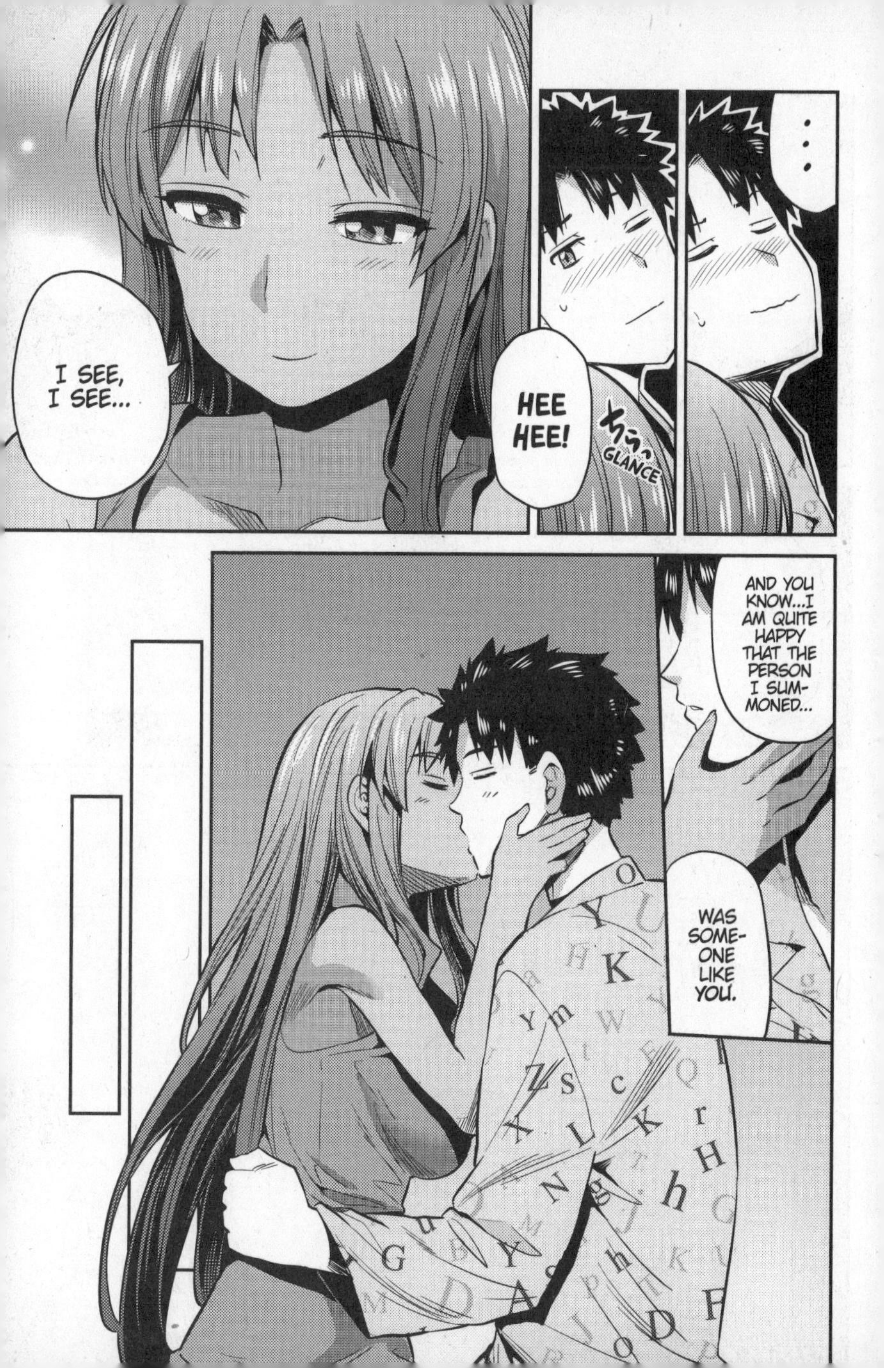
...
HEE HEE!
GLANCE
I SEE, I SEE...
AND YOU KNOW...I AM QUITE HAPPY THAT THE PERSON I SUMMONED...
WAS SOMEONE LIKE YOU.

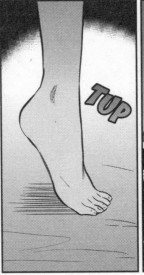

TUP

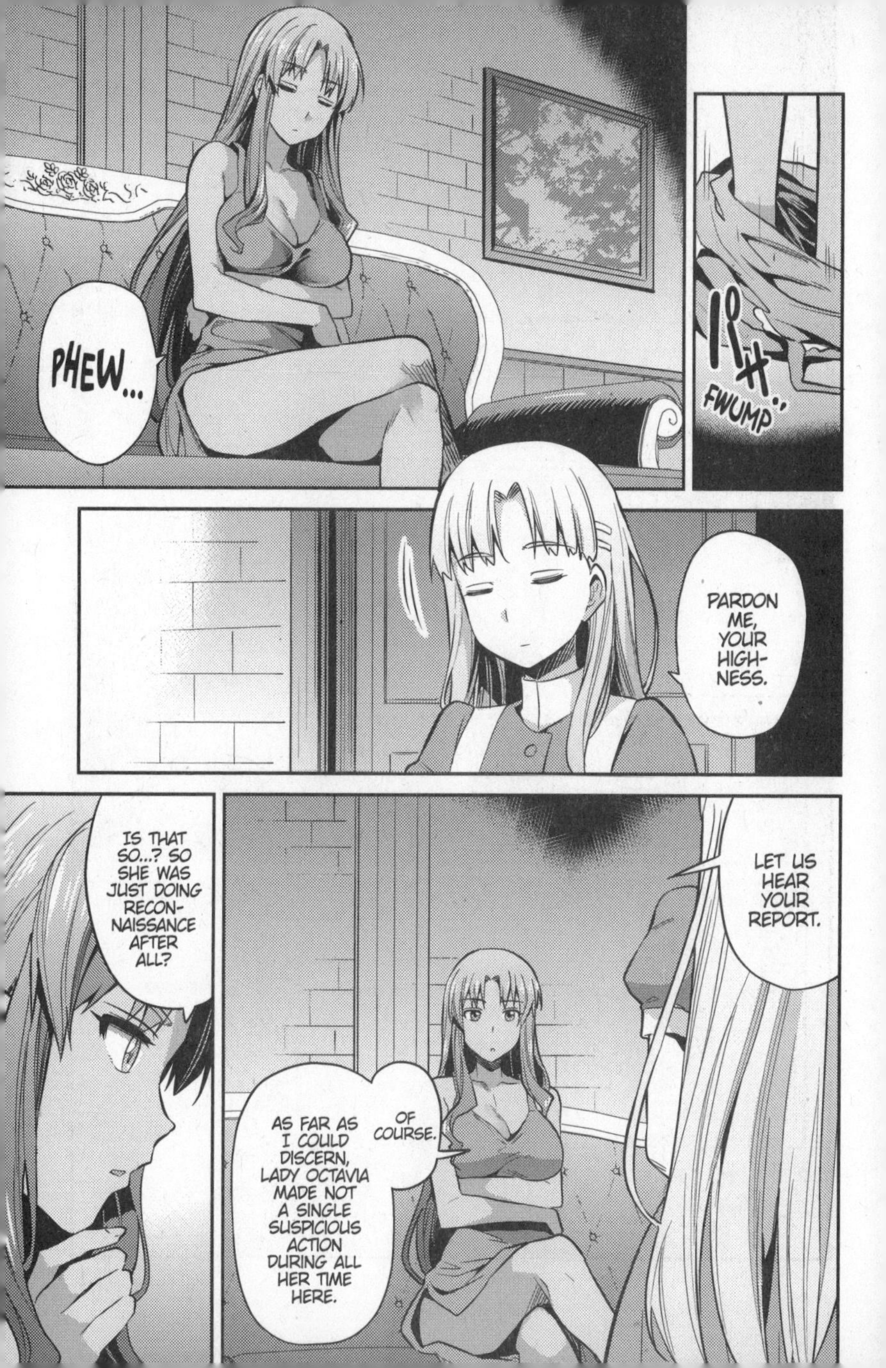
パサ..
FWUMP
PHEW...
PARDON ME, YOUR HIGHNESS.
LET US HEAR YOUR REPORT.
OF COURSE.
AS FAR AS I COULD DISCERN, LADY OCTAVIA MADE NOT A SINGLE SUSPICIOUS ACTION DURING ALL HER TIME HERE.
IS THAT SO...? SO SHE WAS JUST DOING RECONNAISSANCE AFTER ALL?

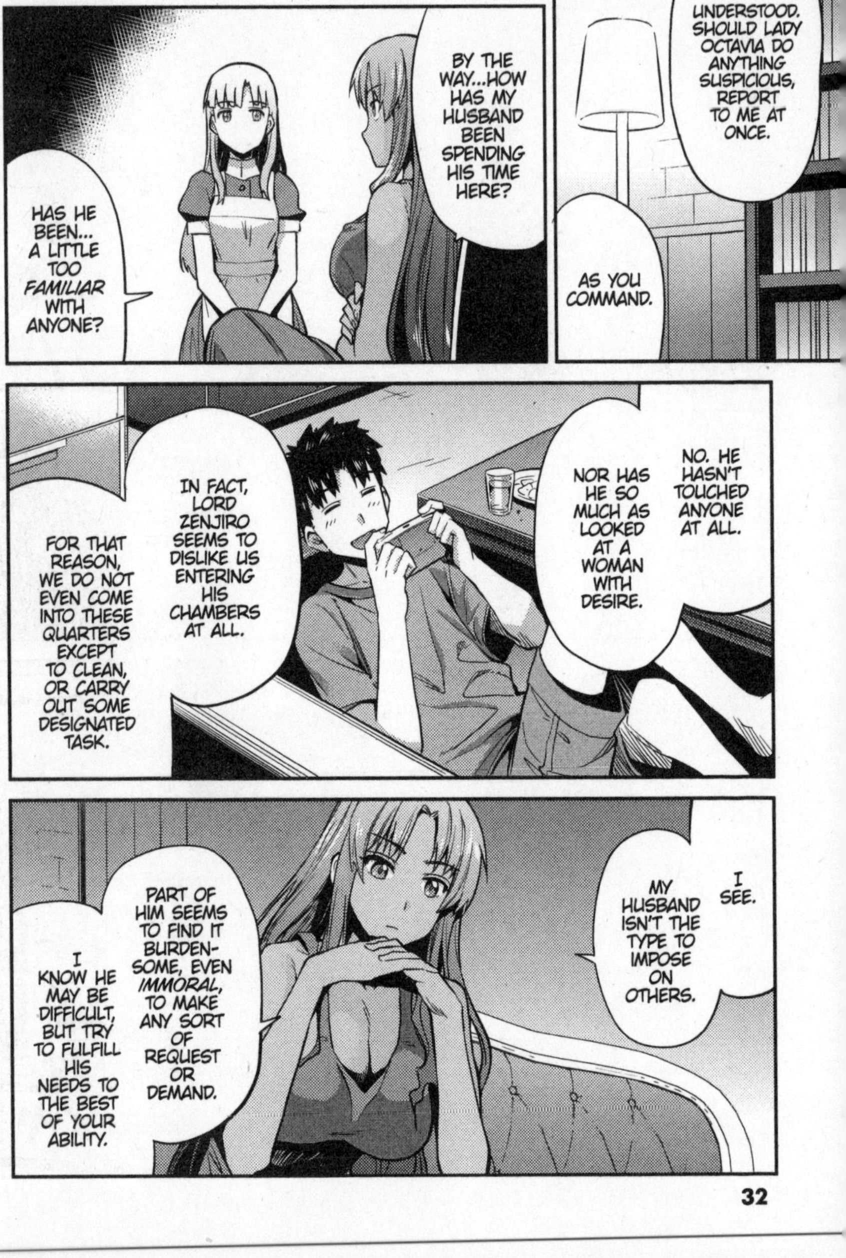
UNDERSTOOD. SHOULD LADY OCTAVIA DO ANYTHING SUSPICIOUS, REPORT TO ME AT ONCE.
AS YOU COMMAND.
BY THE WAY...HOW HAS MY HUSBAND BEEN SPENDING HIS TIME HERE?
HAS HE BEEN... A LITTLE TOO *FAMILIAR* WITH ANYONE?
NO. HE HASN'T TOUCHED ANYONE AT ALL.
NOR HAS HE SO MUCH AS LOOKED AT A WOMAN WITH DESIRE.
IN FACT, LORD ZENJIRO SEEMS TO DISLIKE US ENTERING HIS CHAMBERS AT ALL.
FOR THAT REASON, WE DO NOT EVEN COME INTO THESE QUARTERS EXCEPT TO CLEAN, OR CARRY OUT SOME DESIGNATED TASK.
I SEE.
MY HUSBAND ISN'T THE TYPE TO IMPOSE ON OTHERS.
PART OF HIM SEEMS TO FIND IT BURDEN-SOME, EVEN *IMMORAL*, TO MAKE ANY SORT OF REQUEST OR DEMAND.
I KNOW HE MAY BE DIFFICULT, BUT TRY TO FULFILL HIS NEEDS TO THE BEST OF YOUR ABILITY.

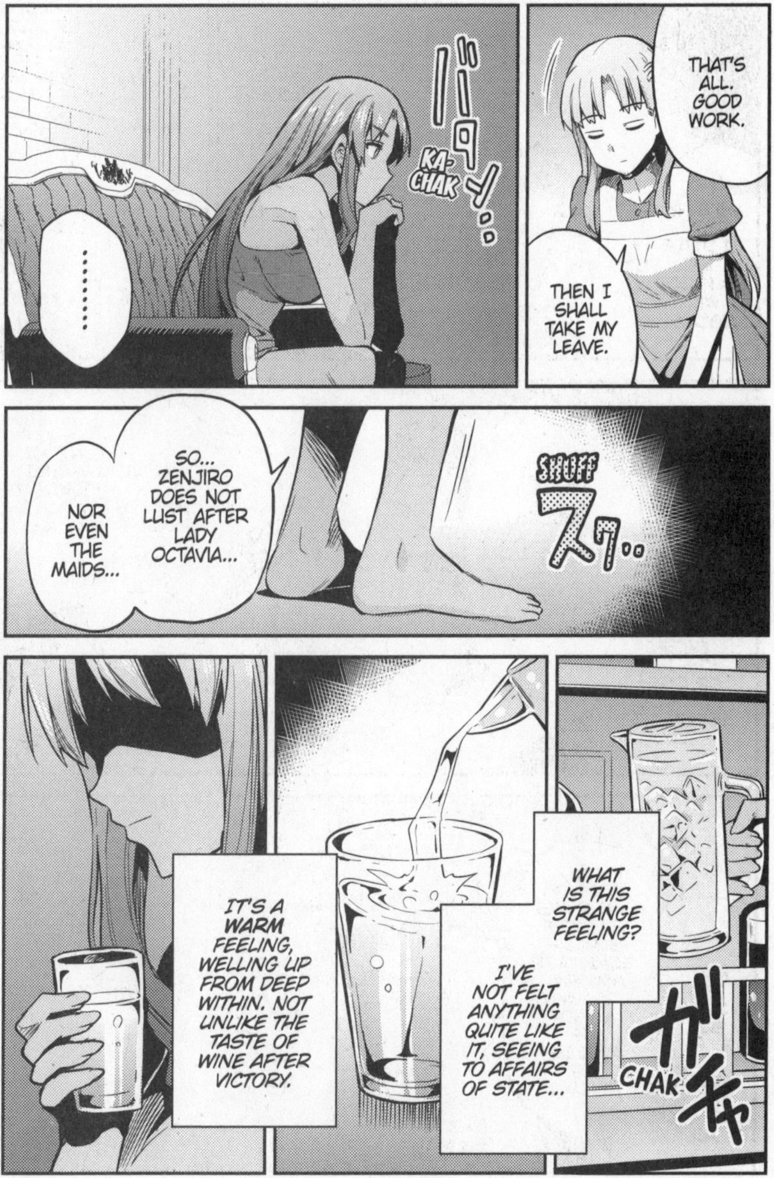
THAT'S ALL. GOOD WORK.
THEN I SHALL TAKE MY LEAVE.
KA-CHAK
......
SHUFF
SO... ZENJIRO DOES NOT LUST AFTER LADY OCTAVIA...
NOR EVEN THE MAIDS...
WHAT IS THIS STRANGE FEELING?
CHAK
I'VE NOT FELT ANYTHING QUITE LIKE IT, SEEING TO AFFAIRS OF STATE...
IT'S A WARM FEELING, WELLING UP FROM DEEP WITHIN. NOT UNLIKE THE TASTE OF WINE AFTER VICTORY.

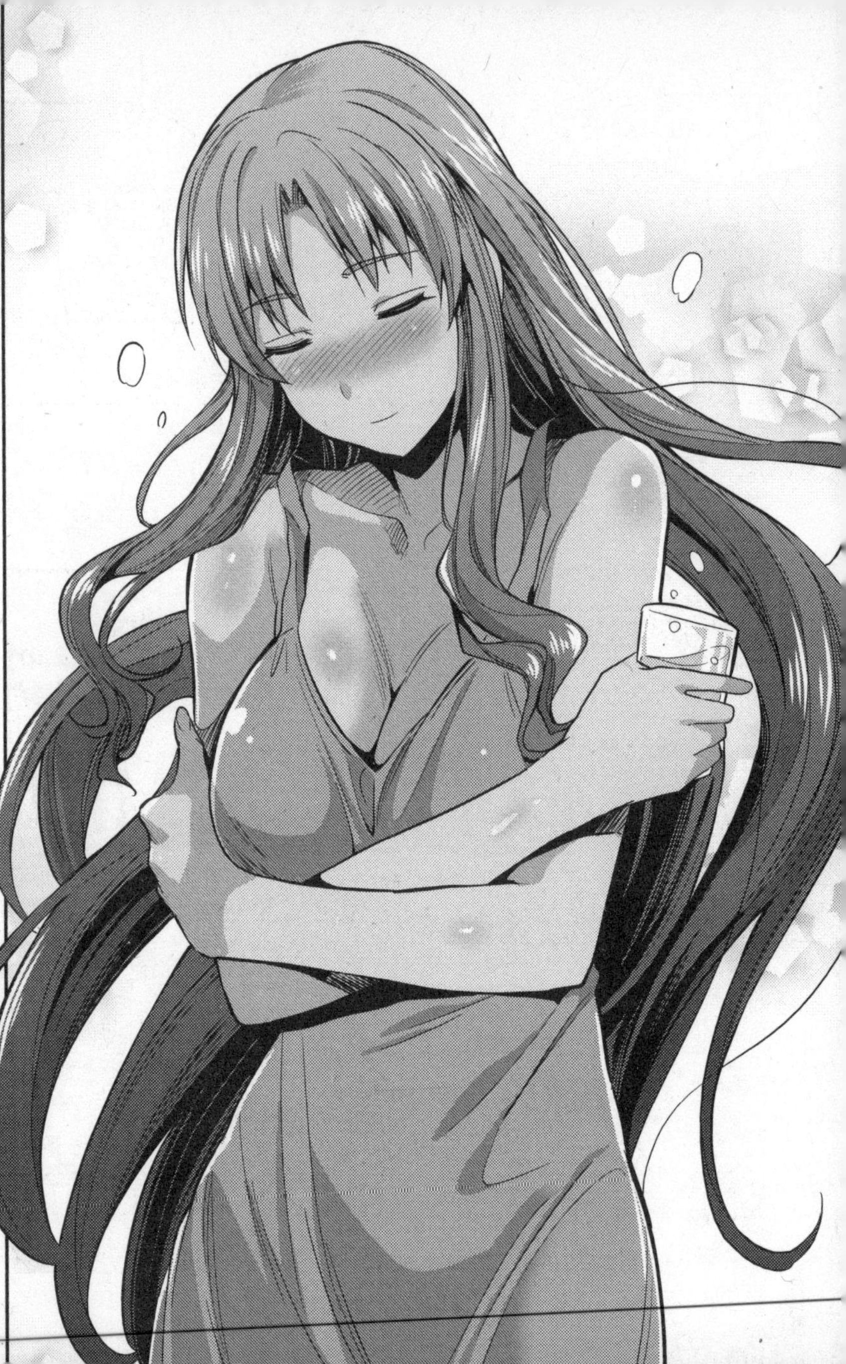

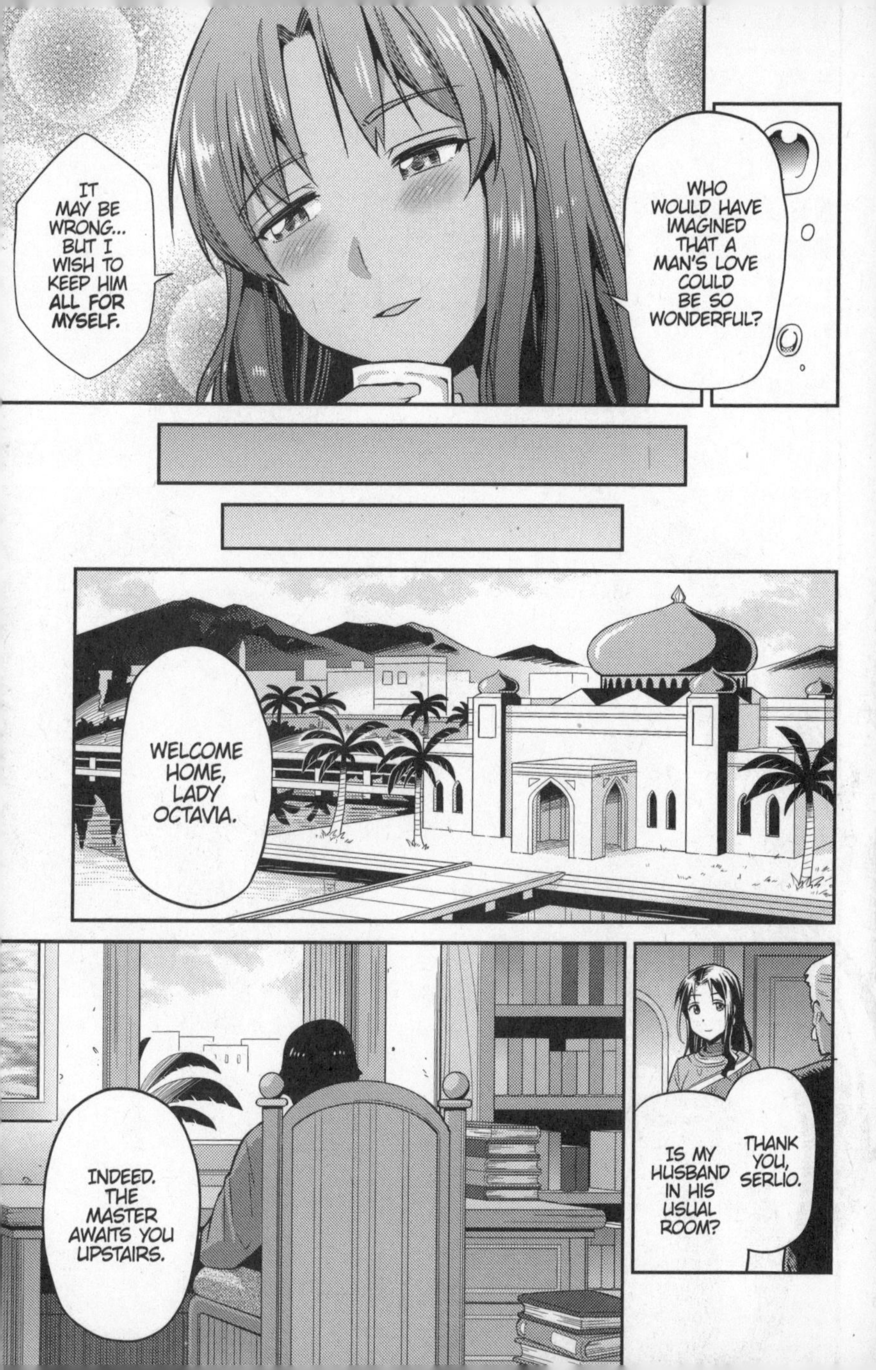
WHO WOULD HAVE IMAGINED THAT A MAN'S LOVE COULD BE SO WONDERFUL?
IT MAY BE WRONG... BUT I WISH TO KEEP HIM ALL FOR MYSELF.
WELCOME HOME, LADY OCTAVIA.
THANK YOU, SERLIO.
IS MY HUSBAND IN HIS USUAL ROOM?
INDEED. THE MASTER AWAITS YOU UPSTAIRS.

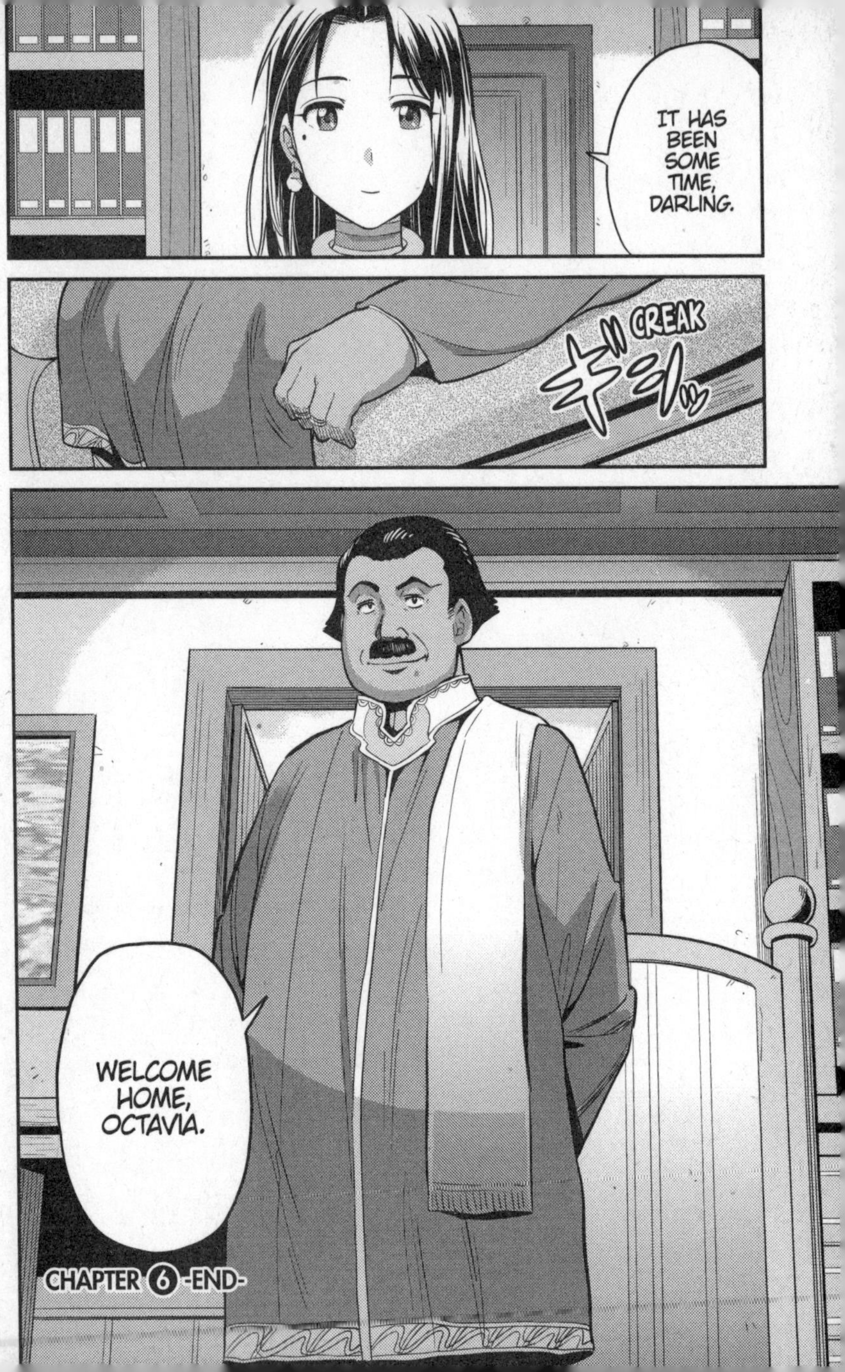
IT HAS BEEN SOME TIME, DARLING.
CREAK
WELCOME HOME, OCTAVIA.
CHAPTER 6 -END-

THE IDEAL SPONGER LIFE
Presented by Tsunehiko Watanabe & Neko Hinotsuki

THE **IDĔAL**
SPONGER LIFE

CHAPTER 7
A Gorgeous Night

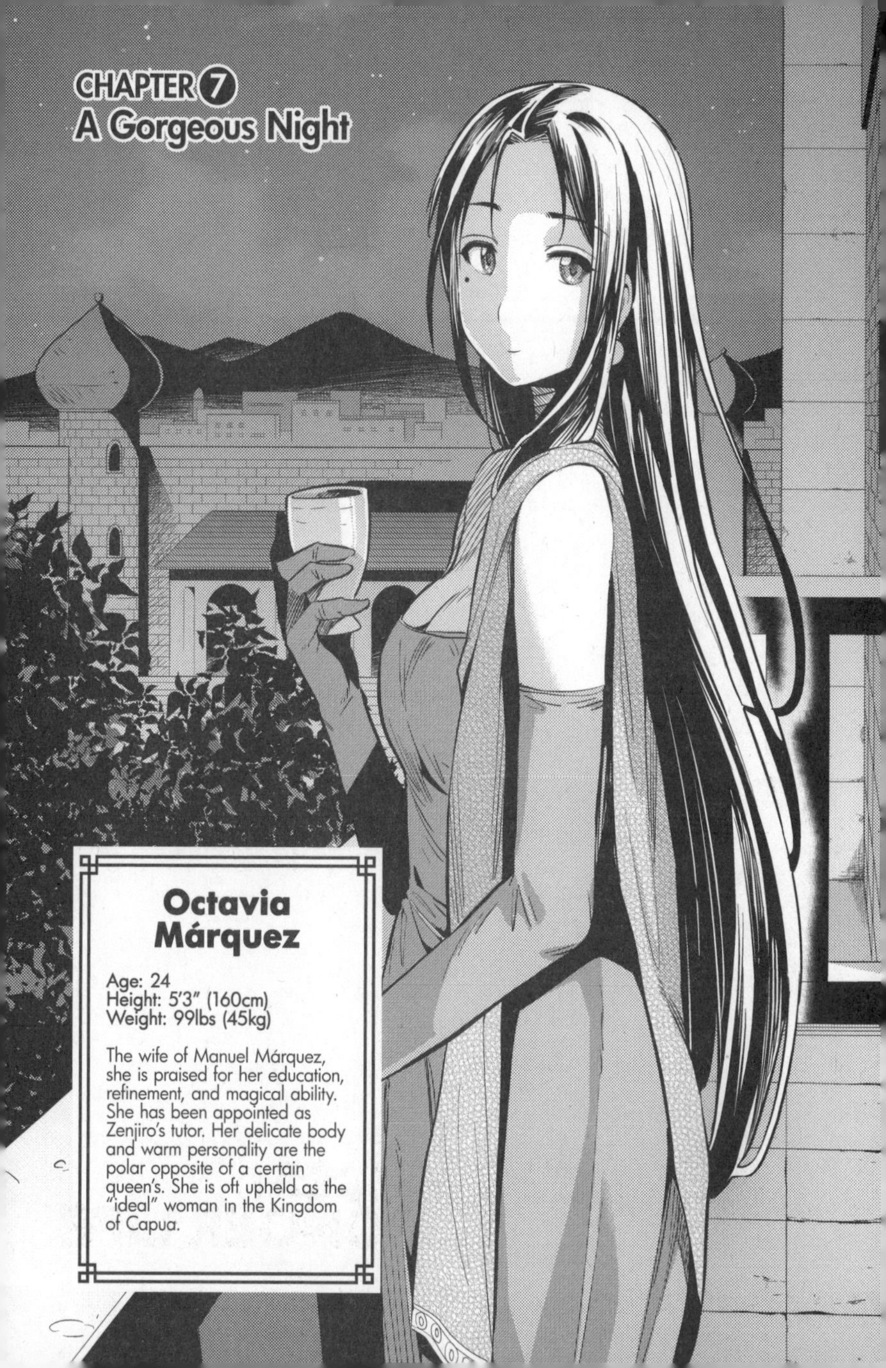
Octavia Márquez
Age: 24
Height: 5'3" (160cm)
Weight: 99lbs (45kg)
The wife of Manuel Márquez, she is praised for her education, refinement, and magical ability. She has been appointed as Zenjiro's tutor. Her delicate body and warm personality are the polar opposite of a certain queen's. She is oft upheld as the "ideal" woman in the Kingdom of Capua.

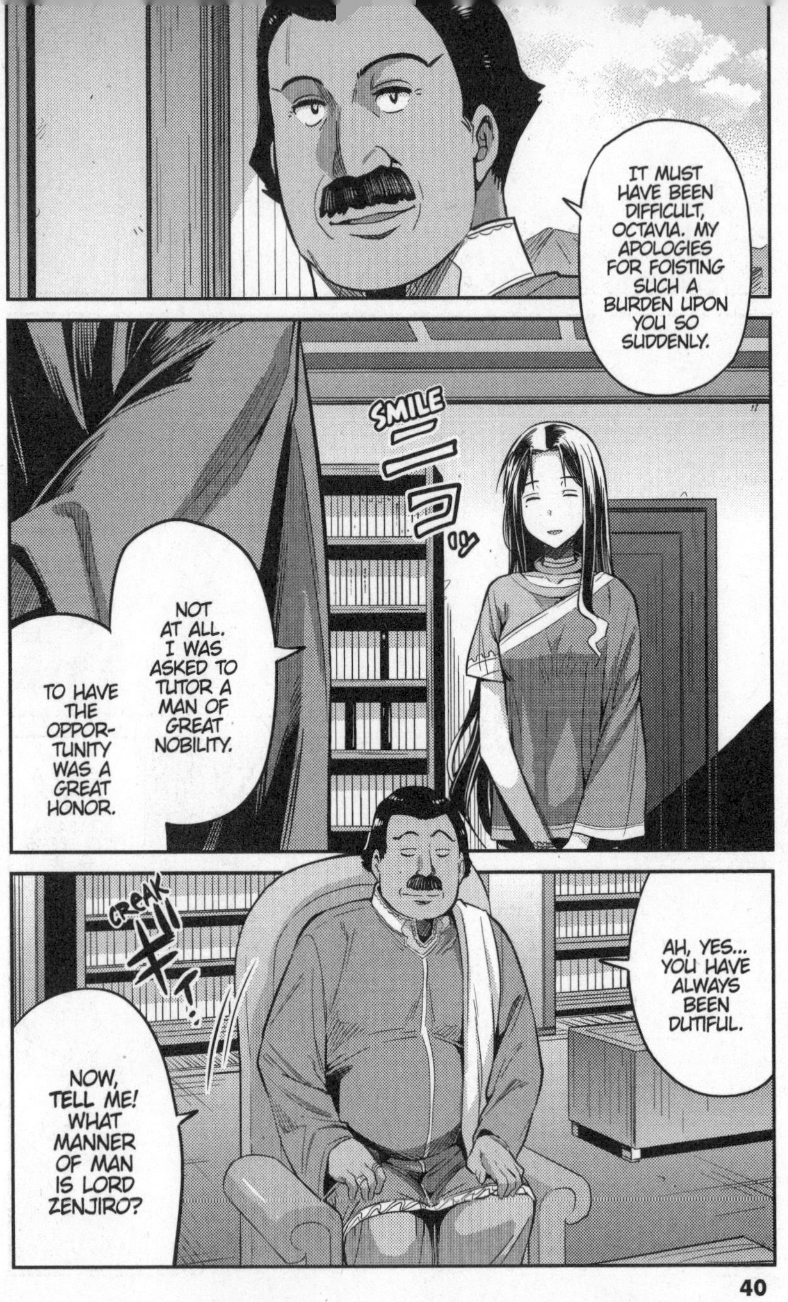
IT MUST HAVE BEEN DIFFICULT, OCTAVIA. MY APOLOGIES FOR FOISTING SUCH A BURDEN UPON YOU SO SUDDENLY.
SMILE
NOT AT ALL. I WAS ASKED TO TUTOR A MAN OF GREAT NOBILITY.
TO HAVE THE OPPORTUNITY WAS A GREAT HONOR.
AH, YES... YOU HAVE ALWAYS BEEN DUTIFUL.
CREAK
NOW, TELL ME! WHAT MANNER OF MAN IS LORD ZENJIRO?

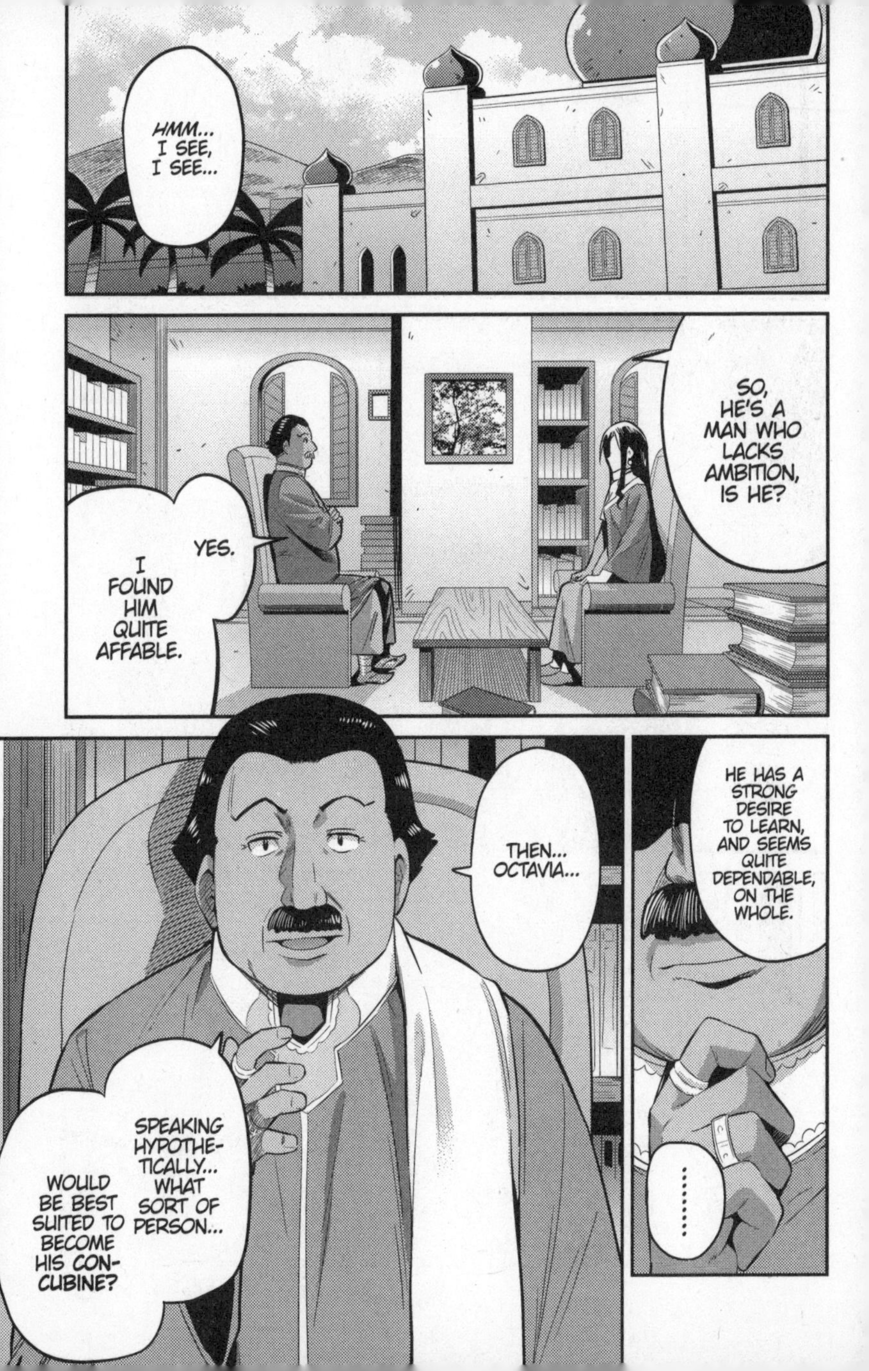
HMM... I SEE, I SEE...
SO, HE'S A MAN WHO LACKS AMBITION, IS HE?
YES.
I FOUND HIM QUITE AFFABLE.
HE HAS A STRONG DESIRE TO LEARN, AND SEEMS QUITE DEPENDABLE, ON THE WHOLE.
THEN... OCTAVIA...
......
SPEAKING HYPOTHE-TICALLY... WHAT SORT OF PERSON...
WOULD BE BEST SUITED TO BECOME HIS CON-CUBINE?

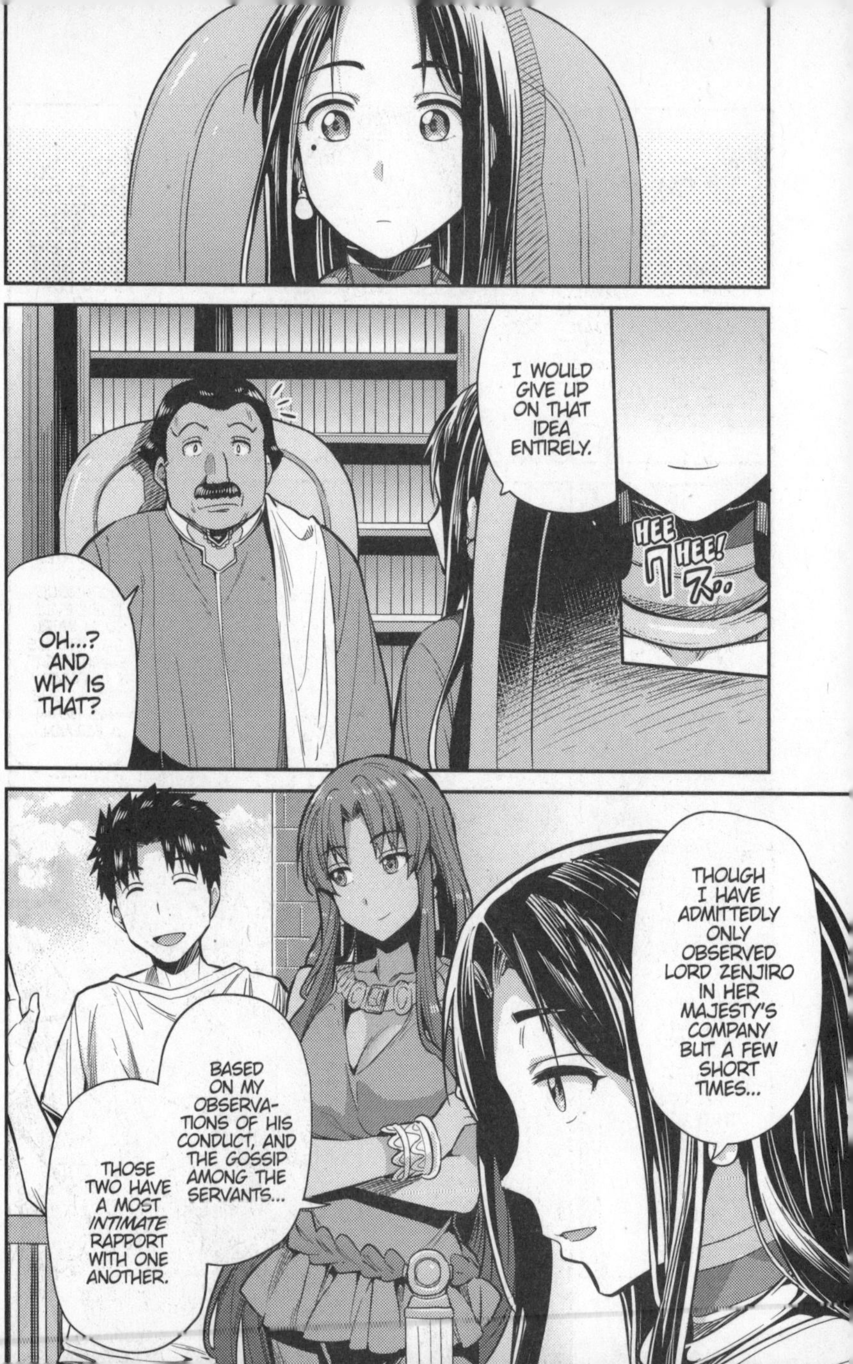
I WOULD GIVE UP ON THAT IDEA ENTIRELY.
HEE HEE!
OH...? AND WHY IS THAT?
THOUGH I HAVE ADMITTEDLY ONLY OBSERVED LORD ZENJIRO IN HER MAJESTY'S COMPANY BUT A FEW SHORT TIMES...
BASED ON MY OBSERVATIONS OF HIS CONDUCT, AND THE GOSSIP AMONG THE SERVANTS...
THOSE TWO HAVE A MOST *INTIMATE* RAPPORT WITH ONE ANOTHER.

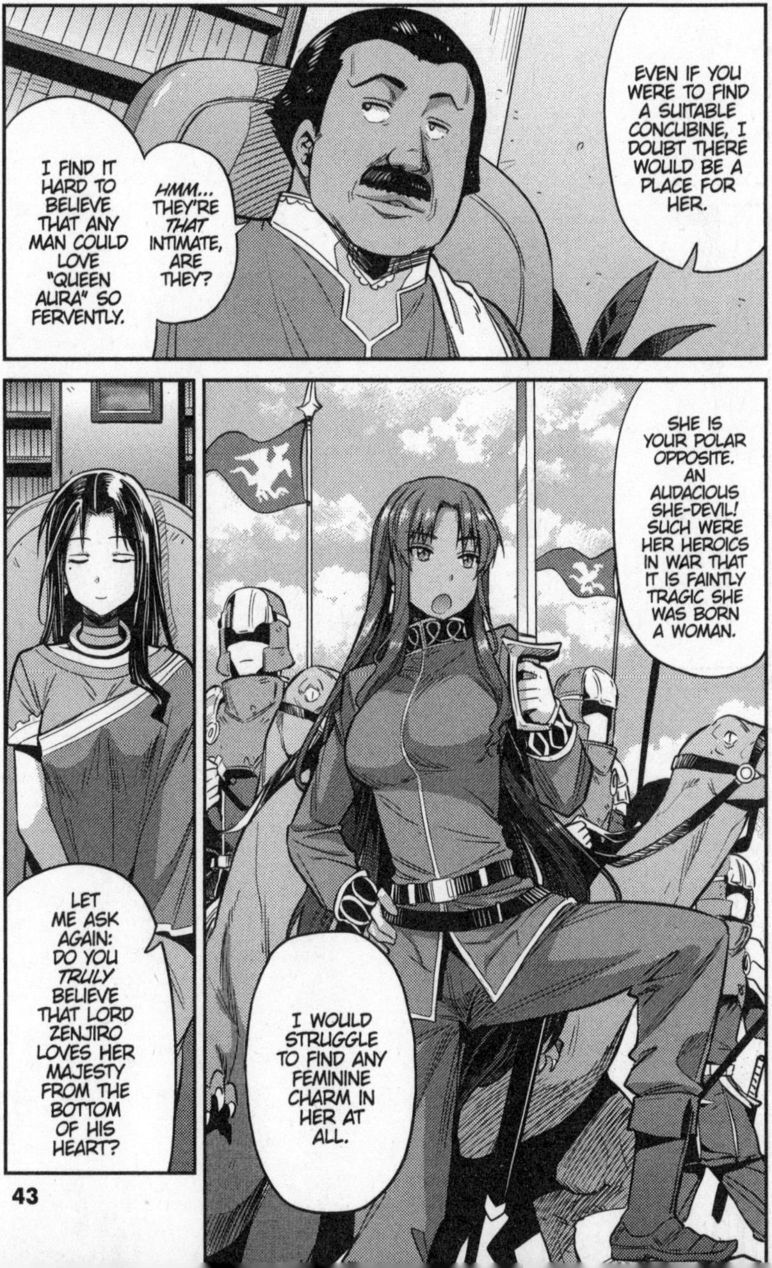

EVEN IF YOU WERE TO FIND A SUITABLE CONCUBINE, I DOUBT THERE WOULD BE A PLACE FOR HER.
HMM... THEY'RE *THAT* INTIMATE, ARE THEY?
I FIND IT HARD TO BELIEVE THAT ANY MAN COULD LOVE "QUEEN AURA" SO FERVENTLY.
SHE IS YOUR POLAR OPPOSITE. AN AUDACIOUS SHE-DEVIL! SUCH WERE HER HEROICS IN WAR THAT IT IS FAINTLY TRAGIC SHE WAS BORN A WOMAN.
I WOULD STRUGGLE TO FIND ANY FEMININE CHARM IN HER AT ALL.
LET ME ASK AGAIN: DO YOU *TRULY* BELIEVE THAT LORD ZENJIRO LOVES HER MAJESTY FROM THE BOTTOM OF HIS HEART?

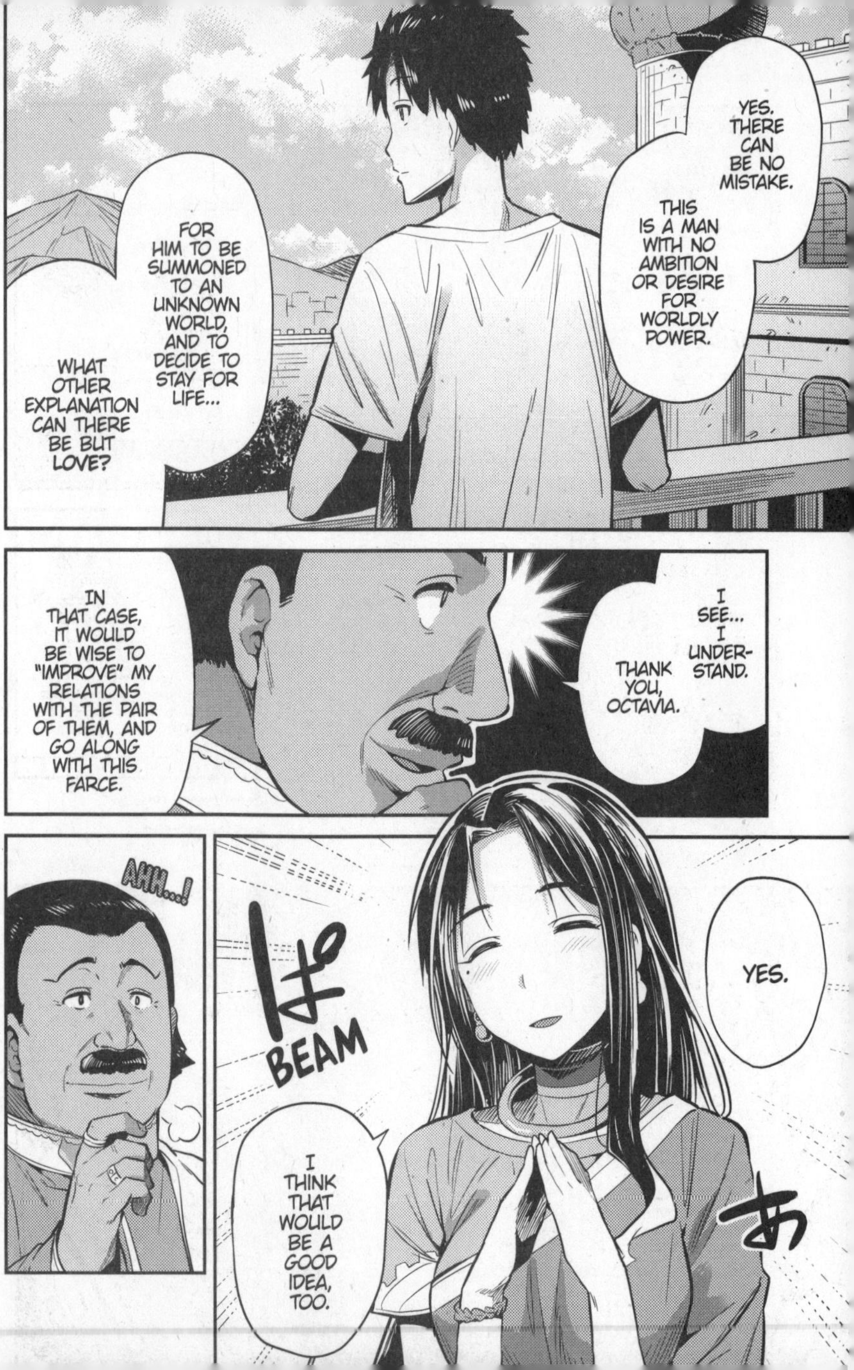
YES. THERE CAN BE NO MISTAKE.
THIS IS A MAN WITH NO AMBITION OR DESIRE FOR WORLDLY POWER.
FOR HIM TO BE SUMMONED TO AN UNKNOWN WORLD, AND TO DECIDE TO STAY FOR LIFE...
WHAT OTHER EXPLANATION CAN THERE BE BUT LOVE?
I SEE... I UNDER-STAND.
THANK YOU, OCTAVIA.
IN THAT CASE, IT WOULD BE WISE TO "IMPROVE" MY RELATIONS WITH THE PAIR OF THEM, AND GO ALONG WITH THIS FARCE.
あ
YES.
ぱ
BEAM
I THINK THAT WOULD BE A GOOD IDEA, TOO.
AHH...!

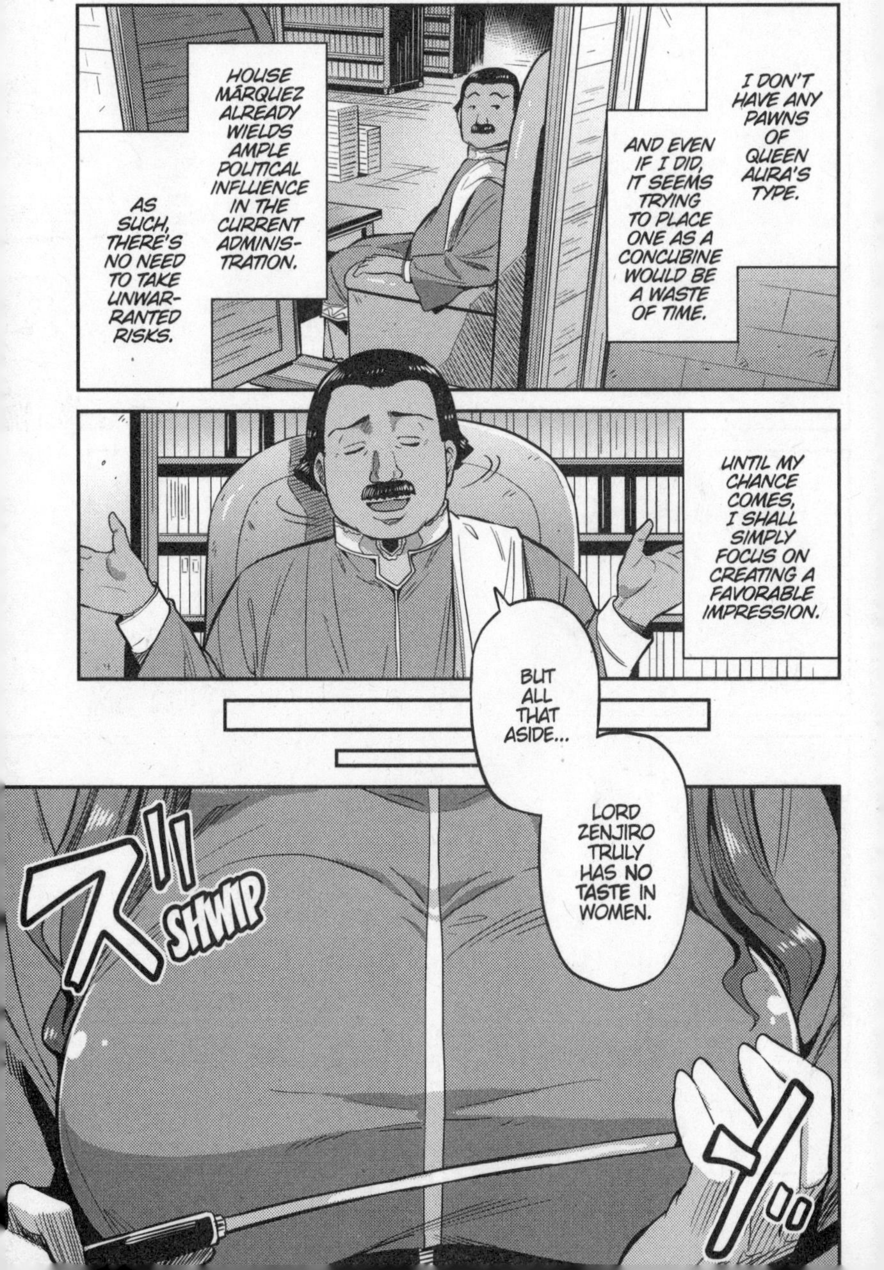
I DON'T HAVE ANY PAWNS OF QUEEN AURA'S TYPE.
AND EVEN IF I DID, IT SEEMS TRYING TO PLACE ONE AS A CONCUBINE WOULD BE A WASTE OF TIME.
HOUSE MÁRQUEZ ALREADY WIELDS AMPLE POLITICAL INFLUENCE IN THE CURRENT ADMINIS-TRATION.
AS SUCH, THERE'S NO NEED TO TAKE UNWAR-RANTED RISKS.
UNTIL MY CHANCE COMES, I SHALL SIMPLY FOCUS ON CREATING A FAVORABLE IMPRESSION.
BUT ALL THAT ASIDE...
LORD ZENJIRO TRULY HAS NO TASTE IN WOMEN.
SHWIP

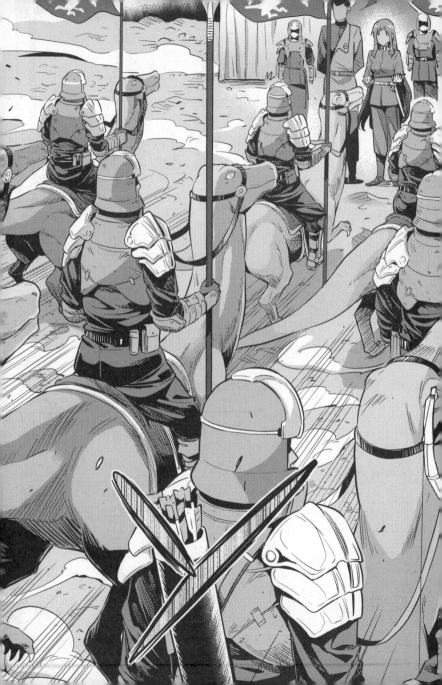

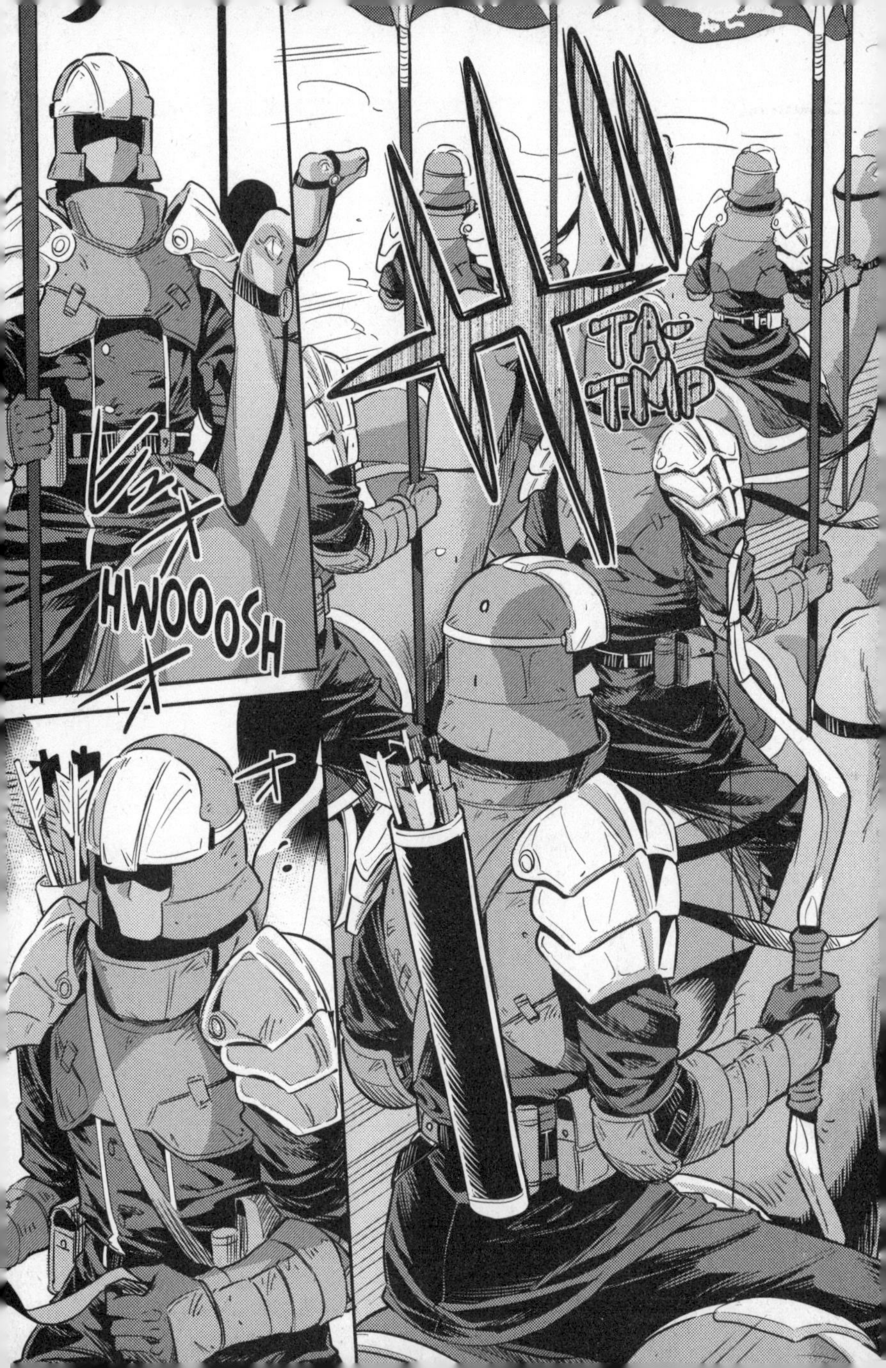
TA-
TMP
HWOOOSH

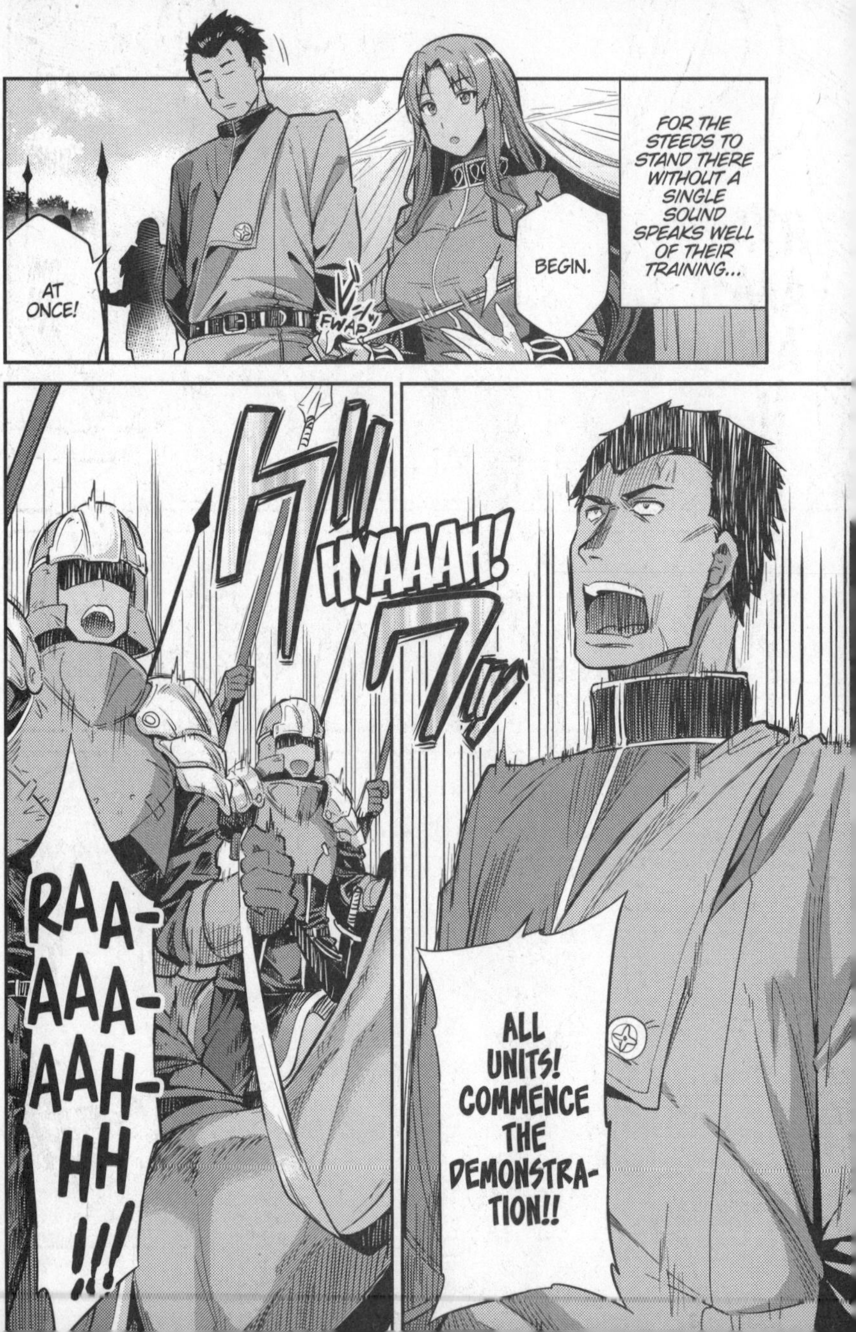
FOR THE STEEDS TO STAND THERE WITHOUT A SINGLE SOUND SPEAKS WELL OF THEIR TRAINING...
BEGIN.
AT ONCE!
FWAP
ALL UNITS! COMMENCE THE DEMONSTRA-TION!!
HYAAAH!
RAA-AAA-AAH-HH !!!

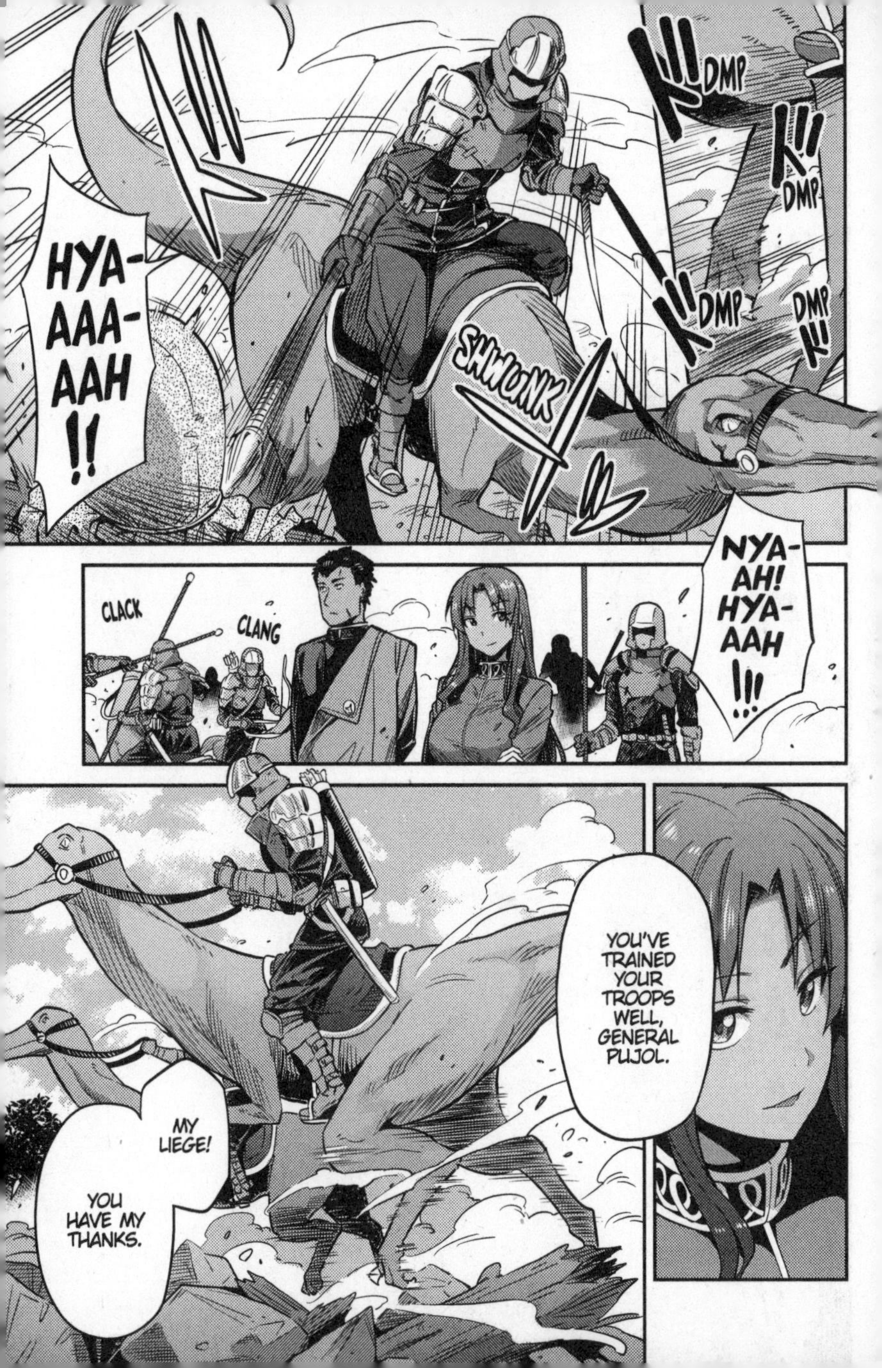
DMP
DMP
DMP
DMP
SHWUNK
HYA-AAA-AAH!!
NYA-AH! HYA-AAH!!!
CLANG
CLACK
YOU'VE TRAINED YOUR TROOPS WELL, GENERAL PUJOL.
MY LIEGE!
YOU HAVE MY THANKS.

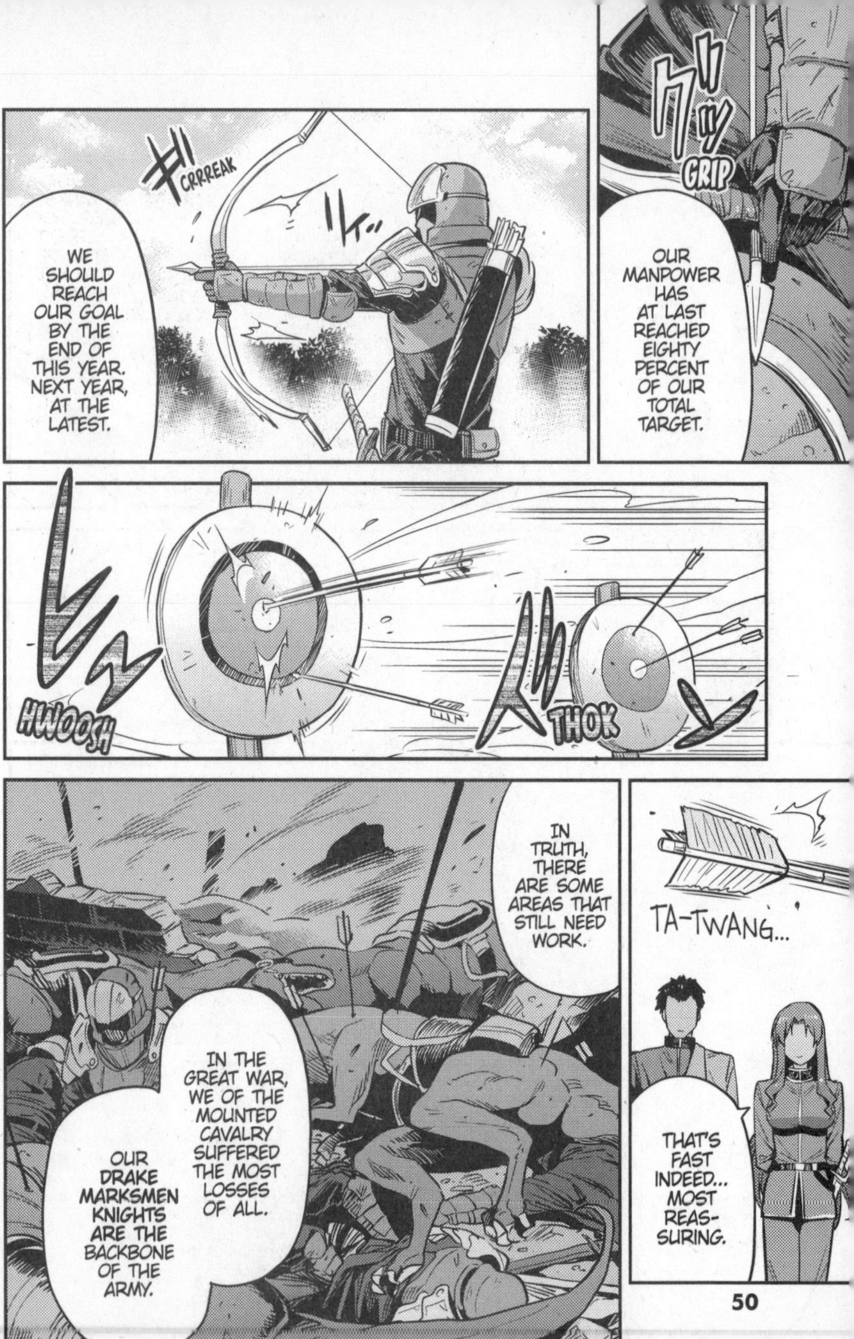
GRIP
OUR MANPOWER HAS AT LAST REACHED EIGHTY PERCENT OF OUR TOTAL TARGET.
CRRREAK
WE SHOULD REACH OUR GOAL BY THE END OF THIS YEAR. NEXT YEAR, AT THE LATEST.
THOK
HWOOSH
TA-TWANG...
THAT'S FAST INDEED... MOST REAS-SURING.
IN TRUTH, THERE ARE SOME AREAS THAT STILL NEED WORK.
IN THE GREAT WAR, WE OF THE MOUNTED CAVALRY SUFFERED THE MOST LOSSES OF ALL.
OUR DRAKE MARKSMEN KNIGHTS ARE THE BACKBONE OF THE ARMY.

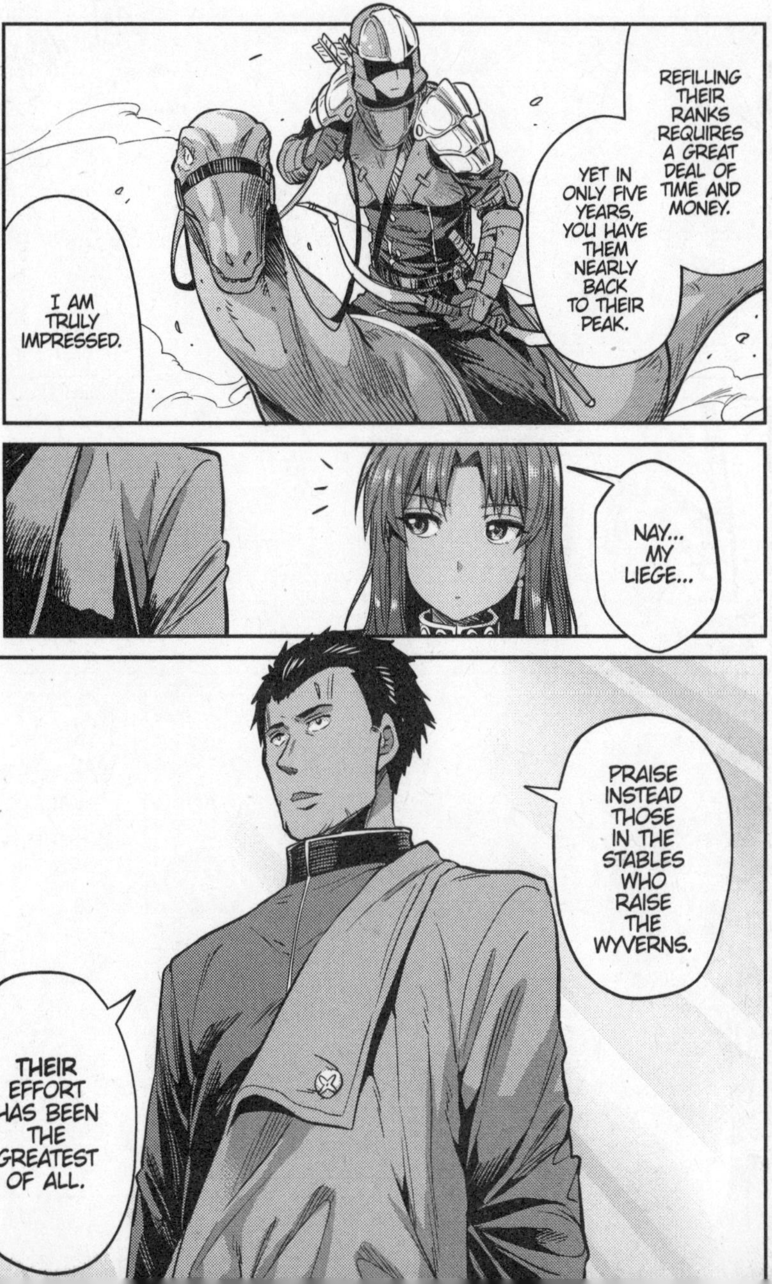
REFILLING THEIR RANKS REQUIRES A GREAT DEAL OF TIME AND MONEY.
YET IN ONLY FIVE YEARS, YOU HAVE THEM NEARLY BACK TO THEIR PEAK.
I AM TRULY IMPRESSED.
NAY... MY LIEGE...
PRAISE INSTEAD THOSE IN THE STABLES WHO RAISE THE WYVERNS.
THEIR EFFORT HAS BEEN THE GREATEST OF ALL.

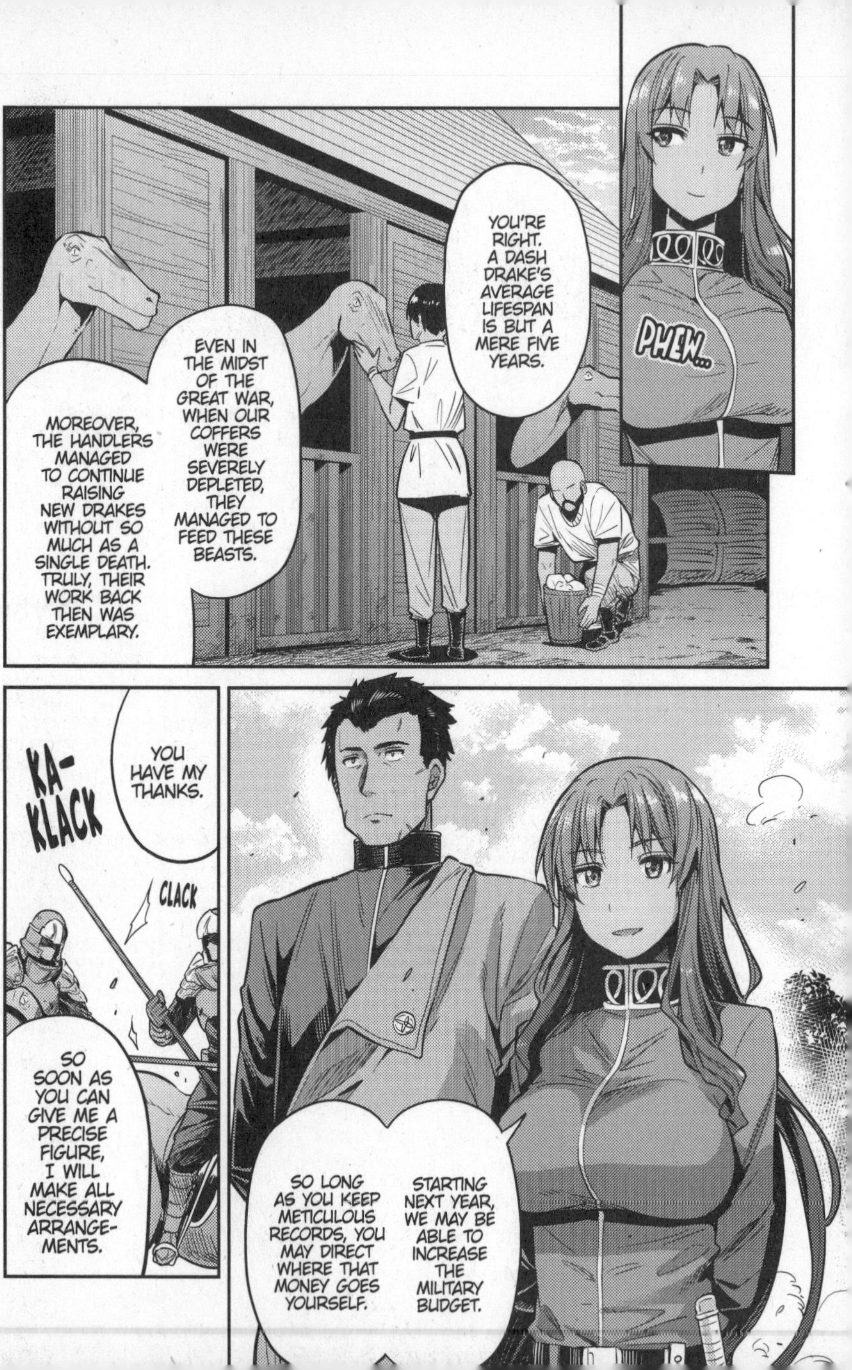
PHEW...
YOU'RE RIGHT. A DASH DRAKE'S AVERAGE LIFESPAN IS BUT A MERE FIVE YEARS.
EVEN IN THE MIDST OF THE GREAT WAR, WHEN OUR COFFERS WERE SEVERELY DEPLETED, THEY MANAGED TO FEED THESE BEASTS.
MOREOVER, THE HANDLERS MANAGED TO CONTINUE RAISING NEW DRAKES WITHOUT SO MUCH AS A SINGLE DEATH. TRULY, THEIR WORK BACK THEN WAS EXEMPLARY.
STARTING NEXT YEAR, WE MAY BE ABLE TO INCREASE THE MILITARY BUDGET.
SO LONG AS YOU KEEP METICULOUS RECORDS, YOU MAY DIRECT WHERE THAT MONEY GOES YOURSELF.
YOU HAVE MY THANKS.
KA-KLACK
CLACK
SO SOON AS YOU CAN GIVE ME A PRECISE FIGURE, I WILL MAKE ALL NECESSARY ARRANGE-MENTS.

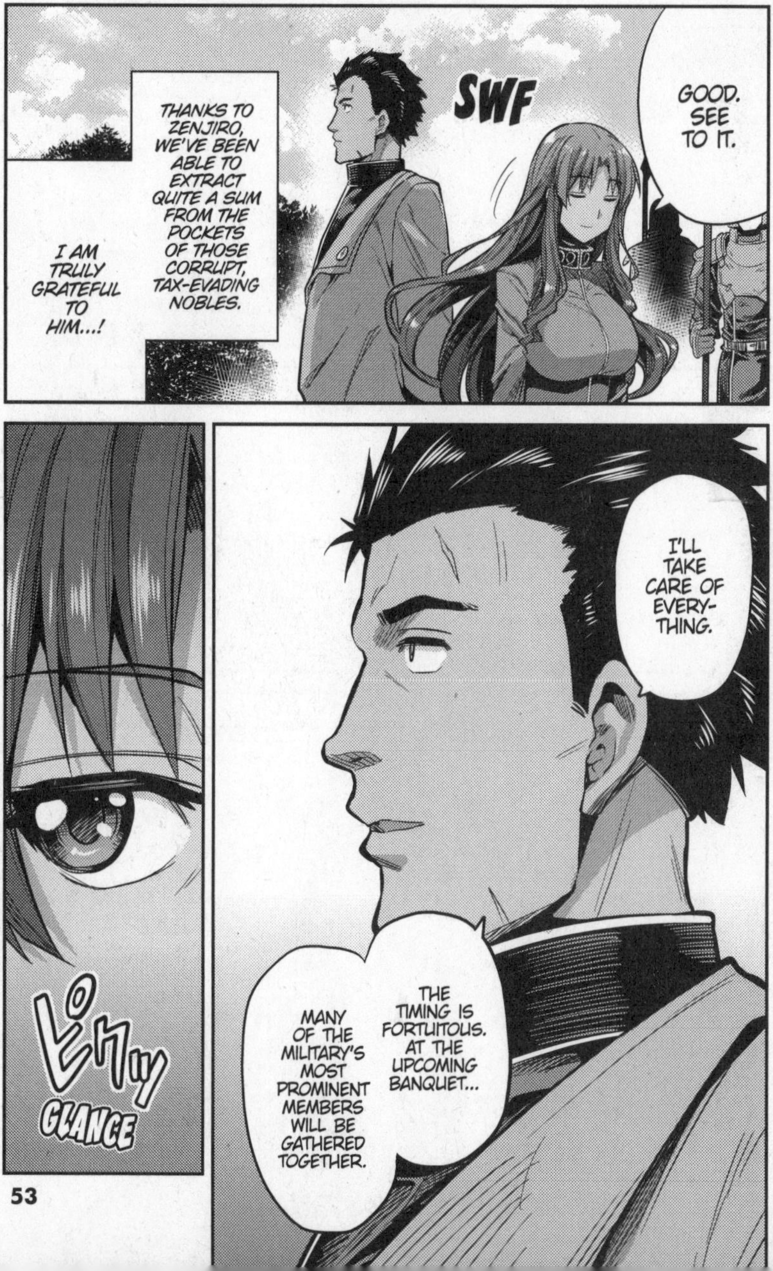
GOOD. SEE TO IT.
SWF
THANKS TO ZENJIRO, WE'VE BEEN ABLE TO EXTRACT QUITE A SUM FROM THE POCKETS OF THOSE CORRUPT, TAX-EVADING NOBLES.
I AM TRULY GRATEFUL TO HIM...!
I'LL TAKE CARE OF EVERY-THING.
THE TIMING IS FORTUITOUS. AT THE UPCOMING BANQUET...
MANY OF THE MILITARY'S MOST PROMINENT MEMBERS WILL BE GATHERED TOGETHER.
GLANCE

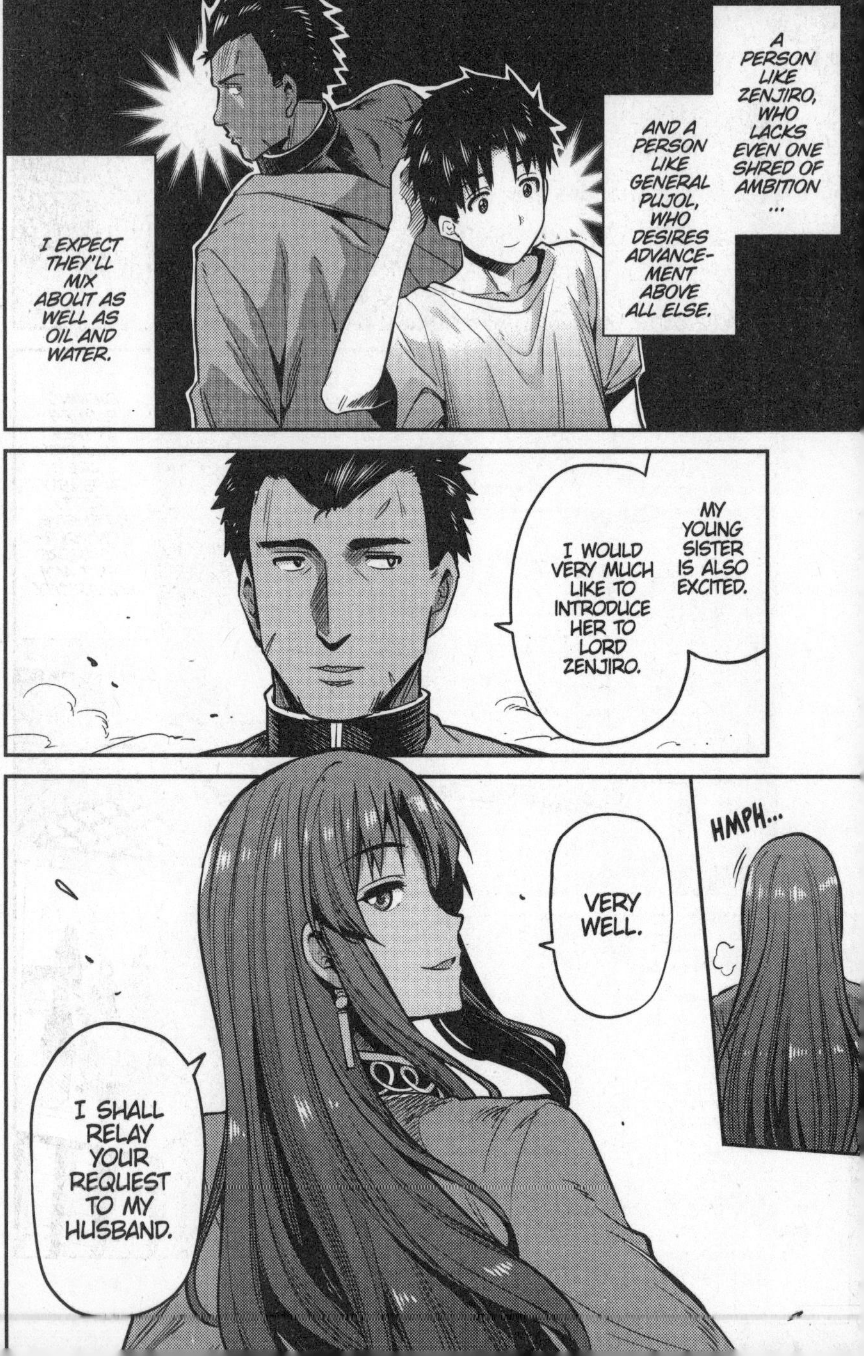
A PERSON LIKE ZENJIRO, WHO LACKS EVEN ONE SHRED OF AMBITION...
AND A PERSON LIKE GENERAL PUJOL, WHO DESIRES ADVANCEMENT ABOVE ALL ELSE.
I EXPECT THEY'LL MIX ABOUT AS WELL AS OIL AND WATER.
MY YOUNG SISTER IS ALSO EXCITED.
I WOULD VERY MUCH LIKE TO INTRODUCE HER TO LORD ZENJIRO.
HMPH...
VERY WELL.
I SHALL RELAY YOUR REQUEST TO MY HUSBAND.

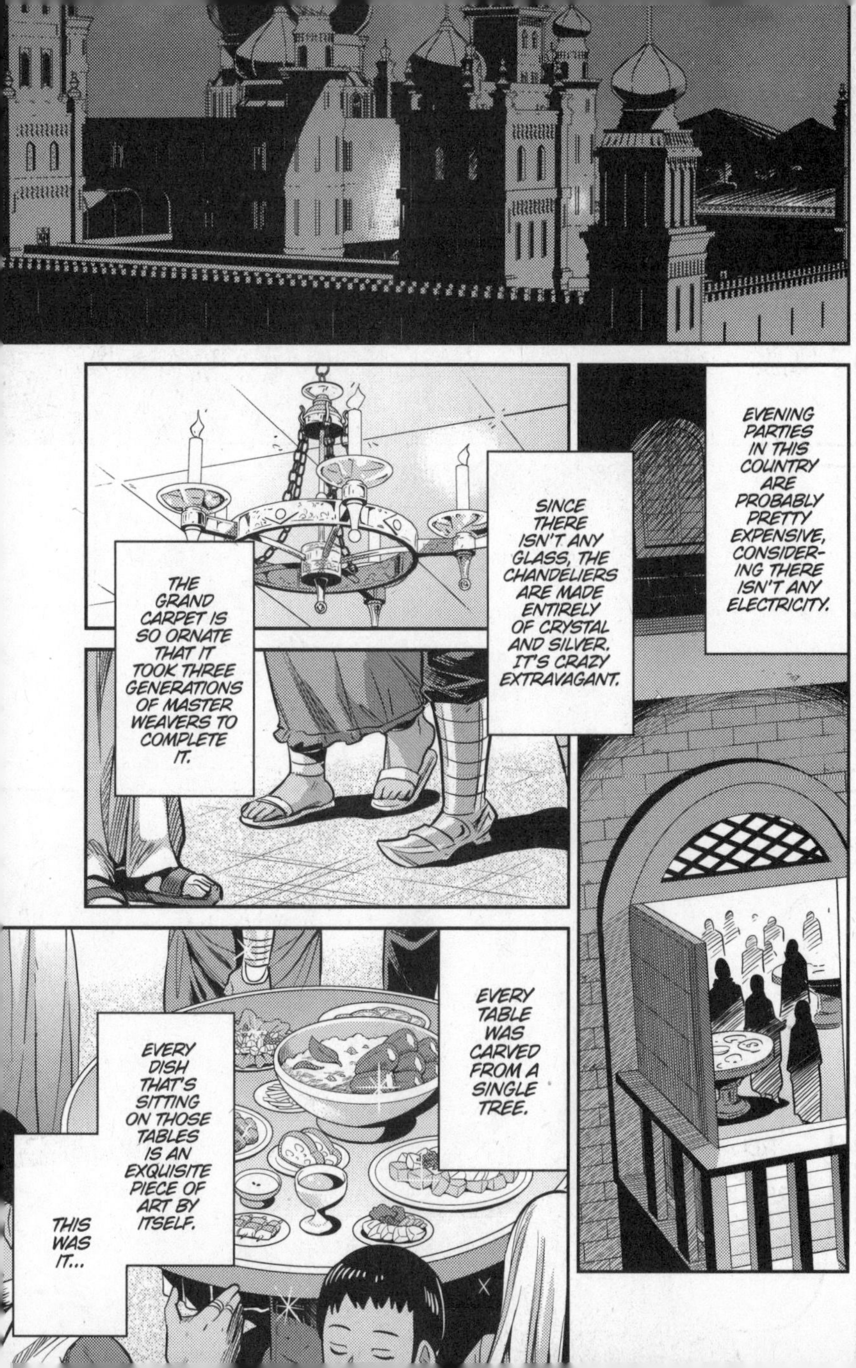
EVENING PARTIES IN THIS COUNTRY ARE PROBABLY PRETTY EXPENSIVE, CONSIDERING THERE ISN'T ANY ELECTRICITY.
SINCE THERE ISN'T ANY GLASS, THE CHANDELIERS ARE MADE ENTIRELY OF CRYSTAL AND SILVER. IT'S CRAZY EXTRAVAGANT.
THE GRAND CARPET IS SO ORNATE THAT IT TOOK THREE GENERATIONS OF MASTER WEAVERS TO COMPLETE IT.
EVERY TABLE WAS CARVED FROM A SINGLE TREE.
EVERY DISH THAT'S SITTING ON THOSE TABLES IS AN EXQUISITE PIECE OF ART BY ITSELF.
THIS WAS IT...

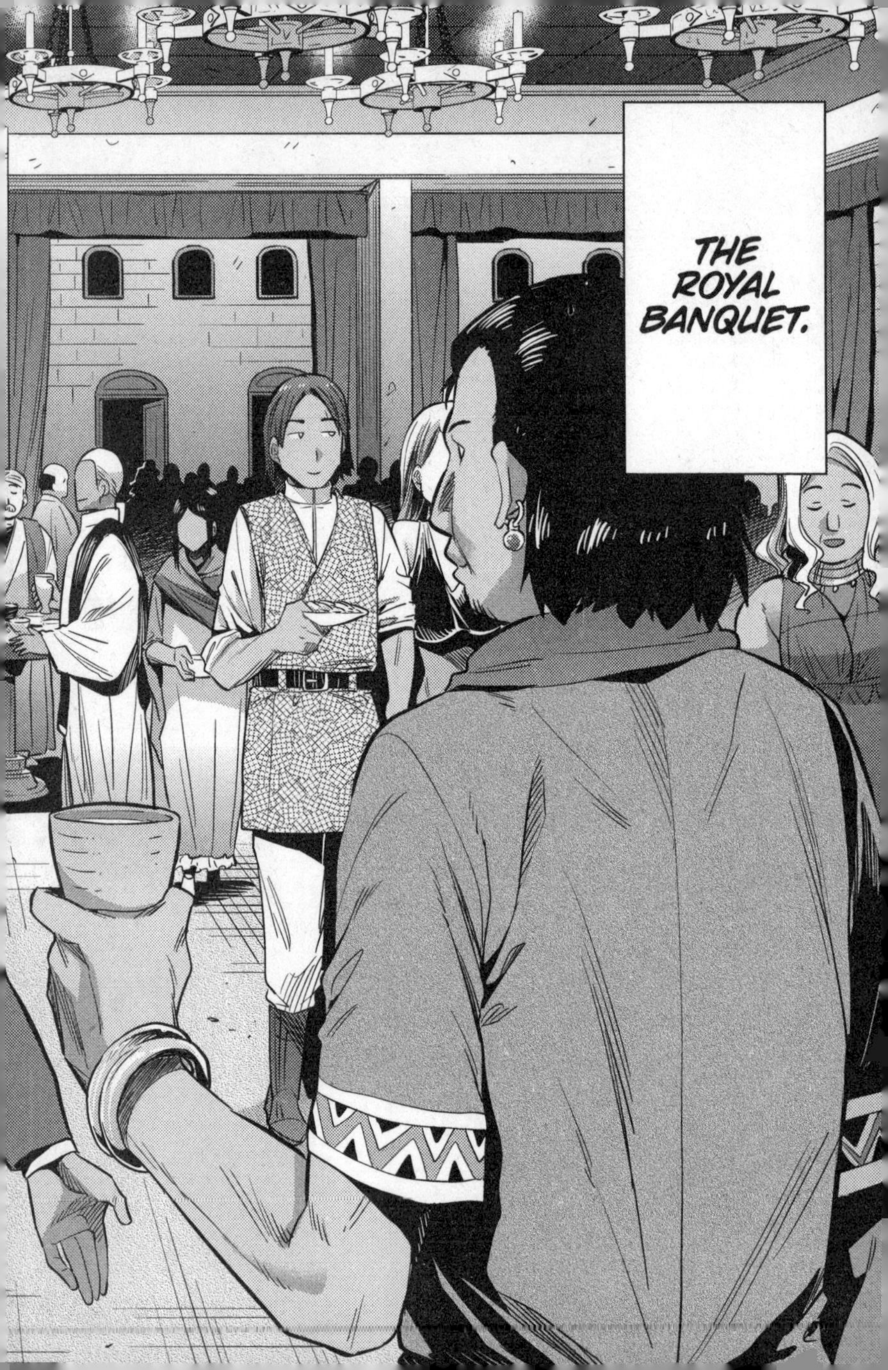
THE ROYAL BANQUET.

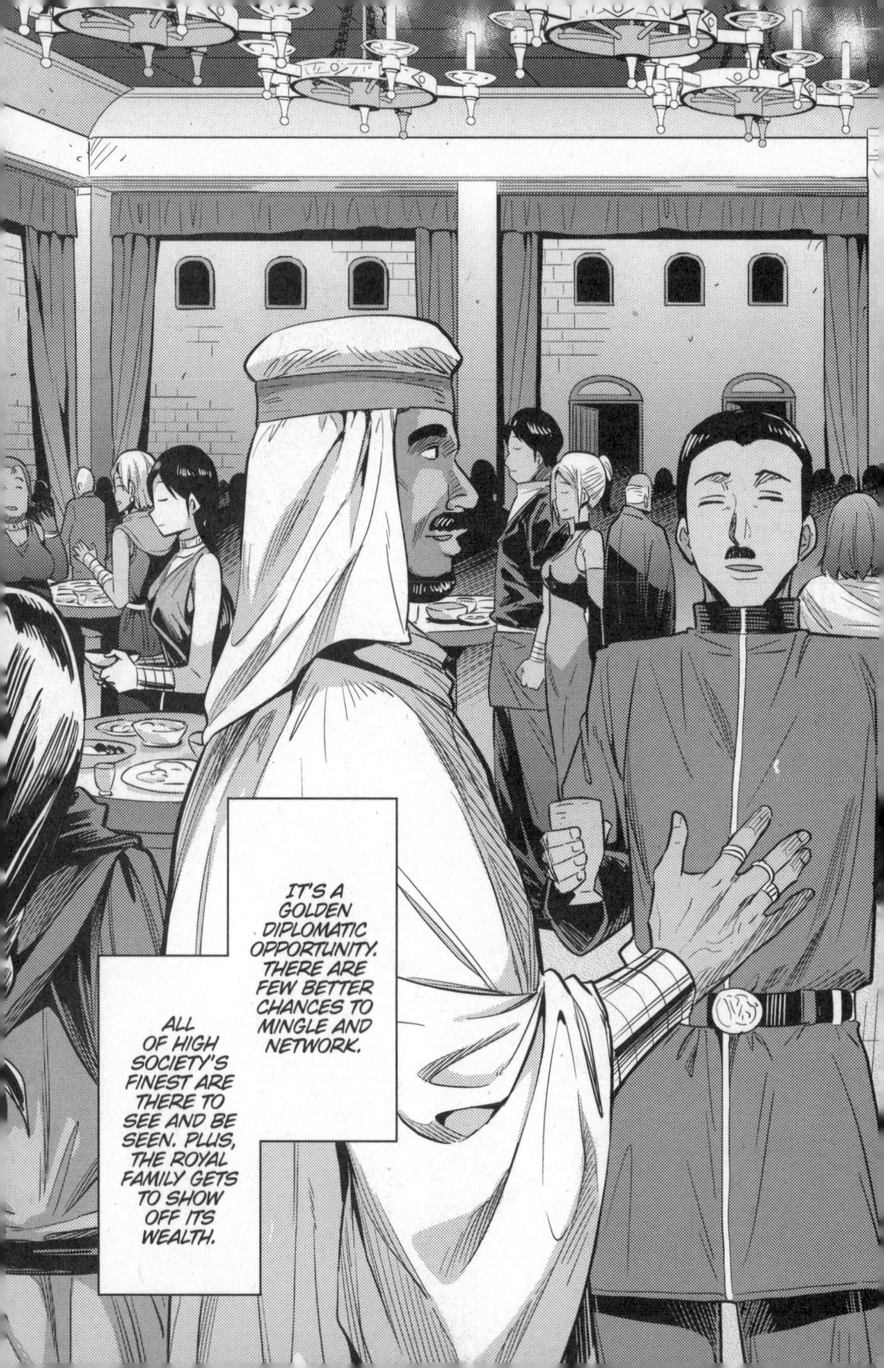
IT'S A GOLDEN DIPLOMATIC OPPORTUNITY. THERE ARE FEW BETTER CHANCES TO MINGLE AND NETWORK.
ALL OF HIGH SOCIETY'S FINEST ARE THERE TO SEE AND BE SEEN. PLUS, THE ROYAL FAMILY GETS TO SHOW OFF ITS WEALTH.

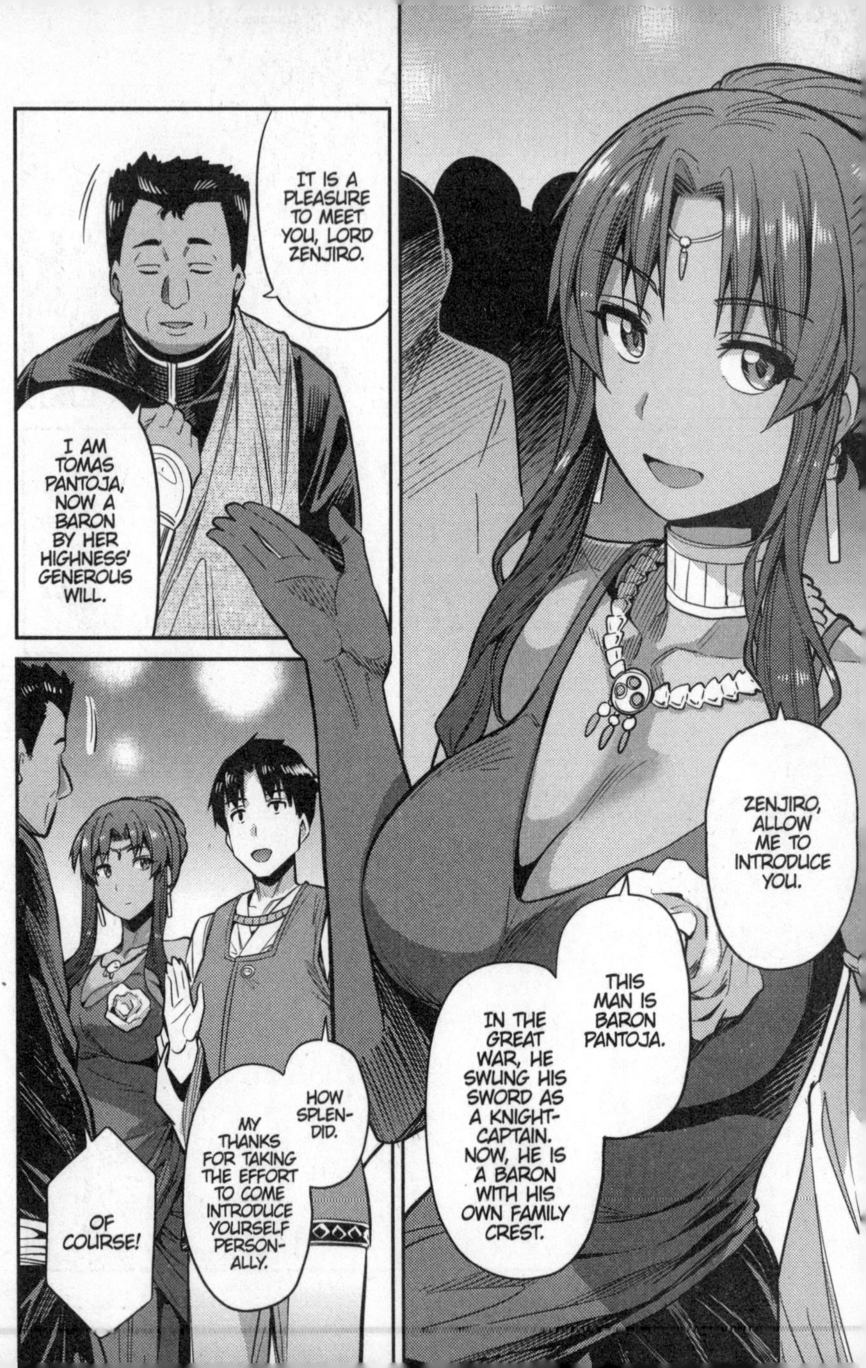
ZENJIRO, ALLOW ME TO INTRODUCE YOU.
THIS MAN IS BARON PANTOJA.
IN THE GREAT WAR, HE SWUNG HIS SWORD AS A KNIGHT-CAPTAIN. NOW, HE IS A BARON WITH HIS OWN FAMILY CREST.
IT IS A PLEASURE TO MEET YOU, LORD ZENJIRO.
I AM TOMAS PANTOJA, NOW A BARON BY HER HIGHNESS' GENEROUS WILL.
HOW SPLEN-DID.
MY THANKS FOR TAKING THE EFFORT TO COME INTRODUCE YOURSELF PERSON-ALLY.
OF COURSE!

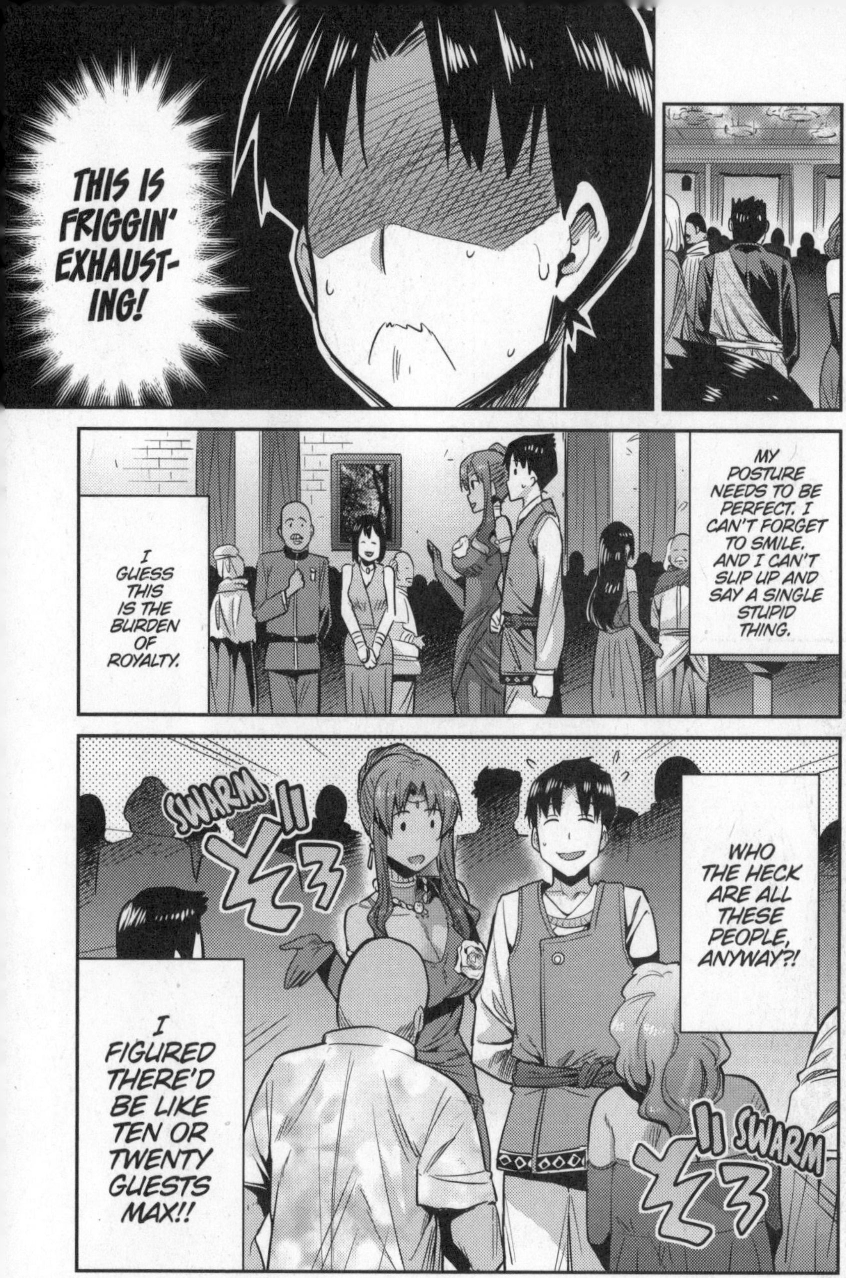
THIS IS FRIGGIN' EXHAUSTING!
MY POSTURE NEEDS TO BE PERFECT. I CAN'T FORGET TO SMILE. AND I CAN'T SLIP UP AND SAY A SINGLE STUPID THING.
I GUESS THIS IS THE BURDEN OF ROYALTY.
WHO THE HECK ARE ALL THESE PEOPLE, ANYWAY?!
SWARM
ぞろ
SWARM
ぞろ
I FIGURED THERE'D BE LIKE TEN OR TWENTY GUESTS MAX!!

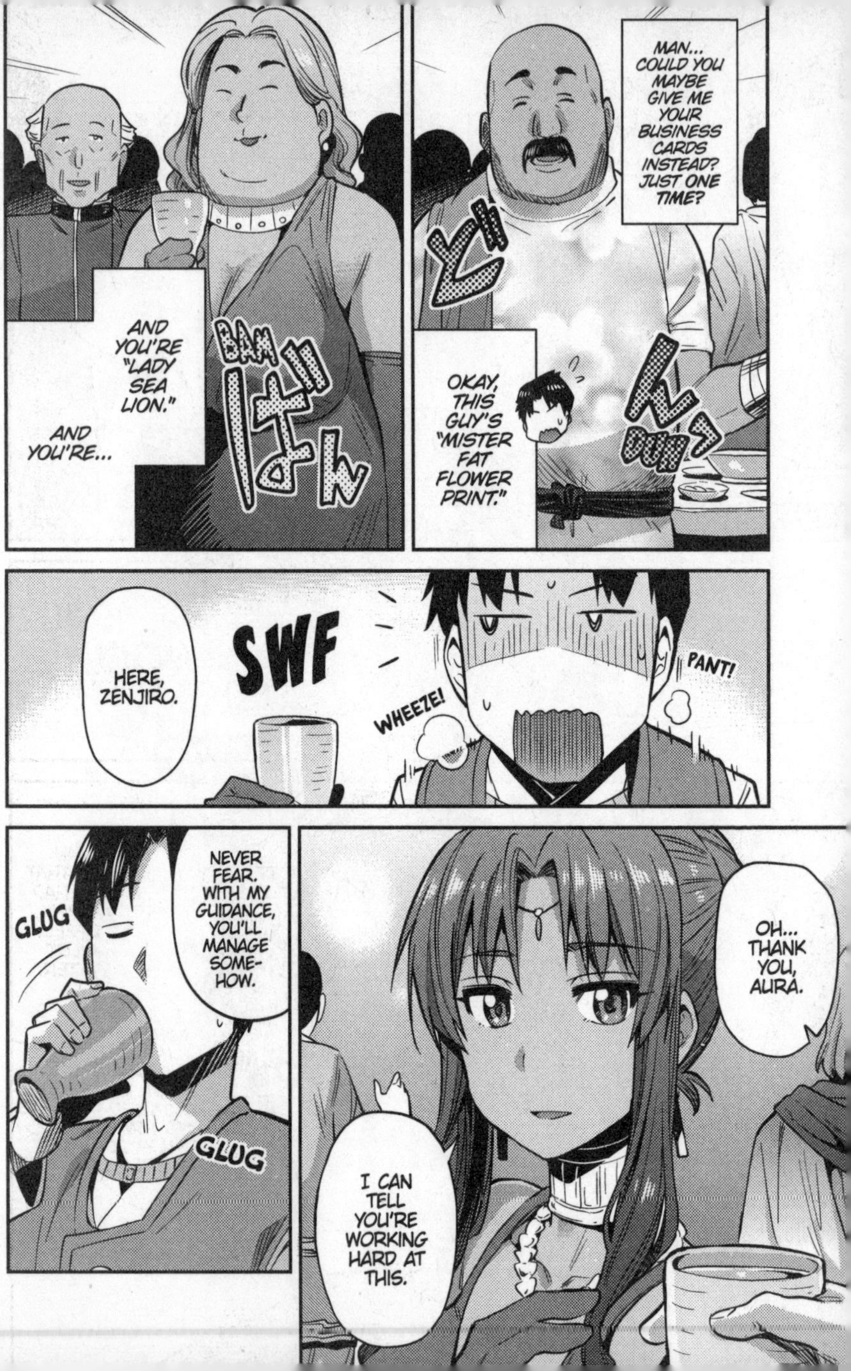
MAN... COULD YOU MAYBE GIVE ME YOUR BUSINESS CARDS INSTEAD? JUST ONE TIME?
どん
DUN
OKAY, THIS GUY'S "MISTER FAT FLOWER PRINT."
BAM
ばん
AND YOU'RE "LADY SEA LION."
AND YOU'RE...
PANT!
WHEEZE!
SWF
HERE, ZENJIRO.
OH... THANK YOU, AURA.
I CAN TELL YOU'RE WORKING HARD AT THIS.
NEVER FEAR. WITH MY GUIDANCE, YOU'LL MANAGE SOME-HOW.
GLUG
GLUG

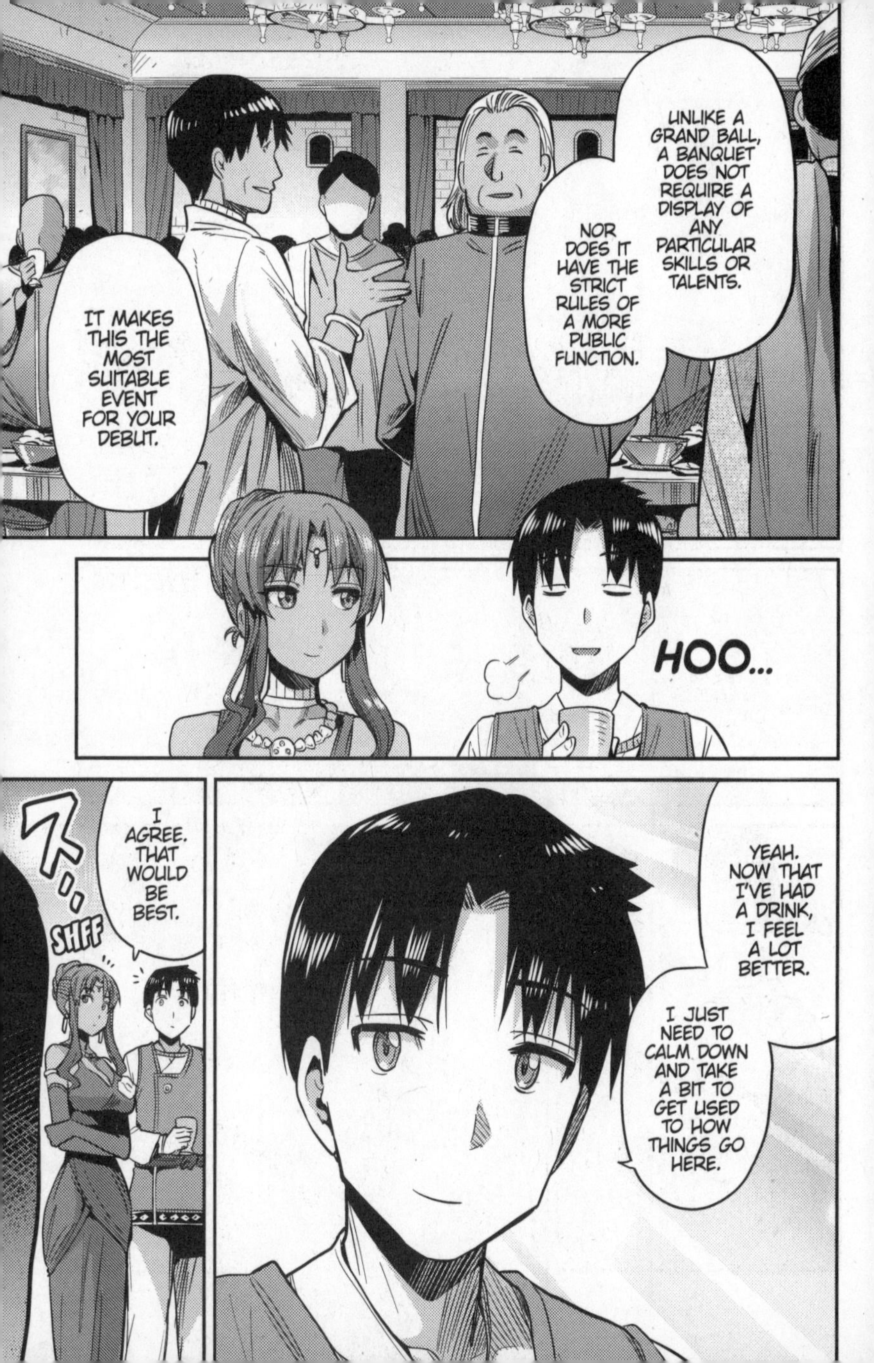
UNLIKE A GRAND BALL, A BANQUET DOES NOT REQUIRE A DISPLAY OF ANY PARTICULAR SKILLS OR TALENTS.
NOR DOES IT HAVE THE STRICT RULES OF A MORE PUBLIC FUNCTION.
IT MAKES THIS THE MOST SUITABLE EVENT FOR YOUR DEBUT.
HOO...
YEAH. NOW THAT I'VE HAD A DRINK, I FEEL A LOT BETTER.
I JUST NEED TO CALM DOWN AND TAKE A BIT TO GET USED TO HOW THINGS GO HERE.
I AGREE. THAT WOULD BE BEST.
SHFF

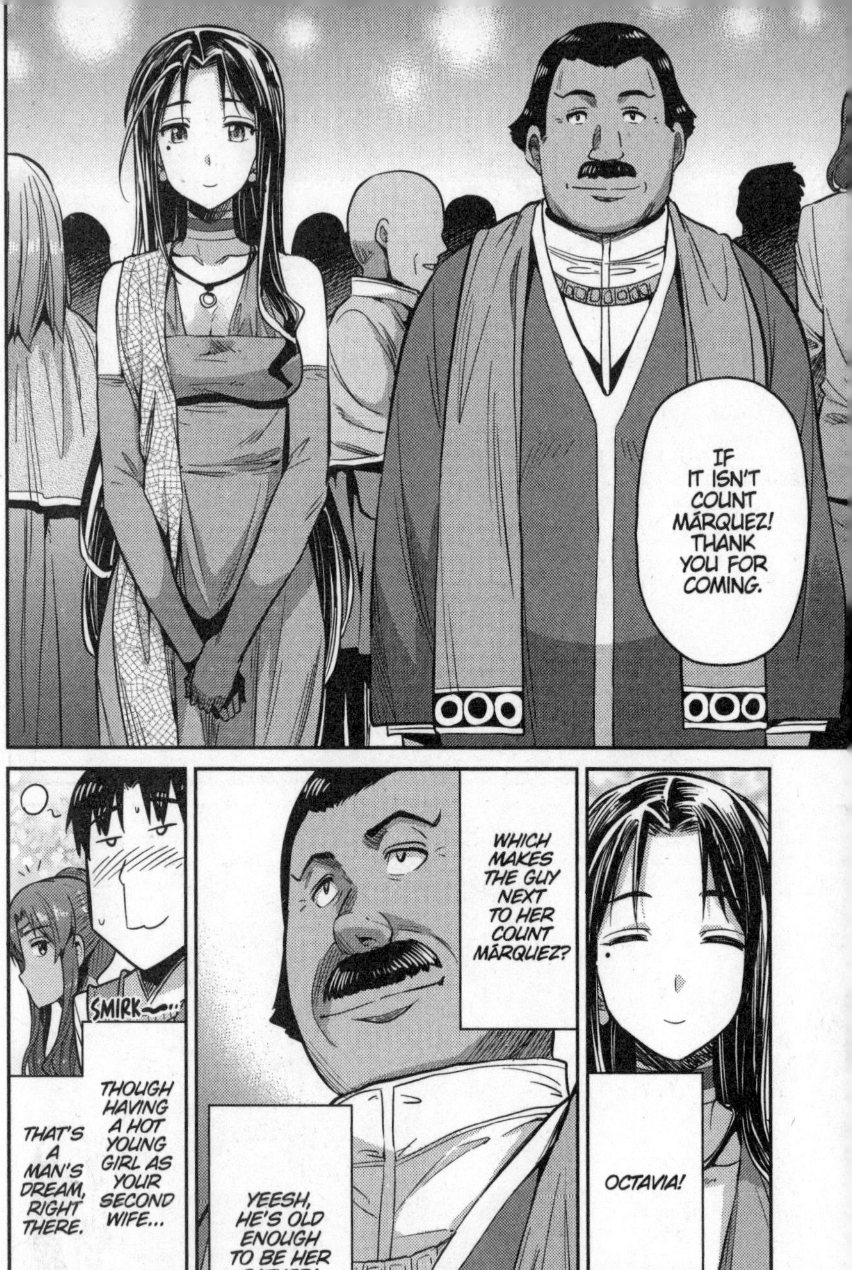
IF IT ISN'T COUNT MÁRQUEZ! THANK YOU FOR COMING.
OCTAVIA!
WHICH MAKES THE GUY NEXT TO HER COUNT MÁRQUEZ?
YEESH, HE'S OLD ENOUGH TO BE HER FATHER!
SMIRK~
THOUGH HAVING A HOT YOUNG GIRL AS YOUR SECOND WIFE...
THAT'S A MAN'S DREAM, RIGHT THERE.

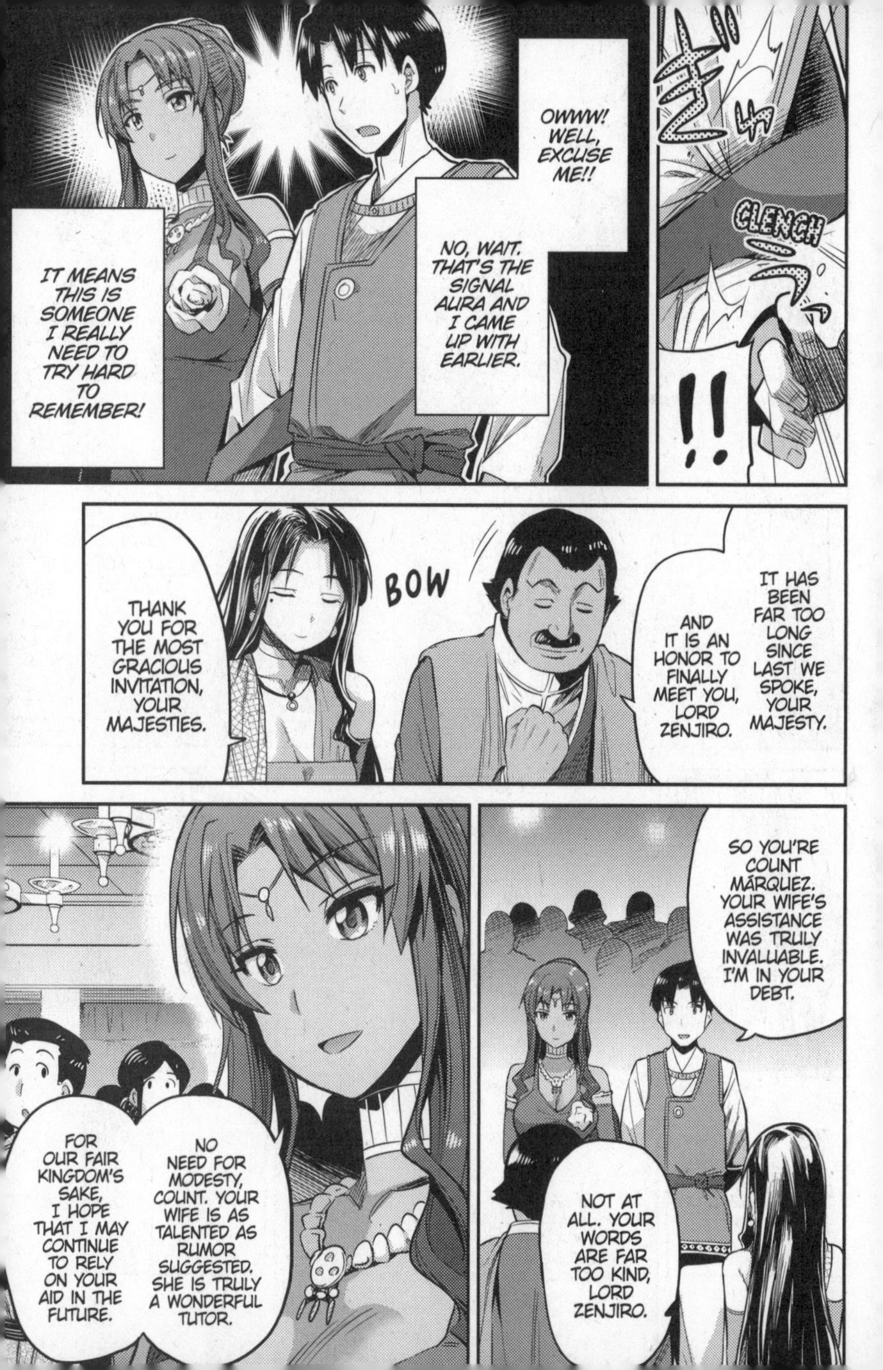
CLENCH
!!
OWWW! WELL, EXCUSE ME!!
NO, WAIT. THAT'S THE SIGNAL AURA AND I CAME UP WITH EARLIER.
IT MEANS THIS IS SOMEONE I REALLY NEED TO TRY HARD TO REMEMBER!
IT HAS BEEN FAR TOO LONG SINCE LAST WE SPOKE, YOUR MAJESTY.
AND IT IS AN HONOR TO FINALLY MEET YOU, LORD ZENJIRO.
BOW
THANK YOU FOR THE MOST GRACIOUS INVITATION, YOUR MAJESTIES.
SO YOU'RE COUNT MÁRQUEZ. YOUR WIFE'S ASSISTANCE WAS TRULY INVALUABLE. I'M IN YOUR DEBT.
NOT AT ALL. YOUR WORDS ARE FAR TOO KIND, LORD ZENJIRO.
NO NEED FOR MODESTY, COUNT. YOUR WIFE IS AS TALENTED AS RUMOR SUGGESTED. SHE IS TRULY A WONDERFUL TUTOR.
FOR OUR FAIR KINGDOM'S SAKE, I HOPE THAT I MAY CONTINUE TO RELY ON YOUR AID IN THE FUTURE.

MURMUR ザワ

MURMUR ザワ

THANK YOU FOR THE MOST GRACIOUS PRAISE, YOUR MAJESTY.

I LEFT EVERYTHING TO AURA, LIKE WE'D AGREED.

IT WASN'T REALLY IMPORTANT THAT I MAKE A GOOD IMPRESSION-- I JUST NEEDED TO AVOID MAKING A BAD ONE.

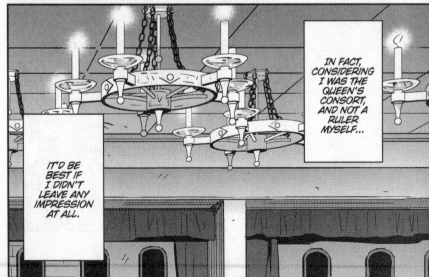

IN FACT, CONSIDERING I WAS THE QUEEN'S CONSORT, AND NOT A RULER MYSELF...

IT'D BE BEST IF I DIDN'T LEAVE ANY IMPRESSION AT ALL.

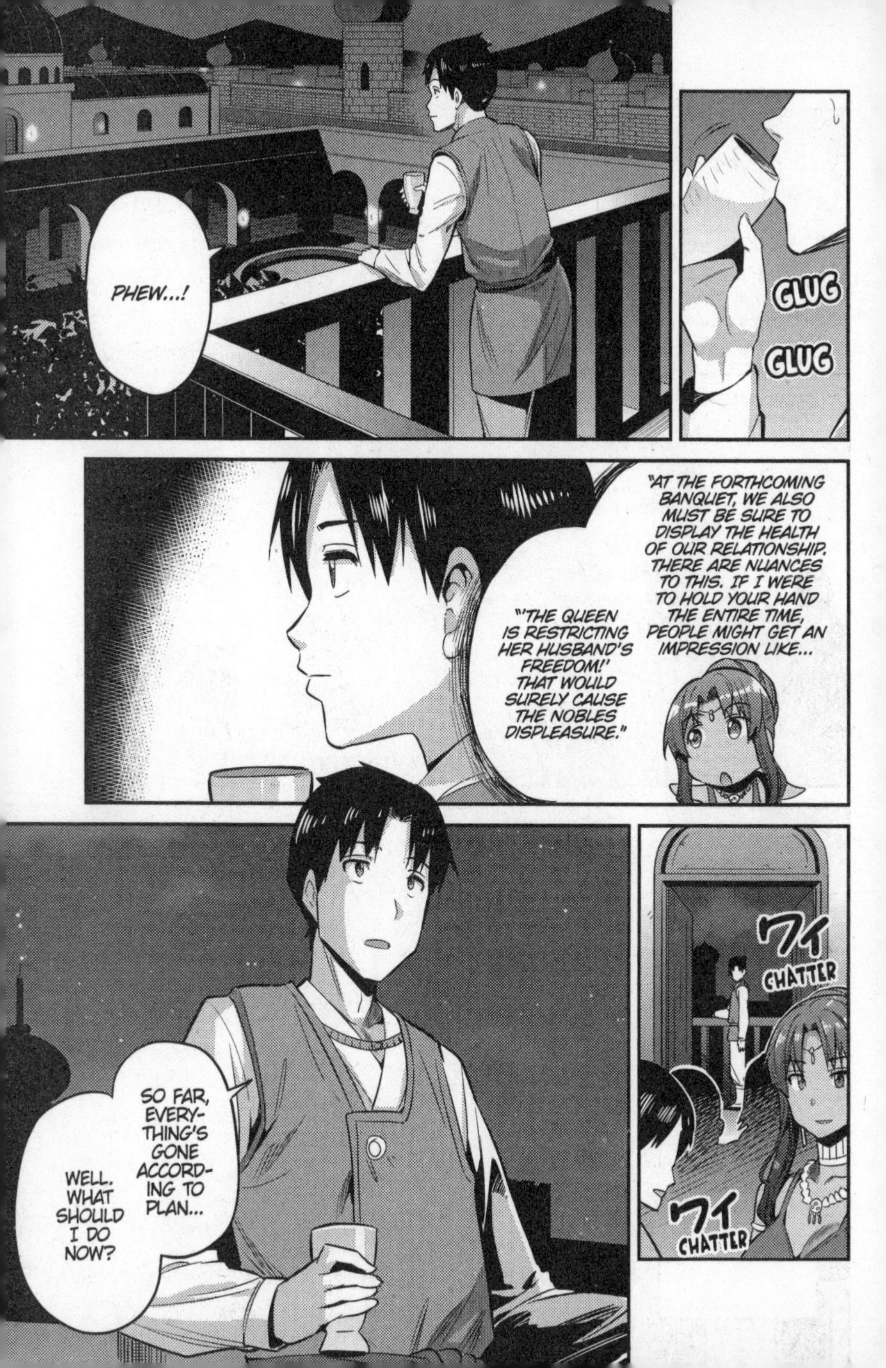
GLUG
GLUG
PHEW...!
"AT THE FORTHCOMING BANQUET, WE ALSO MUST BE SURE TO DISPLAY THE HEALTH OF OUR RELATIONSHIP. THERE ARE NUANCES TO THIS. IF I WERE TO HOLD YOUR HAND THE ENTIRE TIME, PEOPLE MIGHT GET AN IMPRESSION LIKE...
"'THE QUEEN IS RESTRICTING HER HUSBAND'S FREEDOM!' THAT WOULD SURELY CAUSE THE NOBLES DISPLEASURE."
ワイ
CHATTER
ワイ
CHATTER
SO FAR, EVERY-THING'S GONE ACCORD-ING TO PLAN...
WELL. WHAT SHOULD I DO NOW?

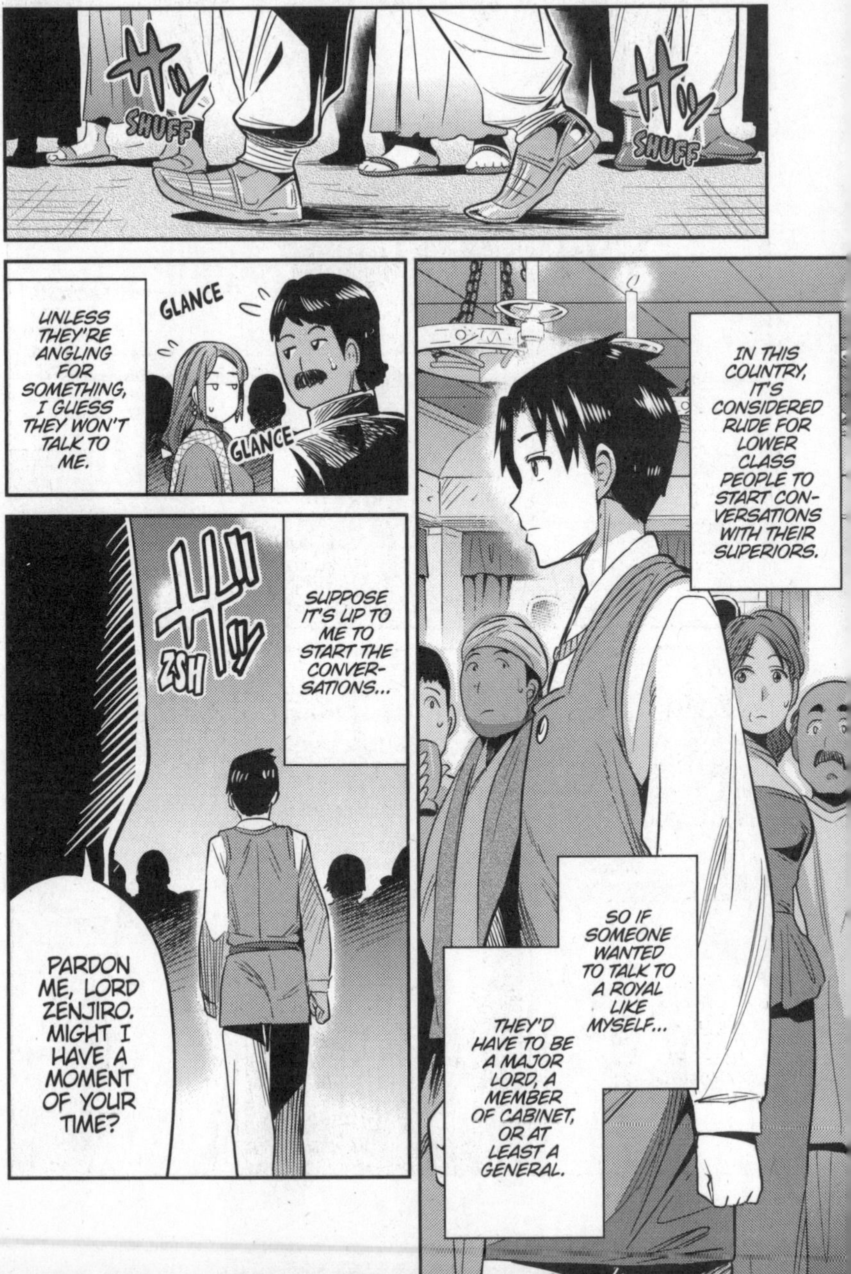
SHUFF
SHUFF
IN THIS COUNTRY, IT'S CONSIDERED RUDE FOR LOWER CLASS PEOPLE TO START CON-VERSATIONS WITH THEIR SUPERIORS.
SO IF SOMEONE WANTED TO TALK TO A ROYAL LIKE MYSELF...
THEY'D HAVE TO BE A MAJOR LORD, A MEMBER OF CABINET, OR AT LEAST A GENERAL.
GLANCE
GLANCE
UNLESS THEY'RE ANGLING FOR SOMETHING, I GUESS THEY WON'T TALK TO ME.
SUPPOSE IT'S UP TO ME TO START THE CONVER-SATIONS...
ZSH
PARDON ME, LORD ZENJIRO. MIGHT I HAVE A MOMENT OF YOUR TIME?

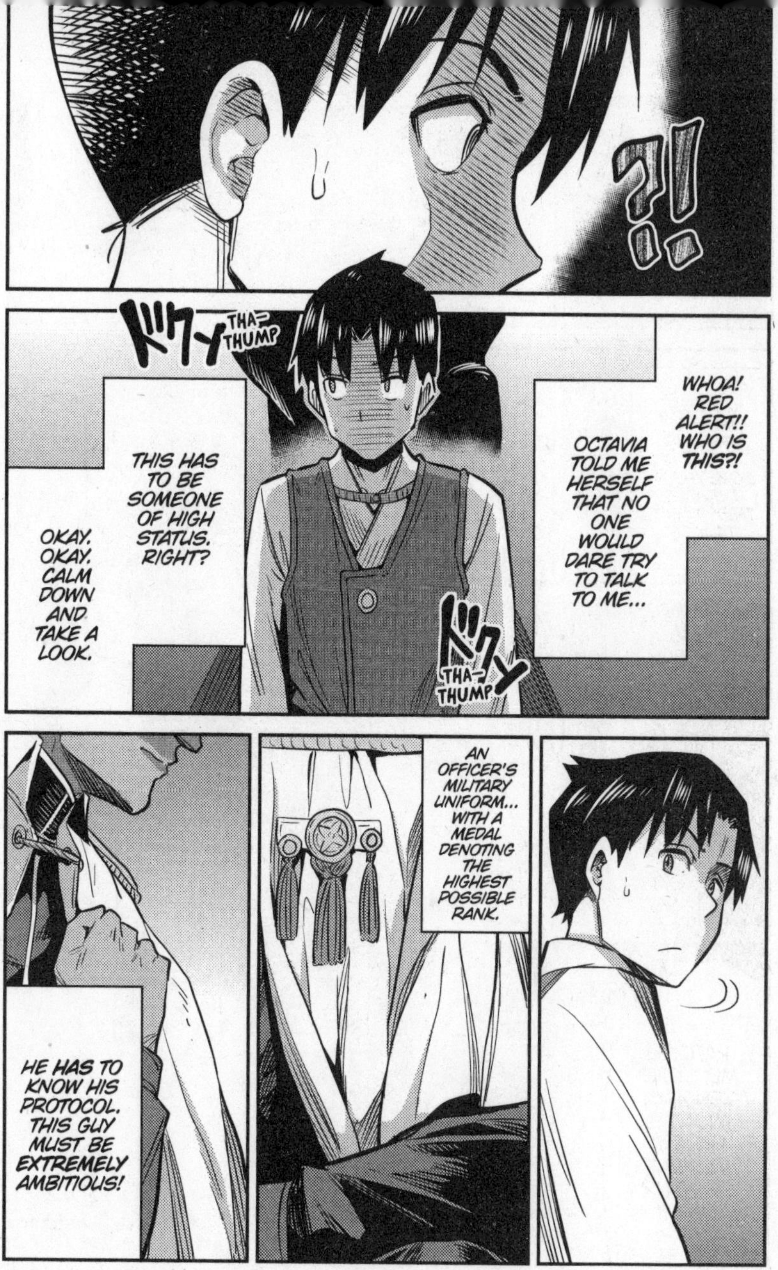
?!
WHOA! RED ALERT!! WHO IS THIS?!
OCTAVIA TOLD ME HERSELF THAT NO ONE WOULD DARE TRY TO TALK TO ME...
ドクン THA-THUMP
THIS HAS TO BE SOMEONE OF HIGH STATUS. RIGHT?
OKAY. OKAY. CALM DOWN AND TAKE A LOOK.
ドクン THA-THUMP
AN OFFICER'S MILITARY UNIFORM... WITH A MEDAL DENOTING THE HIGHEST POSSIBLE RANK.
HE HAS TO KNOW HIS PROTOCOL. THIS GUY MUST BE EXTREMELY AMBITIOUS!

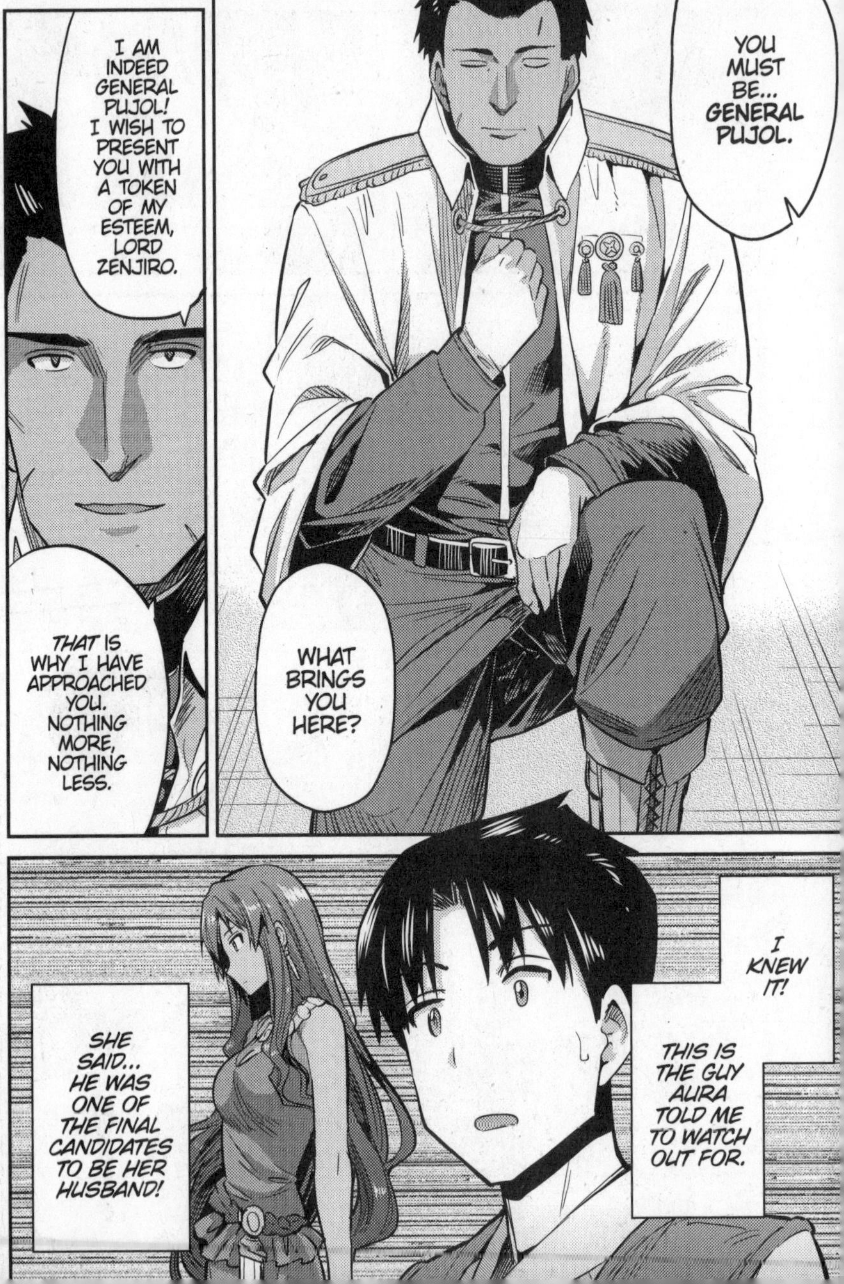
YOU MUST BE... GENERAL PUJOL.
WHAT BRINGS YOU HERE?
I AM INDEED GENERAL PUJOL! I WISH TO PRESENT YOU WITH A TOKEN OF MY ESTEEM, LORD ZENJIRO.
THAT IS WHY I HAVE APPROACHED YOU. NOTHING MORE, NOTHING LESS.
I KNEW IT!
THIS IS THE GUY AURA TOLD ME TO WATCH OUT FOR.
SHE SAID... HE WAS ONE OF THE FINAL CANDIDATES TO BE HER HUSBAND!

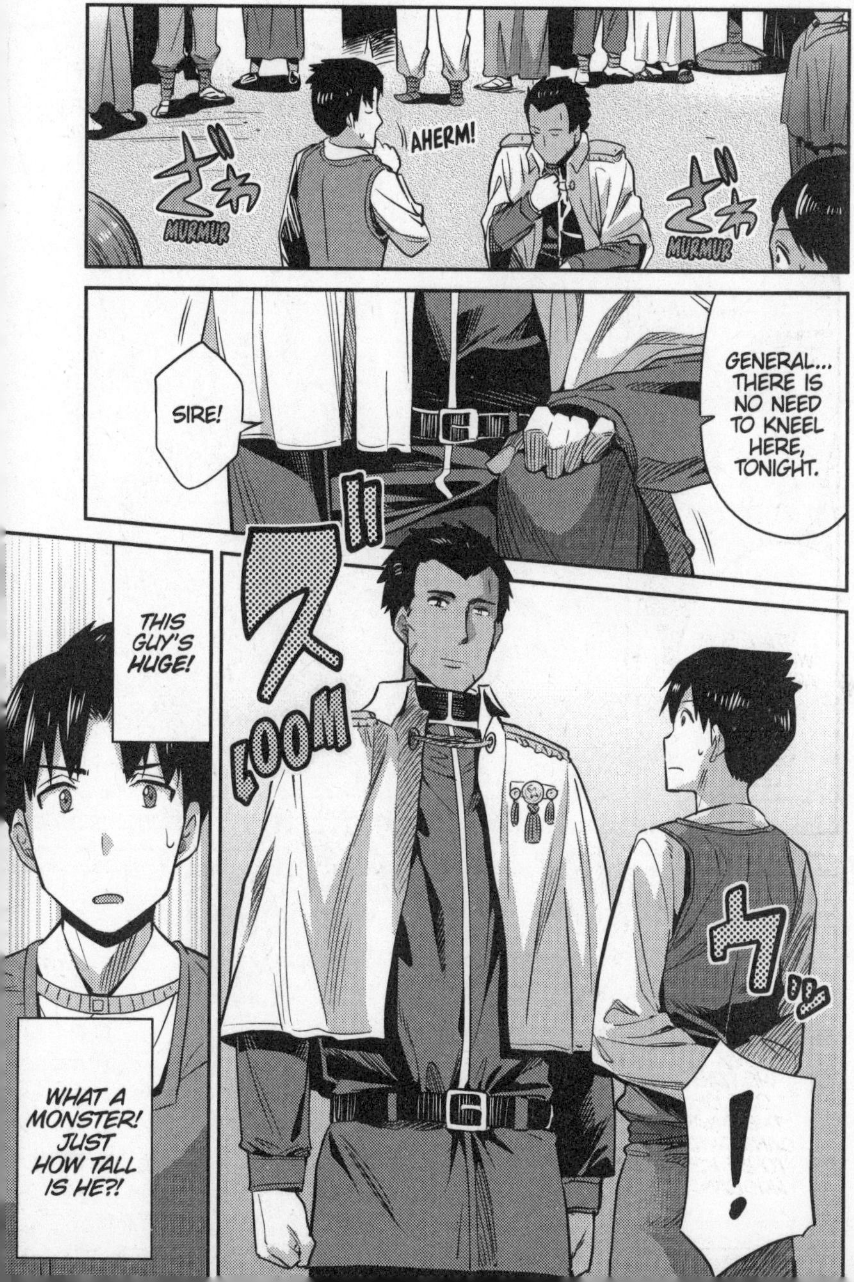
ざわ
MURMUR
AHERM!
ざわ
MURMUR
GENERAL... THERE IS NO NEED TO KNEEL HERE, TONIGHT.
SIRE!
ズ
LOOM
ウッ
!
THIS GUY'S HUGE!
WHAT A MONSTER! JUST HOW TALL IS HE?!

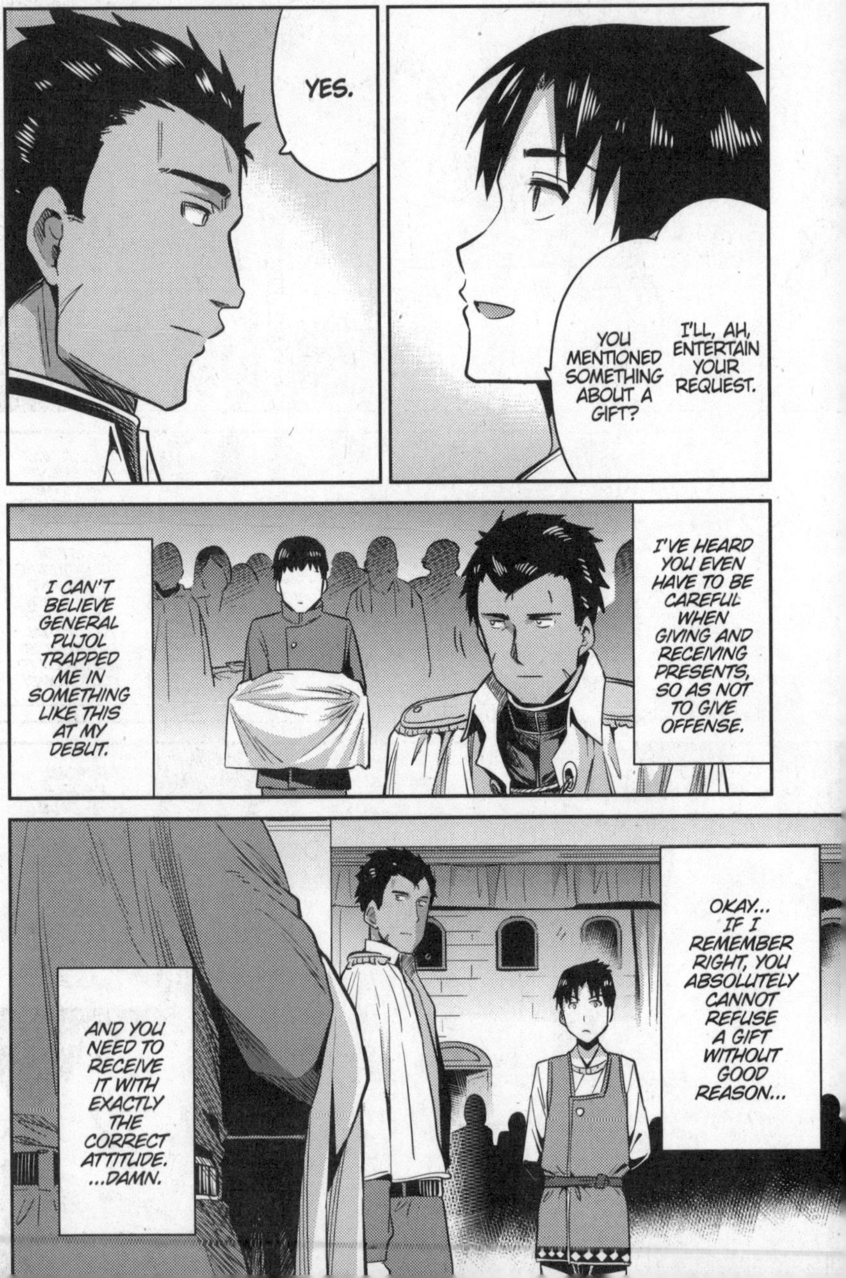
I'LL, AH, ENTERTAIN YOUR REQUEST.
YOU MENTIONED SOMETHING ABOUT A GIFT?
YES.
I'VE HEARD YOU EVEN HAVE TO BE CAREFUL WHEN GIVING AND RECEIVING PRESENTS, SO AS NOT TO GIVE OFFENSE.
I CAN'T BELIEVE GENERAL PUJOL TRAPPED ME IN SOMETHING LIKE THIS AT MY DEBUT.
OKAY... IF I REMEMBER RIGHT, YOU ABSOLUTELY CANNOT REFUSE A GIFT WITHOUT GOOD REASON...
AND YOU NEED TO RECEIVE IT WITH EXACTLY THE CORRECT ATTITUDE. ...DAMN.

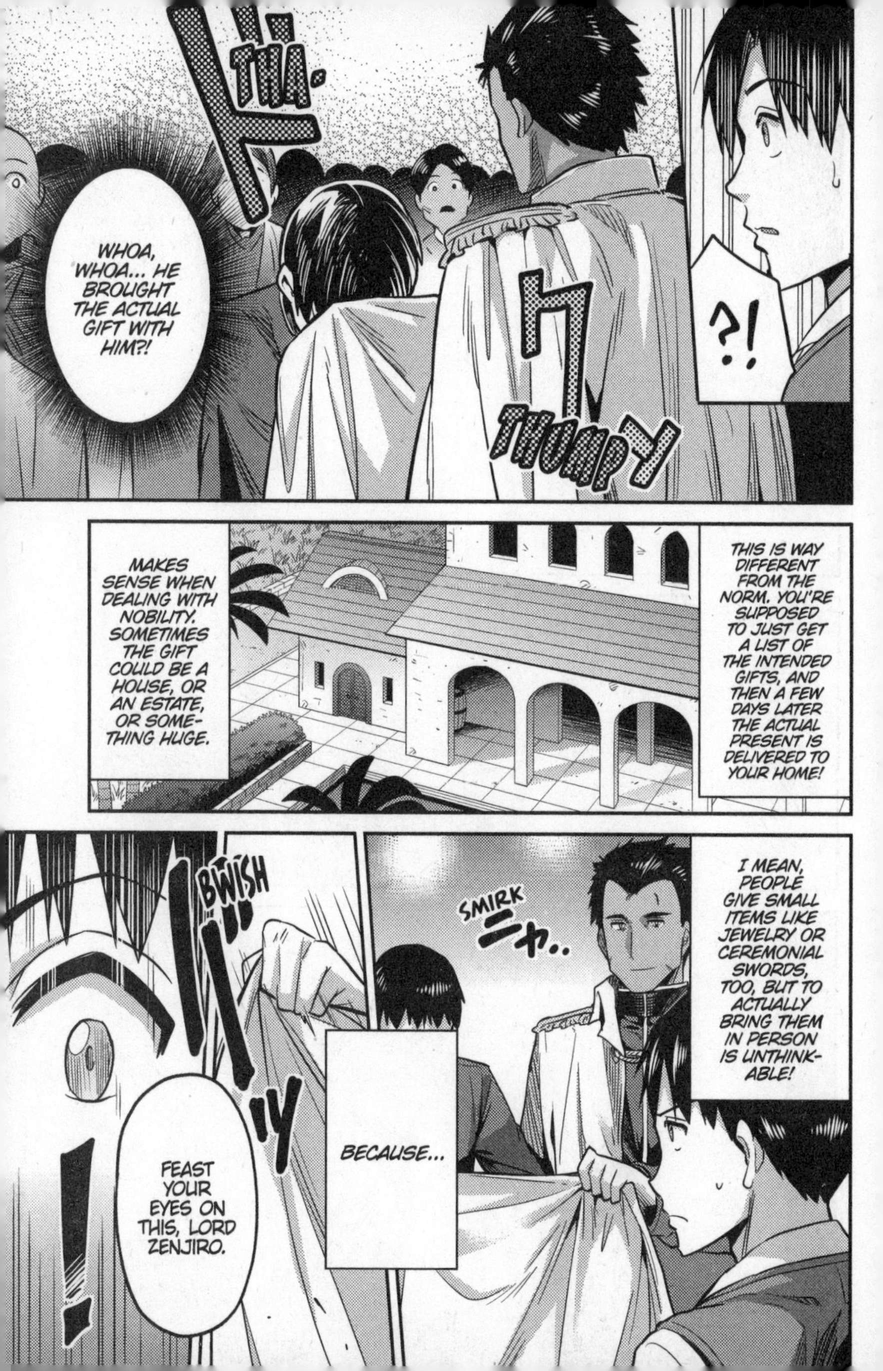

?!
THA-
THUMP
WHOA, WHOA... HE BROUGHT THE ACTUAL GIFT WITH HIM?!
THIS IS WAY DIFFERENT FROM THE NORM. YOU'RE SUPPOSED TO JUST GET A LIST OF THE INTENDED GIFTS, AND THEN A FEW DAYS LATER THE ACTUAL PRESENT IS DELIVERED TO YOUR HOME!
MAKES SENSE WHEN DEALING WITH NOBILITY. SOMETIMES THE GIFT COULD BE A HOUSE, OR AN ESTATE, OR SOME-THING HUGE.
I MEAN, PEOPLE GIVE SMALL ITEMS LIKE JEWELRY OR CEREMONIAL SWORDS, TOO, BUT TO ACTUALLY BRING THEM IN PERSON IS UNTHINK-ABLE!
SMIRK
BECAUSE...
BWISH
FEAST YOUR EYES ON THIS, LORD ZENJIRO.
!

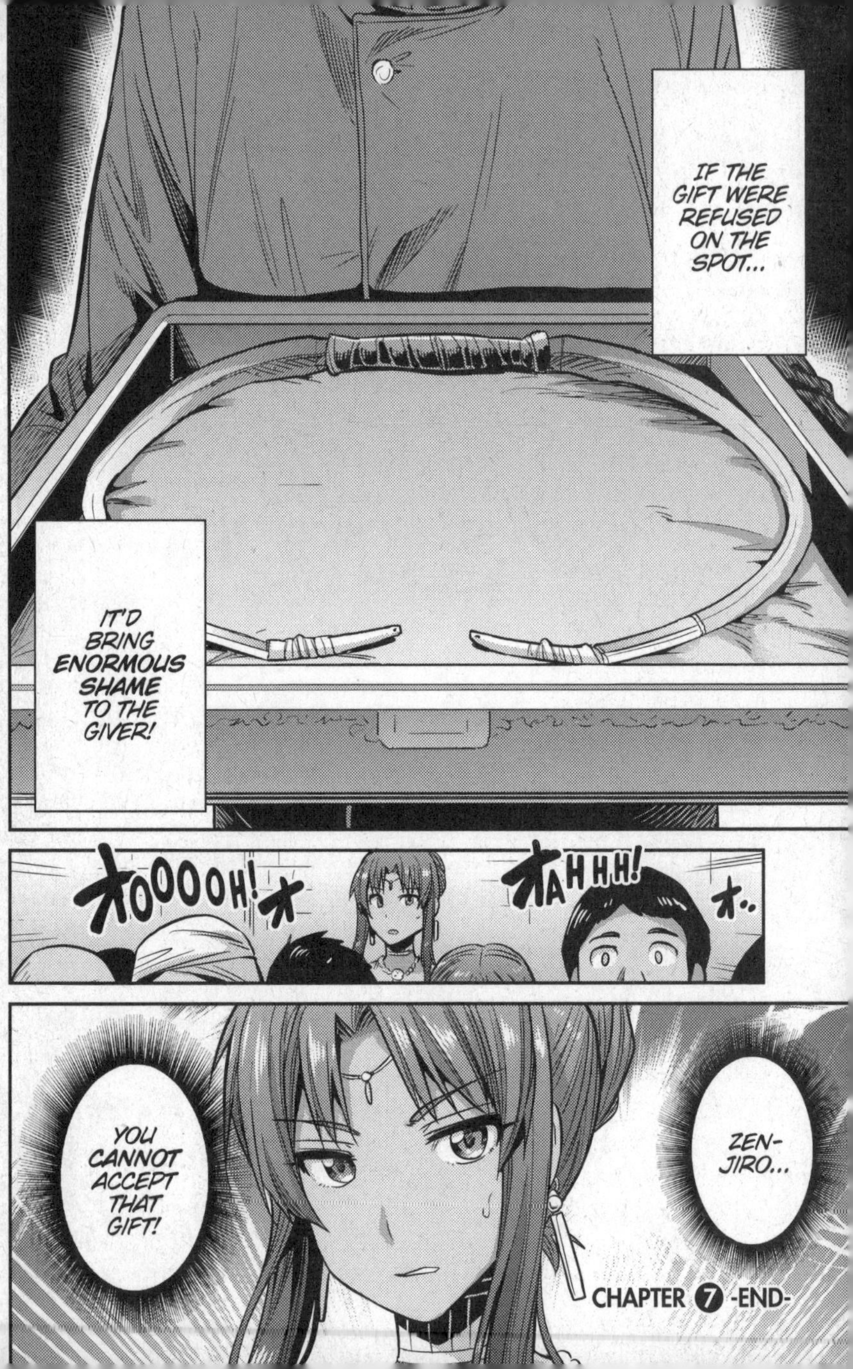
IF THE GIFT WERE REFUSED ON THE SPOT...
IT'D BRING ENORMOUS SHAME TO THE GIVER!
AHHH!
OOOOH!
ZEN-JIRO...
YOU CANNOT ACCEPT THAT GIFT!
CHAPTER 7 -END-

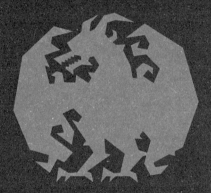

+THE IDEAL SPONGER LIFE+
Presented by Tsunehiko Watanabe & Neko Hinotsuki

THE IDEAL SPONGER LIFE

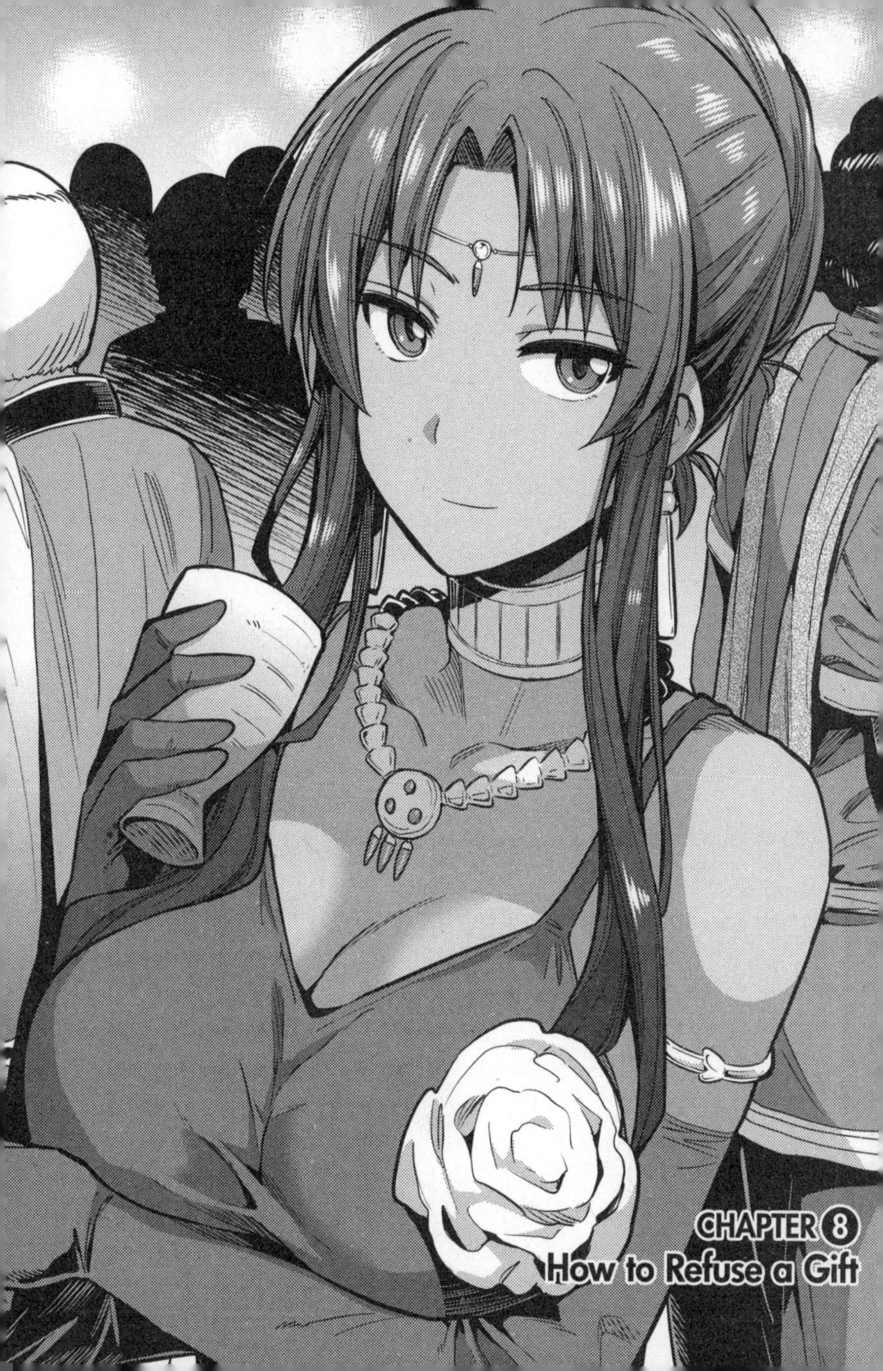
CHAPTER 8
How to Refuse a Gift

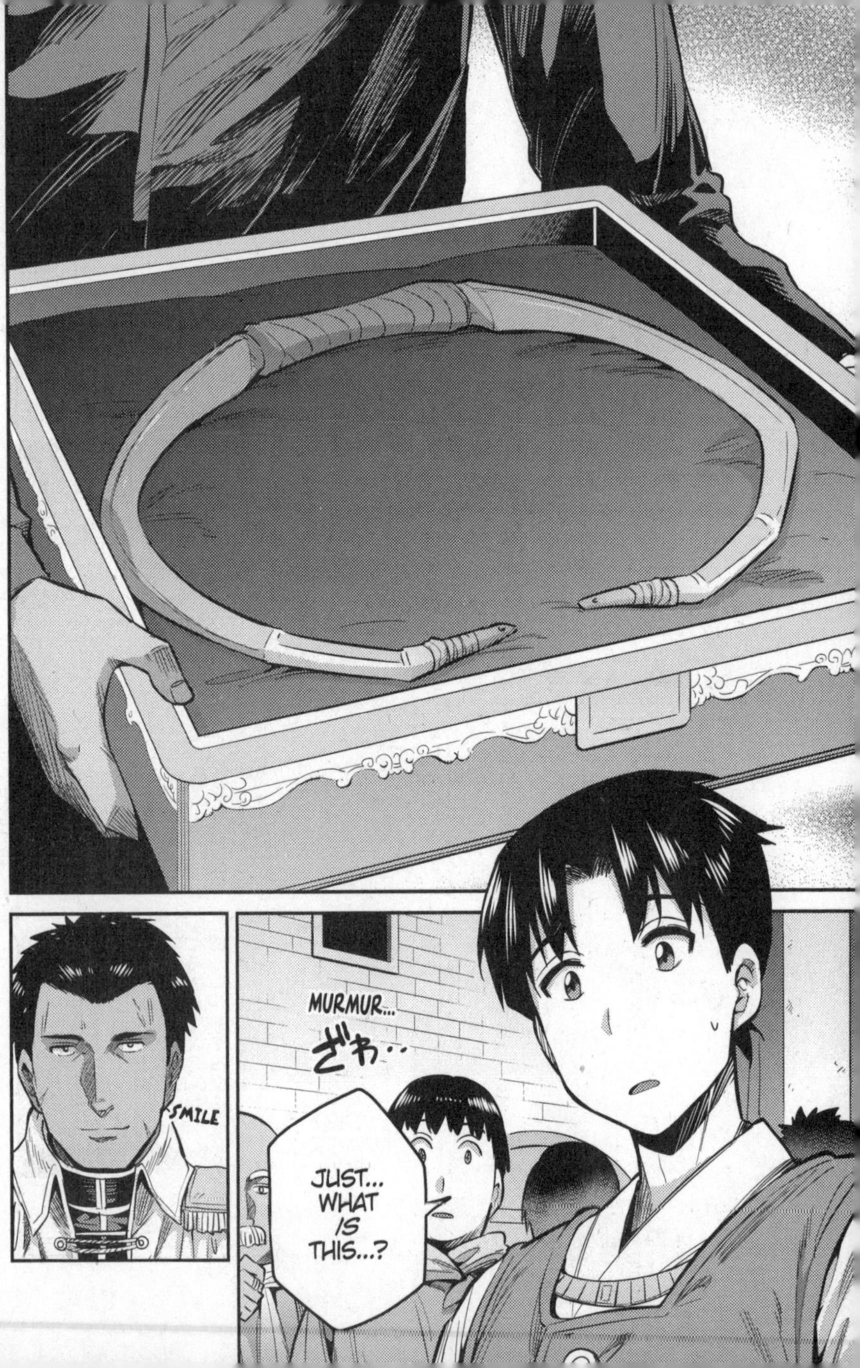
MURMUR...
ざわ‥
JUST... WHAT IS THIS...?
SMILE

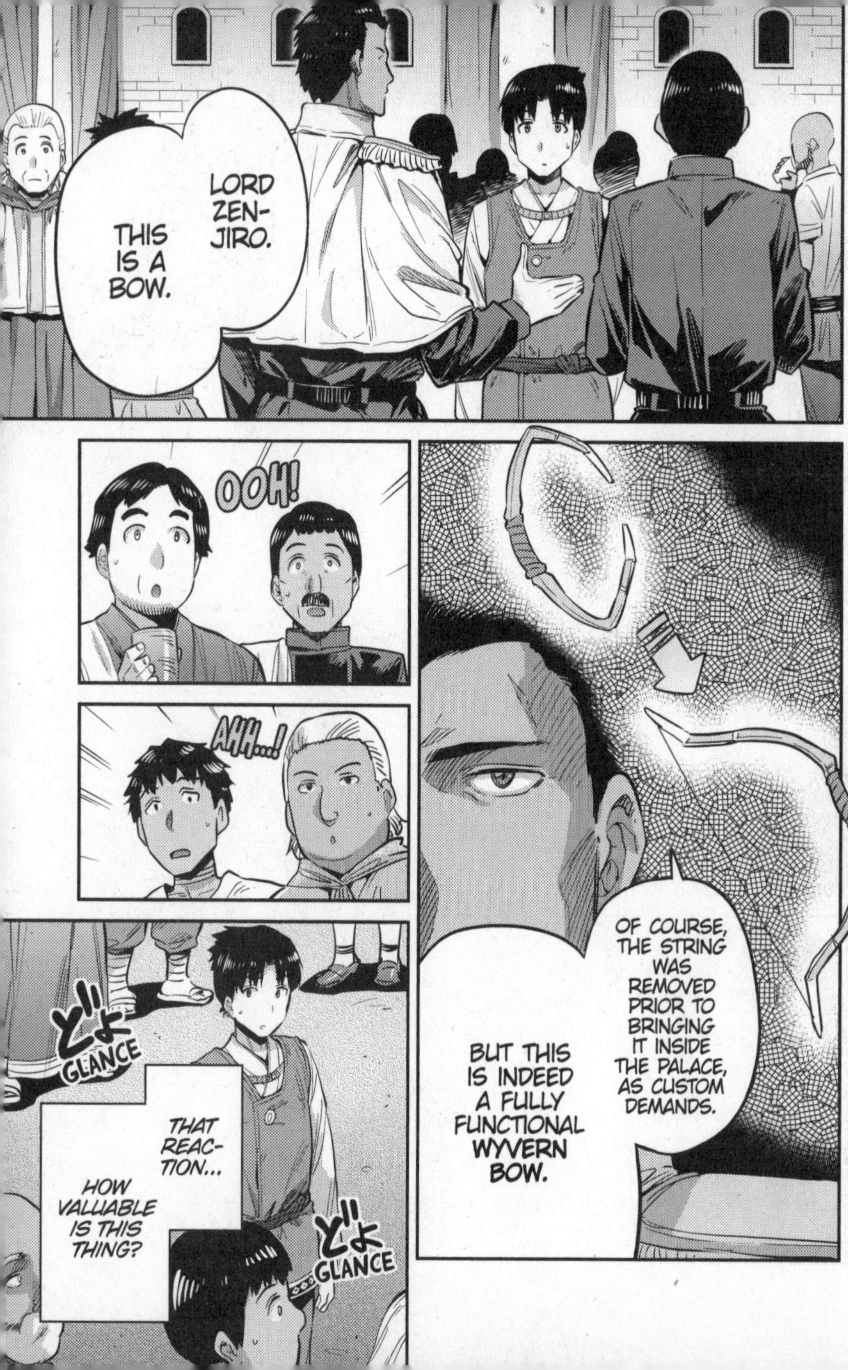
LORD ZEN-JIRO.
THIS IS A BOW.
OF COURSE, THE STRING WAS REMOVED PRIOR TO BRINGING IT INSIDE THE PALACE, AS CUSTOM DEMANDS.
BUT THIS IS INDEED A FULLY FUNCTIONAL WYVERN BOW.
OOH!
AHH...!
どよ
GLANCE
THAT REAC-TION...
HOW VALUABLE IS THIS THING?
どよ
GLANCE

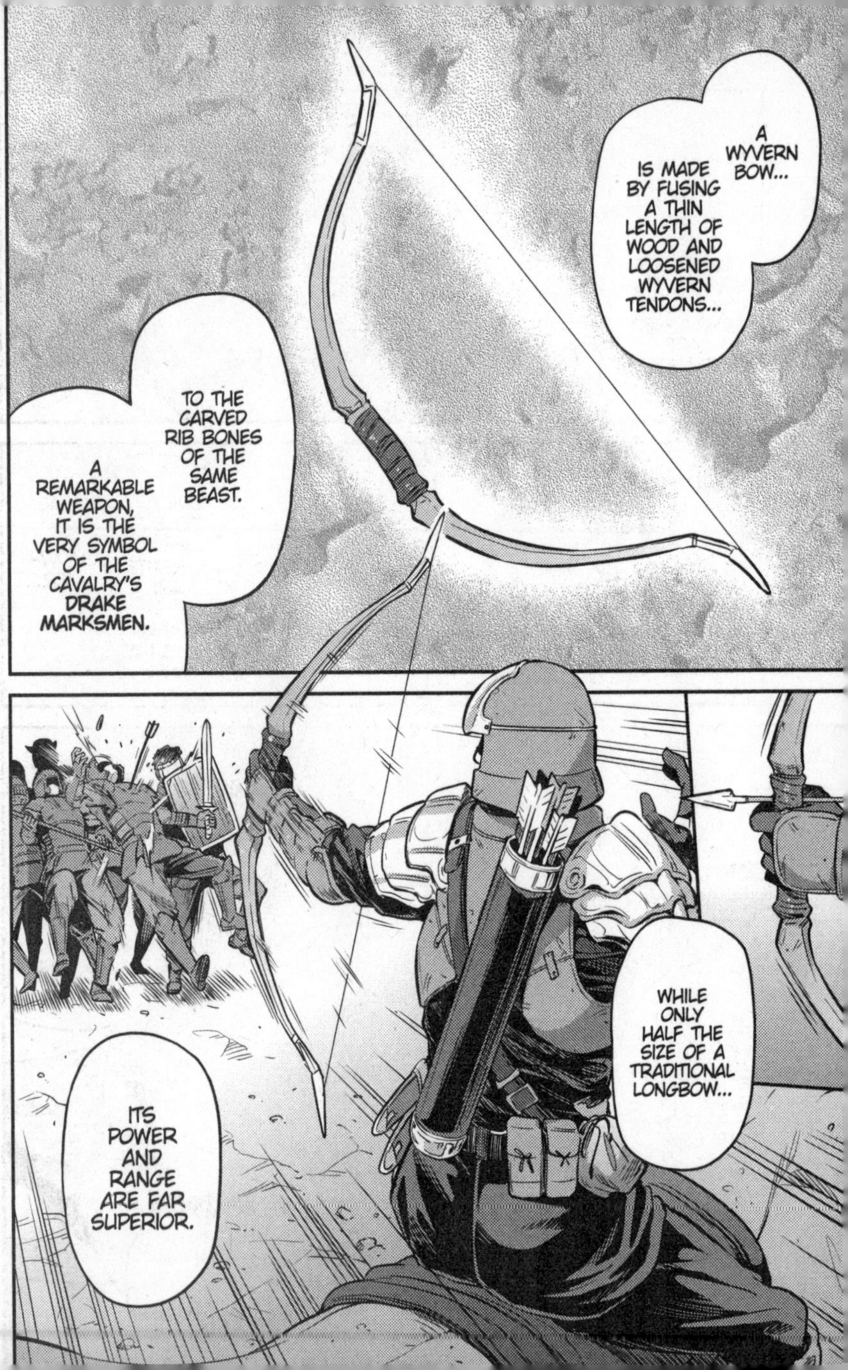
A WYVERN BOW...
IS MADE BY FUSING A THIN LENGTH OF WOOD AND LOOSENED WYVERN TENDONS...
TO THE CARVED RIB BONES OF THE SAME BEAST.
A REMARKABLE WEAPON, IT IS THE VERY SYMBOL OF THE CAVALRY'S DRAKE MARKSMEN.
WHILE ONLY HALF THE SIZE OF A TRADITIONAL LONGBOW...
ITS POWER AND RANGE ARE FAR SUPERIOR.

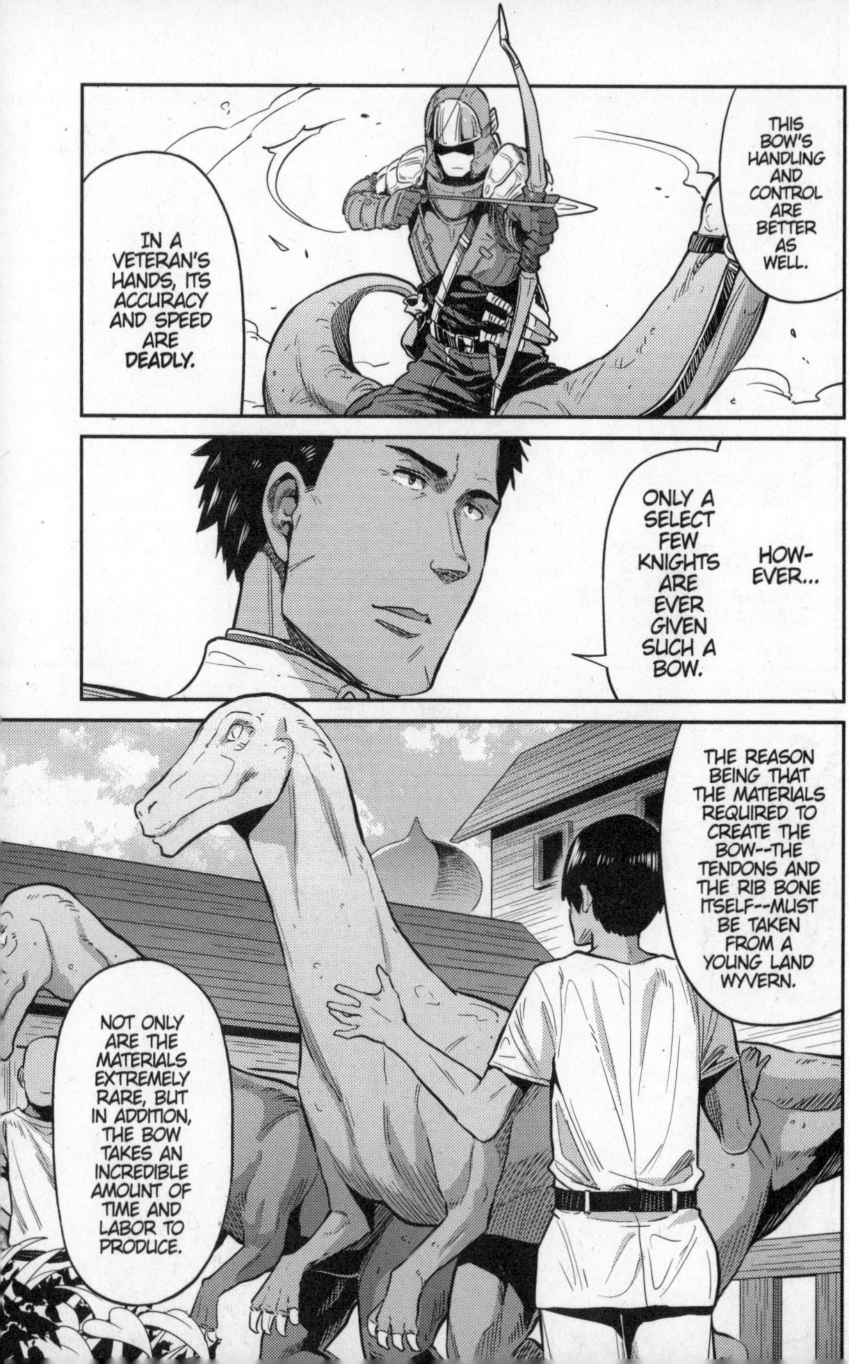
THIS BOW'S HANDLING AND CONTROL ARE BETTER AS WELL.
IN A VETERAN'S HANDS, ITS ACCURACY AND SPEED ARE DEADLY.
HOW-EVER...
ONLY A SELECT FEW KNIGHTS ARE EVER GIVEN SUCH A BOW.
THE REASON BEING THAT THE MATERIALS REQUIRED TO CREATE THE BOW--THE TENDONS AND THE RIB BONE ITSELF--MUST BE TAKEN FROM A YOUNG LAND WYVERN.
NOT ONLY ARE THE MATERIALS EXTREMELY RARE, BUT IN ADDITION, THE BOW TAKES AN INCREDIBLE AMOUNT OF TIME AND LABOR TO PRODUCE.

GULP

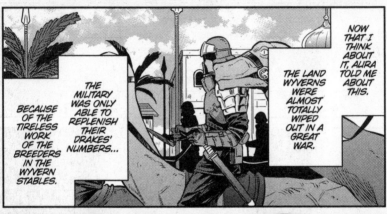

NOW THAT I THINK ABOUT IT, ALIRA TOLD ME ABOUT THIS.

THE LAND WYVERNS WERE ALMOST TOTALLY WIPED OUT IN A GREAT WAR.

THE MILITARY WAS ONLY ABLE TO REPLENISH THEIR DRAKES' NUMBERS...

BECAUSE OF THE TIRELESS WORK OF THE BREEDERS IN THE WYVERN STABLES.

FOR SUCH A PRECIOUS CREATURE TO BE KILLED WHILE IT'S STILL YOUNG, ALL TO BECOME A WEAPON...

THAT WOULD MEAN... THE BOW'S VALUE AS A WEAPON MUST BE JUST AS HIGH AS THE WYVERN THAT DIED TO MAKE IT...!

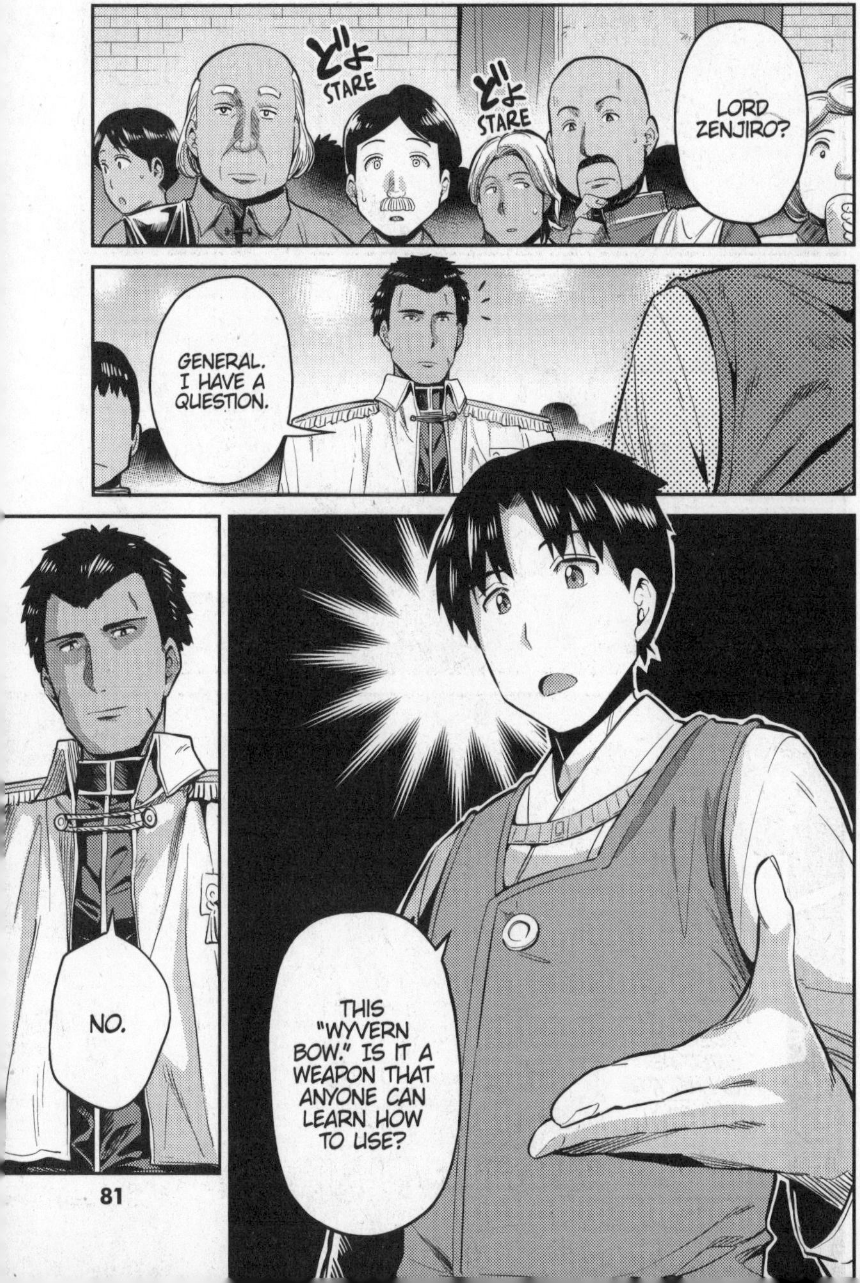
LORD ZENJIRO?
どよ STARE
どよ STARE
GENERAL. I HAVE A QUESTION.
THIS "WYVERN BOW." IS IT A WEAPON THAT ANYONE CAN LEARN HOW TO USE?
NO.

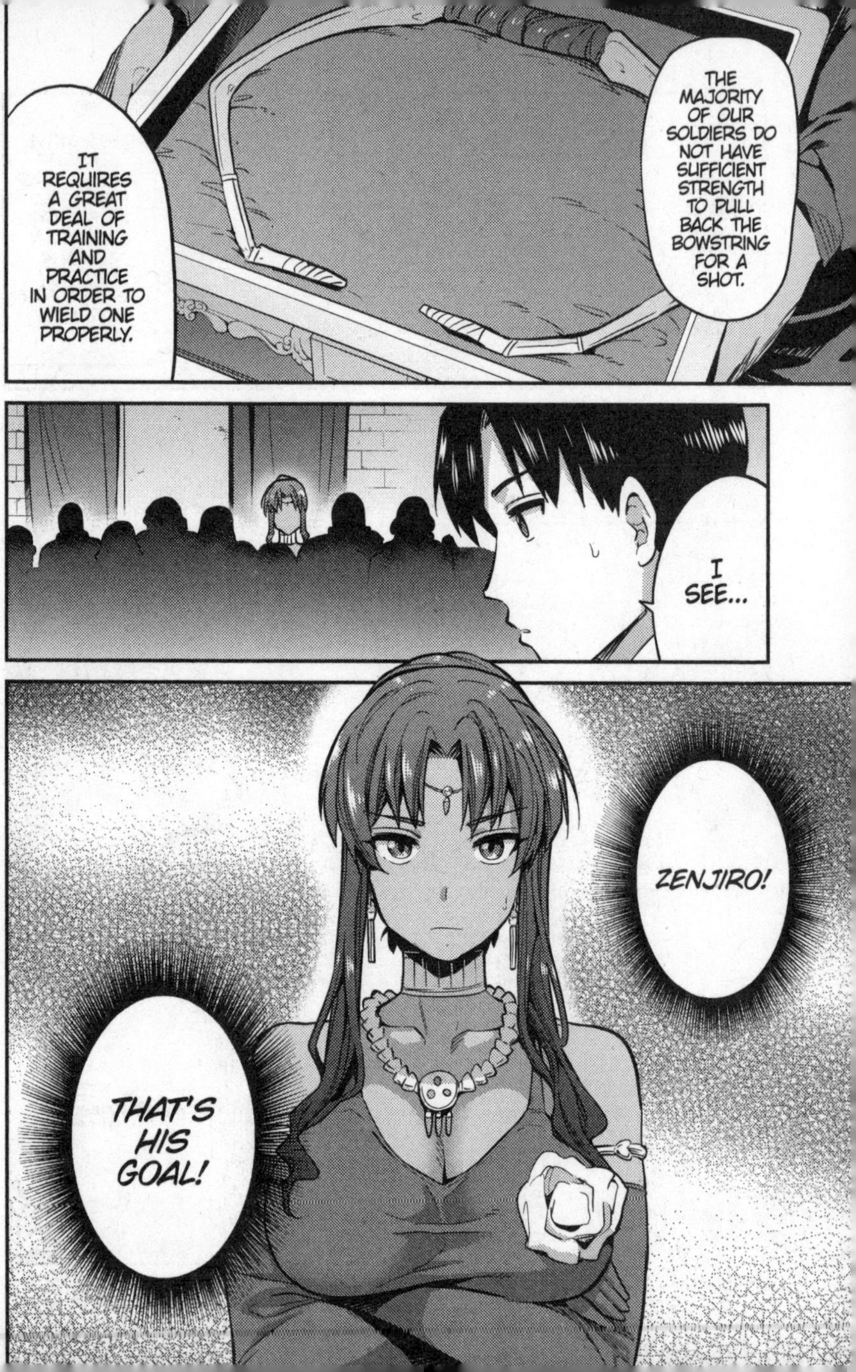
THE MAJORITY OF OUR SOLDIERS DO NOT HAVE SUFFICIENT STRENGTH TO PULL BACK THE BOWSTRING FOR A SHOT.
IT REQUIRES A GREAT DEAL OF TRAINING AND PRACTICE IN ORDER TO WIELD ONE PROPERLY.
I SEE...
ZENJIRO!
THAT'S HIS GOAL!

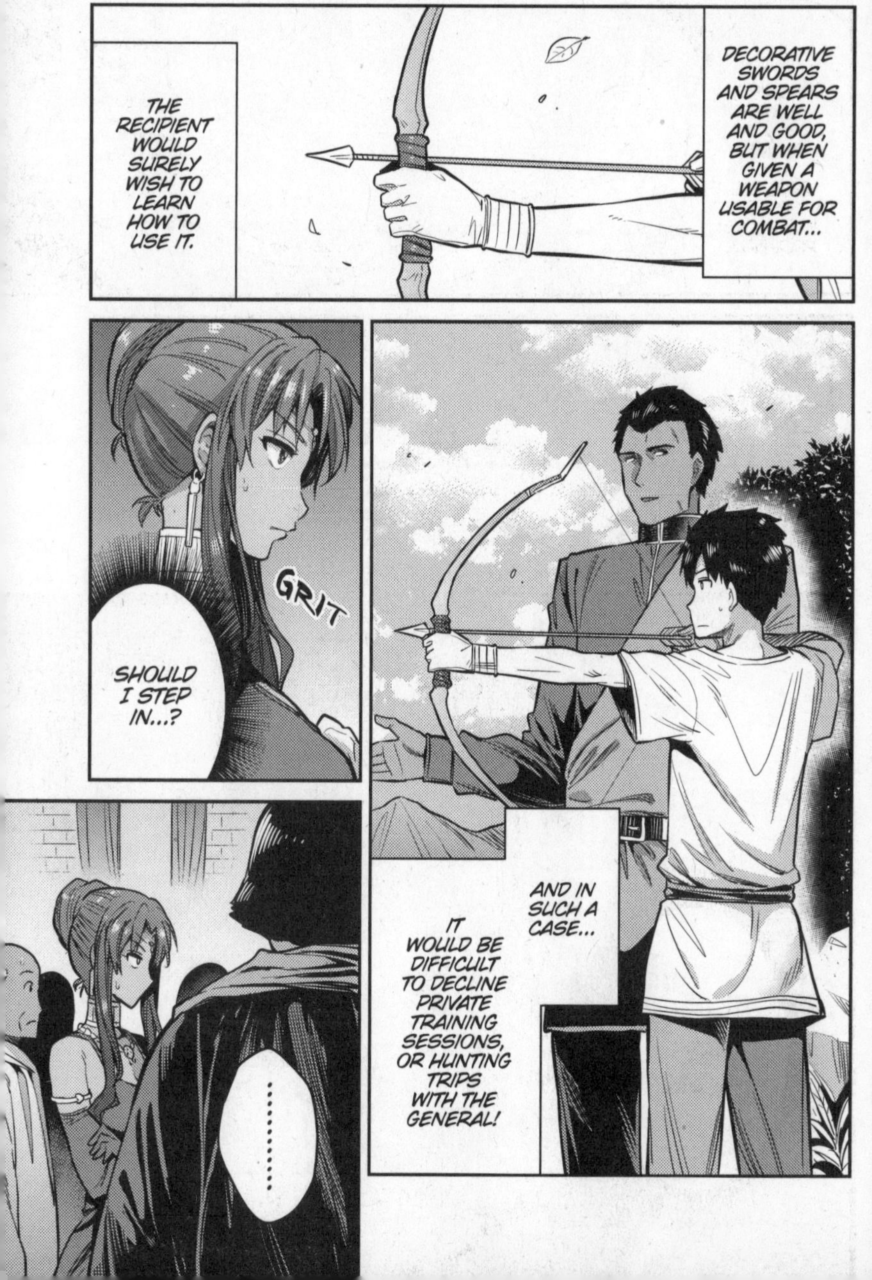
DECORATIVE SWORDS AND SPEARS ARE WELL AND GOOD, BUT WHEN GIVEN A WEAPON USABLE FOR COMBAT...
THE RECIPIENT WOULD SURELY WISH TO LEARN HOW TO USE IT.
AND IN SUCH A CASE...
IT WOULD BE DIFFICULT TO DECLINE PRIVATE TRAINING SESSIONS, OR HUNTING TRIPS WITH THE GENERAL!
GRIT
SHOULD I STEP IN...?
......

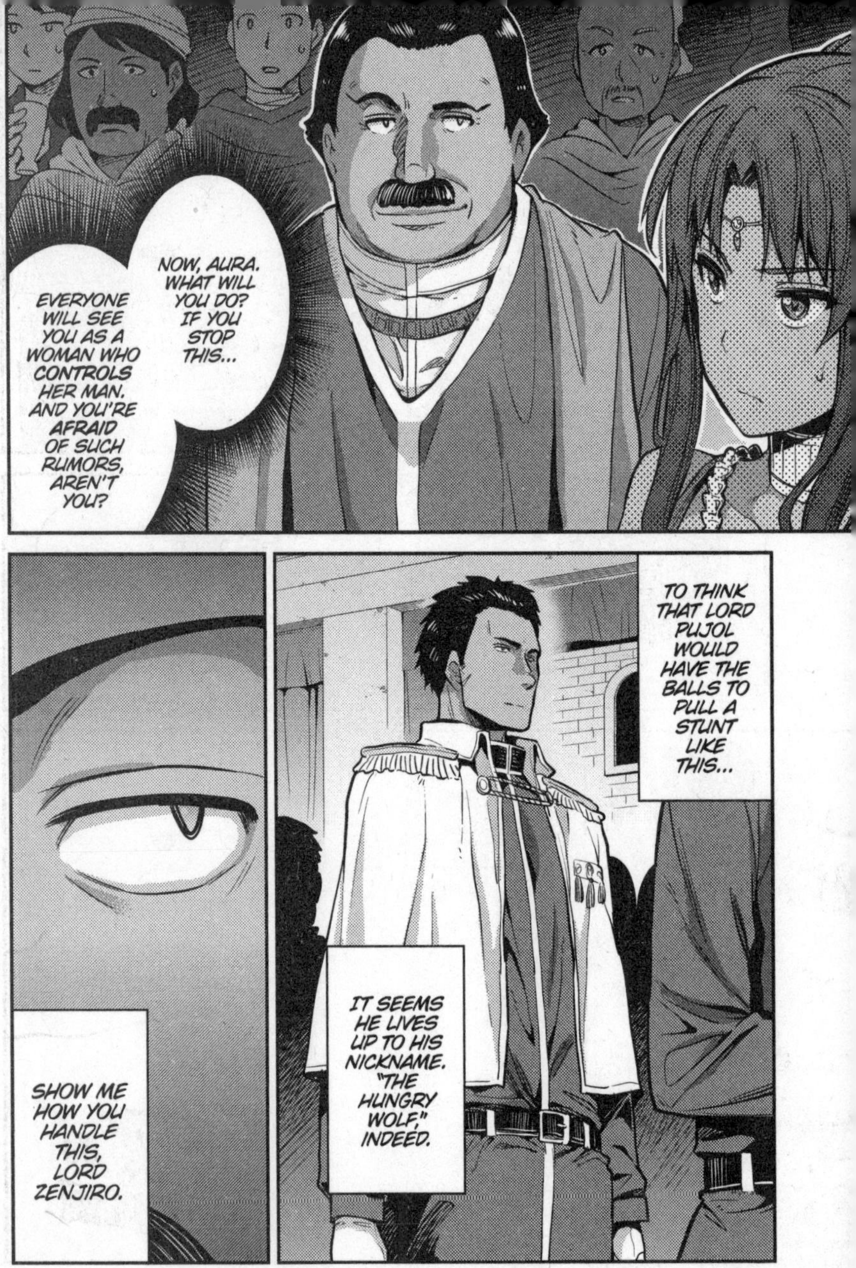
NOW, AURA. WHAT WILL YOU DO? IF YOU STOP THIS...
EVERYONE WILL SEE YOU AS A WOMAN WHO CONTROLS HER MAN. AND YOU'RE AFRAID OF SUCH RUMORS, AREN'T YOU?
TO THINK THAT LORD PUJOL WOULD HAVE THE BALLS TO PULL A STUNT LIKE THIS...
IT SEEMS HE LIVES UP TO HIS NICKNAME. "THE HUNGRY WOLF," INDEED.
SHOW ME HOW YOU HANDLE THIS, LORD ZENJIRO.

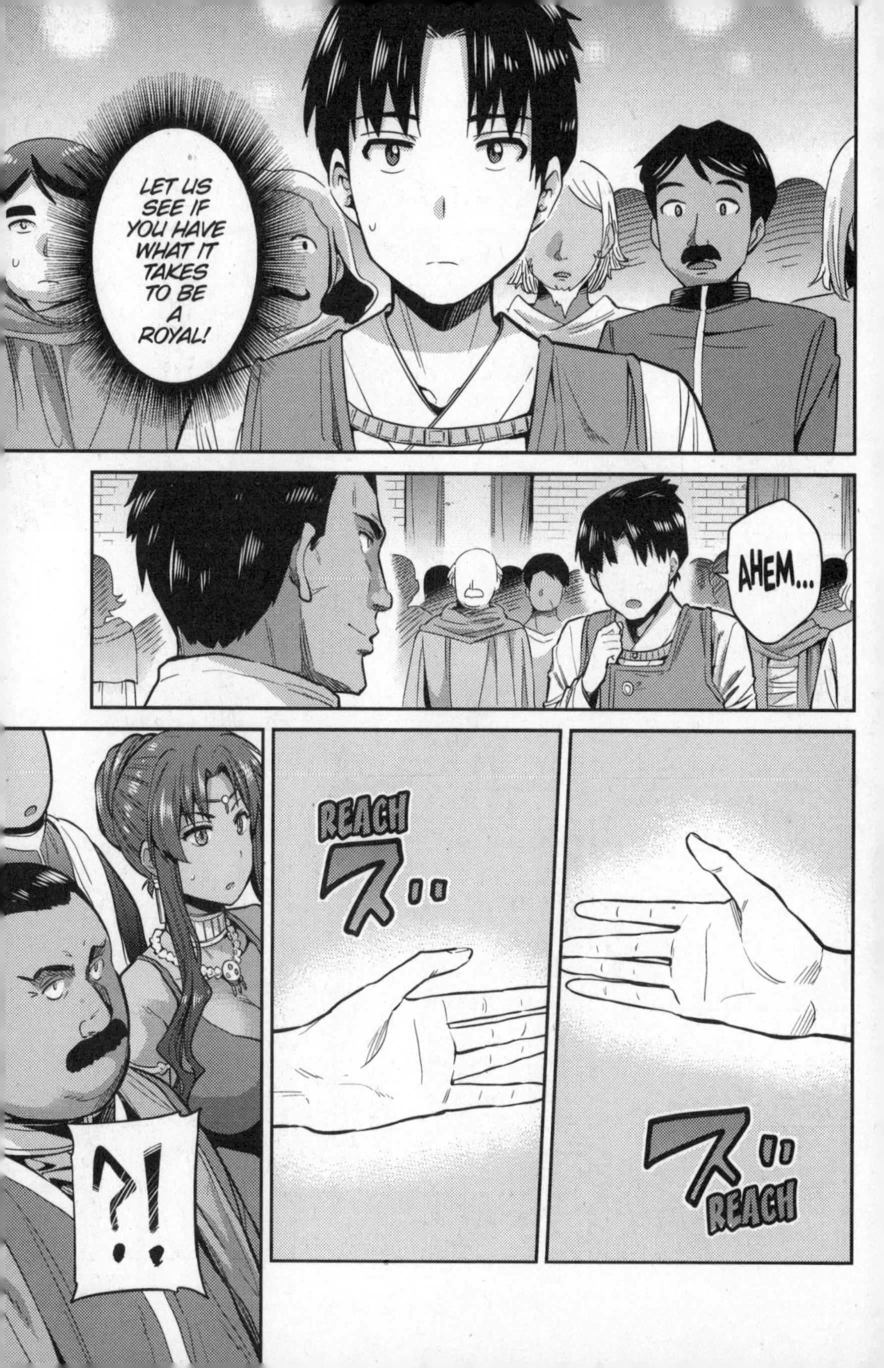
LET US SEE IF YOU HAVE WHAT IT TAKES TO BE A ROYAL!
AHEM...
ス
REACH
REACH
ス
?!

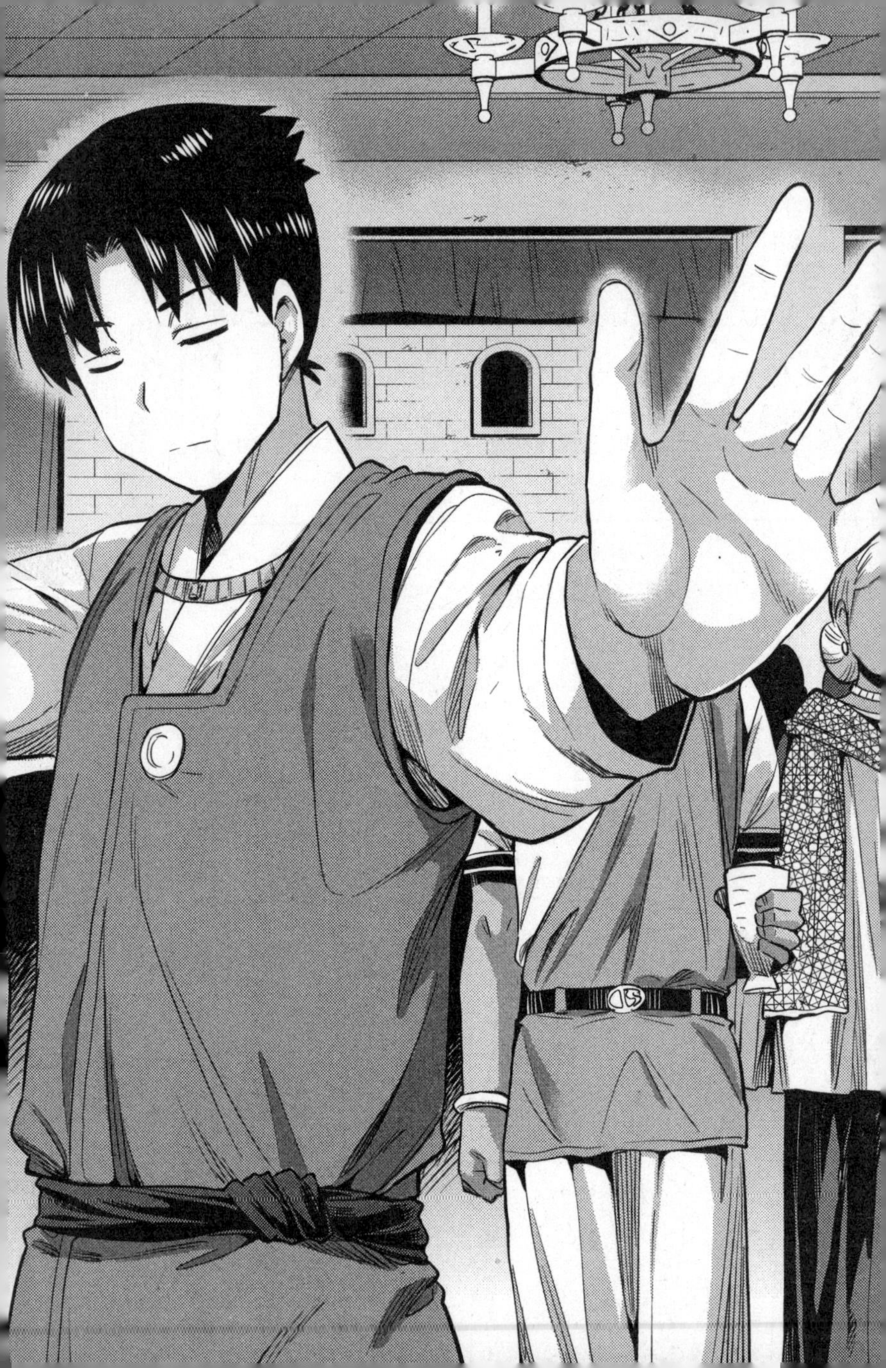

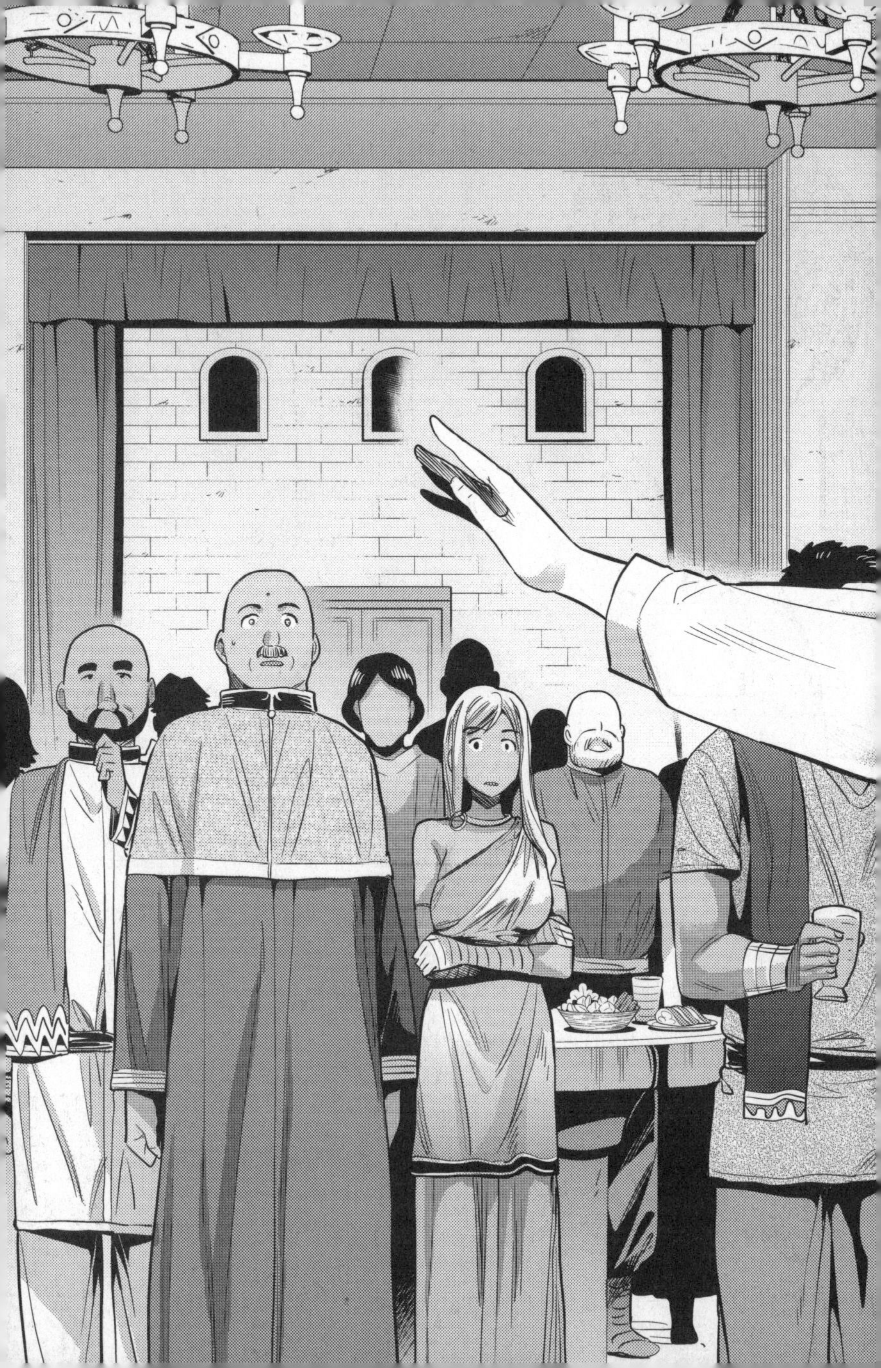

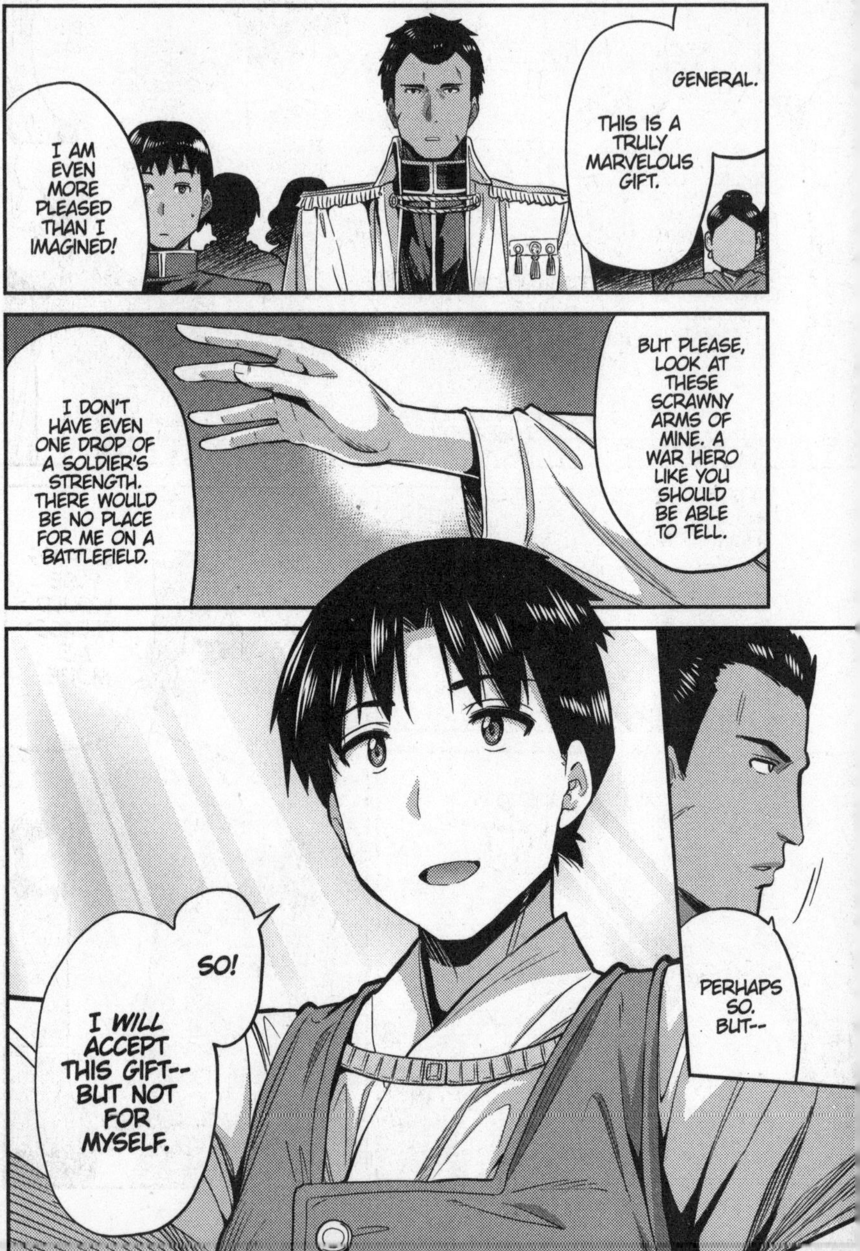
GENERAL.
THIS IS A TRULY MARVELOUS GIFT.
I AM EVEN MORE PLEASED THAN I IMAGINED!
BUT PLEASE, LOOK AT THESE SCRAWNY ARMS OF MINE. A WAR HERO LIKE YOU SHOULD BE ABLE TO TELL.
I DON'T HAVE EVEN ONE DROP OF A SOLDIER'S STRENGTH. THERE WOULD BE NO PLACE FOR ME ON A BATTLEFIELD.
PERHAPS SO. BUT--
SO!
I *WILL* ACCEPT THIS GIFT--BUT NOT FOR MYSELF.

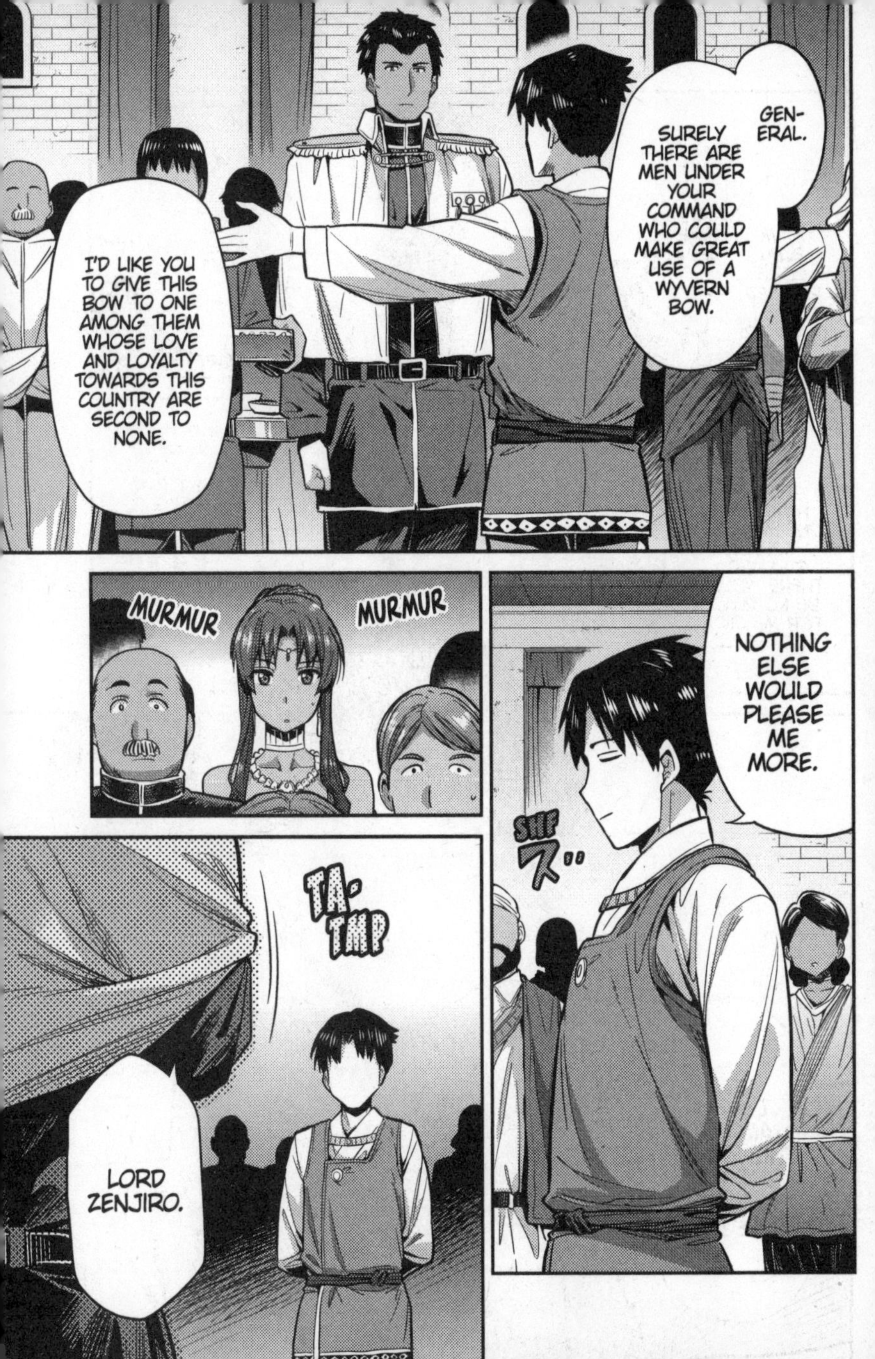
GEN-ERAL.
SURELY THERE ARE MEN UNDER YOUR COMMAND WHO COULD MAKE GREAT USE OF A WYVERN BOW.
I'D LIKE YOU TO GIVE THIS BOW TO ONE AMONG THEM WHOSE LOVE AND LOYALTY TOWARDS THIS COUNTRY ARE SECOND TO NONE.
NOTHING ELSE WOULD PLEASE ME MORE.
SHF
MURMUR
MURMUR
TA-TMP
LORD ZENJIRO.

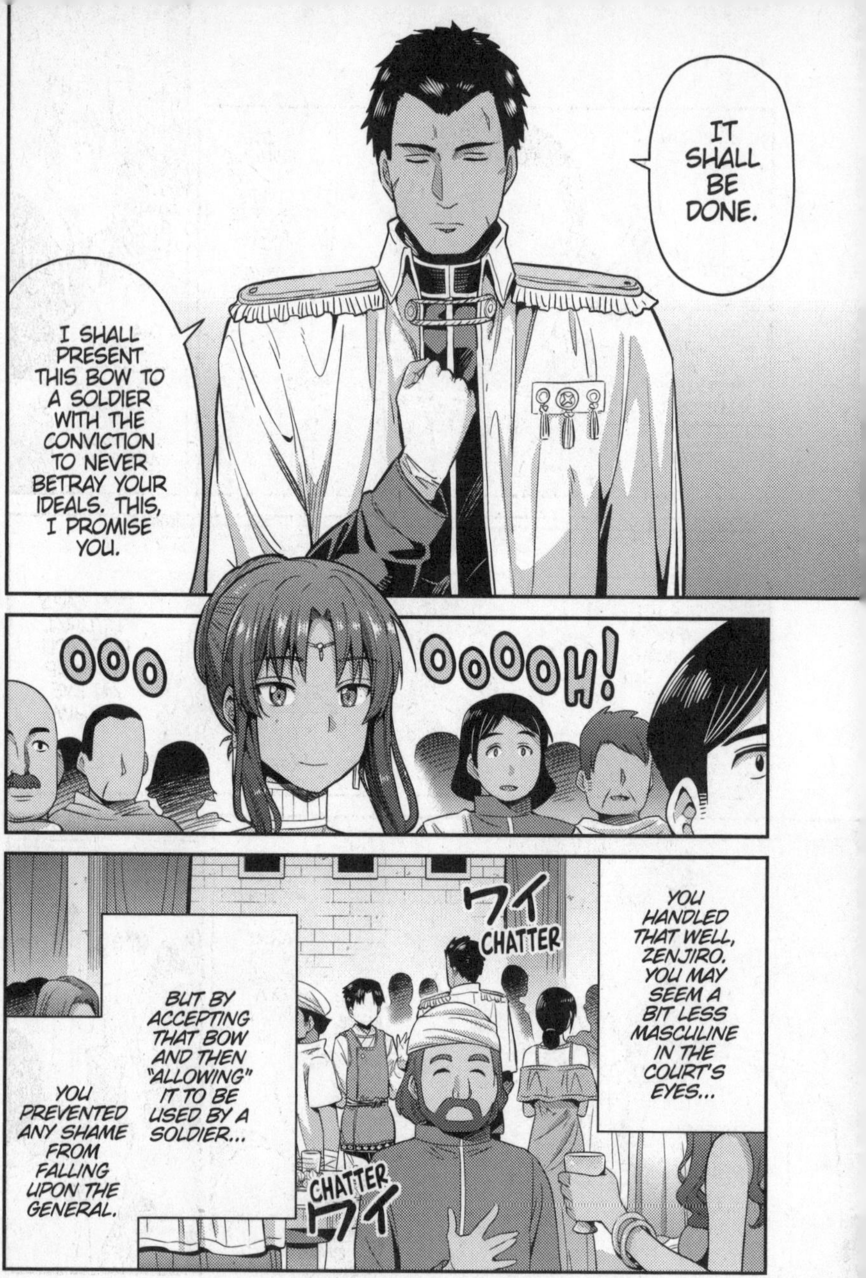
IT SHALL BE DONE.
I SHALL PRESENT THIS BOW TO A SOLDIER WITH THE CONVICTION TO NEVER BETRAY YOUR IDEALS. THIS, I PROMISE YOU.
OOO OOOOH!
YOU HANDLED THAT WELL, ZENJIRO. YOU MAY SEEM A BIT LESS MASCULINE IN THE COURT'S EYES...
ワイ CHATTER
BUT BY ACCEPTING THAT BOW AND THEN "ALLOWING" IT TO BE USED BY A SOLDIER...
YOU PREVENTED ANY SHAME FROM FALLING UPON THE GENERAL.
CHATTER ワイ

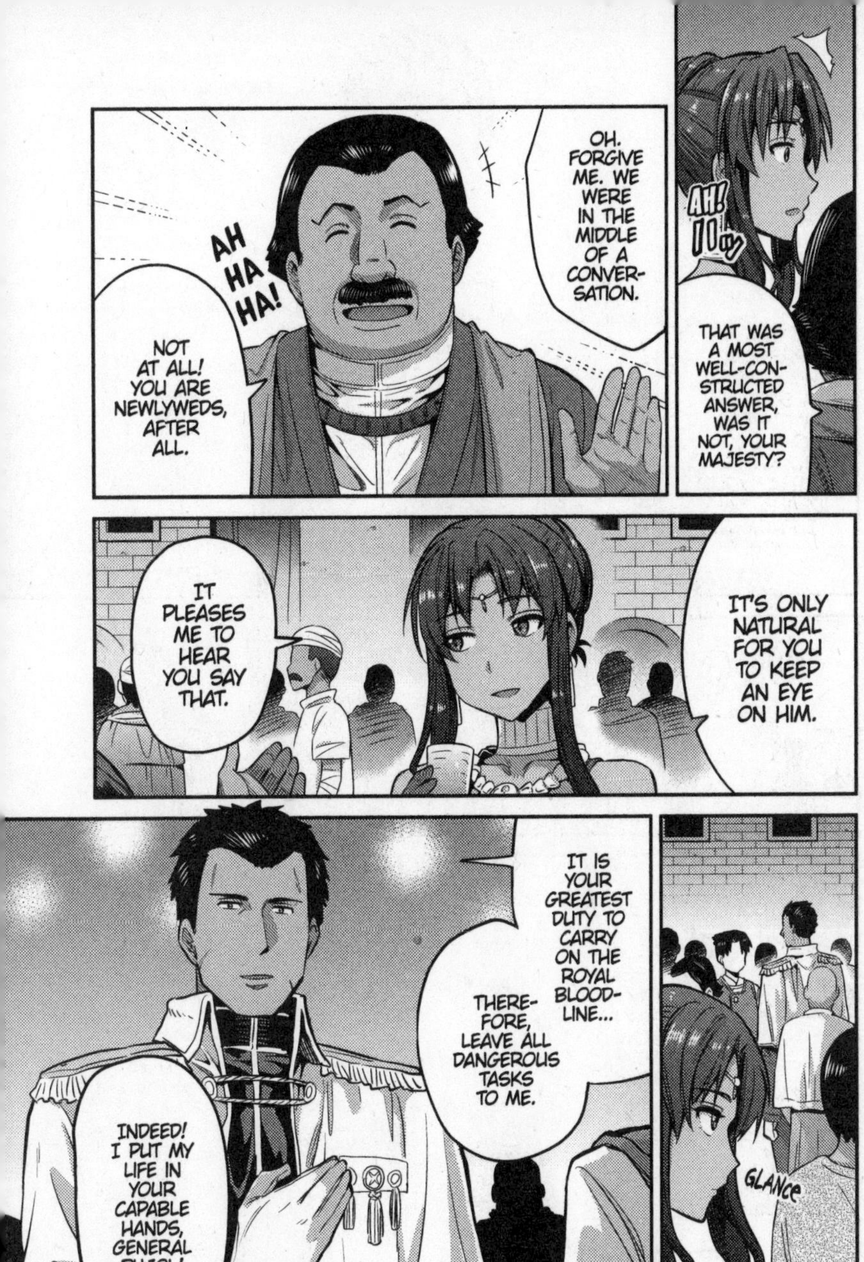
AH! !!
THAT WAS A MOST WELL-CONSTRUCTED ANSWER, WAS IT NOT, YOUR MAJESTY?
OH. FORGIVE ME. WE WERE IN THE MIDDLE OF A CONVERSATION.
AH HA HA!
NOT AT ALL! YOU ARE NEWLYWEDS, AFTER ALL.
IT'S ONLY NATURAL FOR YOU TO KEEP AN EYE ON HIM.
IT PLEASES ME TO HEAR YOU SAY THAT.
GLANCE
IT IS YOUR GREATEST DUTY TO CARRY ON THE ROYAL BLOODLINE...
THEREFORE, LEAVE ALL DANGEROUS TASKS TO ME.
INDEED! I PUT MY LIFE IN YOUR CAPABLE HANDS, GENERAL PUJOL!

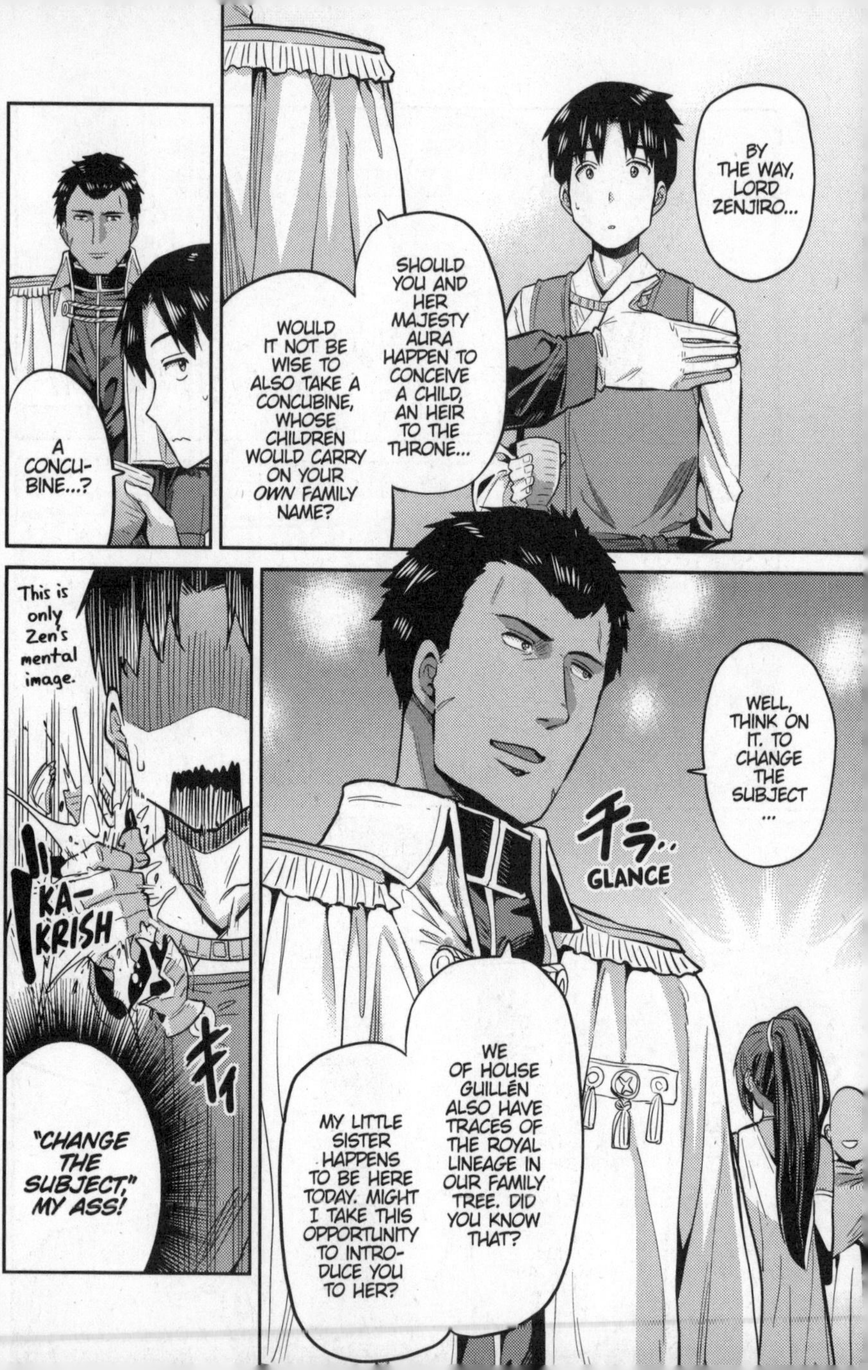
BY THE WAY, LORD ZENJIRO...
SHOULD YOU AND HER MAJESTY AURA HAPPEN TO CONCEIVE A CHILD, AN HEIR TO THE THRONE...
WOULD IT NOT BE WISE TO ALSO TAKE A CONCUBINE, WHOSE CHILDREN WOULD CARRY ON YOUR OWN FAMILY NAME?
A CONCUBINE...?
WELL, THINK ON IT. TO CHANGE THE SUBJECT ...
チラ..
GLANCE
WE OF HOUSE GUILLÉN ALSO HAVE TRACES OF THE ROYAL LINEAGE IN OUR FAMILY TREE. DID YOU KNOW THAT?
MY LITTLE SISTER HAPPENS TO BE HERE TODAY. MIGHT I TAKE THIS OPPORTUNITY TO INTRODUCE YOU TO HER?
This is only Zen's mental image.
KA-KRISH
キィ
"CHANGE THE SUBJECT," MY ASS!

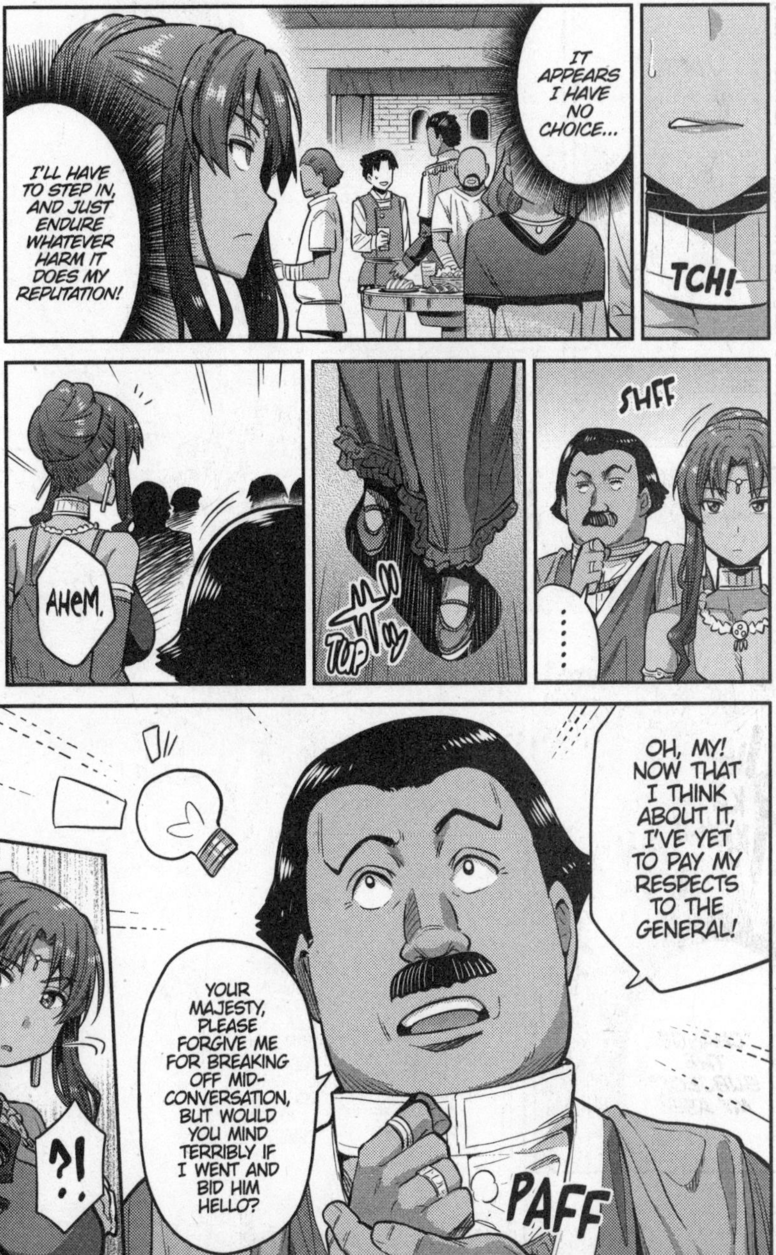
TCH!
IT APPEARS I HAVE NO CHOICE...
I'LL HAVE TO STEP IN, AND JUST ENDURE WHATEVER HARM IT DOES MY REPUTATION!
SHFF
......
TUP
AHEM.
OH, MY! NOW THAT I THINK ABOUT IT, I'VE YET TO PAY MY RESPECTS TO THE GENERAL!
YOUR MAJESTY, PLEASE FORGIVE ME FOR BREAKING OFF MID-CONVERSATION, BUT WOULD YOU MIND TERRIBLY IF I WENT AND BID HIM HELLO?
?!
PAFF

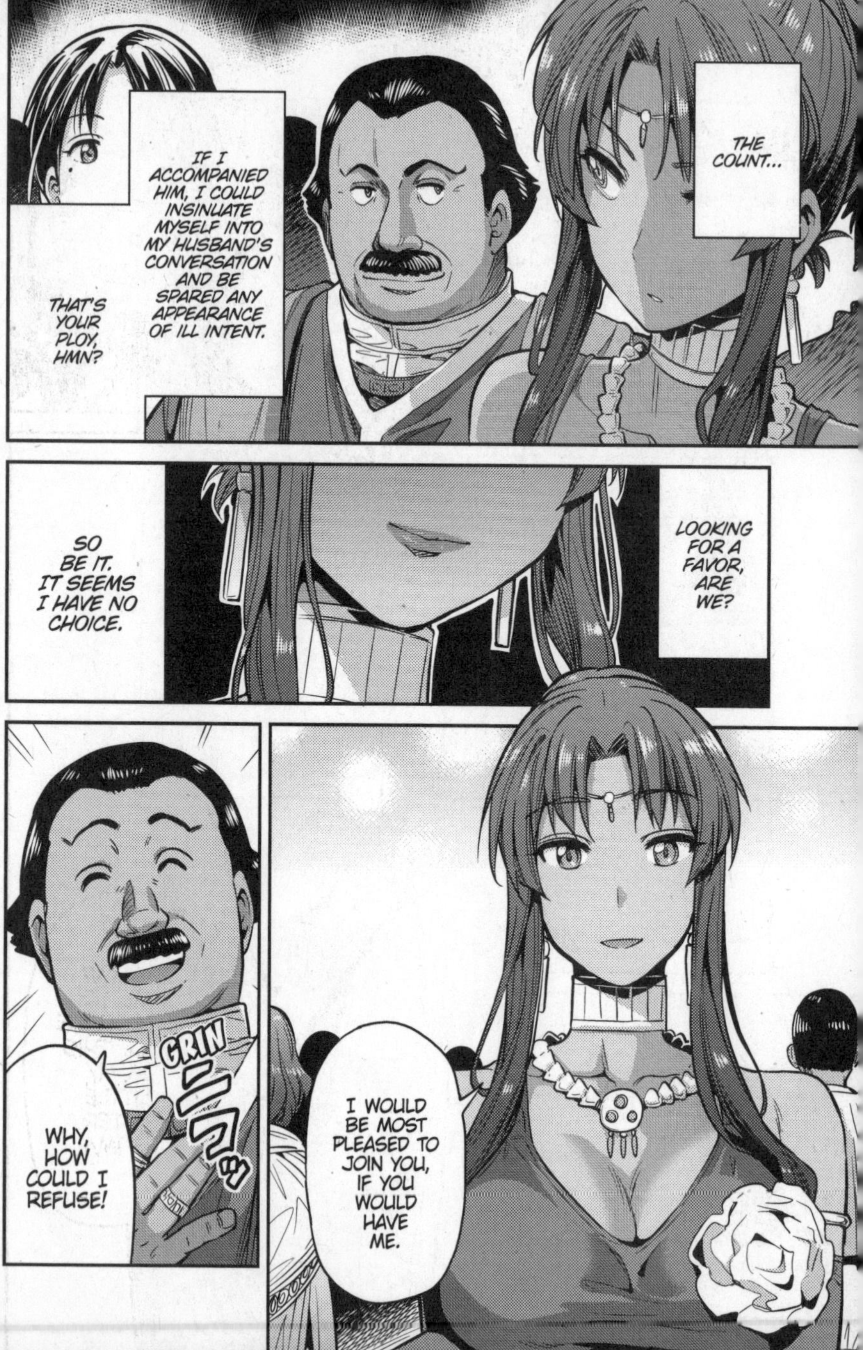
THE COUNT...
IF I ACCOMPANIED HIM, I COULD INSINUATE MYSELF INTO MY HUSBAND'S CONVERSATION AND BE SPARED ANY APPEARANCE OF ILL INTENT.
THAT'S YOUR PLOY, HMN?
LOOKING FOR A FAVOR, ARE WE?
SO BE IT. IT SEEMS I HAVE NO CHOICE.
I WOULD BE MOST PLEASED TO JOIN YOU, IF YOU WOULD HAVE ME.
GRIN
ニコッ
WHY, HOW COULD I REFUSE!

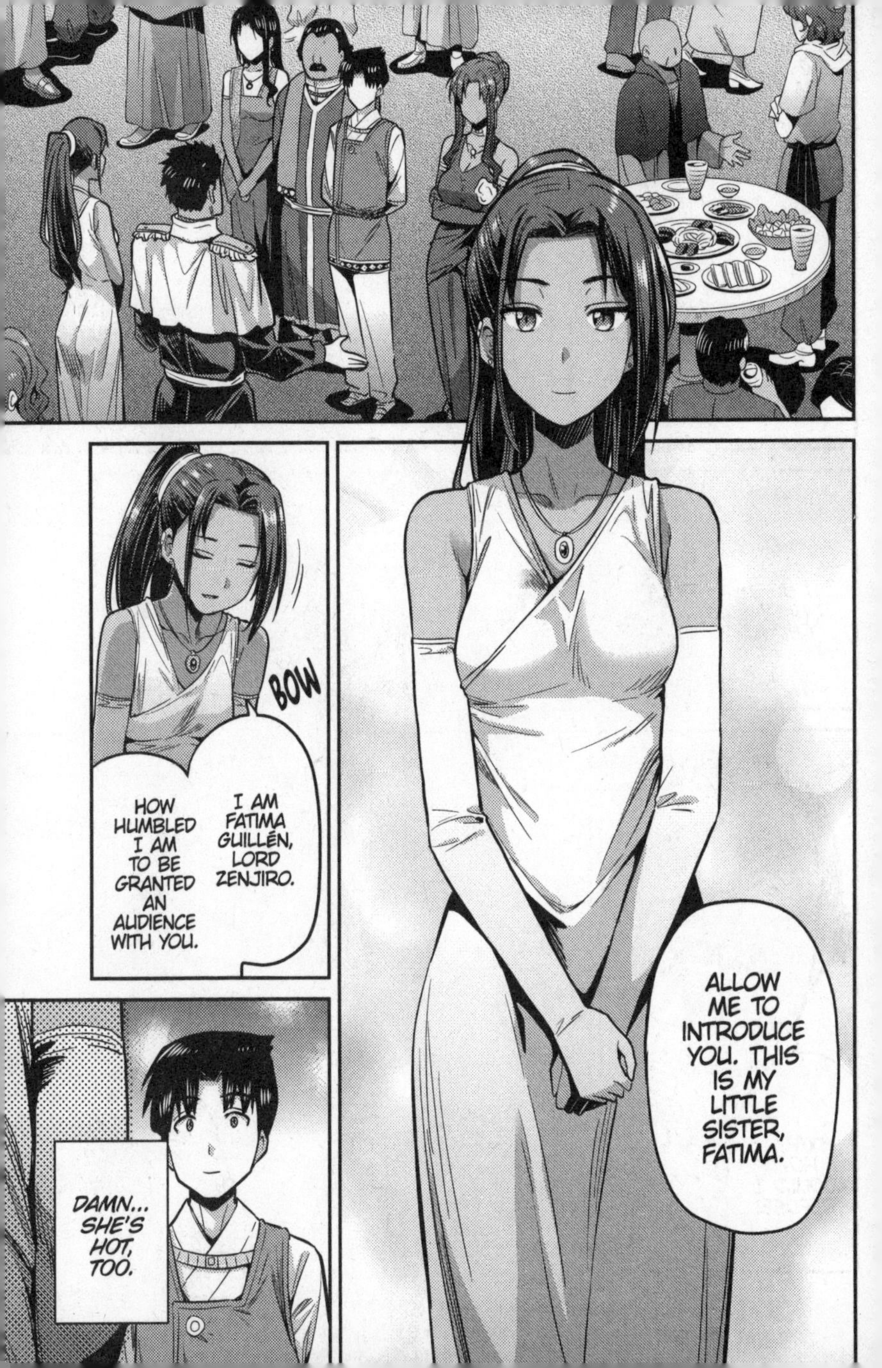
ALLOW ME TO INTRODUCE YOU. THIS IS MY LITTLE SISTER, FATIMA.
BOW
I AM FATIMA GUILLÉN, LORD ZENJIRO.
HOW HUMBLED I AM TO BE GRANTED AN AUDIENCE WITH YOU.
DAMN... SHE'S HOT, TOO.

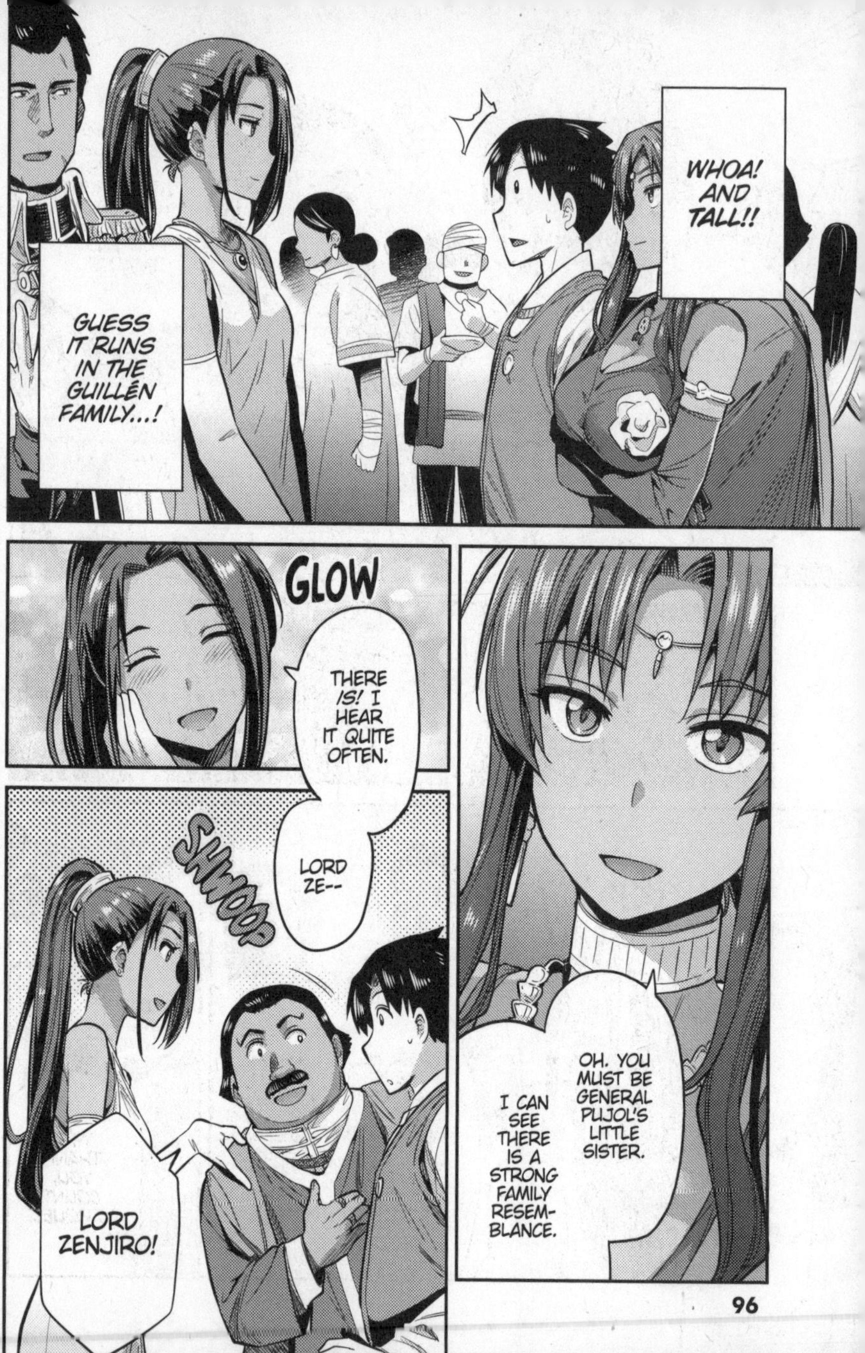
WHOA! AND TALL!!
GUESS IT RUNS IN THE GUILLÉN FAMILY...!
OH. YOU MUST BE GENERAL PUJOL'S LITTLE SISTER.
I CAN SEE THERE IS A STRONG FAMILY RESEMBLANCE.
GLOW
THERE IS! I HEAR IT QUITE OFTEN.
LORD ZE--
SWOOP
LORD ZENJIRO!

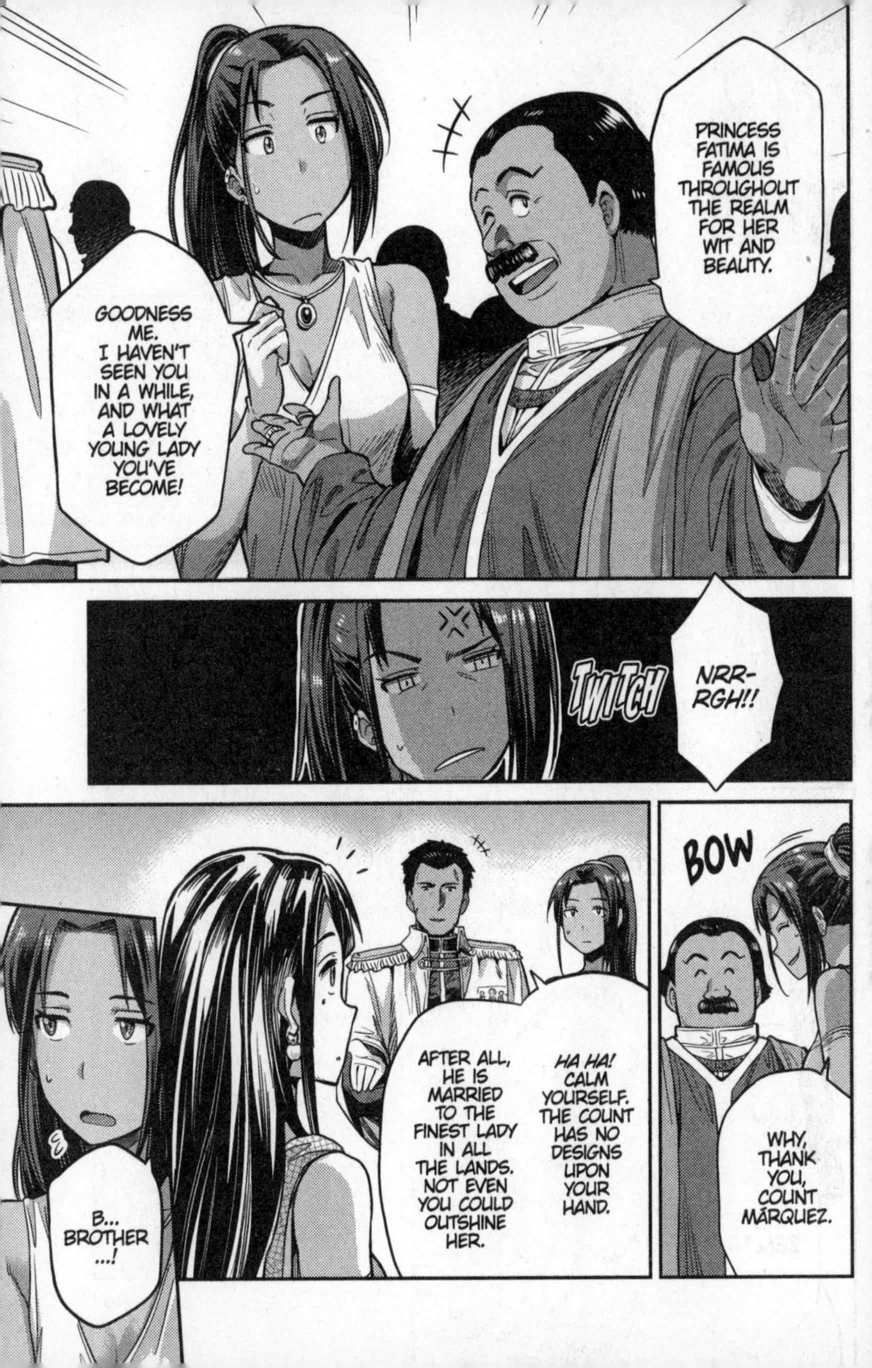
PRINCESS FATIMA IS FAMOUS THROUGHOUT THE REALM FOR HER WIT AND BEAUTY.
GOODNESS ME. I HAVEN'T SEEN YOU IN A WHILE, AND WHAT A LOVELY YOUNG LADY YOU'VE BECOME!
NRR-RGH!!
TWITCH
BOW
WHY, THANK YOU, COUNT MÁRQUEZ.
HA HA! CALM YOURSELF. THE COUNT HAS NO DESIGNS UPON YOUR HAND.
AFTER ALL, HE IS MARRIED TO THE FINEST LADY IN ALL THE LANDS. NOT EVEN YOU COULD OUTSHINE HER.
B... BROTHER ...!

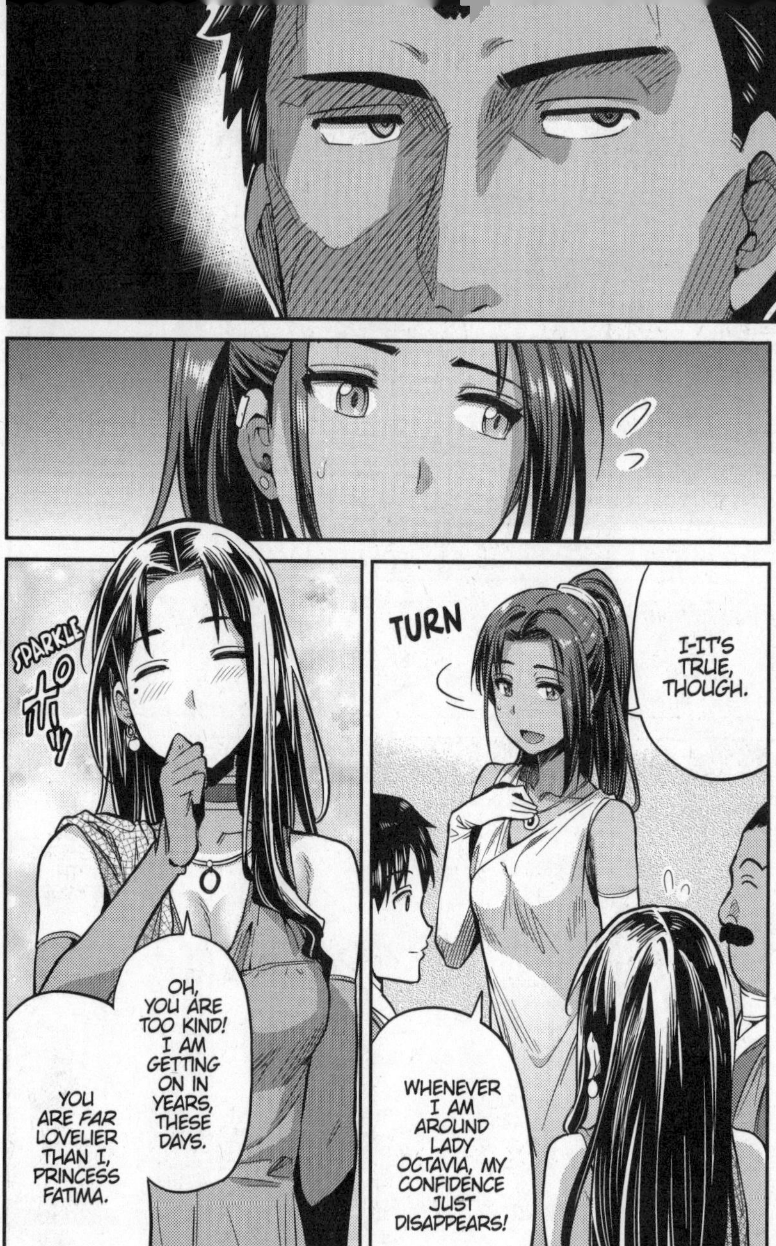
TURN
I-IT'S TRUE, THOUGH.
WHENEVER I AM AROUND LADY OCTAVIA, MY CONFIDENCE JUST DISAPPEARS!
SPARKLE
OH, YOU ARE TOO KIND! I AM GETTING ON IN YEARS, THESE DAYS.
YOU ARE *FAR* LOVELIER THAN I, PRINCESS FATIMA.

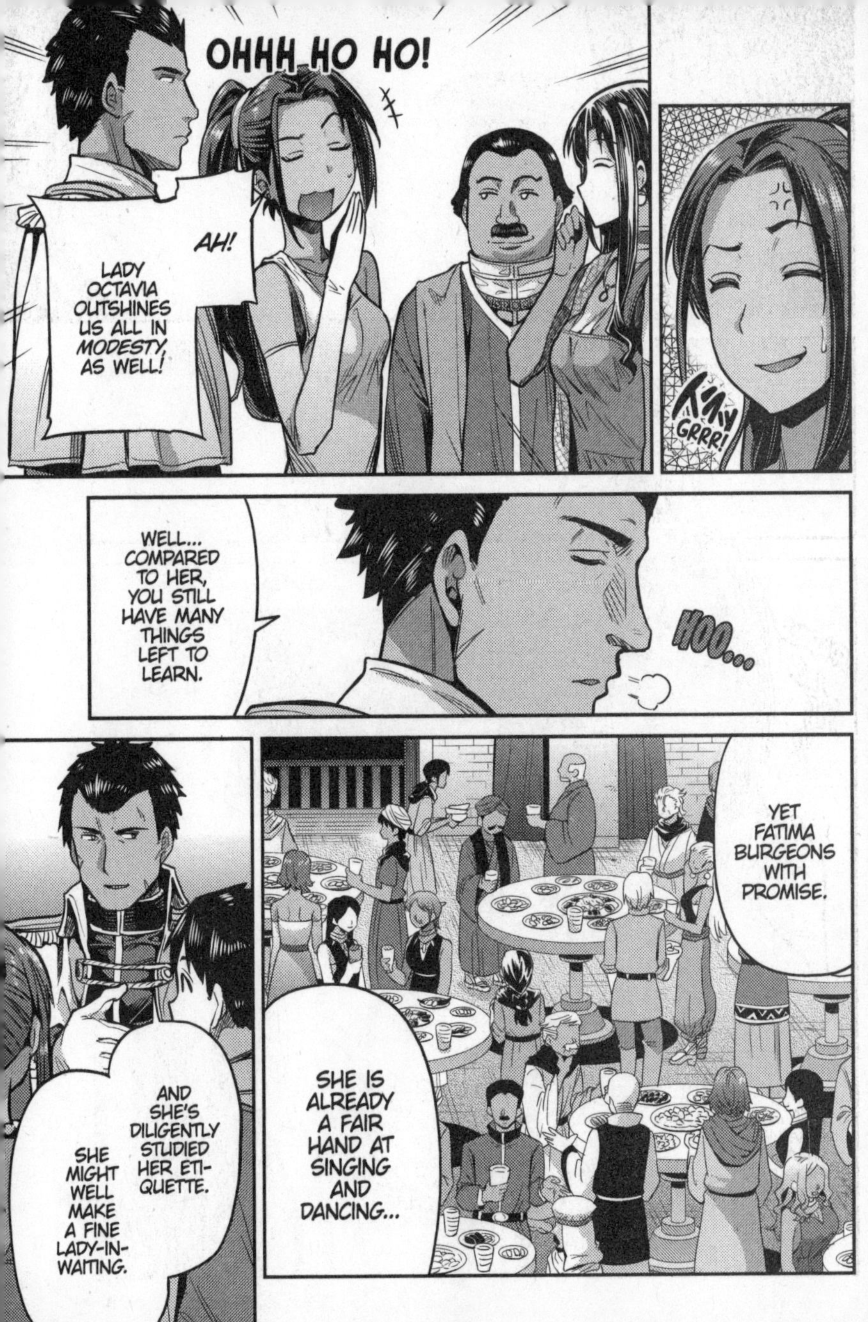
GRRR!
OHHH HO HO!
AH! LADY OCTAVIA OUTSHINES US ALL IN MODESTY, AS WELL!
HOO...
WELL... COMPARED TO HER, YOU STILL HAVE MANY THINGS LEFT TO LEARN.
YET FATIMA BURGEONS WITH PROMISE.
SHE IS ALREADY A FAIR HAND AT SINGING AND DANCING...
AND SHE'S DILIGENTLY STUDIED HER ETI-QUETTE.
SHE MIGHT WELL MAKE A FINE LADY-IN-WAITING.

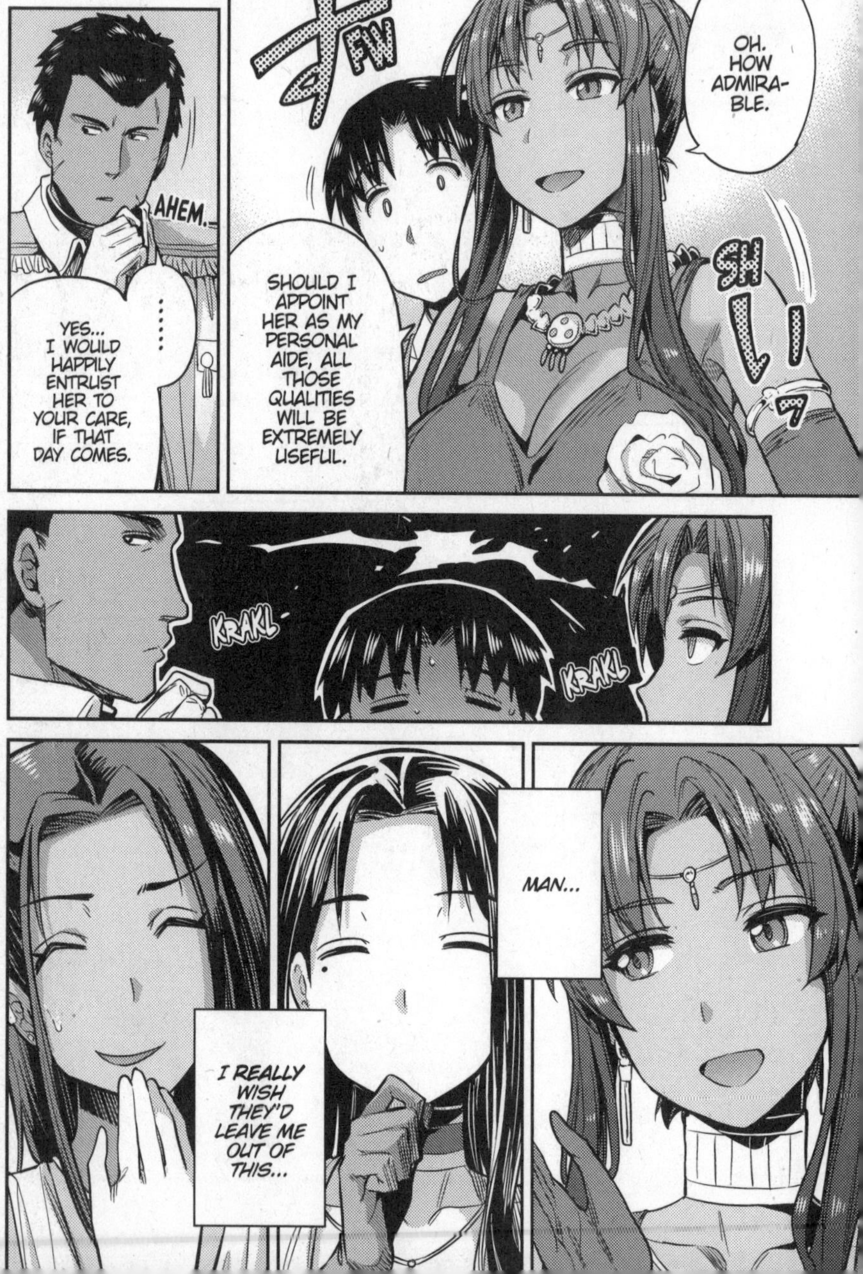
OH. HOW ADMIRA-BLE.
SH
FV
SHOULD I APPOINT HER AS MY PERSONAL AIDE, ALL THOSE QUALITIES WILL BE EXTREMELY USEFUL.
AHEM.
......
YES... I WOULD HAPPILY ENTRUST HER TO YOUR CARE, IF THAT DAY COMES.
KRAKL
KRAKL
MAN...
I REALLY WISH THEY'D LEAVE ME OUT OF THIS...

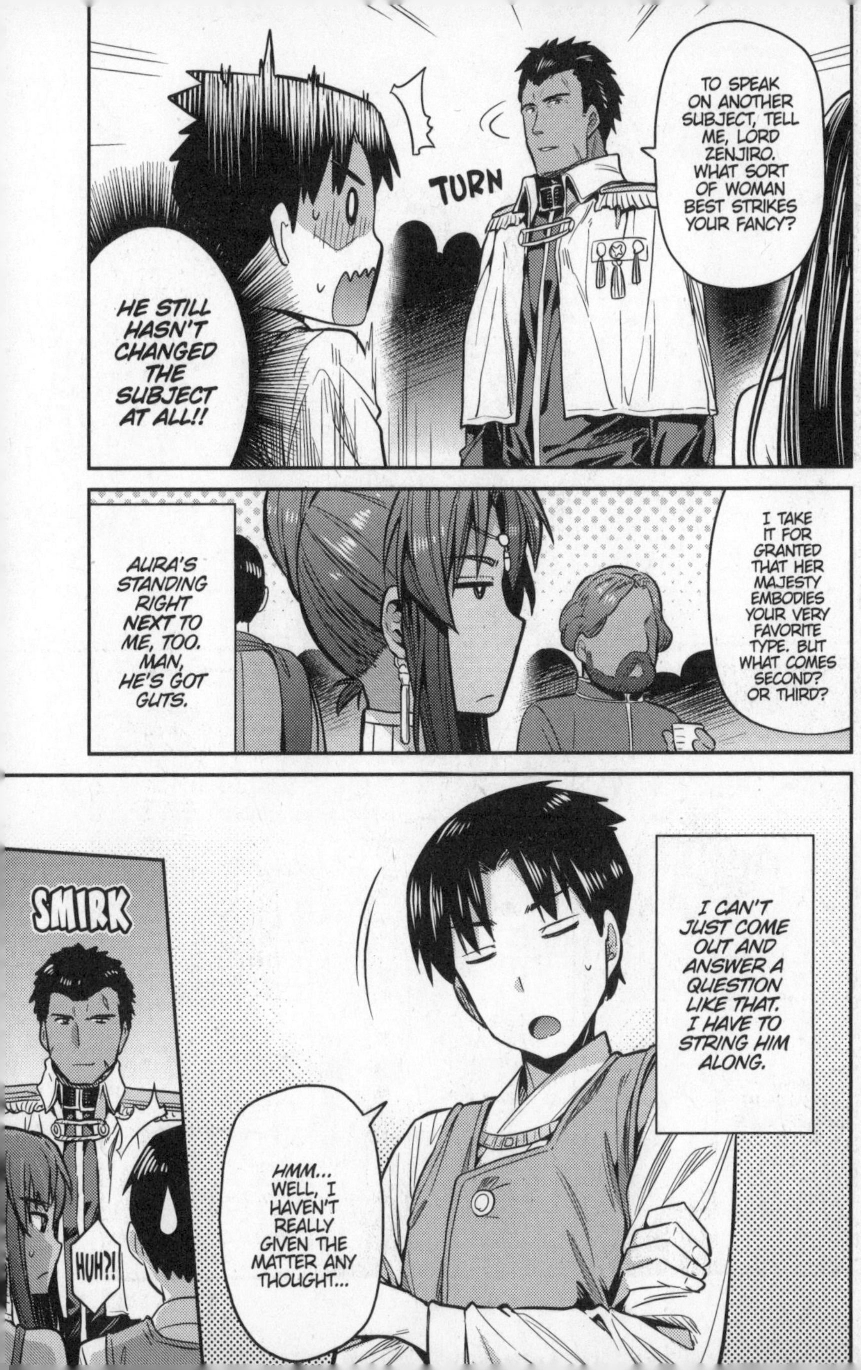
TO SPEAK ON ANOTHER SUBJECT, TELL ME, LORD ZENJIRO. WHAT SORT OF WOMAN BEST STRIKES YOUR FANCY?
TURN
HE STILL HASN'T CHANGED THE SUBJECT AT ALL!!
I TAKE IT FOR GRANTED THAT HER MAJESTY EMBODIES YOUR VERY FAVORITE TYPE. BUT WHAT COMES SECOND? OR THIRD?
AURA'S STANDING RIGHT NEXT TO ME, TOO. MAN, HE'S GOT GUTS.
I CAN'T JUST COME OUT AND ANSWER A QUESTION LIKE THAT. I HAVE TO STRING HIM ALONG.
HMM... WELL, I HAVEN'T REALLY GIVEN THE MATTER ANY THOUGHT...
SMIRK
HUH?!

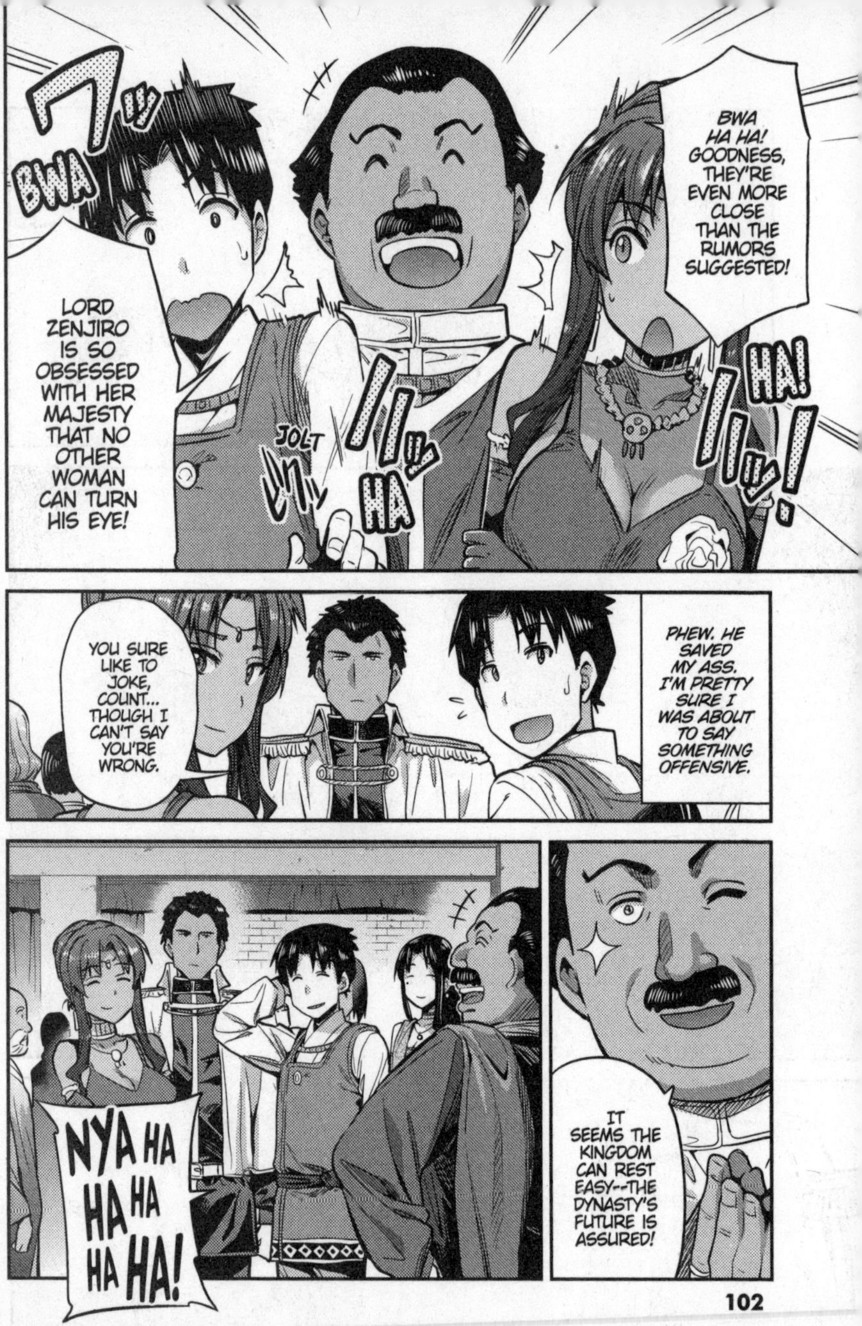
BWA HA HA! GOODNESS, THEY'RE EVEN MORE CLOSE THAN THE RUMORS SUGGESTED!
HA!
HA
LORD ZENJIRO IS SO OBSESSED WITH HER MAJESTY THAT NO OTHER WOMAN CAN TURN HIS EYE!
JOLT
BWA
PHEW. HE SAVED MY ASS. I'M PRETTY SURE I WAS ABOUT TO SAY SOMETHING OFFENSIVE.
YOU SURE LIKE TO JOKE, COUNT... THOUGH I CAN'T SAY YOU'RE WRONG.
IT SEEMS THE KINGDOM CAN REST EASY--THE DYNASTY'S FUTURE IS ASSURED!
NYA HA HA HA HA HA HA HA!

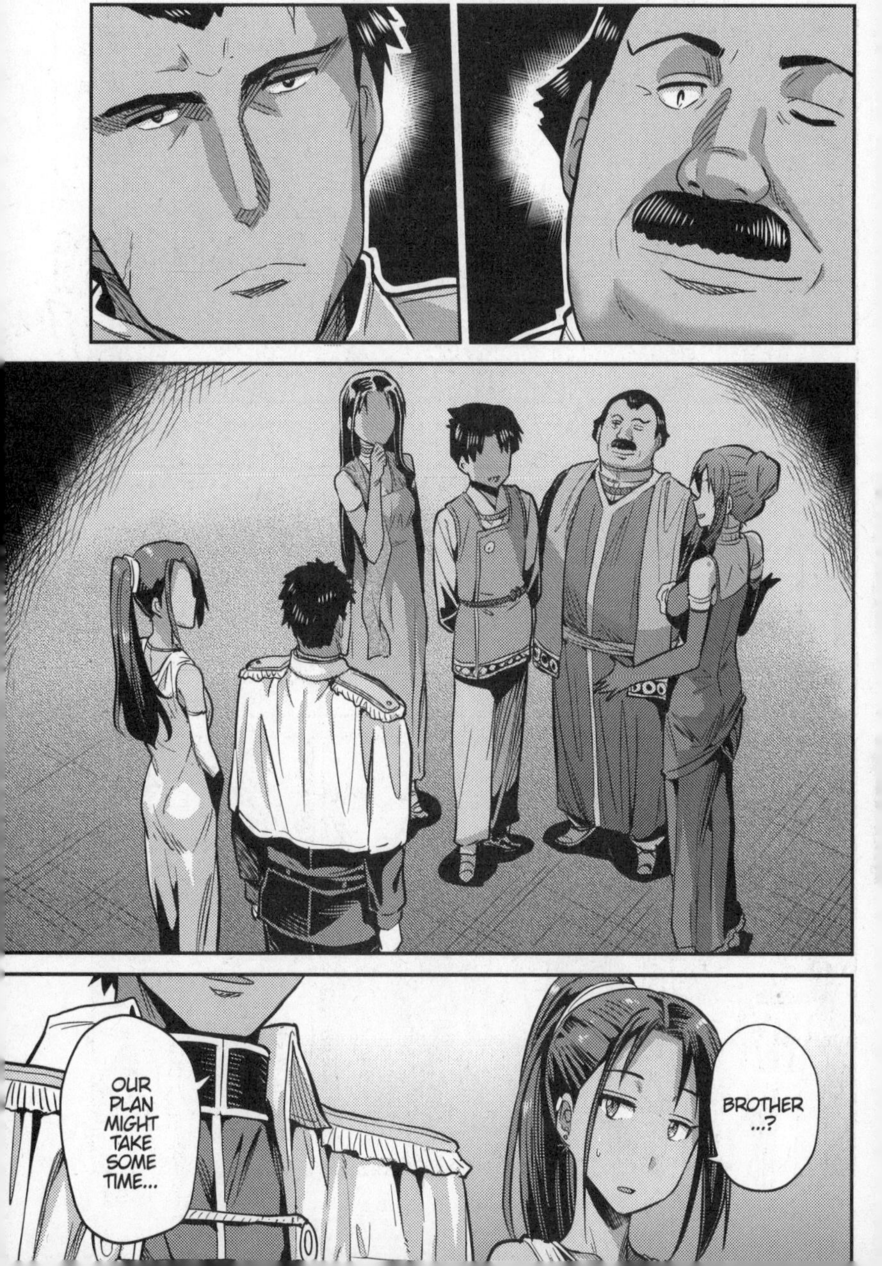
BROTHER ...?
OUR PLAN MIGHT TAKE SOME TIME...

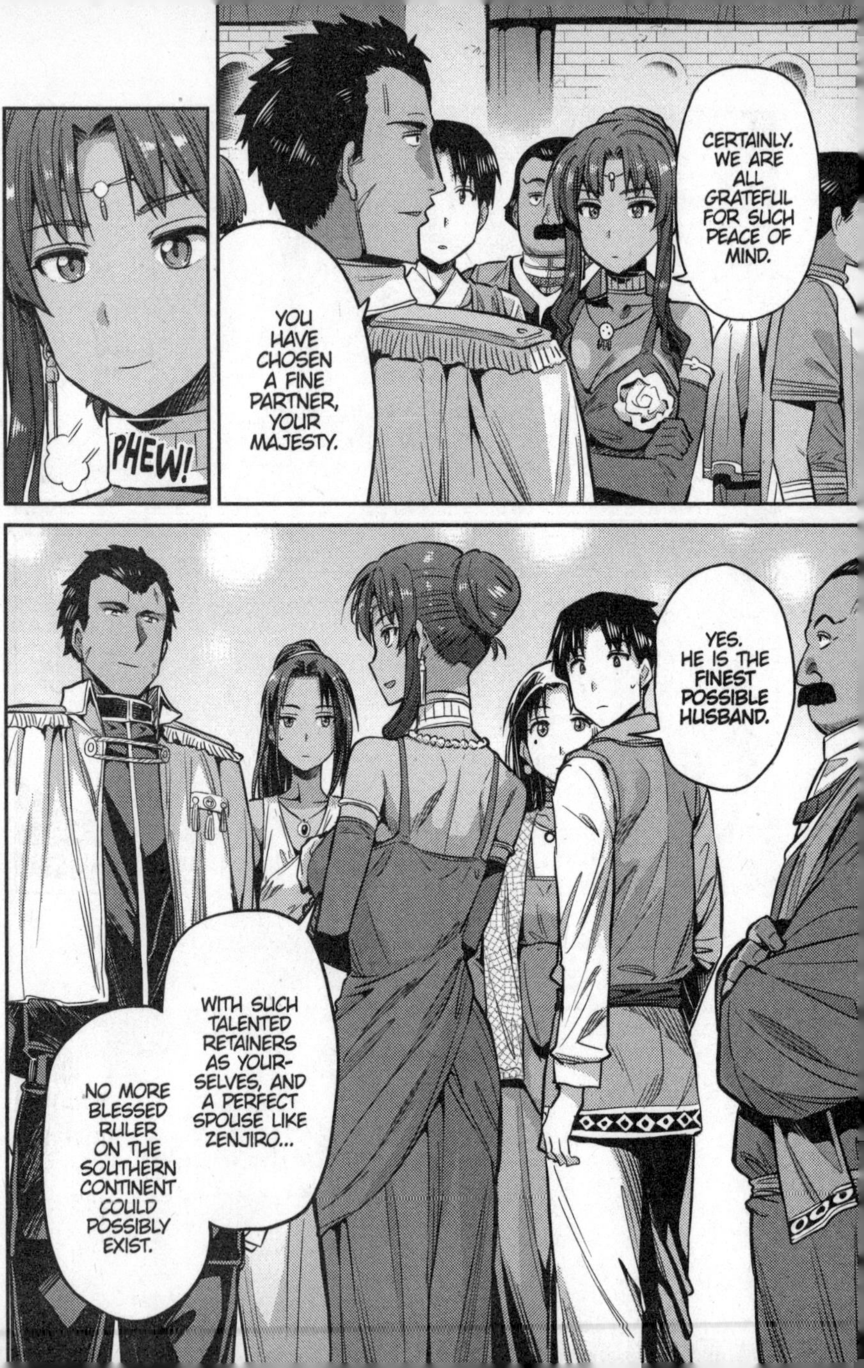
CERTAINLY. WE ARE ALL GRATEFUL FOR SUCH PEACE OF MIND.
YOU HAVE CHOSEN A FINE PARTNER, YOUR MAJESTY.
PHEW!
YES. HE IS THE FINEST POSSIBLE HUSBAND.
WITH SUCH TALENTED RETAINERS AS YOURSELVES, AND A PERFECT SPOUSE LIKE ZENJIRO...
NO MORE BLESSED RULER ON THE SOUTHERN CONTINENT COULD POSSIBLY EXIST.

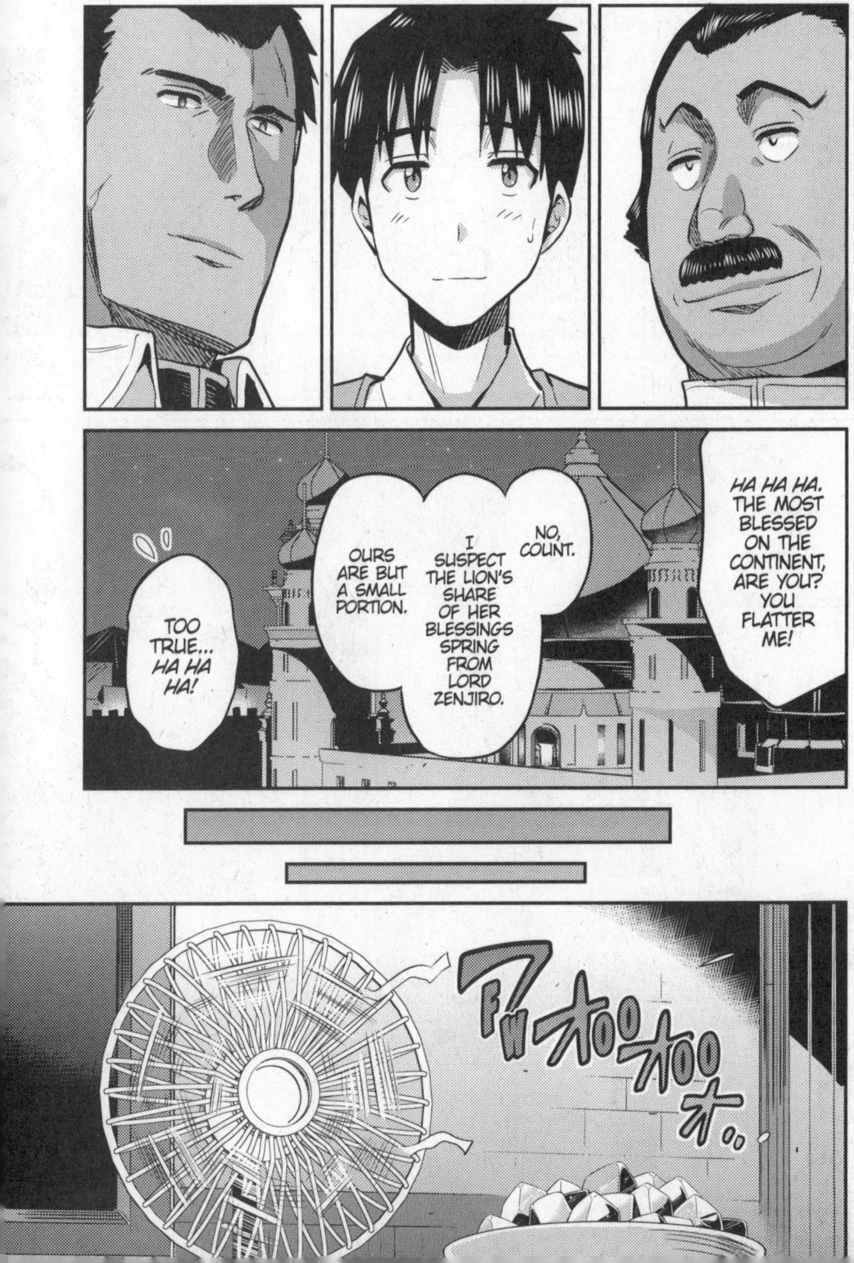
HA HA HA. THE MOST BLESSED ON THE CONTINENT, ARE YOU? YOU FLATTER ME!
NO, COUNT.
I SUSPECT THE LION'S SHARE OF HER BLESSINGS SPRING FROM LORD ZENJIRO.
OURS ARE BUT A SMALL PORTION.
TOO TRUE... HA HA HA!
FWOOOOOO...

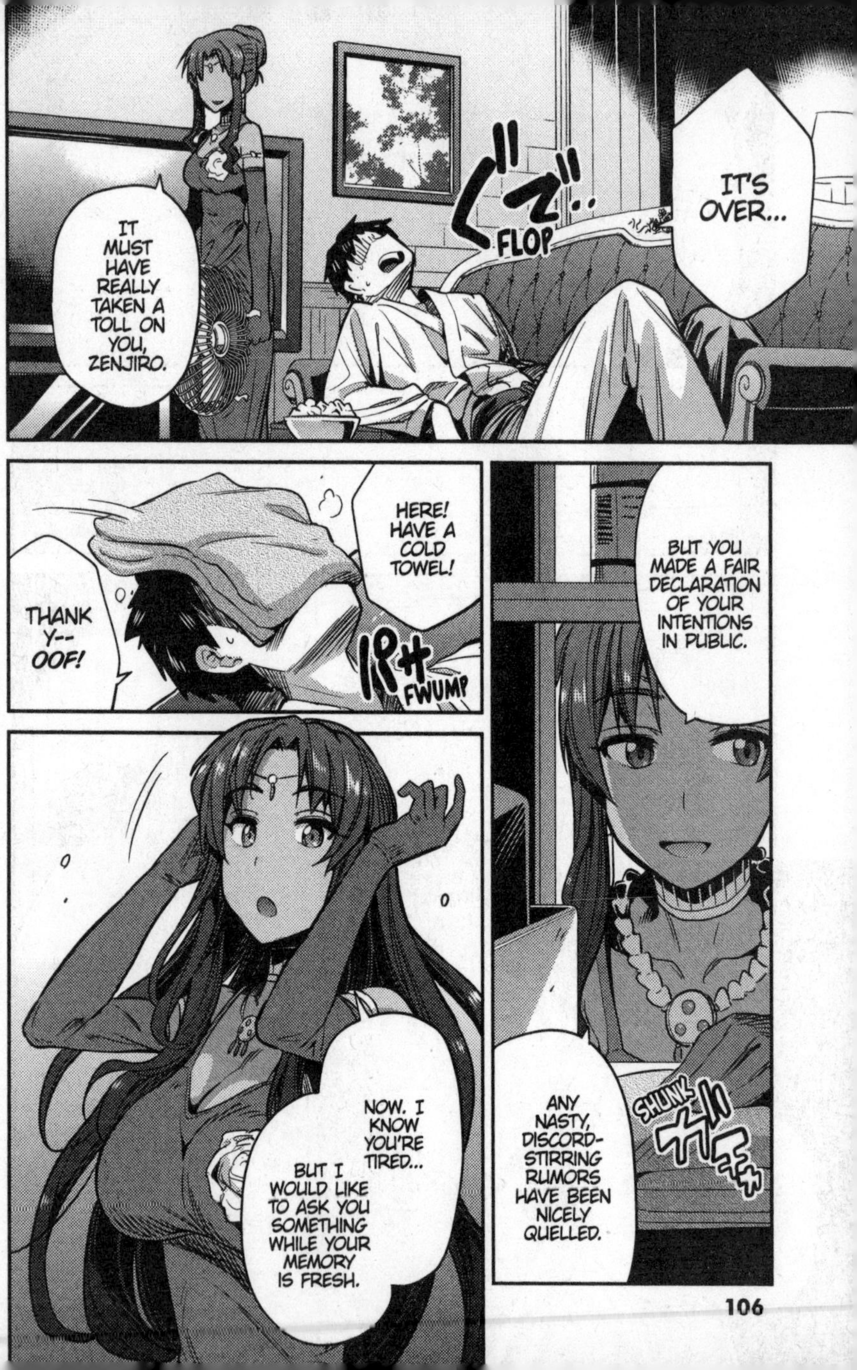
IT'S OVER...
FLOP
IT MUST HAVE REALLY TAKEN A TOLL ON YOU, ZENJIRO.
BUT YOU MADE A FAIR DECLARATION OF YOUR INTENTIONS IN PUBLIC.
ANY NASTY, DISCORD-STIRRING RUMORS HAVE BEEN NICELY QUELLED.
SHUNK
HERE! HAVE A COLD TOWEL!
FWUMP
THANK Y-- OOF!
NOW. I KNOW YOU'RE TIRED...
BUT I WOULD LIKE TO ASK YOU SOMETHING WHILE YOUR MEMORY IS FRESH.

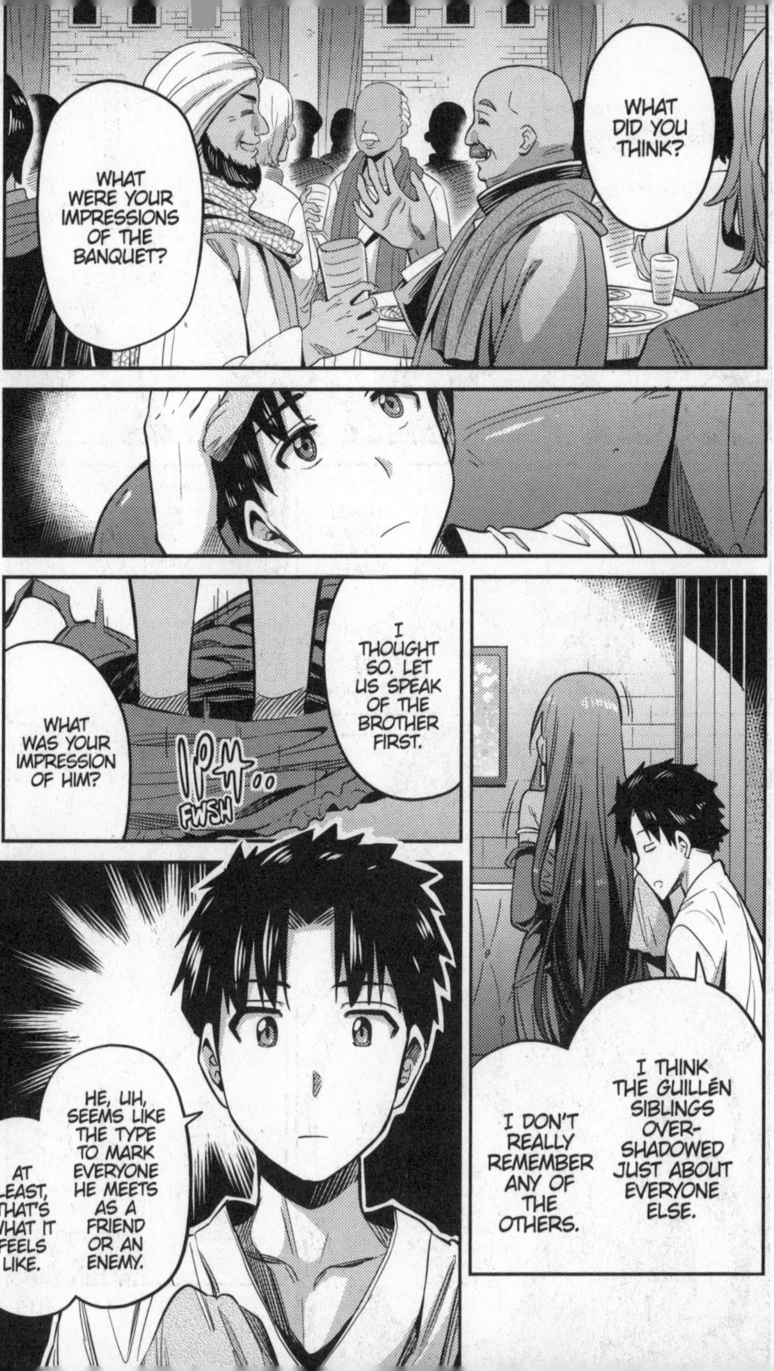
WHAT DID YOU THINK?
WHAT WERE YOUR IMPRESSIONS OF THE BANQUET?
I THINK THE GUILLÉN SIBLINGS OVER-SHADOWED JUST ABOUT EVERYONE ELSE.
I DON'T REALLY REMEMBER ANY OF THE OTHERS.
I THOUGHT SO. LET US SPEAK OF THE BROTHER FIRST.
WHAT WAS YOUR IMPRESSION OF HIM?
FWSH
HE, UH, SEEMS LIKE THE TYPE TO MARK EVERYONE HE MEETS AS A FRIEND OR AN ENEMY.
AT LEAST, THAT'S WHAT IT FEELS LIKE.

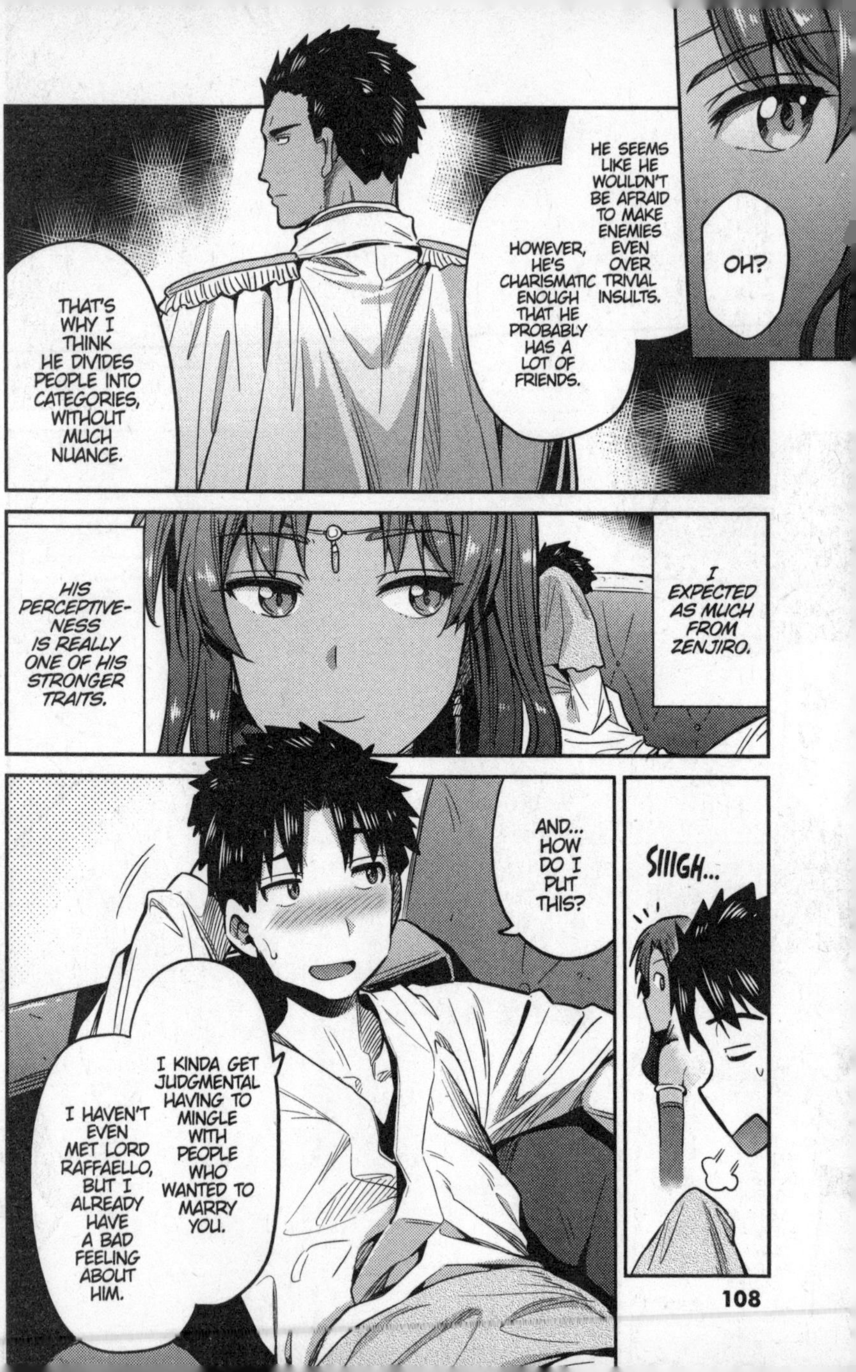
OH?
HE SEEMS LIKE HE WOULDN'T BE AFRAID TO MAKE ENEMIES EVEN OVER TRIVIAL INSULTS.
HOWEVER, HE'S CHARISMATIC ENOUGH THAT HE PROBABLY HAS A LOT OF FRIENDS.
THAT'S WHY I THINK HE DIVIDES PEOPLE INTO CATEGORIES, WITHOUT MUCH NUANCE.
I EXPECTED AS MUCH FROM ZENJIRO.
HIS PERCEPTIVENESS IS REALLY ONE OF HIS STRONGER TRAITS.
SIIIGH...
AND... HOW DO I PUT THIS?
I KINDA GET JUDGMENTAL HAVING TO MINGLE WITH PEOPLE WHO WANTED TO MARRY YOU.
I HAVEN'T EVEN MET LORD RAFFAELLO, BUT I ALREADY HAVE A BAD FEELING ABOUT HIM.

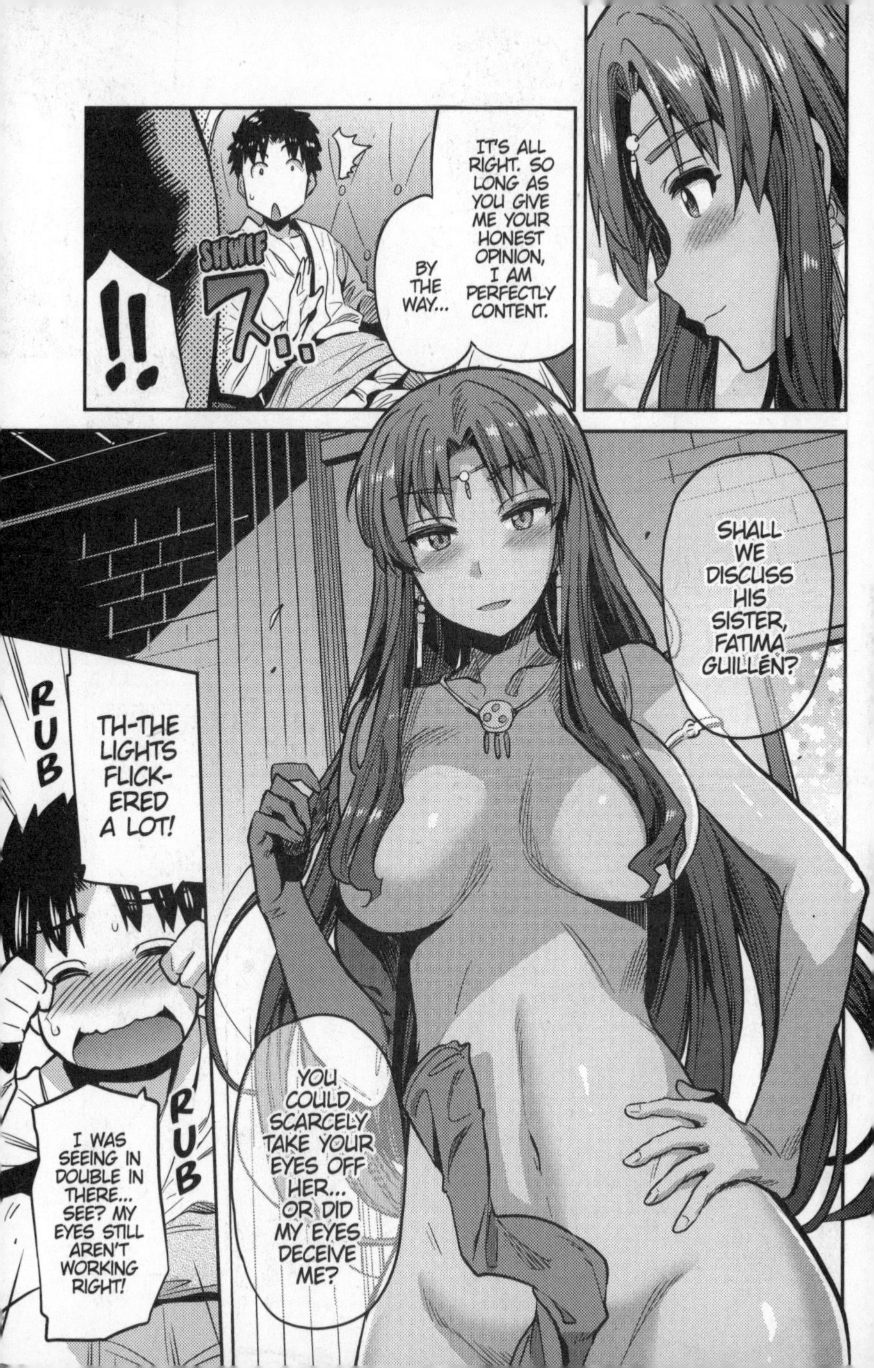
IT'S ALL RIGHT. SO LONG AS YOU GIVE ME YOUR HONEST OPINION, I AM PERFECTLY CONTENT.
BY THE WAY...
SHWIF
!!
SHALL WE DISCUSS HIS SISTER, FATIMA GUILLÉN?
YOU COULD SCARCELY TAKE YOUR EYES OFF HER... OR DID MY EYES DECEIVE ME?
RUB
TH-THE LIGHTS FLICK-ERED A LOT!
RUB
I WAS SEEING IN DOUBLE IN THERE... SEE? MY EYES STILL AREN'T WORKING RIGHT!

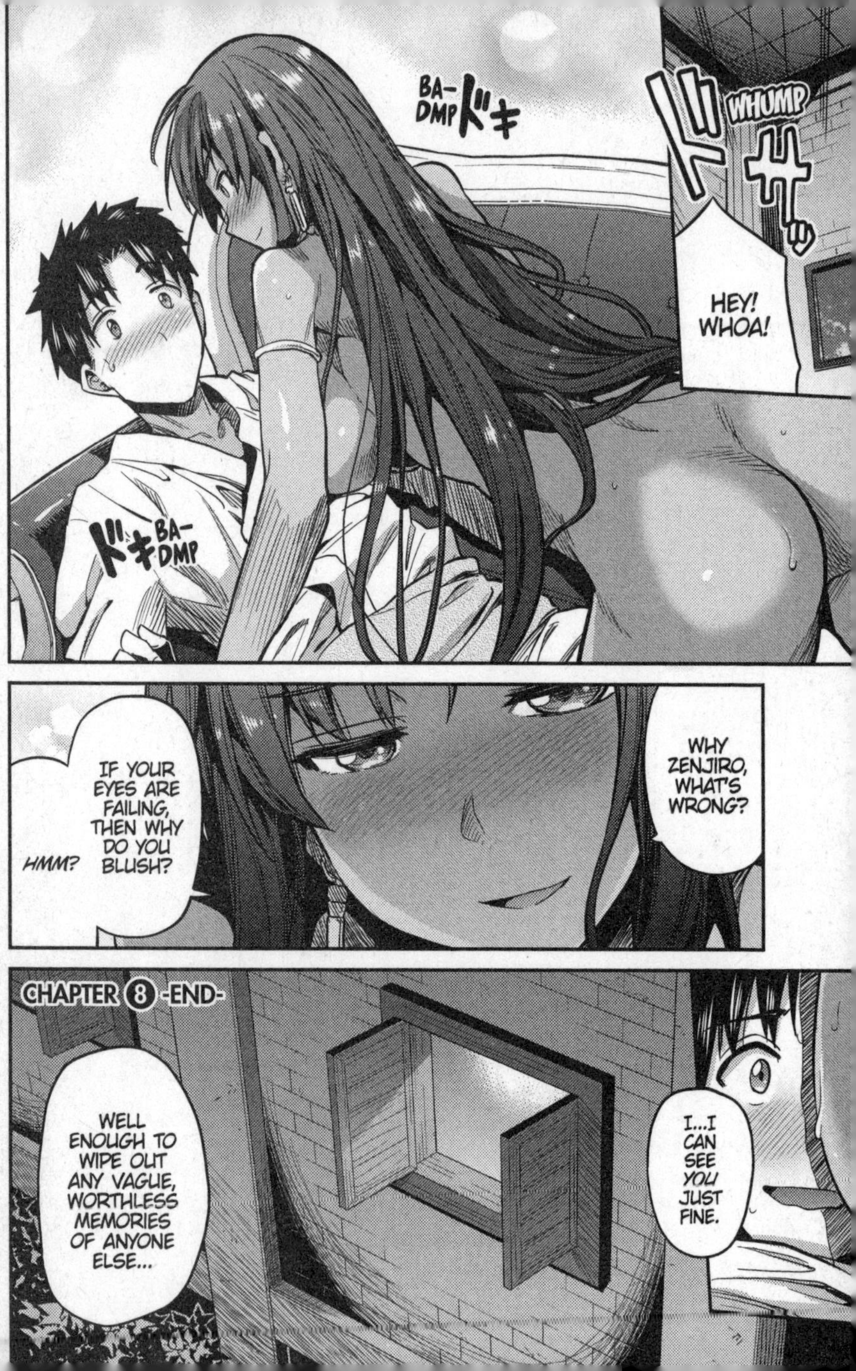
ドサッ
WHUMP
HEY! WHOA!
BA-DMP ドキ
ドキ BA-DMP
WHY ZENJIRO, WHAT'S WRONG?
IF YOUR EYES ARE FAILING, THEN WHY DO YOU BLUSH?
HMM?
I...I CAN SEE YOU JUST FINE.
WELL ENOUGH TO WIPE OUT ANY VAGUE, WORTHLESS MEMORIES OF ANYONE ELSE...
CHAPTER 8 -END-

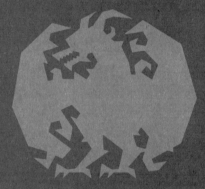

THE IDEAL SPONGER LIFE
Presented by Tsunehiko Watanabe & Neko Hinotsuki

THE IDEAL SPONGER LIFE

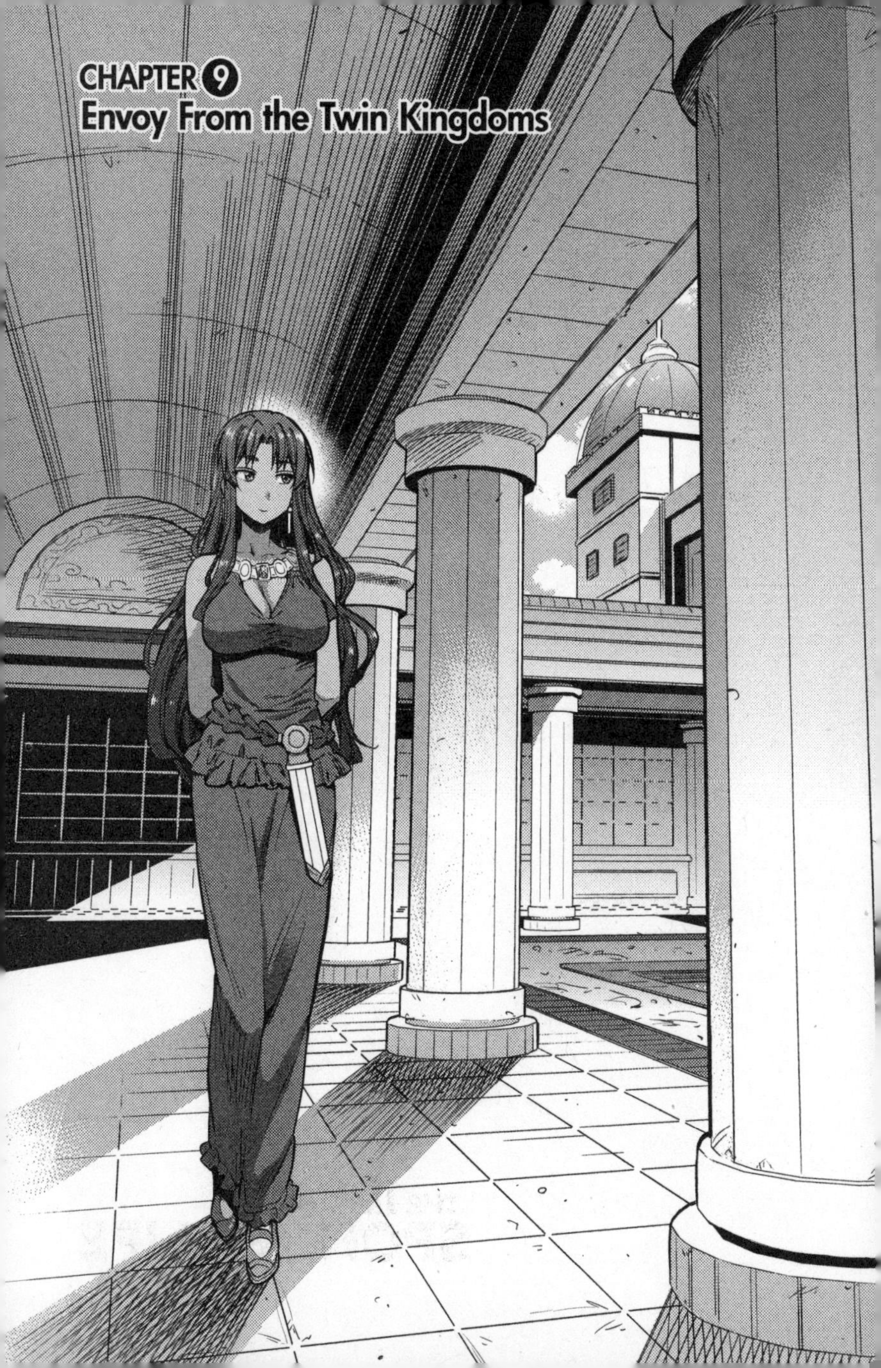
CHAPTER 9
Envoy From the Twin Kingdoms

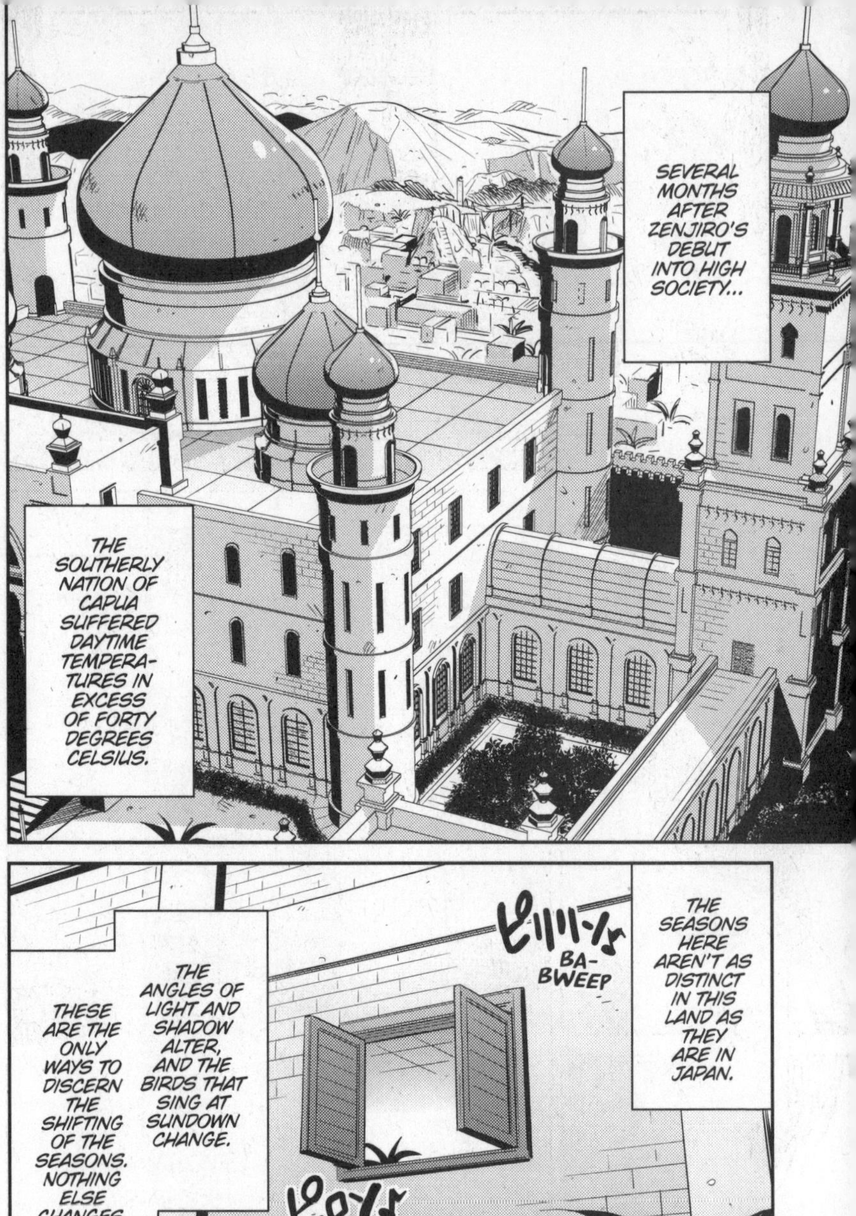

SEVERAL MONTHS AFTER ZENJIRO'S DEBUT INTO HIGH SOCIETY...
THE SOUTHERLY NATION OF CAPUA SUFFERED DAYTIME TEMPERA-TURES IN EXCESS OF FORTY DEGREES CELSIUS.
THE SEASONS HERE AREN'T AS DISTINCT IN THIS LAND AS THEY ARE IN JAPAN.
ピリリ-ィ♪ BA-BWEEP
THE ANGLES OF LIGHT AND SHADOW ALTER, AND THE BIRDS THAT SING AT SUNDOWN CHANGE.
THESE ARE THE ONLY WAYS TO DISCERN THE SHIFTING OF THE SEASONS. NOTHING ELSE CHANGES.
ピロ-ィ♪ PLONK

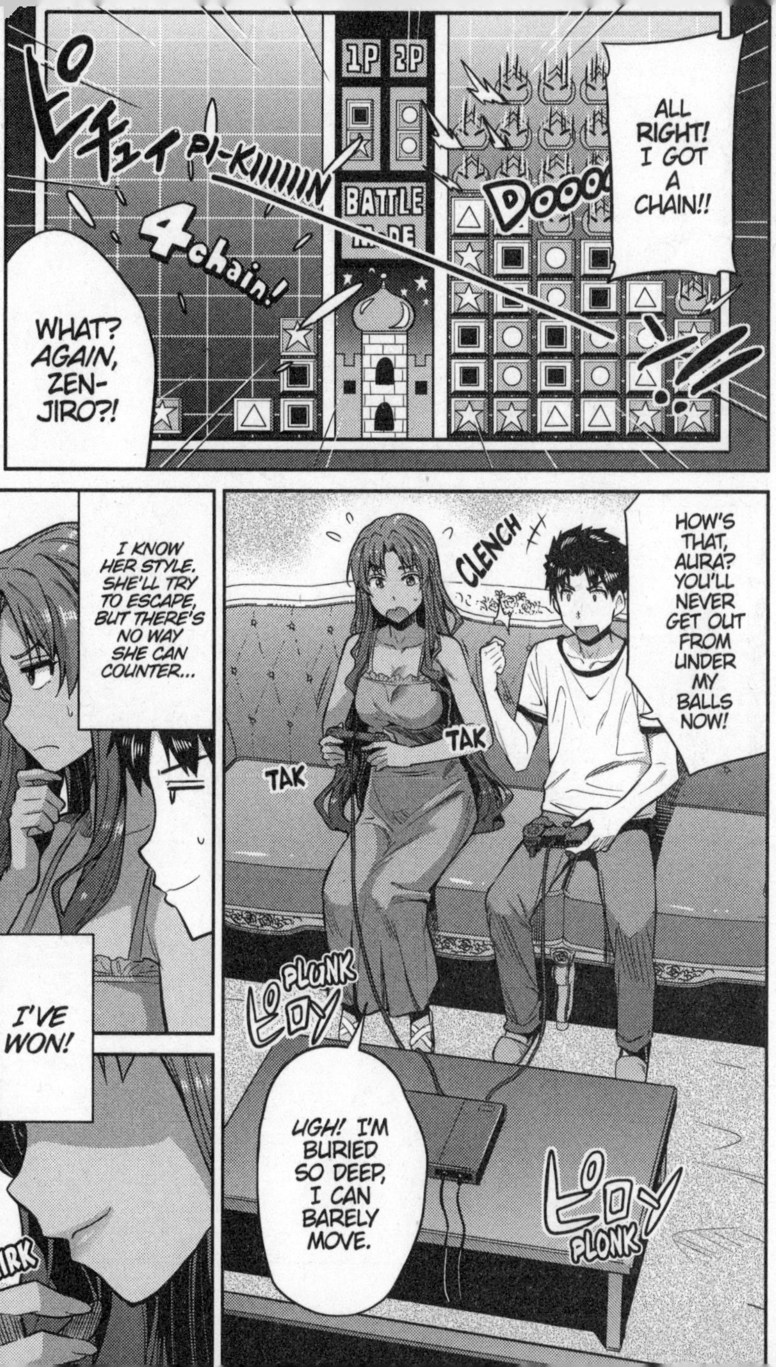
1P 2P
BATTLE
ALL RIGHT! I GOT A CHAIN!!
Dooo
ピキュイ PI-KIIIIIIIN
4chain!
WHAT? AGAIN, ZEN-JIRO?!
HOW'S THAT, AURA? YOU'LL NEVER GET OUT FROM UNDER MY BALLS NOW!
CLENCH
TAK
TAK
ピロッ PLONK
UGH! I'M BURIED SO DEEP, I CAN BARELY MOVE.
ピロッ PLONK
I KNOW HER STYLE. SHE'LL TRY TO ESCAPE, BUT THERE'S NO WAY SHE CAN COUNTER...
HMM...
I'VE WON!
SMIRK

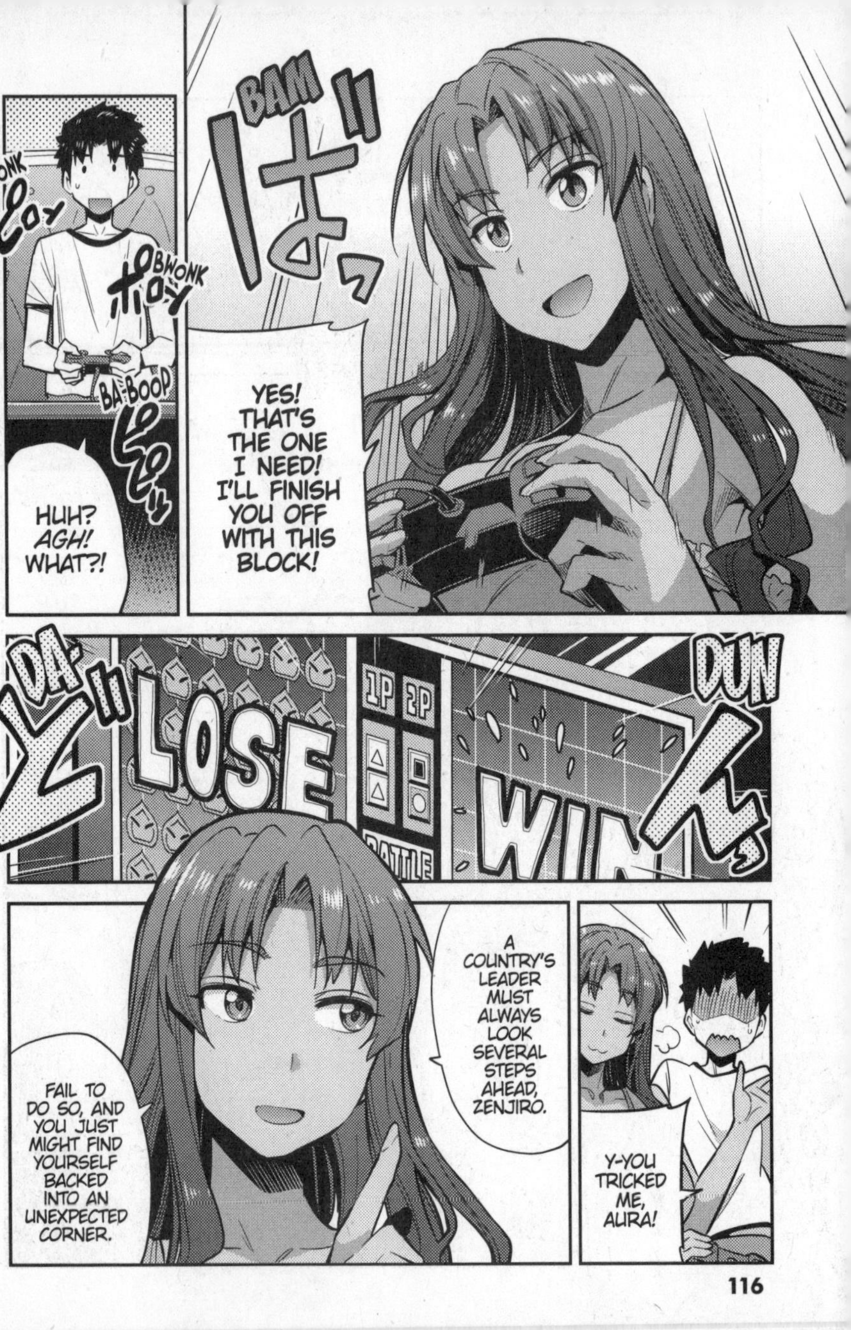
BAM
YES! THAT'S THE ONE I NEED! I'LL FINISH YOU OFF WITH THIS BLOCK!
PLONK
BWONK
BA-BOOP
HUH? AGH! WHAT?!
DUN
DA
LOSE
1P 2P
WIN
Y-YOU TRICKED ME, AURA!
A COUNTRY'S LEADER MUST ALWAYS LOOK SEVERAL STEPS AHEAD, ZENJIRO.
FAIL TO DO SO, AND YOU JUST MIGHT FIND YOURSELF BACKED INTO AN UNEXPECTED CORNER.

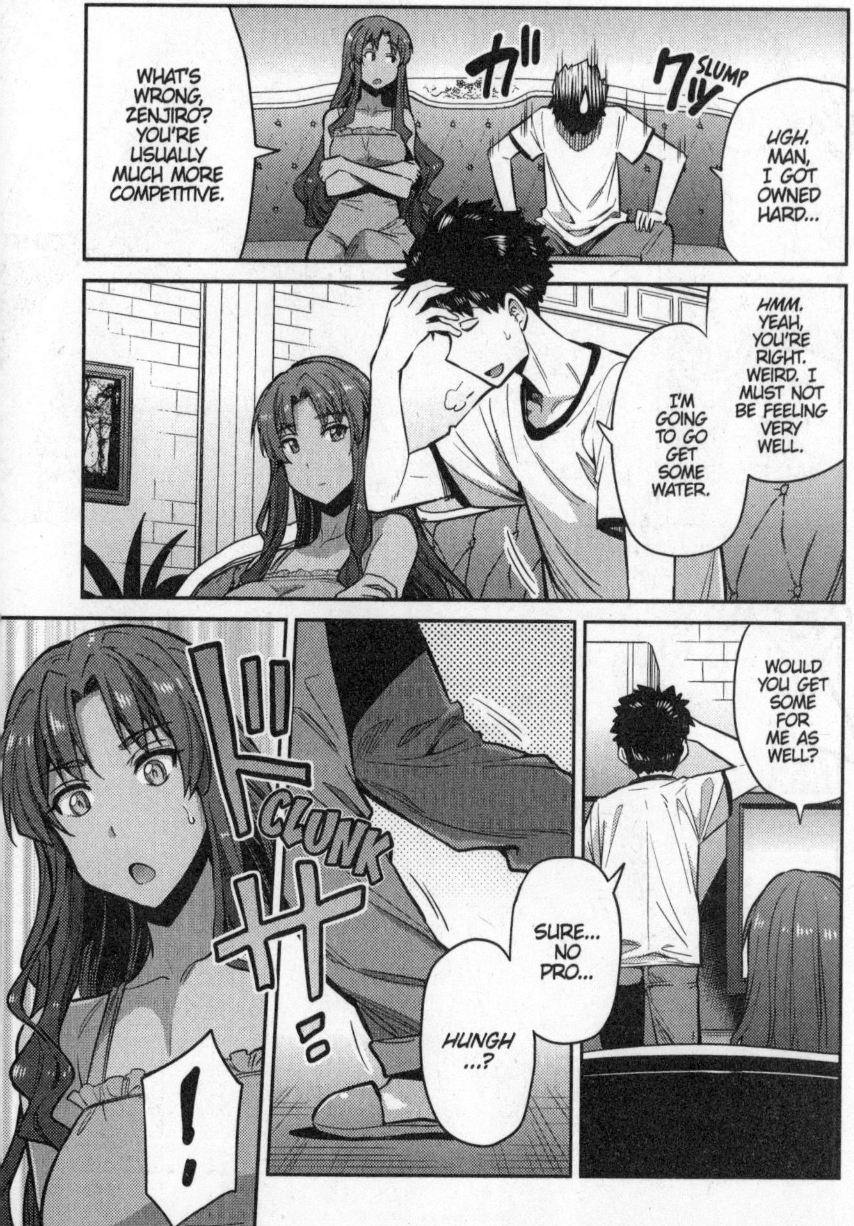
SLUMP
UGH. MAN, I GOT OWNED HARD...
WHAT'S WRONG, ZENJIRO? YOU'RE USUALLY MUCH MORE COMPETITIVE.
HMM. YEAH, YOU'RE RIGHT. WEIRD. I MUST NOT BE FEELING VERY WELL.
I'M GOING TO GO GET SOME WATER.
WOULD YOU GET SOME FOR ME AS WELL?
SURE... NO PRO...
HUNGH ...?
CLUNK
!

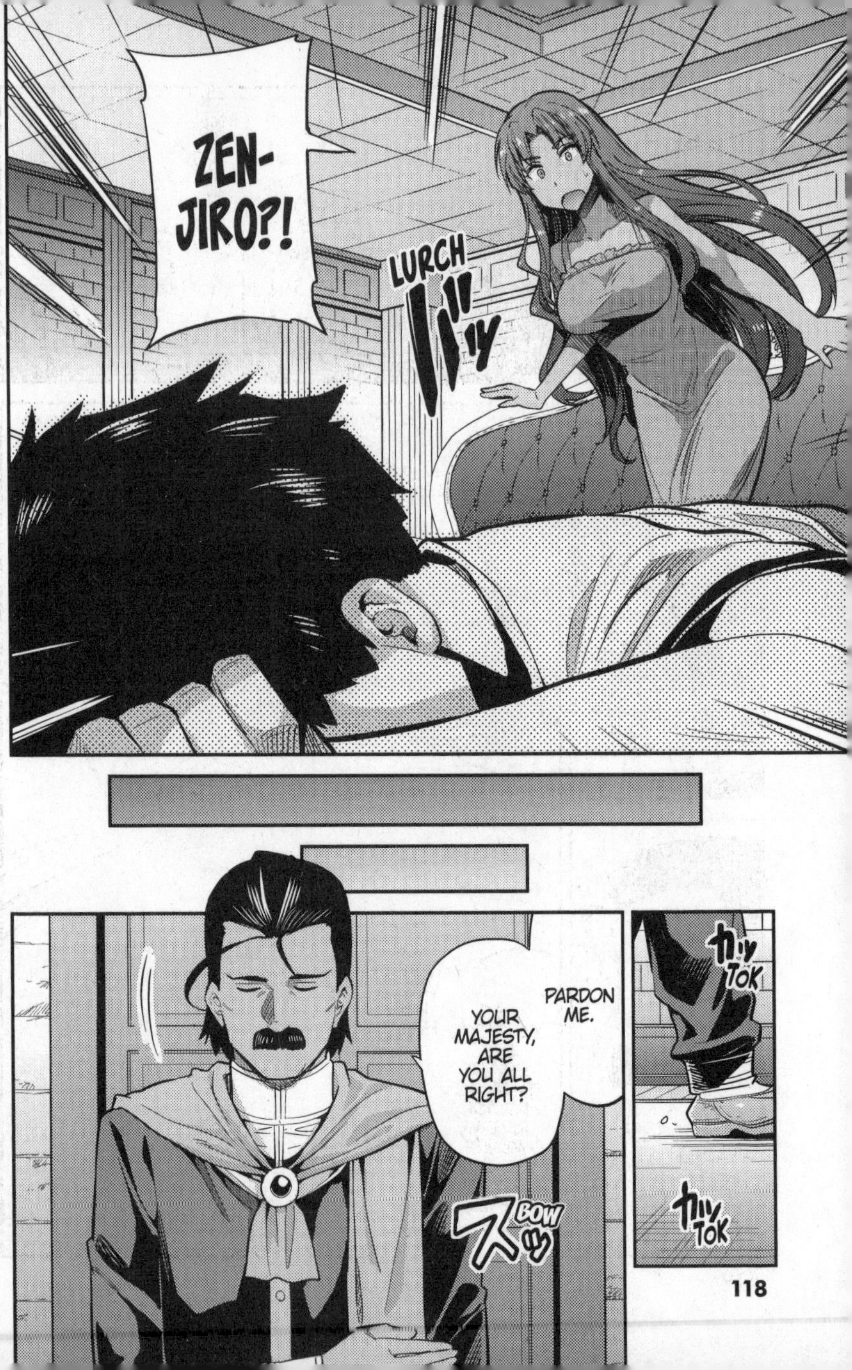
ZEN-JIRO?!
LURCH
TOK
TOK
PARDON ME.
YOUR MAJESTY, ARE YOU ALL RIGHT?
BOW

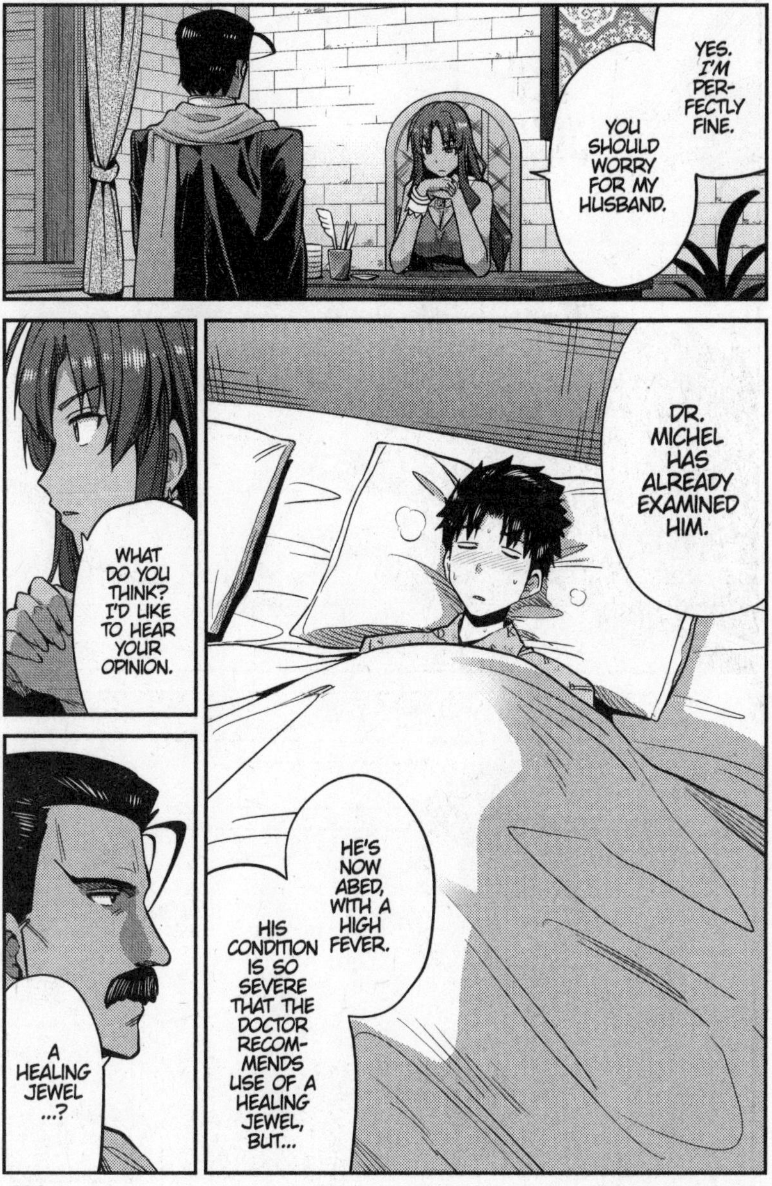
YES. I'M PER-FECTLY FINE.
YOU SHOULD WORRY FOR MY HUSBAND.
DR. MICHEL HAS ALREADY EXAMINED HIM.
HE'S NOW ABED, WITH A HIGH FEVER.
HIS CONDITION IS SO SEVERE THAT THE DOCTOR RECOMMENDS USE OF A HEALING JEWEL, BUT...
WHAT DO YOU THINK? I'D LIKE TO HEAR YOUR OPINION.
A HEALING JEWEL ...?

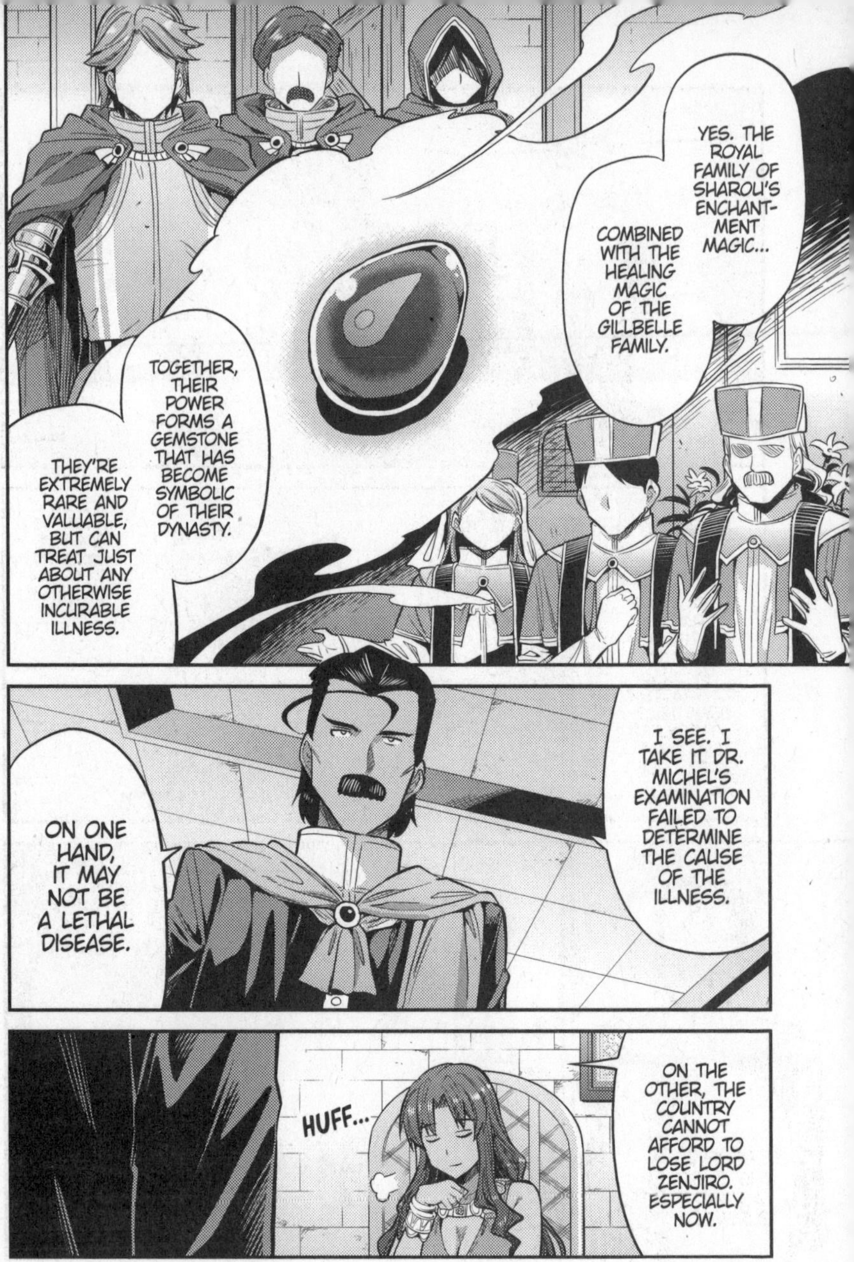
YES. THE ROYAL FAMILY OF SHAROU'S ENCHANT-MENT MAGIC...
COMBINED WITH THE HEALING MAGIC OF THE GILLBELLE FAMILY.
TOGETHER, THEIR POWER FORMS A GEMSTONE THAT HAS BECOME SYMBOLIC OF THEIR DYNASTY.
THEY'RE EXTREMELY RARE AND VALUABLE, BUT CAN TREAT JUST ABOUT ANY OTHERWISE INCURABLE ILLNESS.
I SEE. I TAKE IT DR. MICHEL'S EXAMINATION FAILED TO DETERMINE THE CAUSE OF THE ILLNESS.
ON ONE HAND, IT MAY NOT BE A LETHAL DISEASE.
ON THE OTHER, THE COUNTRY CANNOT AFFORD TO LOSE LORD ZENJIRO. ESPECIALLY NOW.
HUFF...

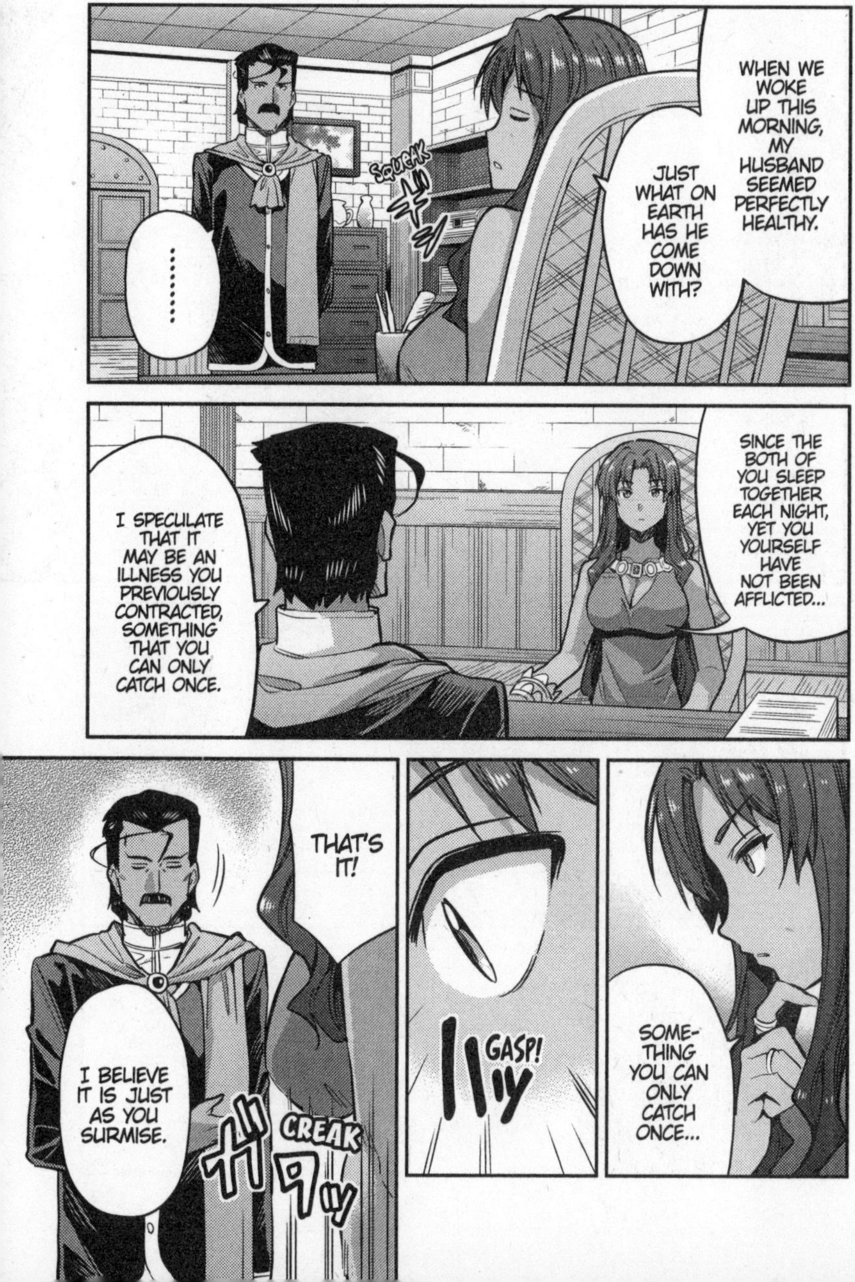
WHEN WE WOKE UP THIS MORNING, MY HUSBAND SEEMED PERFECTLY HEALTHY.
JUST WHAT ON EARTH HAS HE COME DOWN WITH?
SQUEAK
......
SINCE THE BOTH OF YOU SLEEP TOGETHER EACH NIGHT, YET YOU YOURSELF HAVE NOT BEEN AFFLICTED...
I SPECULATE THAT IT MAY BE AN ILLNESS YOU PREVIOUSLY CONTRACTED, SOMETHING THAT YOU CAN ONLY CATCH ONCE.
SOME-THING YOU CAN ONLY CATCH ONCE...
GASP!
THAT'S IT!
CREAK
I BELIEVE IT IS JUST AS YOU SURMISE.

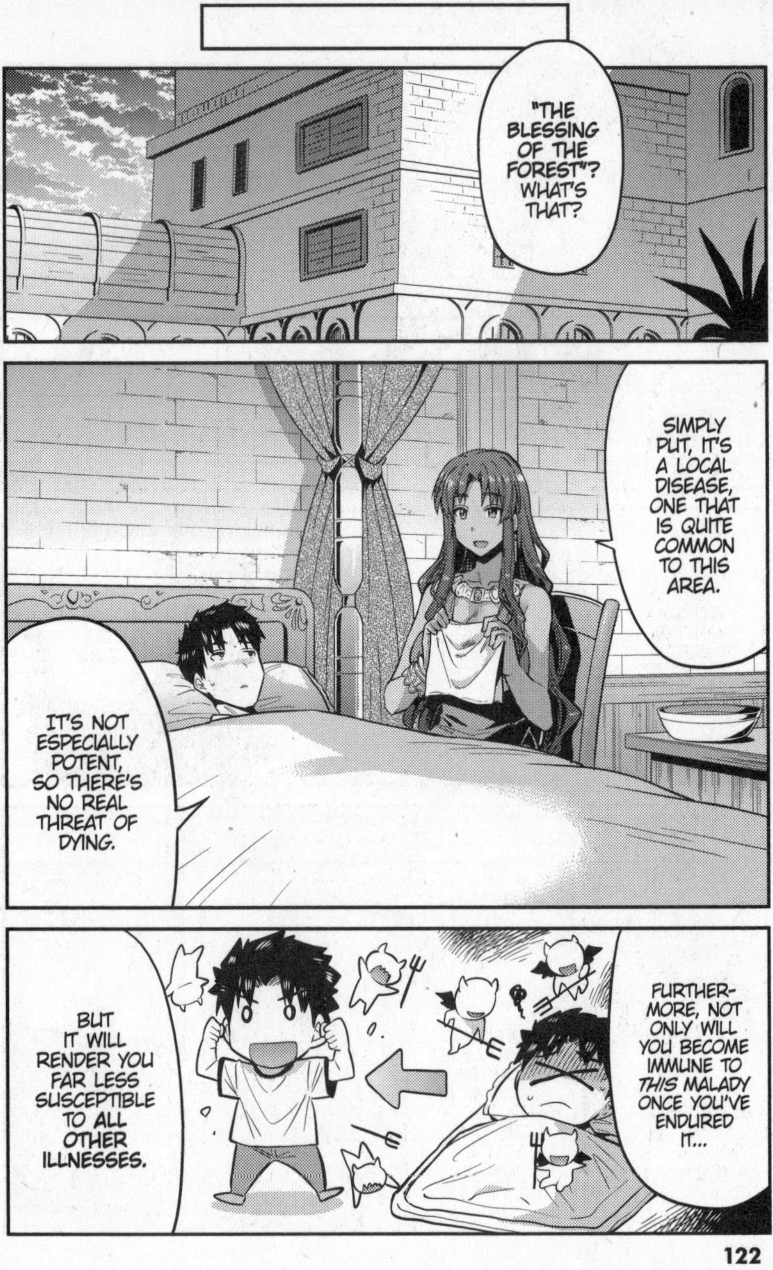
"THE BLESSING OF THE FOREST"? WHAT'S THAT?
SIMPLY PUT, IT'S A LOCAL DISEASE, ONE THAT IS QUITE COMMON TO THIS AREA.
IT'S NOT ESPECIALLY POTENT, SO THERE'S NO REAL THREAT OF DYING.
FURTHER-MORE, NOT ONLY WILL YOU BECOME IMMUNE TO *THIS* MALADY ONCE YOU'VE ENDURED IT...
BUT IT WILL RENDER YOU FAR LESS SUSCEPTIBLE TO ALL OTHER ILLNESSES.

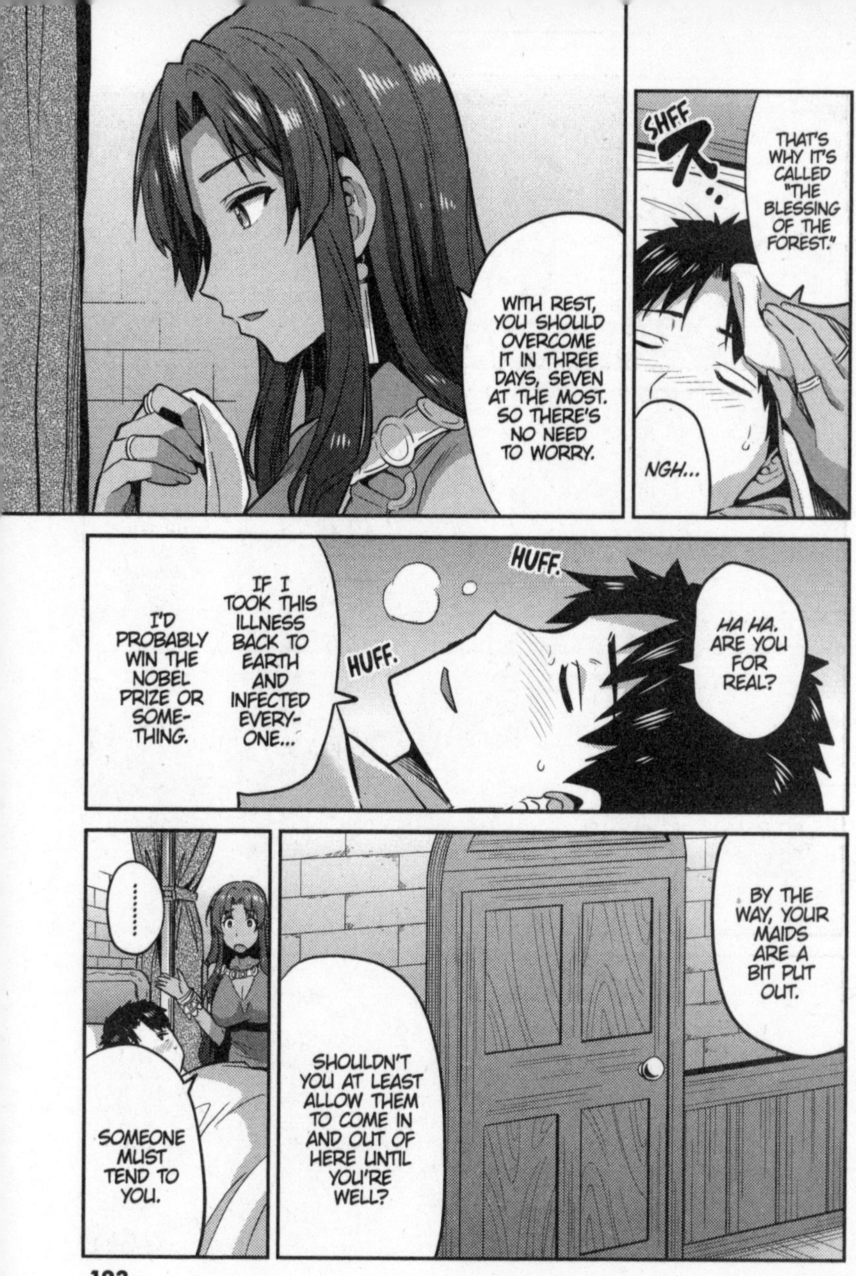
SHFF
THAT'S WHY IT'S CALLED "THE BLESSING OF THE FOREST."
NGH...
WITH REST, YOU SHOULD OVERCOME IT IN THREE DAYS, SEVEN AT THE MOST. SO THERE'S NO NEED TO WORRY.
HA HA. ARE YOU FOR REAL?
HUFF.
HUFF.
IF I TOOK THIS ILLNESS BACK TO EARTH AND INFECTED EVERY-ONE...
I'D PROBABLY WIN THE NOBEL PRIZE OR SOME-THING.
BY THE WAY, YOUR MAIDS ARE A BIT PUT OUT.
SHOULDN'T YOU AT LEAST ALLOW THEM TO COME IN AND OUT OF HERE UNTIL YOU'RE WELL?
......
SOMEONE MUST TEND TO YOU.

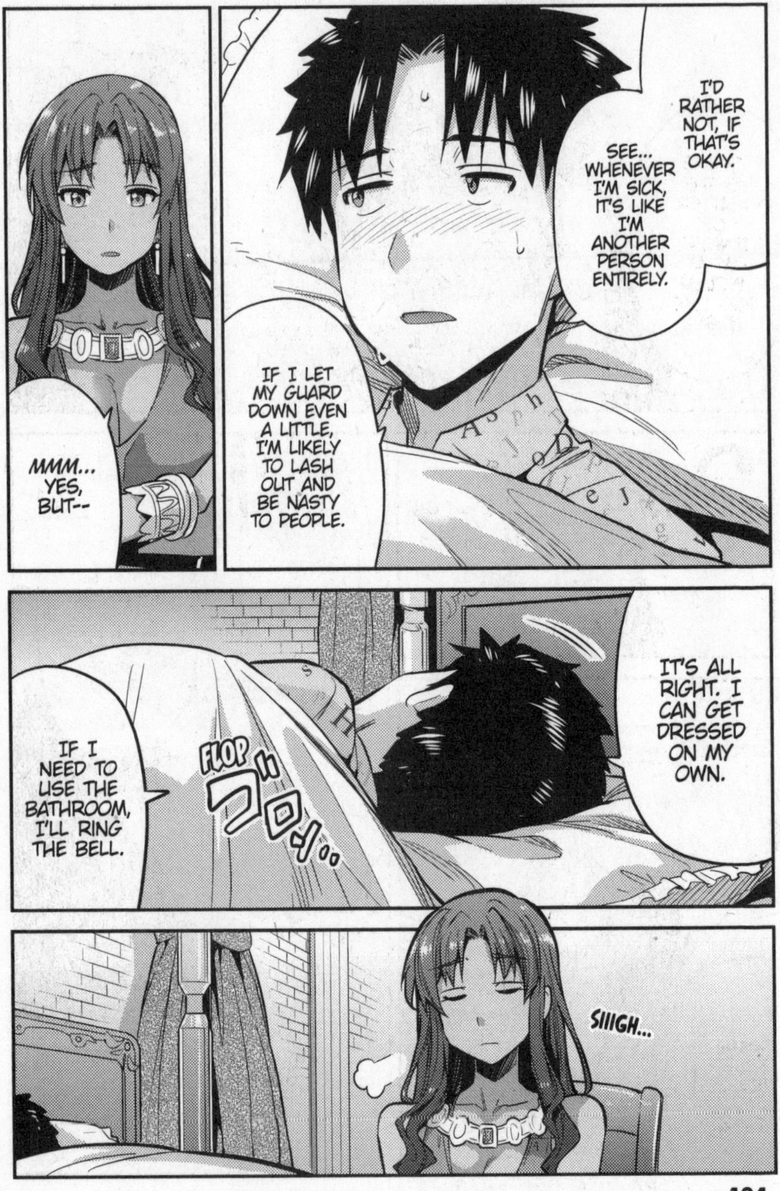
I'D RATHER NOT, IF THAT'S OKAY.
SEE... WHENEVER I'M SICK, IT'S LIKE I'M ANOTHER PERSON ENTIRELY.
IF I LET MY GUARD DOWN EVEN A LITTLE, I'M LIKELY TO LASH OUT AND BE NASTY TO PEOPLE.
MMM... YES, BUT--
IT'S ALL RIGHT. I CAN GET DRESSED ON MY OWN.
FLOP
ゴロッ
IF I NEED TO USE THE BATHROOM, I'LL RING THE BELL.
SIIIGH...

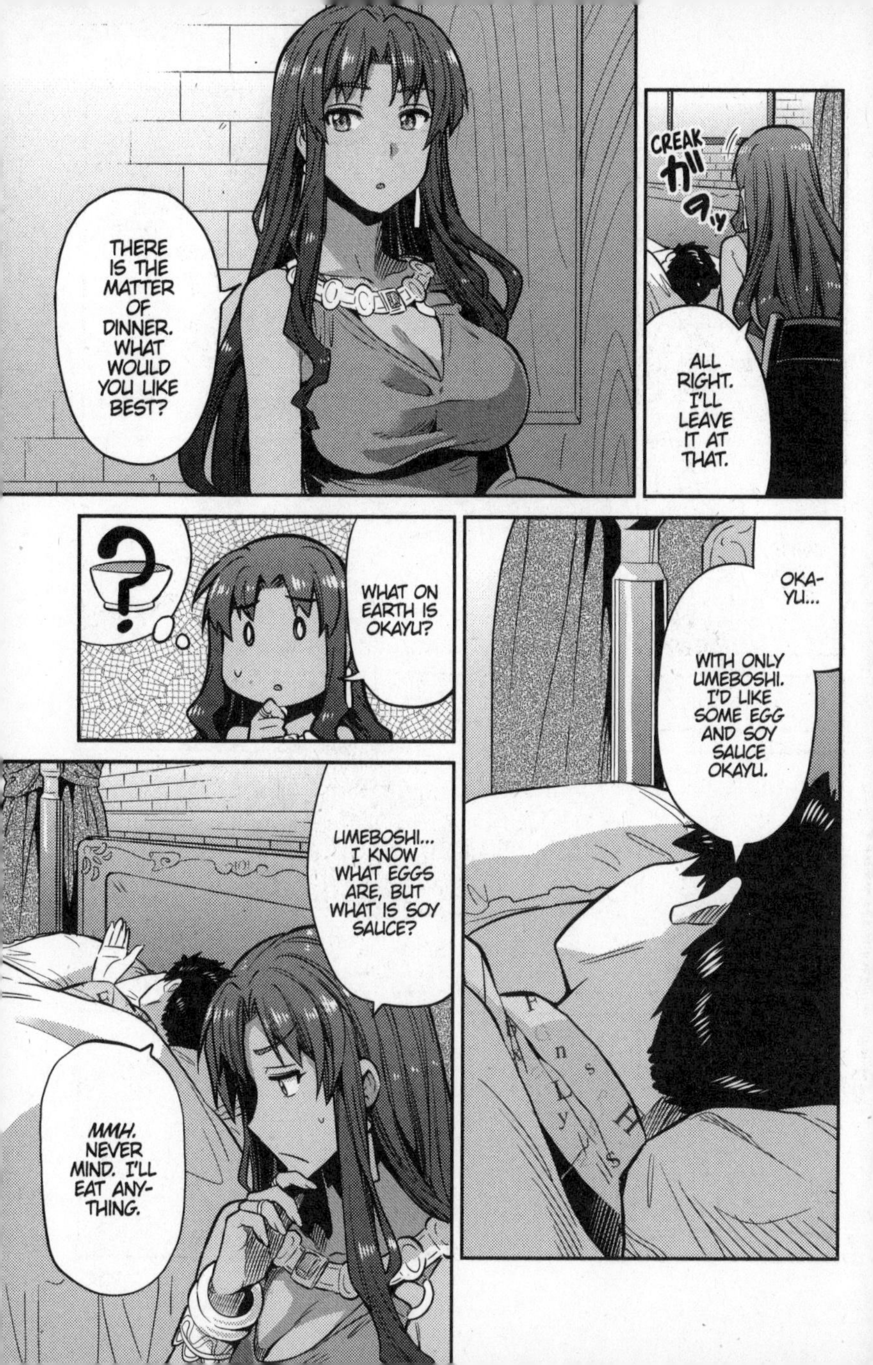
CREAK
ガタッ
ALL RIGHT. I'LL LEAVE IT AT THAT.
THERE IS THE MATTER OF DINNER. WHAT WOULD YOU LIKE BEST?
OKA-YU...
WITH ONLY UMEBOSHI. I'D LIKE SOME EGG AND SOY SAUCE OKAYU.
?
WHAT ON EARTH IS OKAYU?
UMEBOSHI... I KNOW WHAT EGGS ARE, BUT WHAT IS SOY SAUCE?
MMH. NEVER MIND. I'LL EAT ANY-THING.

SORRY. I'LL ASK THE KITCHEN STAFF TO MAKE YOU SOMETHING SPECIAL.

THANK YOU. I'M LOOKING FORWARD TO IT.

BTAM

ガチャ KA-CHAK

ROLL...

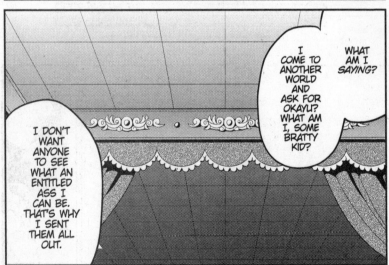

WHAT AM I SAYING?

I COME TO ANOTHER WORLD AND ASK FOR OKAYU? WHAT AM I, SOME BRATTY KID?

I DON'T WANT ANYONE TO SEE WHAT AN ENTITLED ASS I CAN BE. THAT'S WHY I SENT THEM ALL OUT.

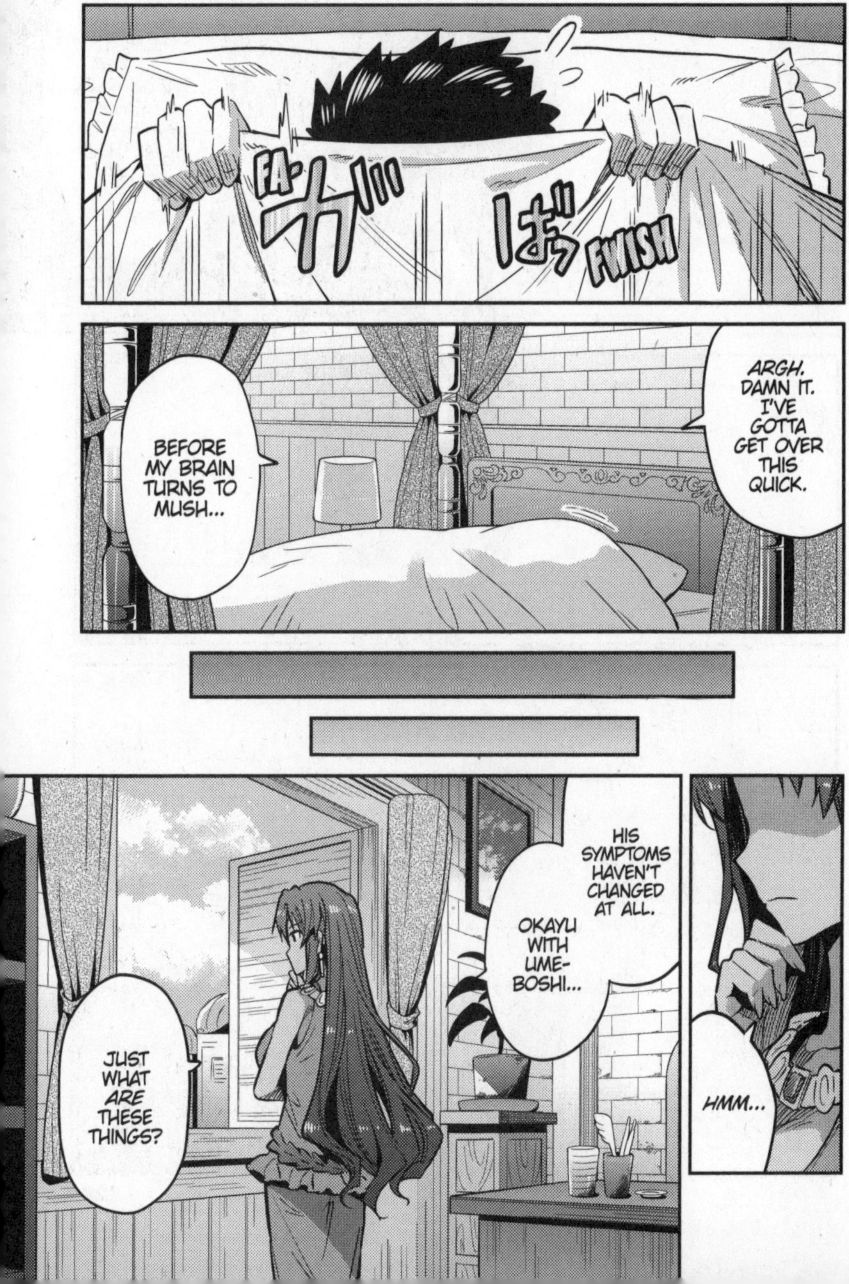
FA-
FWISH
ARGH. DAMN IT. I'VE GOTTA GET OVER THIS QUICK.
BEFORE MY BRAIN TURNS TO MUSH...
HMM...
HIS SYMPTOMS HAVEN'T CHANGED AT ALL.
OKAYU WITH UME-BOSHI...
JUST WHAT *ARE* THESE THINGS?

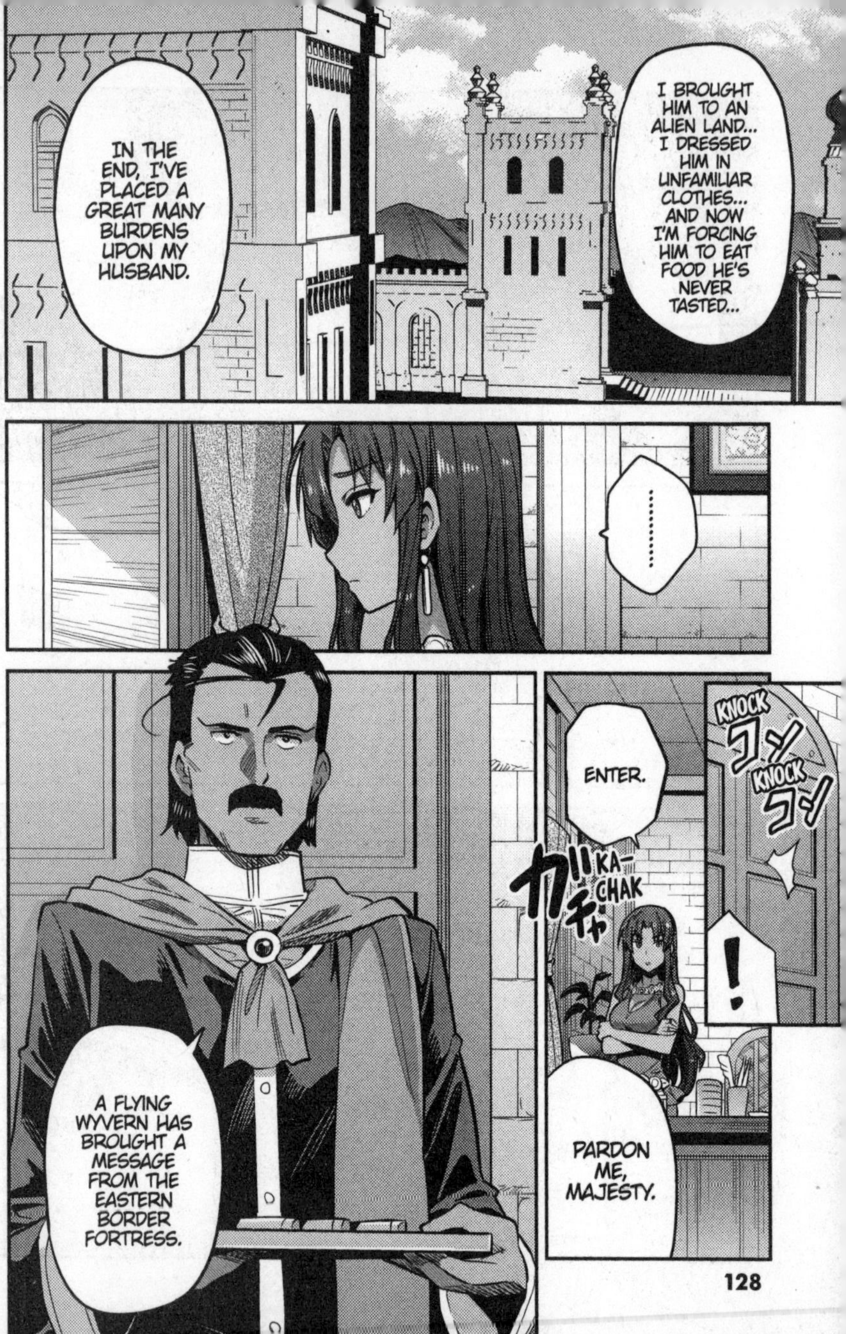
I BROUGHT HIM TO AN ALIEN LAND... I DRESSED HIM IN UNFAMILIAR CLOTHES... AND NOW I'M FORCING HIM TO EAT FOOD HE'S NEVER TASTED...
IN THE END, I'VE PLACED A GREAT MANY BURDENS UPON MY HUSBAND.
......
KNOCK
KNOCK
!
ENTER.
KA-CHAK
PARDON ME, MAJESTY.
A FLYING WYVERN HAS BROUGHT A MESSAGE FROM THE EASTERN BORDER FORTRESS.

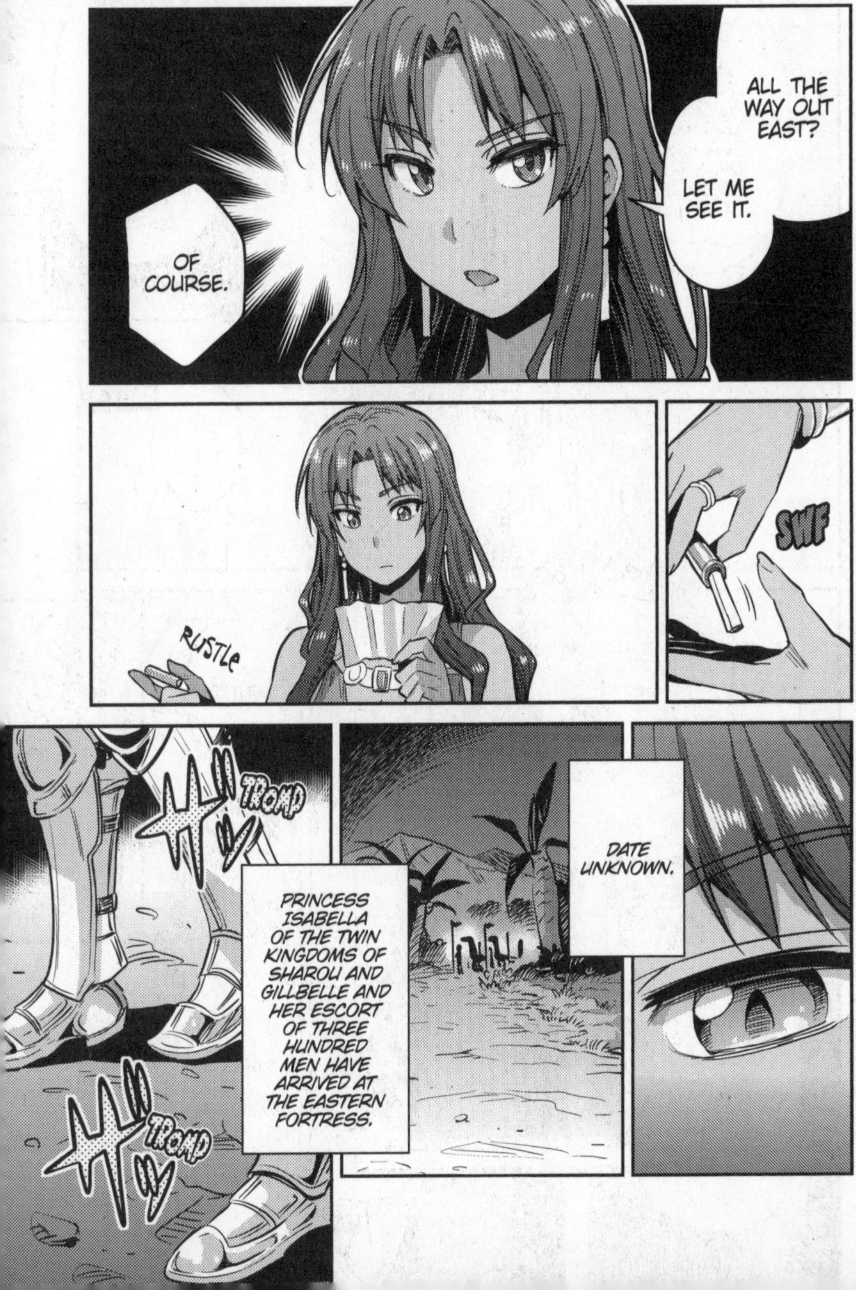
ALL THE WAY OUT EAST?
LET ME SEE IT.
OF COURSE.
SWF
RUSTLE
DATE UNKNOWN.
PRINCESS ISABELLA OF THE TWIN KINGDOMS OF SHAROU AND GILLBELLE AND HER ESCORT OF THREE HUNDRED MEN HAVE ARRIVED AT THE EASTERN FORTRESS.
TROMP
TROMP

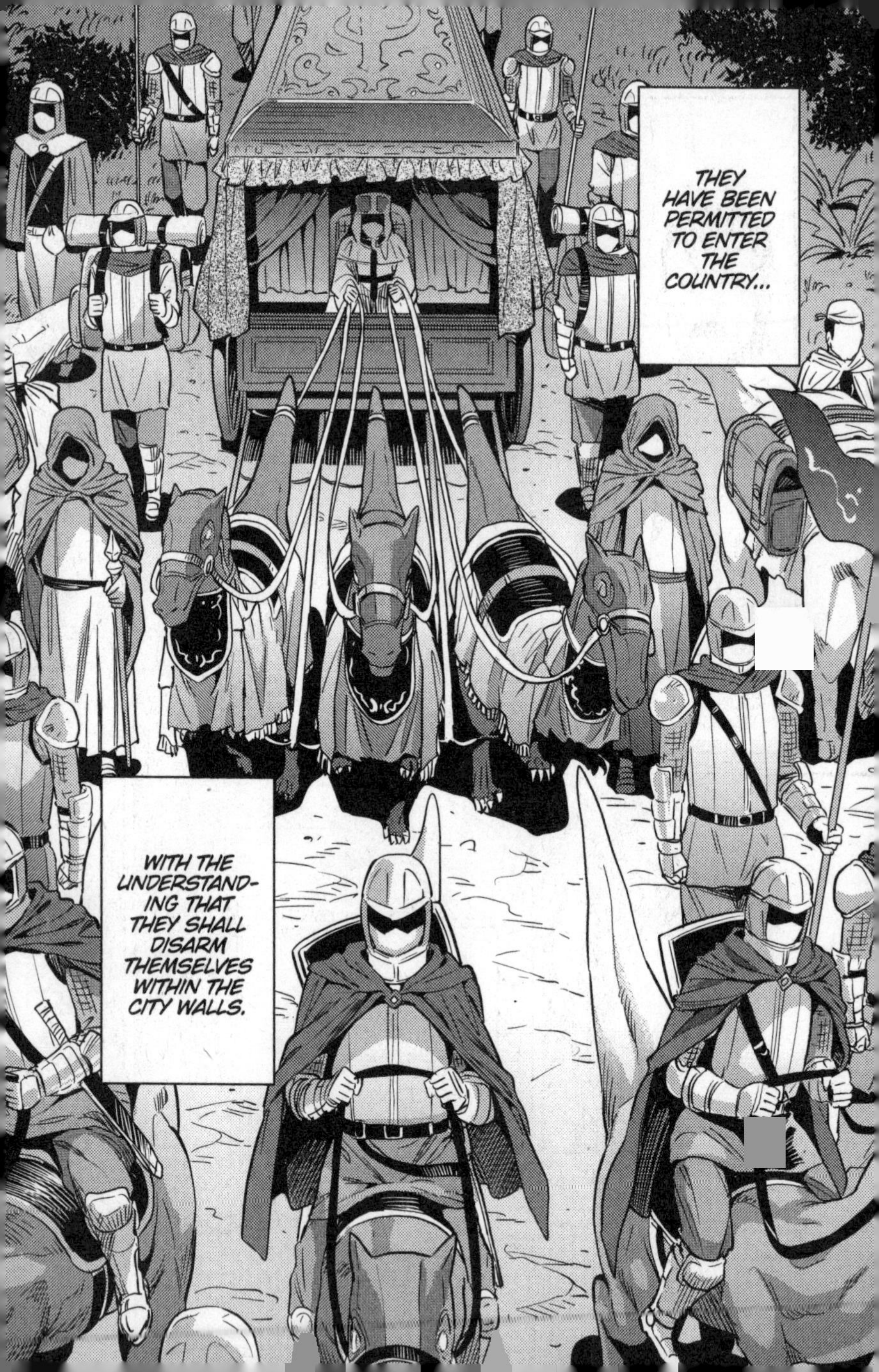
THEY HAVE BEEN PERMITTED TO ENTER THE COUNTRY...
WITH THE UNDERSTANDING THAT THEY SHALL DISARM THEMSELVES WITHIN THE CITY WALLS.

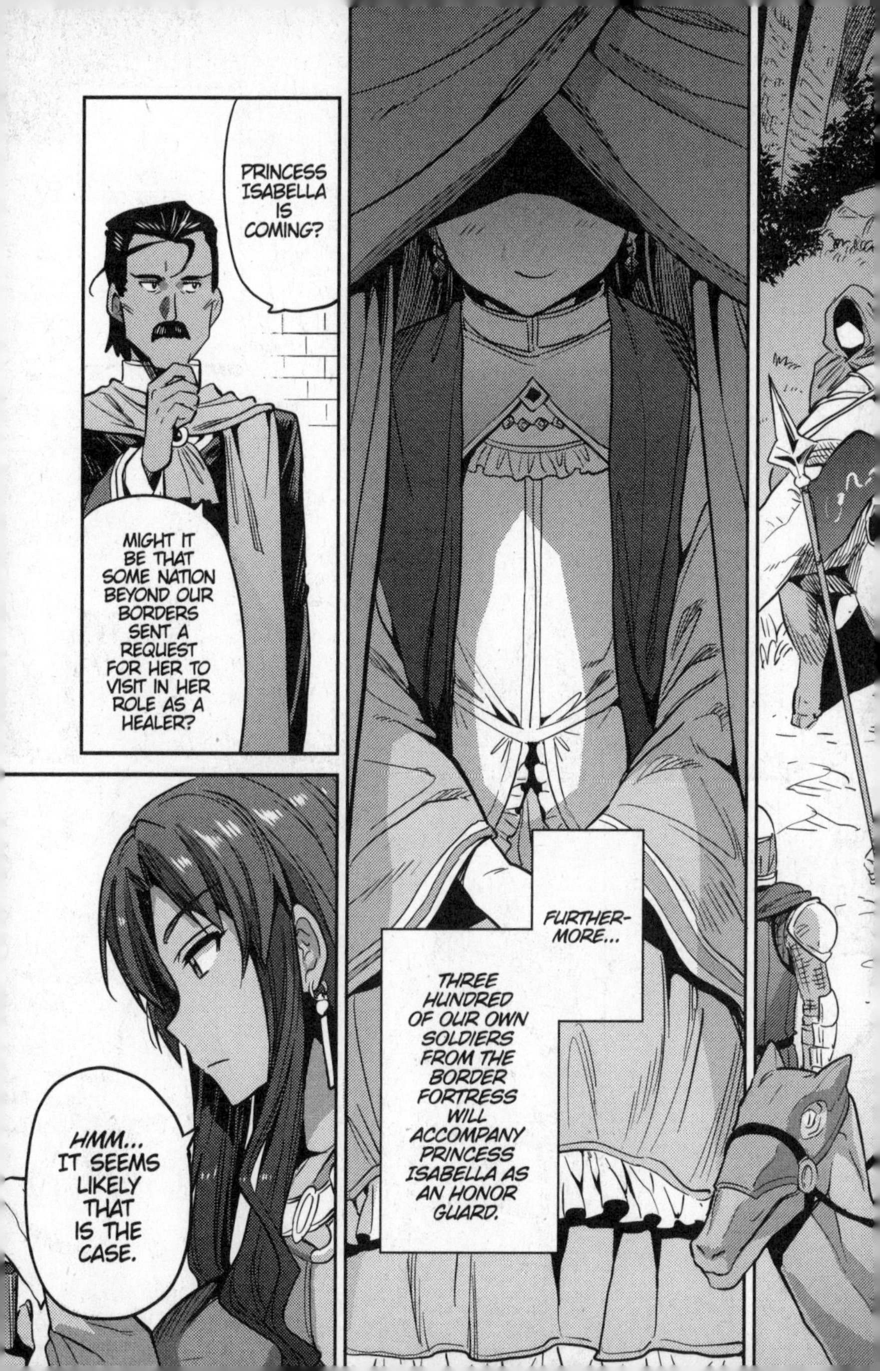
FURTHER-MORE...
THREE HUNDRED OF OUR OWN SOLDIERS FROM THE BORDER FORTRESS WILL ACCOMPANY PRINCESS ISABELLA AS AN HONOR GUARD.
PRINCESS ISABELLA IS COMING?
MIGHT IT BE THAT SOME NATION BEYOND OUR BORDERS SENT A REQUEST FOR HER TO VISIT IN HER ROLE AS A HEALER?
HMM... IT SEEMS LIKELY THAT IS THE CASE.

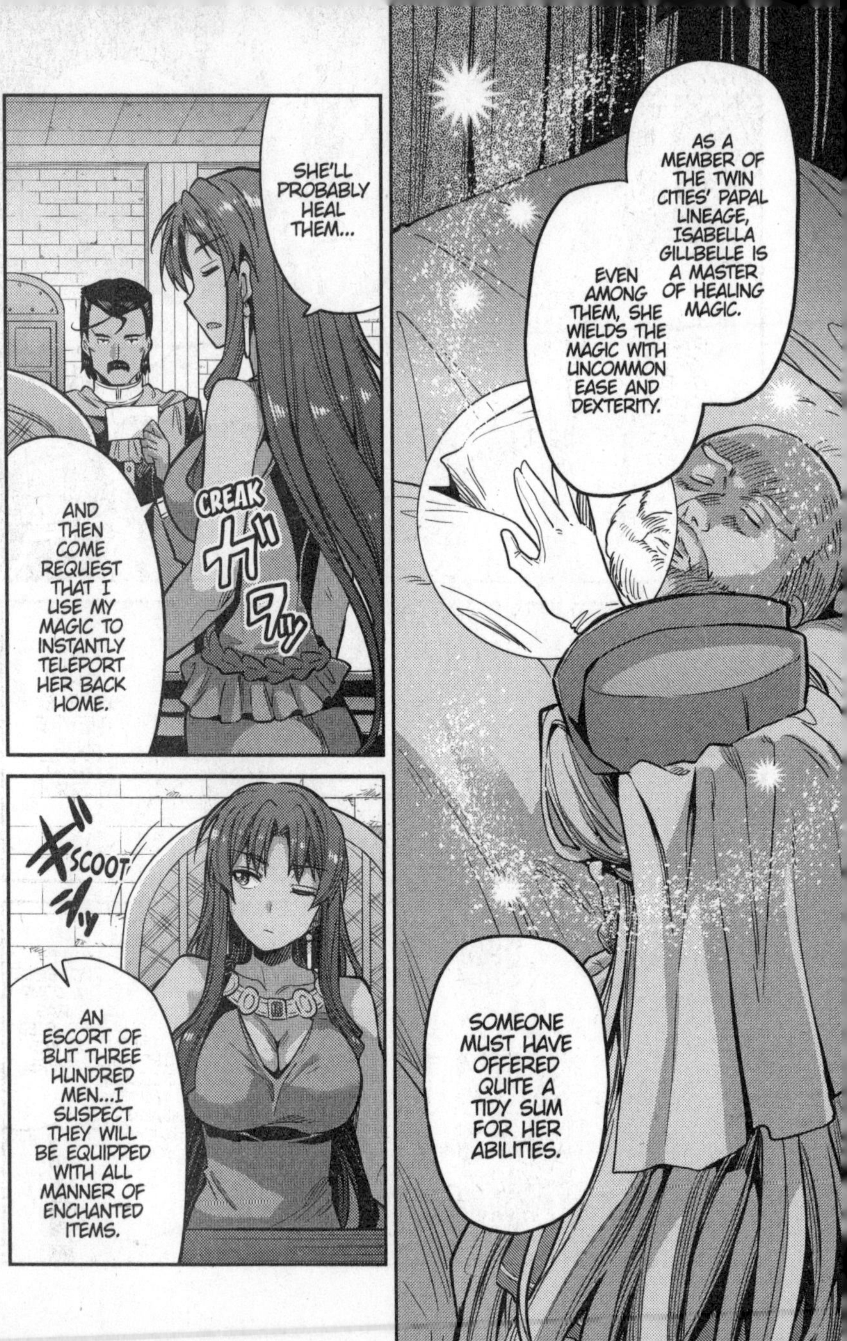
AS A MEMBER OF THE TWIN CITIES' PAPAL LINEAGE, ISABELLA GILLBELLE IS A MASTER OF HEALING MAGIC.
EVEN AMONG THEM, SHE WIELDS THE MAGIC WITH UNCOMMON EASE AND DEXTERITY.
SOMEONE MUST HAVE OFFERED QUITE A TIDY SUM FOR HER ABILITIES.
SHE'LL PROBABLY HEAL THEM...
CREAK
AND THEN COME REQUEST THAT I USE MY MAGIC TO INSTANTLY TELEPORT HER BACK HOME.
SCOOT
AN ESCORT OF BUT THREE HUNDRED MEN...I SUSPECT THEY WILL BE EQUIPPED WITH ALL MANNER OF ENCHANTED ITEMS.

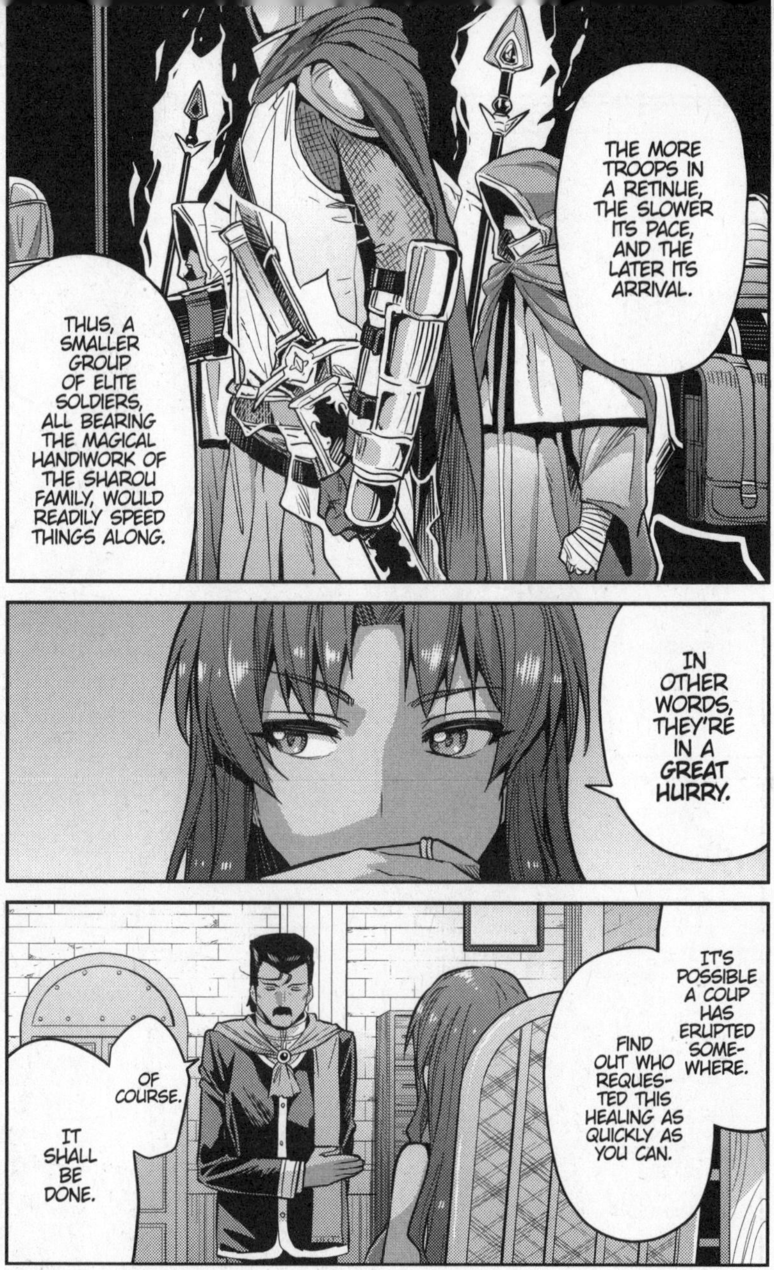
THE MORE TROOPS IN A RETINUE, THE SLOWER ITS PACE, AND THE LATER ITS ARRIVAL.
THUS, A SMALLER GROUP OF ELITE SOLDIERS, ALL BEARING THE MAGICAL HANDIWORK OF THE SHAROU FAMILY, WOULD READILY SPEED THINGS ALONG.
IN OTHER WORDS, THEY'RE IN A GREAT HURRY.
IT'S POSSIBLE A COUP HAS ERUPTED SOME-WHERE.
FIND OUT WHO REQUES-TED THIS HEALING AS QUICKLY AS YOU CAN.
OF COURSE.
IT SHALL BE DONE.

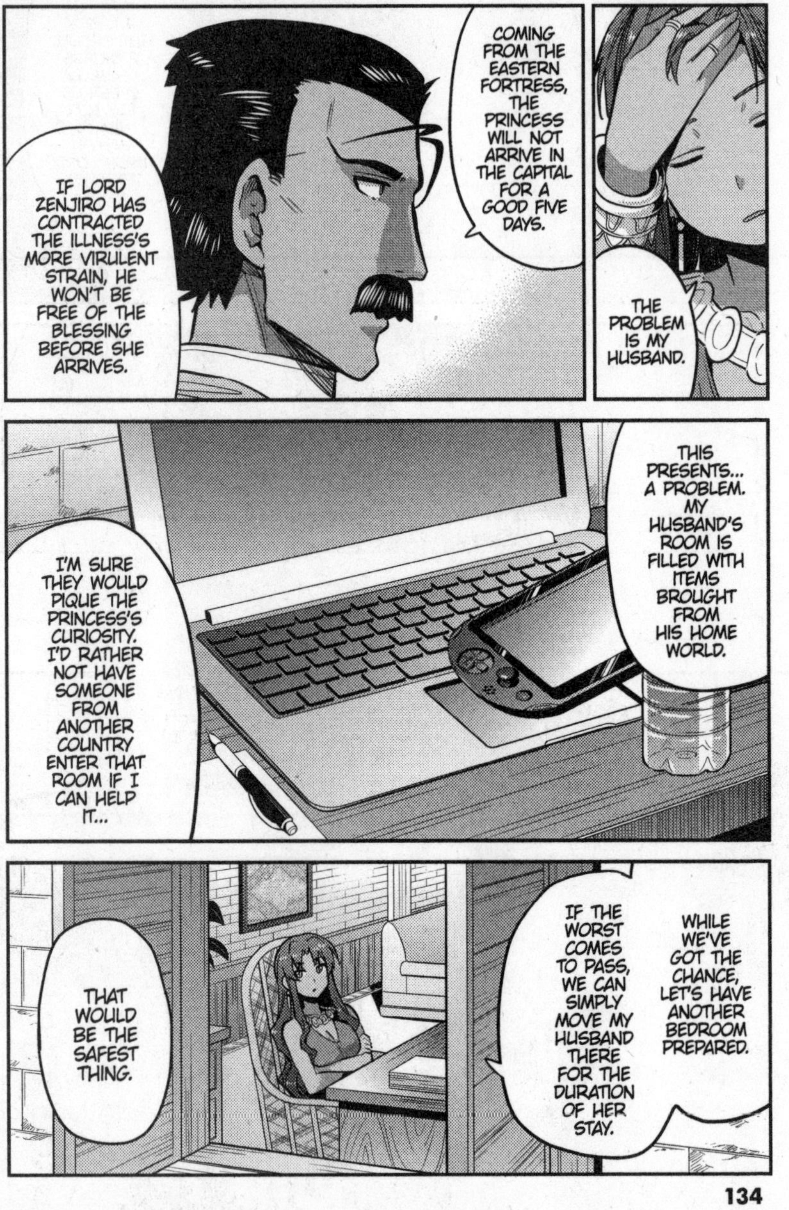
THE PROBLEM IS MY HUSBAND.
COMING FROM THE EASTERN FORTRESS, THE PRINCESS WILL NOT ARRIVE IN THE CAPITAL FOR A GOOD FIVE DAYS.
IF LORD ZENJIRO HAS CONTRACTED THE ILLNESS'S MORE VIRULENT STRAIN, HE WON'T BE FREE OF THE BLESSING BEFORE SHE ARRIVES.
THIS PRESENTS... A PROBLEM. MY HUSBAND'S ROOM IS FILLED WITH ITEMS BROUGHT FROM HIS HOME WORLD.
I'M SURE THEY WOULD PIQUE THE PRINCESS'S CURIOSITY. I'D RATHER NOT HAVE SOMEONE FROM ANOTHER COUNTRY ENTER THAT ROOM IF I CAN HELP IT...
WHILE WE'VE GOT THE CHANCE, LET'S HAVE ANOTHER BEDROOM PREPARED.
IF THE WORST COMES TO PASS, WE CAN SIMPLY MOVE MY HUSBAND THERE FOR THE DURATION OF HER STAY.
THAT WOULD BE THE SAFEST THING.

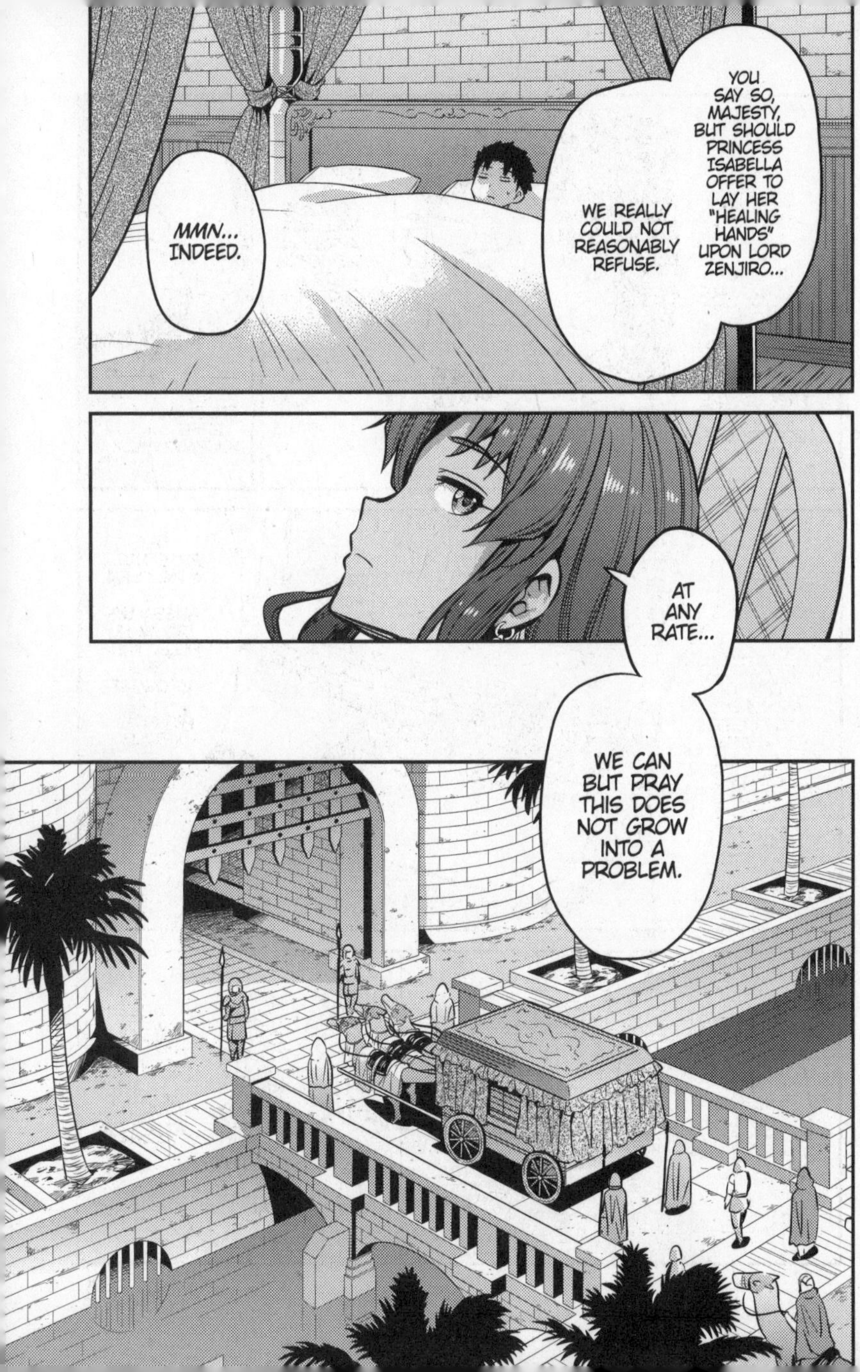
YOU SAY SO, MAJESTY, BUT SHOULD PRINCESS ISABELLA OFFER TO LAY HER "HEALING HANDS" UPON LORD ZENJIRO...
WE REALLY COULD NOT REASONABLY REFUSE.
MMN... INDEED.
AT ANY RATE...
WE CAN BUT PRAY THIS DOES NOT GROW INTO A PROBLEM.

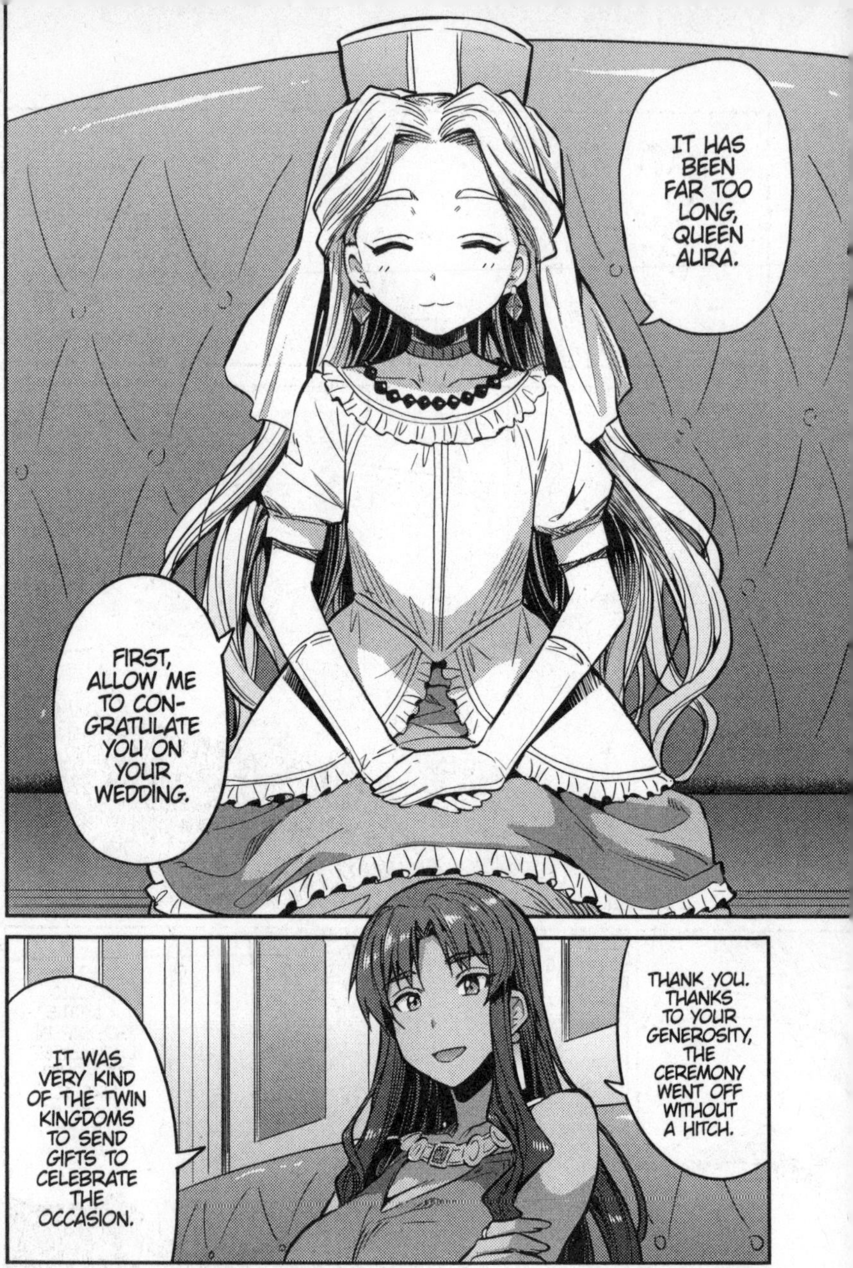
IT HAS BEEN FAR TOO LONG, QUEEN AURA.
FIRST, ALLOW ME TO CON-GRATULATE YOU ON YOUR WEDDING.
THANK YOU. THANKS TO YOUR GENEROSITY, THE CEREMONY WENT OFF WITHOUT A HITCH.
IT WAS VERY KIND OF THE TWIN KINGDOMS TO SEND GIFTS TO CELEBRATE THE OCCASION.

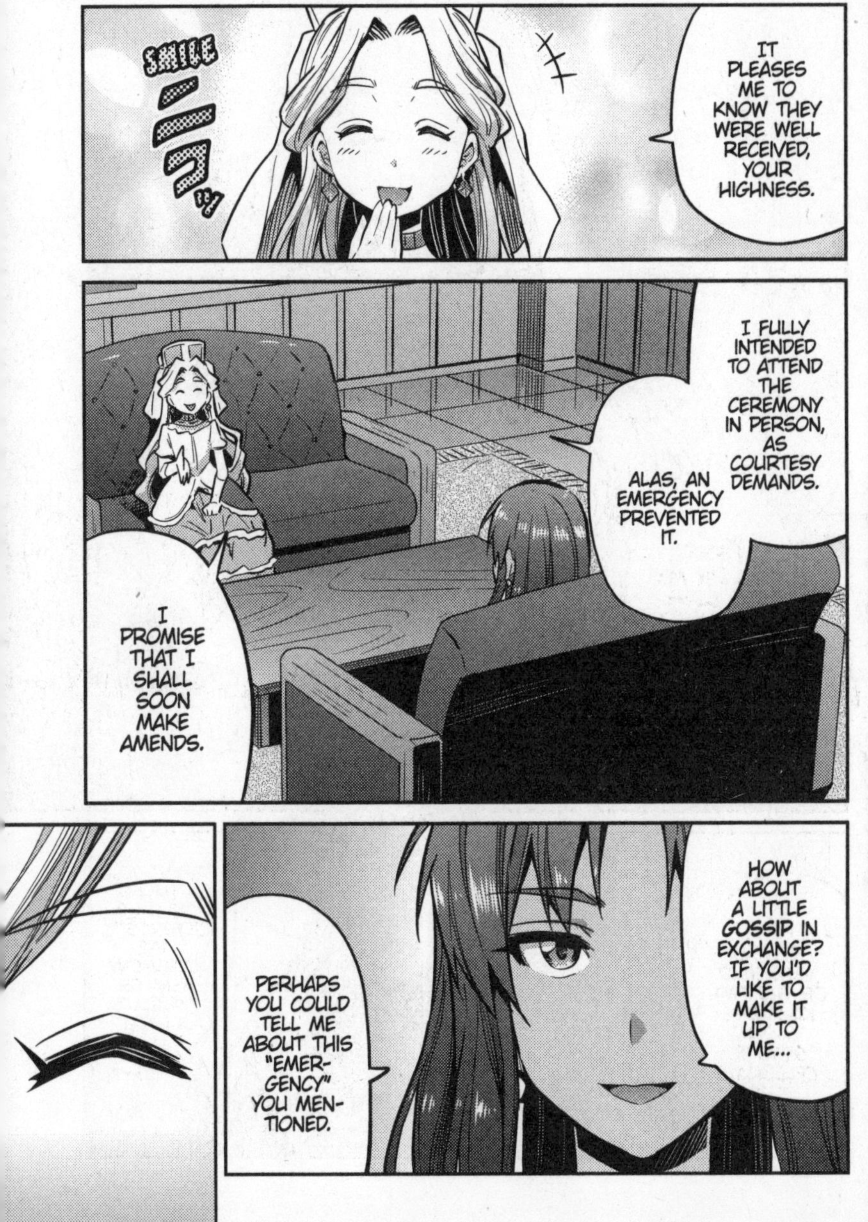
IT PLEASES ME TO KNOW THEY WERE WELL RECEIVED, YOUR HIGHNESS.
SMILE
I FULLY INTENDED TO ATTEND THE CEREMONY IN PERSON, AS COURTESY DEMANDS.
ALAS, AN EMERGENCY PREVENTED IT.
I PROMISE THAT I SHALL SOON MAKE AMENDS.
HOW ABOUT A LITTLE GOSSIP IN EXCHANGE? IF YOU'D LIKE TO MAKE IT UP TO ME...
PERHAPS YOU COULD TELL ME ABOUT THIS "EMER-GENCY" YOU MEN-TIONED.

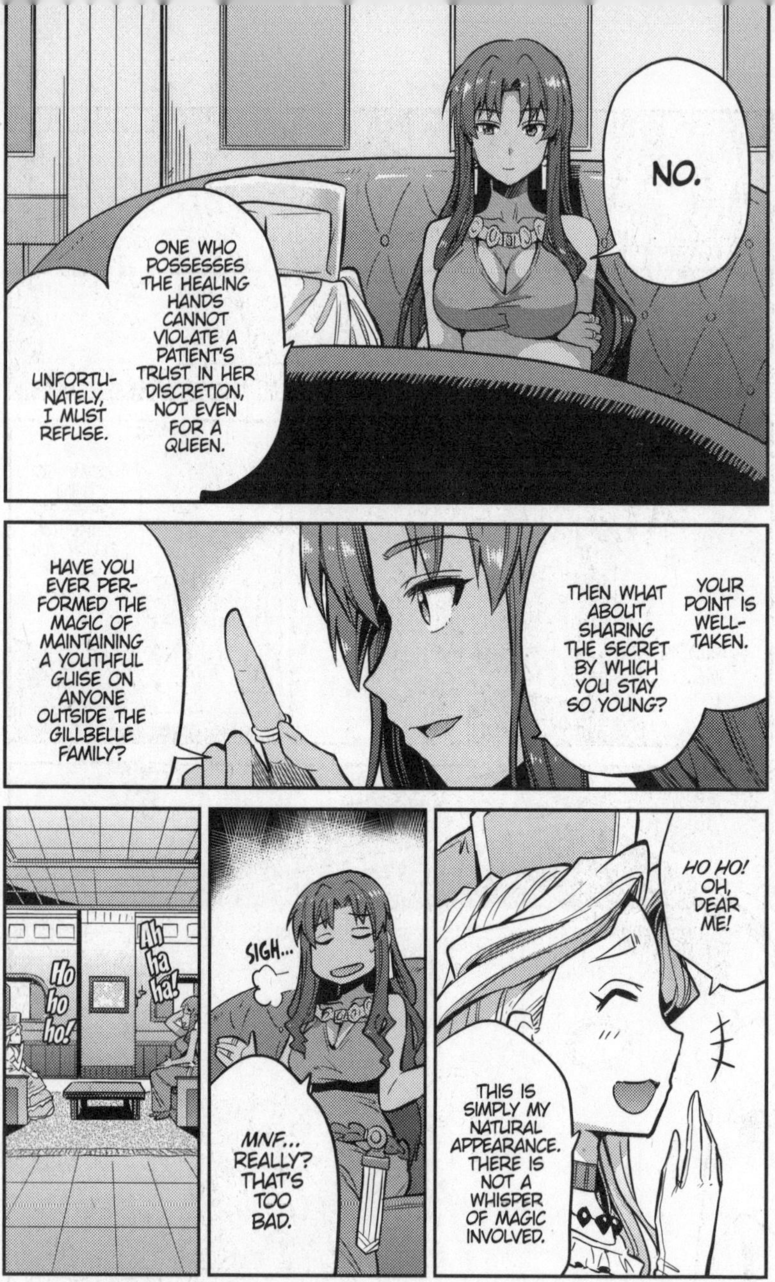
NO.
ONE WHO POSSESSES THE HEALING HANDS CANNOT VIOLATE A PATIENT'S TRUST IN HER DISCRETION, NOT EVEN FOR A QUEEN.
UNFORTU-NATELY, I MUST REFUSE.
YOUR POINT IS WELL-TAKEN.
THEN WHAT ABOUT SHARING THE SECRET BY WHICH YOU STAY SO YOUNG?
HAVE YOU EVER PER-FORMED THE MAGIC OF MAINTAINING A YOUTHFUL GUISE ON ANYONE OUTSIDE THE GILLBELLE FAMILY?
HO HO! OH, DEAR ME!
THIS IS SIMPLY MY NATURAL APPEARANCE. THERE IS NOT A WHISPER OF MAGIC INVOLVED.
SIGH...
MNF... REALLY? THAT'S TOO BAD.
Ah ha ha!
Ho ho ho!

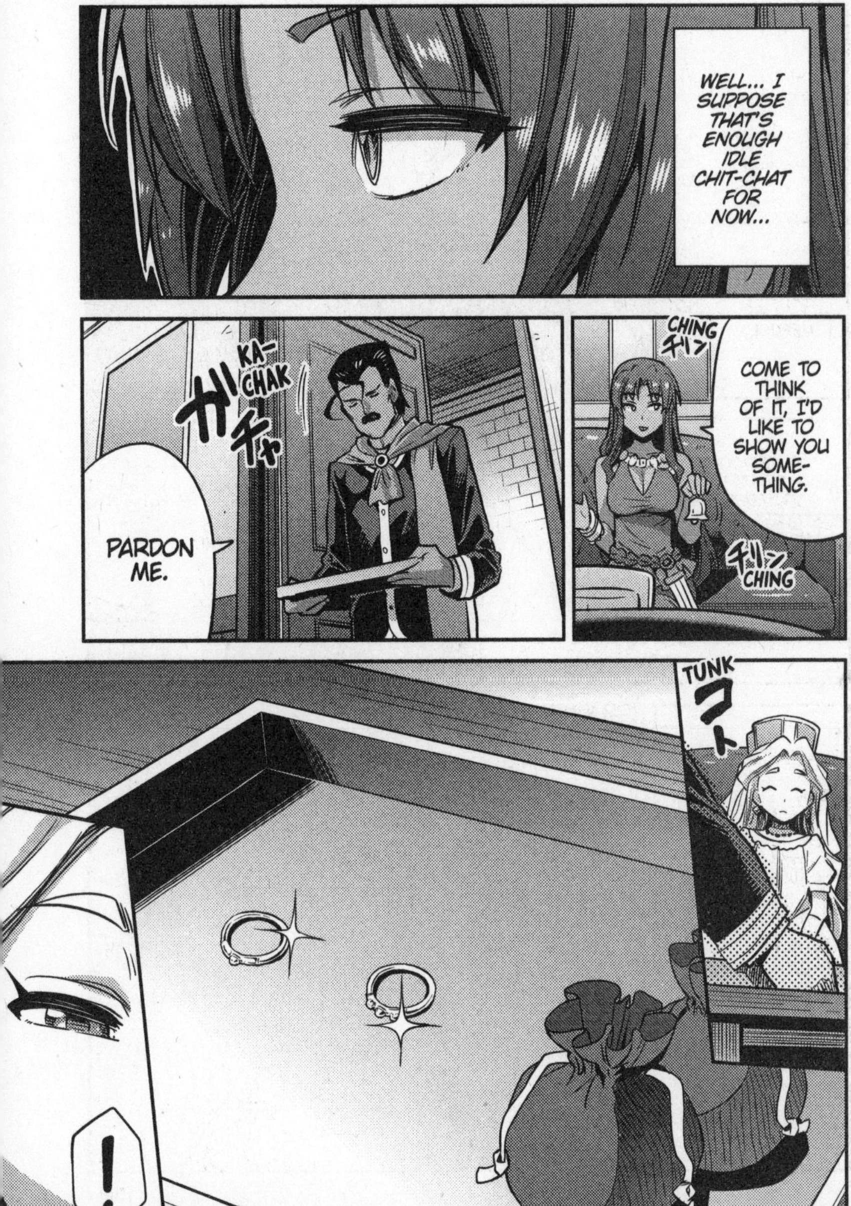
WELL... I SUPPOSE THAT'S ENOUGH IDLE CHIT-CHAT FOR NOW...
CHING
チリン
COME TO THINK OF IT, I'D LIKE TO SHOW YOU SOME-THING.
チリン
CHING
KA-CHAK
ガチャ
PARDON ME.
TUNK
コト
!

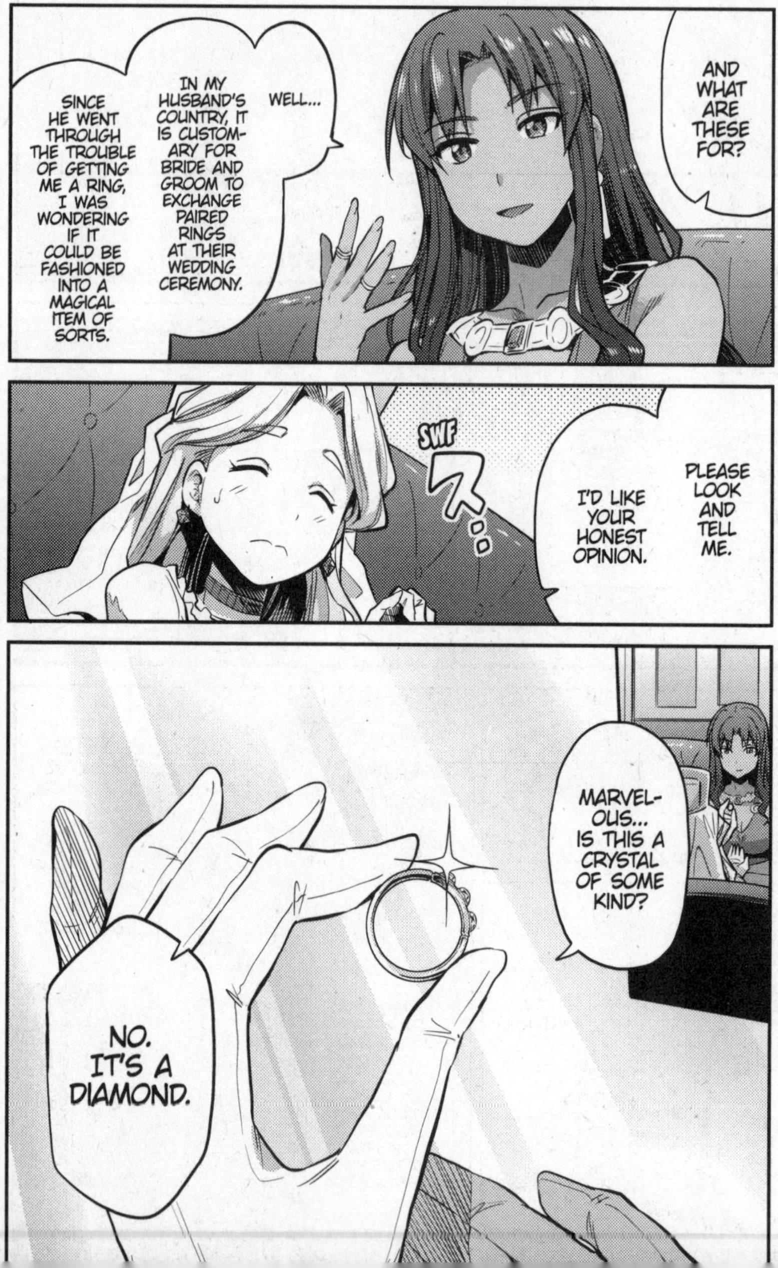
AND WHAT ARE THESE FOR?
WELL...
IN MY HUSBAND'S COUNTRY, IT IS CUSTOMARY FOR BRIDE AND GROOM TO EXCHANGE PAIRED RINGS AT THEIR WEDDING CEREMONY.
SINCE HE WENT THROUGH THE TROUBLE OF GETTING ME A RING, I WAS WONDERING IF IT COULD BE FASHIONED INTO A MAGICAL ITEM OF SORTS.
PLEASE LOOK AND TELL ME.
I'D LIKE YOUR HONEST OPINION.
SWF
MARVELOUS... IS THIS A CRYSTAL OF SOME KIND?
NO. IT'S A DIAMOND.

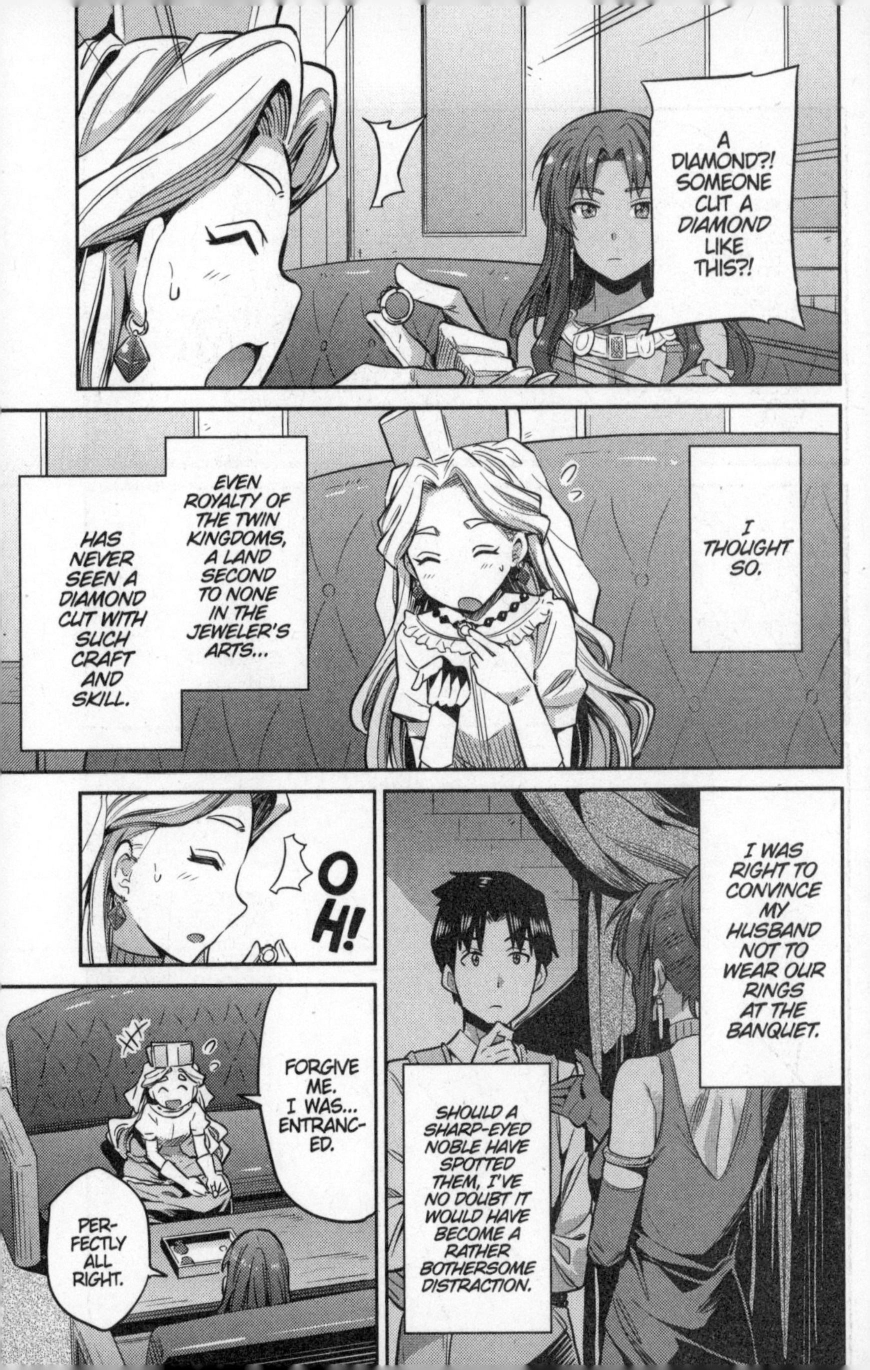
A DIAMOND?! SOMEONE CUT A DIAMOND LIKE THIS?!
I THOUGHT SO.
EVEN ROYALTY OF THE TWIN KINGDOMS, A LAND SECOND TO NONE IN THE JEWELER'S ARTS...
HAS NEVER SEEN A DIAMOND CUT WITH SUCH CRAFT AND SKILL.
I WAS RIGHT TO CONVINCE MY HUSBAND NOT TO WEAR OUR RINGS AT THE BANQUET.
SHOULD A SHARP-EYED NOBLE HAVE SPOTTED THEM, I'VE NO DOUBT IT WOULD HAVE BECOME A RATHER BOTHERSOME DISTRACTION.
OH!
FORGIVE ME. I WAS... ENTRANC-ED.
PER-FECTLY ALL RIGHT.

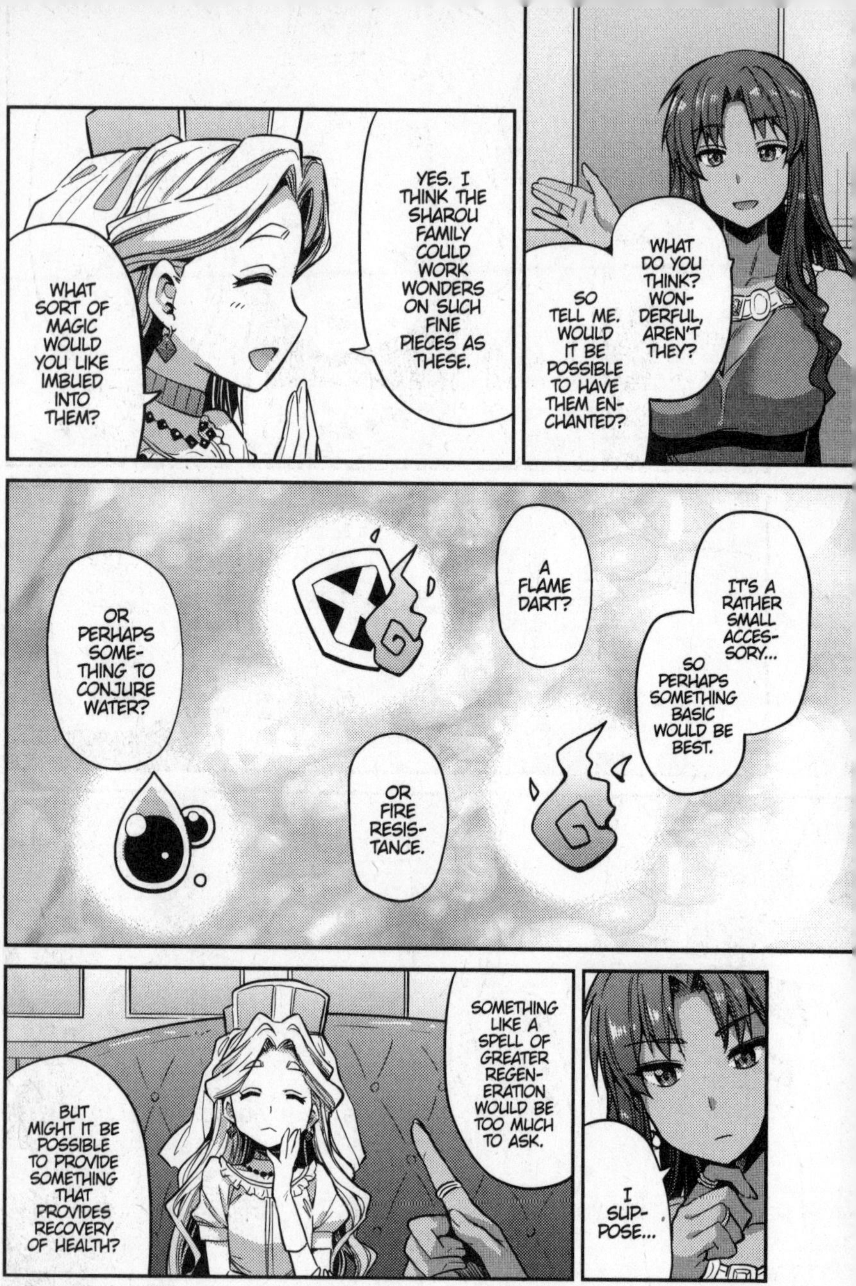
WHAT DO YOU THINK? WONDERFUL, AREN'T THEY?
SO TELL ME. WOULD IT BE POSSIBLE TO HAVE THEM ENCHANTED?
YES. I THINK THE SHAROU FAMILY COULD WORK WONDERS ON SUCH FINE PIECES AS THESE.
WHAT SORT OF MAGIC WOULD YOU LIKE IMBUED INTO THEM?
IT'S A RATHER SMALL ACCESSORY...
SO PERHAPS SOMETHING BASIC WOULD BE BEST.
A FLAME DART?
OR FIRE RESISTANCE.
OR PERHAPS SOMETHING TO CONJURE WATER?
I SUPPOSE...
SOMETHING LIKE A SPELL OF GREATER REGENERATION WOULD BE TOO MUCH TO ASK.
BUT MIGHT IT BE POSSIBLE TO PROVIDE SOMETHING THAT PROVIDES RECOVERY OF HEALTH?

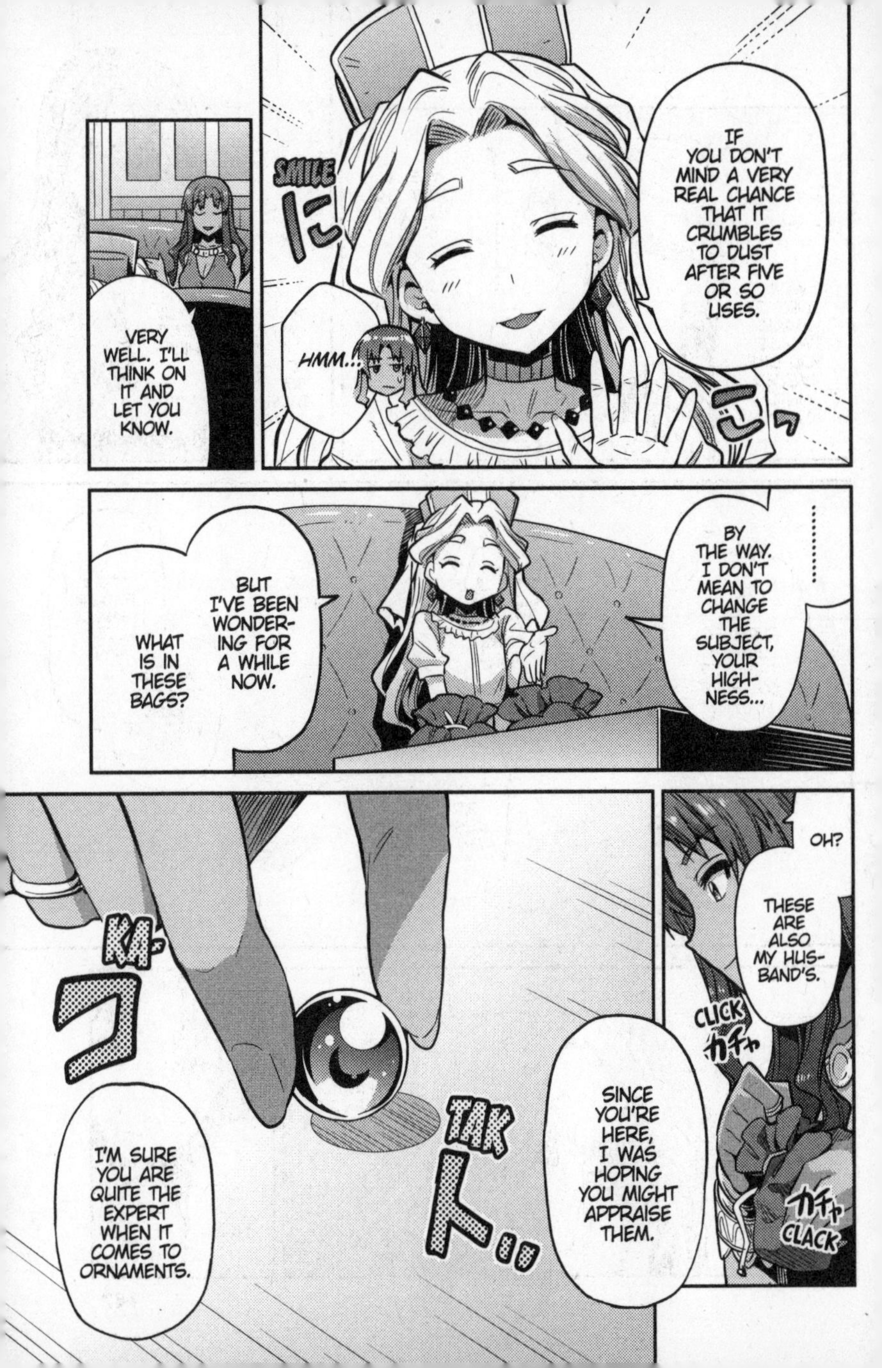
IF YOU DON'T MIND A VERY REAL CHANCE THAT IT CRUMBLES TO DUST AFTER FIVE OR SO USES.
SMILE
に
HMM...
こっ
VERY WELL. I'LL THINK ON IT AND LET YOU KNOW.
......
BY THE WAY. I DON'T MEAN TO CHANGE THE SUBJECT, YOUR HIGHNESS...
BUT I'VE BEEN WONDERING FOR A WHILE NOW.
WHAT IS IN THESE BAGS?
OH?
THESE ARE ALSO MY HUSBAND'S.
CLICK
カチャ
カチャ
CLACK
SINCE YOU'RE HERE, I WAS HOPING YOU MIGHT APPRAISE THEM.
KA
コ
TAK
ト..
I'M SURE YOU ARE QUITE THE EXPERT WHEN IT COMES TO ORNAMENTS.

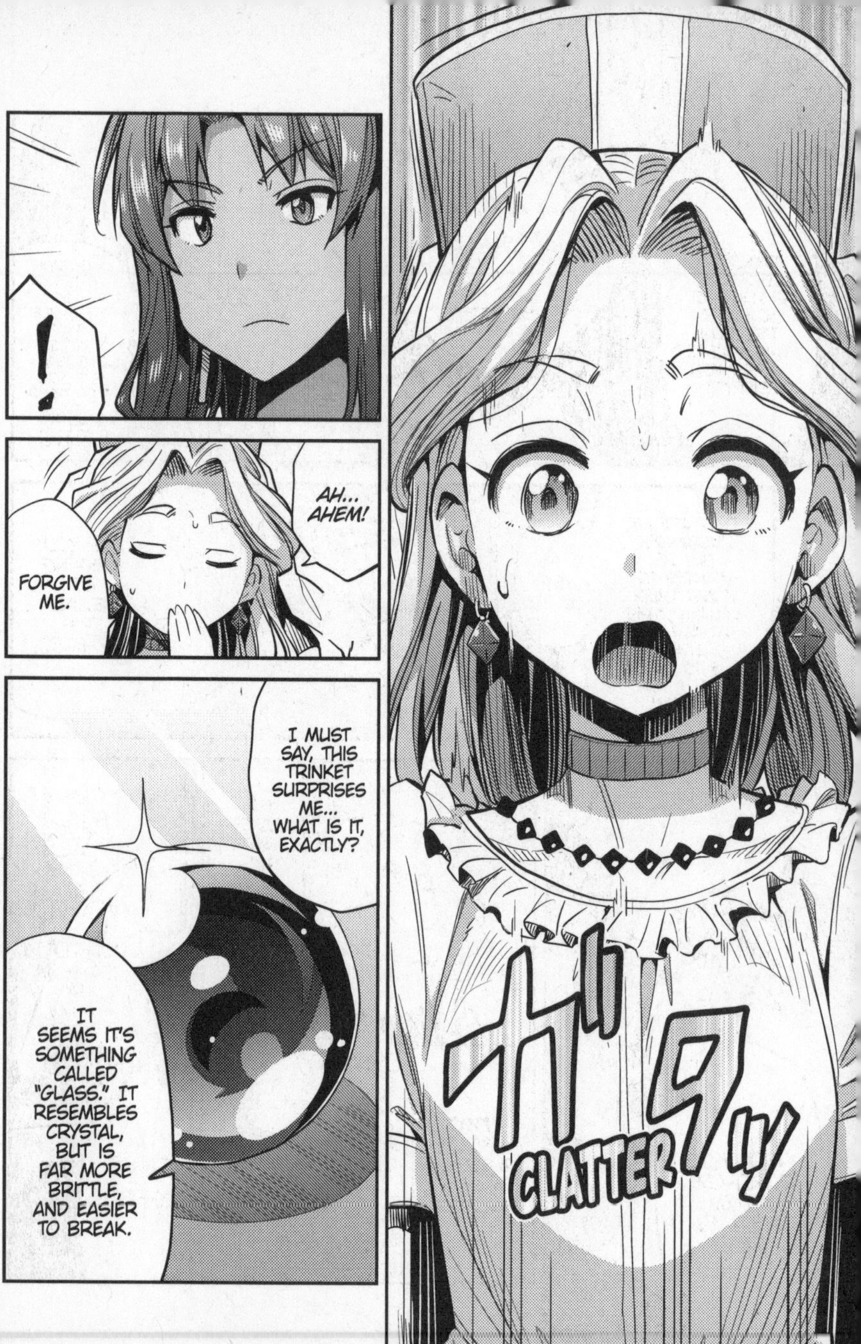
ガタッ
CLATTER
!
AH... AHEM!
FORGIVE ME.
I MUST SAY, THIS TRINKET SURPRISES ME... WHAT IS IT, EXACTLY?
IT SEEMS IT'S SOMETHING CALLED "GLASS." IT RESEMBLES CRYSTAL, BUT IS FAR MORE BRITTLE, AND EASIER TO BREAK.

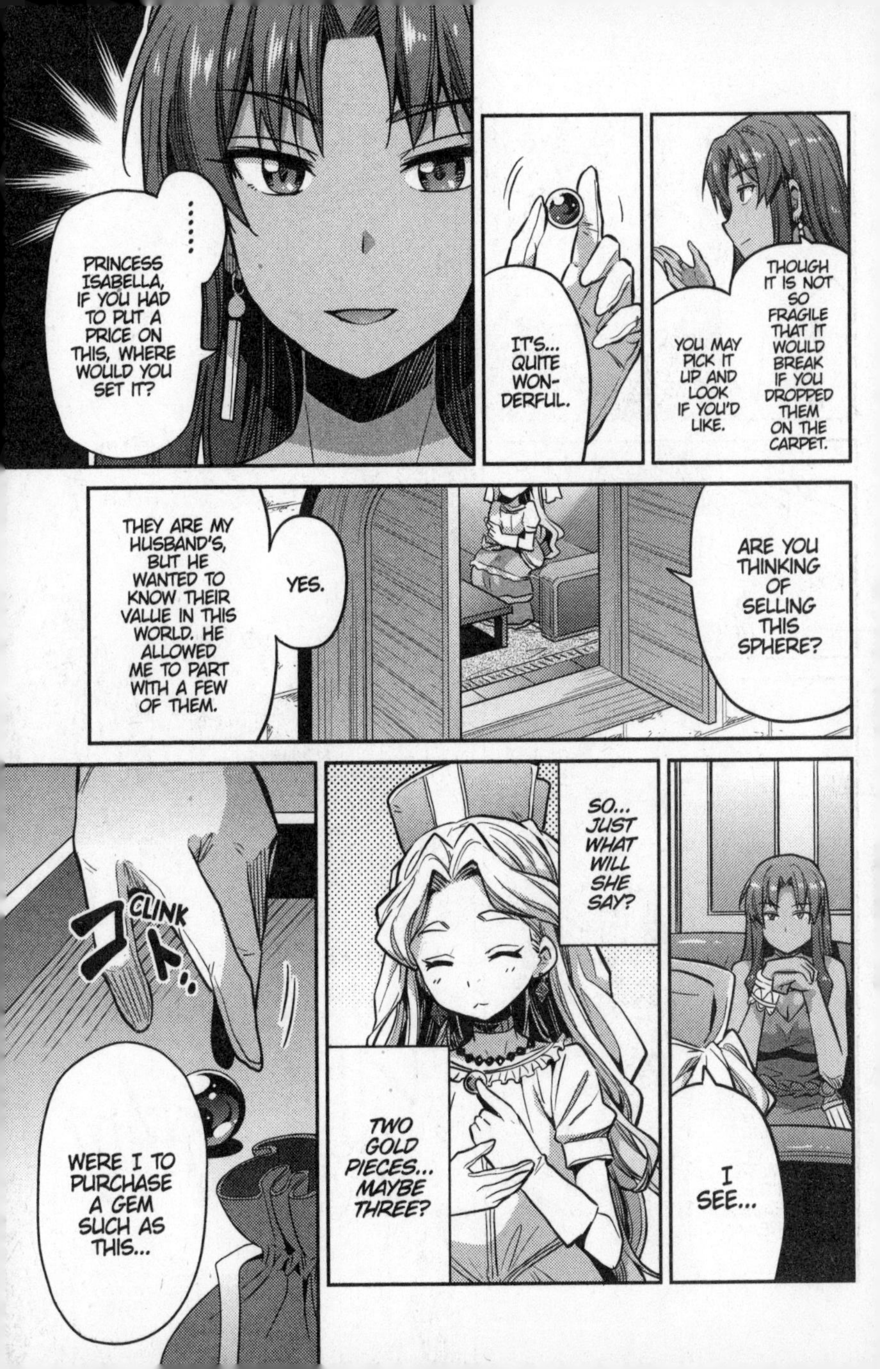
THOUGH IT IS NOT SO FRAGILE THAT IT WOULD BREAK IF YOU DROPPED THEM ON THE CARPET.
YOU MAY PICK IT UP AND LOOK IF YOU'D LIKE.
IT'S... QUITE WON-DERFUL.
......
PRINCESS ISABELLA, IF YOU HAD TO PUT A PRICE ON THIS, WHERE WOULD YOU SET IT?
ARE YOU THINKING OF SELLING THIS SPHERE?
YES.
THEY ARE MY HUSBAND'S, BUT HE WANTED TO KNOW THEIR VALUE IN THIS WORLD. HE ALLOWED ME TO PART WITH A FEW OF THEM.
I SEE...
SO... JUST WHAT WILL SHE SAY?
TWO GOLD PIECES... MAYBE THREE?
CLINK
WERE I TO PURCHASE A GEM SUCH AS THIS...

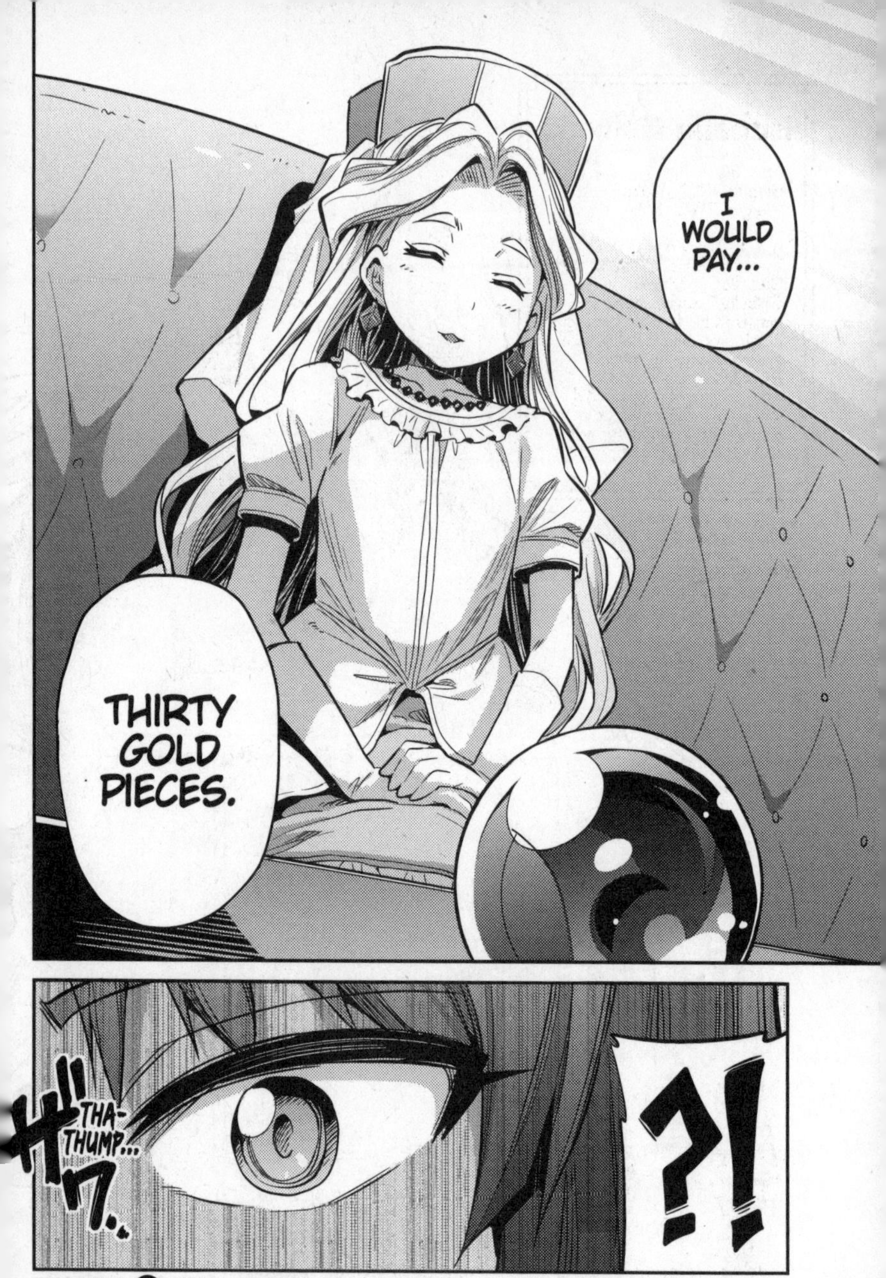
I WOULD PAY...
THIRTY GOLD PIECES.
?!
THA-THUMP...

CHAPTER 9 -END-

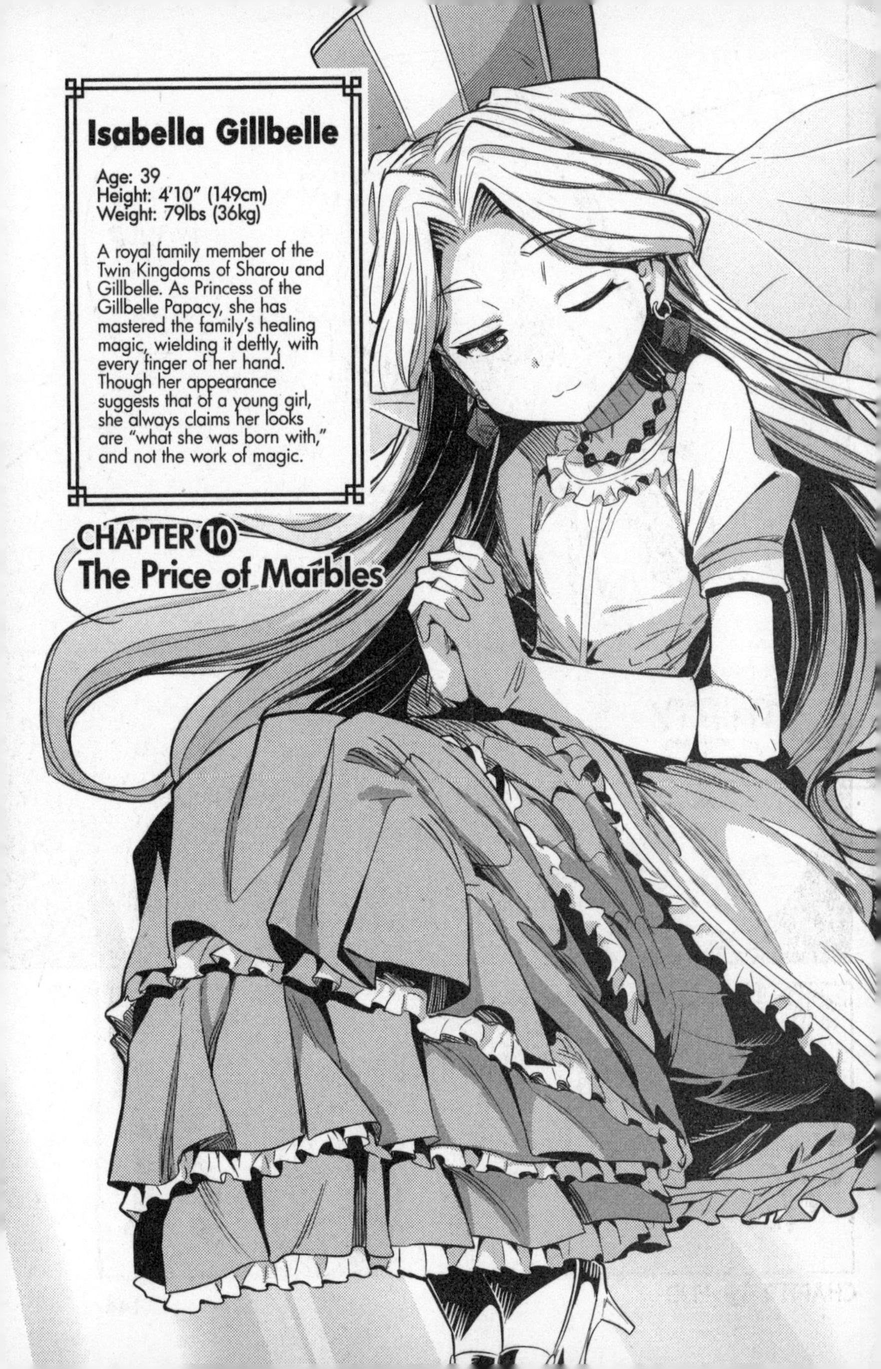
Isabella Gillbelle
Age: 39
Height: 4'10" (149cm)
Weight: 79lbs (36kg)
A royal family member of the Twin Kingdoms of Sharou and Gillbelle. As Princess of the Gillbelle Papacy, she has mastered the family's healing magic, wielding it deftly, with every finger of her hand. Though her appearance suggests that of a young girl, she always claims her looks are "what she was born with," and not the work of magic.

CHAPTER 10
The Price of Marbles

IN THE KINGDOM OF CAPUA, ONE GOLD COIN IS WORTH A HUNDRED SILVER COINS.

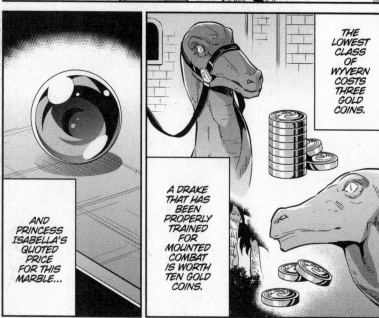

THE LOWEST CLASS OF WYVERN COSTS THREE GOLD COINS.

A DRAKE THAT HAS BEEN PROPERLY TRAINED FOR MOUNTED COMBAT IS WORTH TEN GOLD COINS.

AND PRINCESS ISABELLA'S QUOTED PRICE FOR THIS MARBLE...

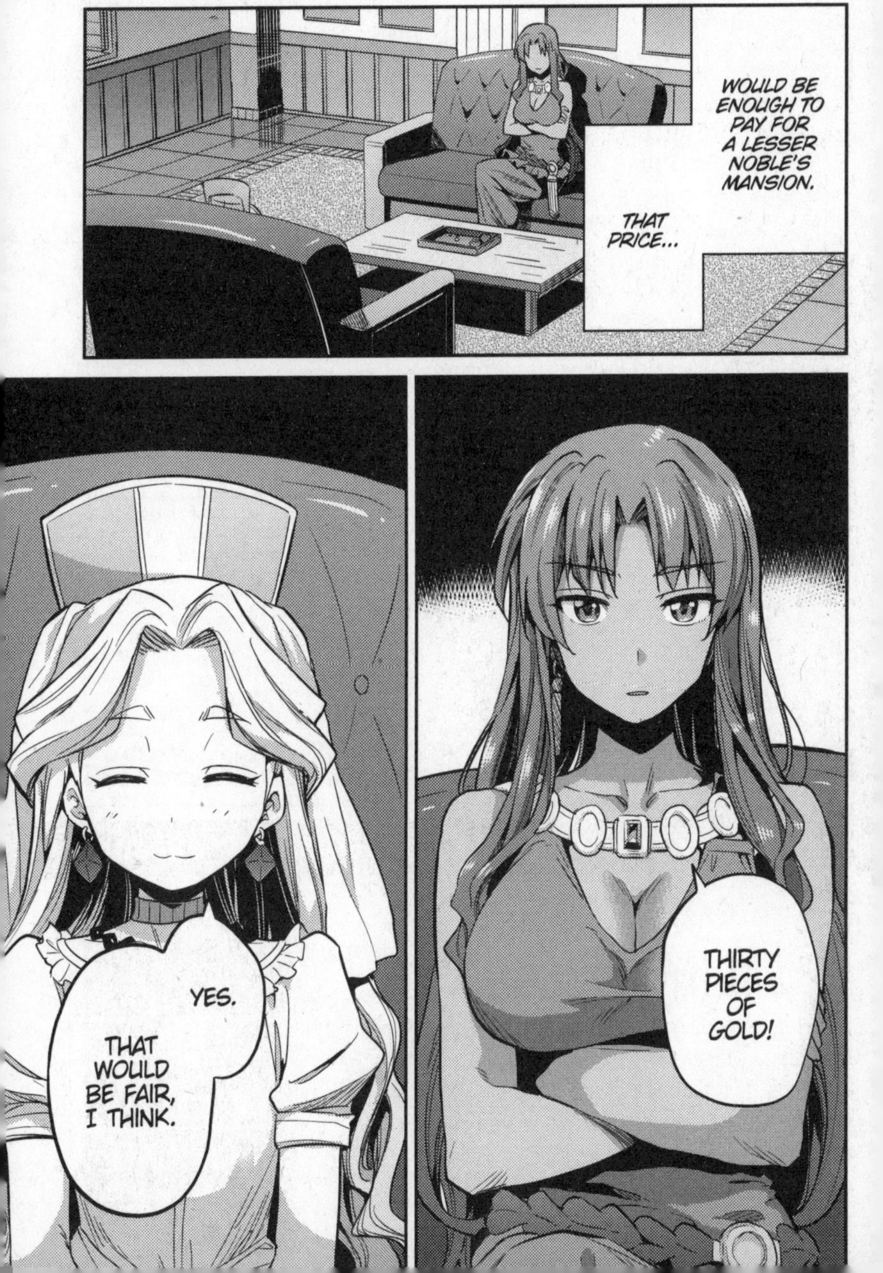
THAT PRICE...
WOULD BE ENOUGH TO PAY FOR A LESSER NOBLE'S MANSION.
THIRTY PIECES OF GOLD!
YES.
THAT WOULD BE FAIR, I THINK.

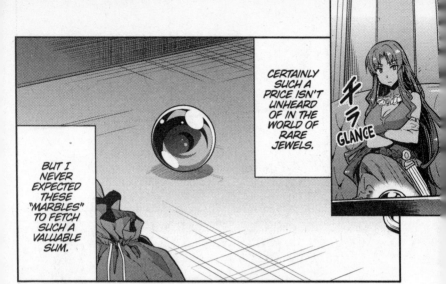

CERTAINLY SUCH A PRICE ISN'T UNHEARD OF IN THE WORLD OF RARE JEWELS.

BUT I NEVER EXPECTED THESE "MARBLES" TO FETCH SUCH A VALUABLE SUM.

GLANCE

ARE YOU SERIOUS ABOUT THAT OFFER?

HMM, LET ME SEE...

PHEW...

· · · · · · · · ·

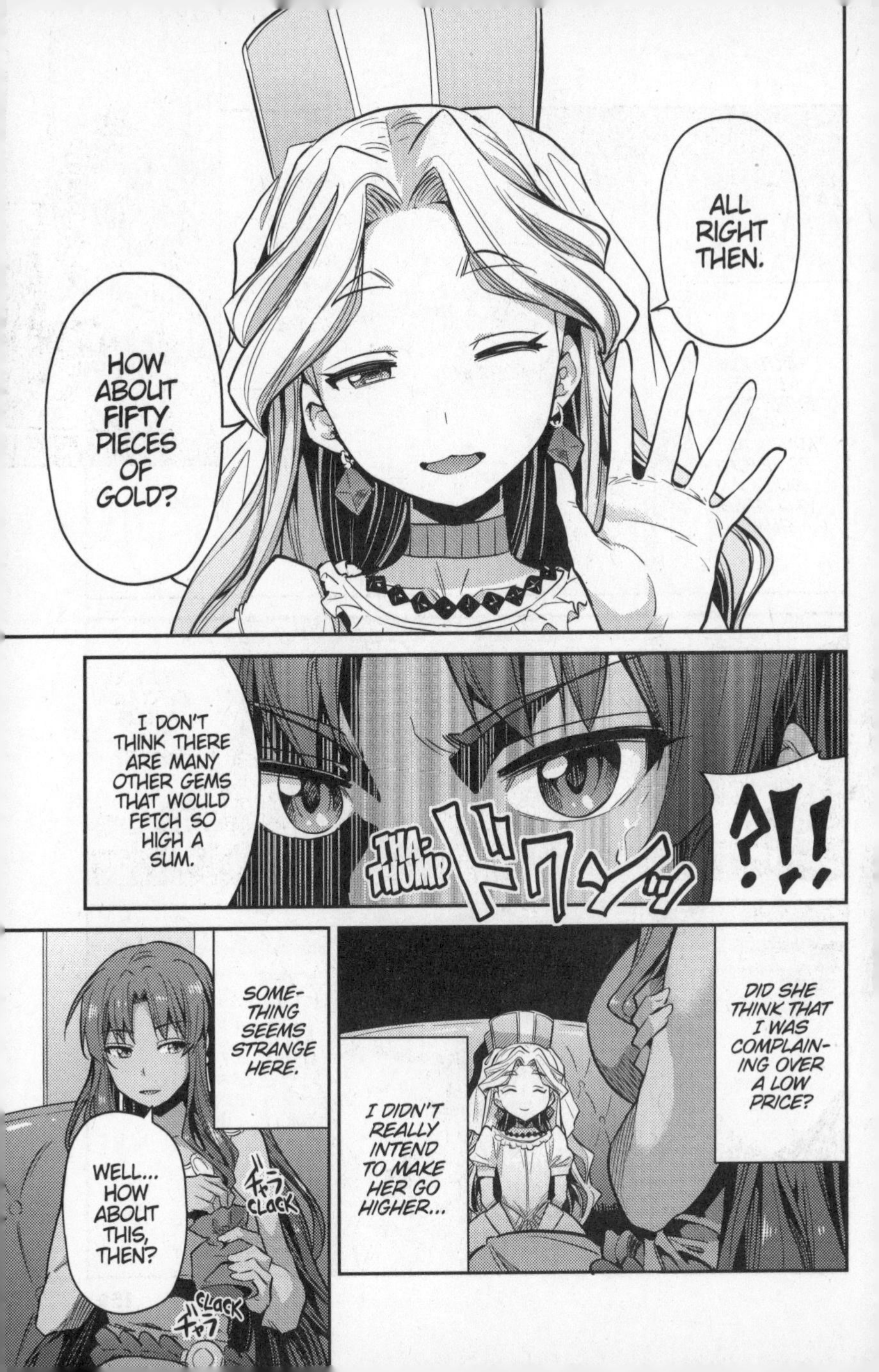
ALL RIGHT THEN.
HOW ABOUT FIFTY PIECES OF GOLD?
?!!
ドクンッ THA-THUMP
I DON'T THINK THERE ARE MANY OTHER GEMS THAT WOULD FETCH SO HIGH A SUM.
DID SHE THINK THAT I WAS COMPLAIN-ING OVER A LOW PRICE?
I DIDN'T REALLY INTEND TO MAKE HER GO HIGHER...
SOME-THING SEEMS STRANGE HERE.
チャラ CLACK
WELL... HOW ABOUT THIS, THEN?
チャラ CLACK

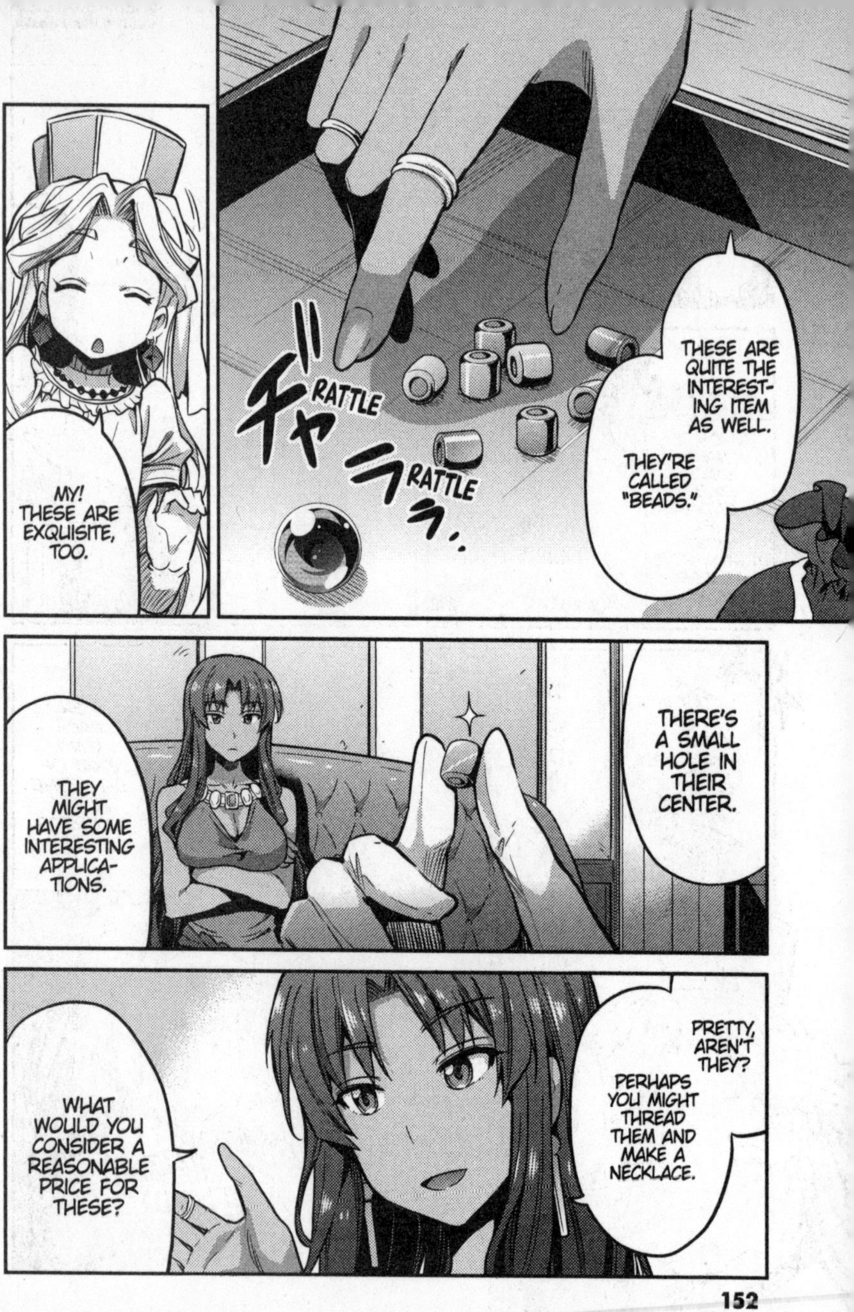
THESE ARE QUITE THE INTEREST-ING ITEM AS WELL.
THEY'RE CALLED "BEADS."
チャ RATTLE
ラ RATTLE
ラ...
MY! THESE ARE EXQUISITE, TOO.
THERE'S A SMALL HOLE IN THEIR CENTER.
THEY MIGHT HAVE SOME INTERESTING APPLICA-TIONS.
PRETTY, AREN'T THEY?
PERHAPS YOU MIGHT THREAD THEM AND MAKE A NECKLACE.
WHAT WOULD YOU CONSIDER A REASONABLE PRICE FOR THESE?

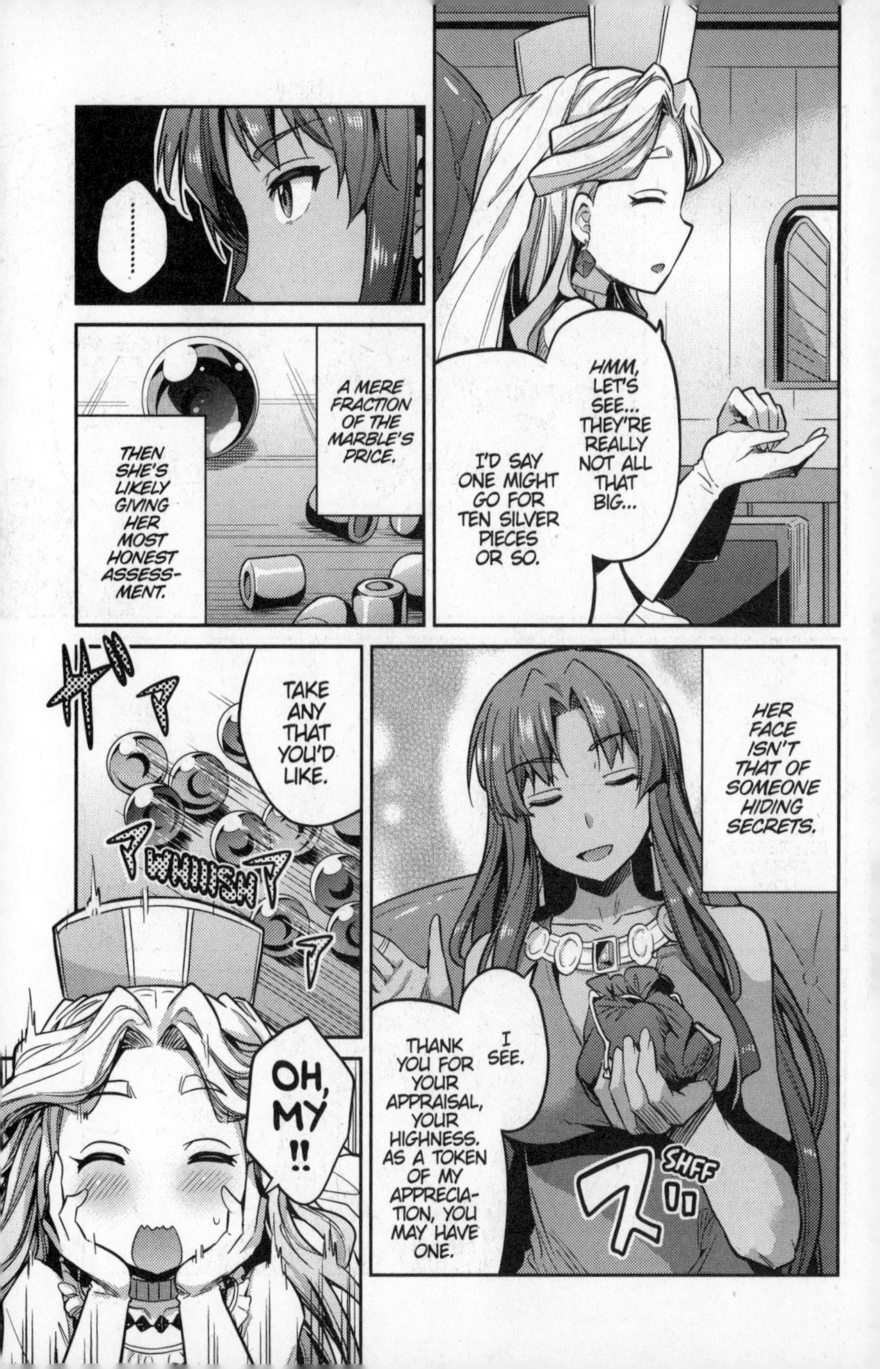
HMM, LET'S SEE... THEY'RE REALLY NOT ALL THAT BIG...
I'D SAY ONE MIGHT GO FOR TEN SILVER PIECES OR SO.
......
A MERE FRACTION OF THE MARBLE'S PRICE.
THEN SHE'S LIKELY GIVING HER MOST HONEST ASSESSMENT.
HER FACE ISN'T THAT OF SOMEONE HIDING SECRETS.
I SEE.
THANK YOU FOR YOUR APPRAISAL, YOUR HIGHNESS. AS A TOKEN OF MY APPRECIATION, YOU MAY HAVE ONE.
SHFF
TAKE ANY THAT YOU'D LIKE.
WHIIISH
OH, MY!!

NO NEED TO HOLD BACK.

TAKE YOUR TIME. LOOK THEM OVER. CHOOSE WHICHEVER ONE YOU'D BEST PREFER.

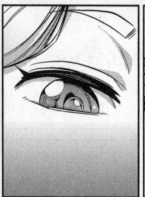

IT'S SUCH A HARD CHOICE TO MAKE! ♥

THEN...

I THINK I'LL OBLIGE YOU, AND TAKE THIS ONE.

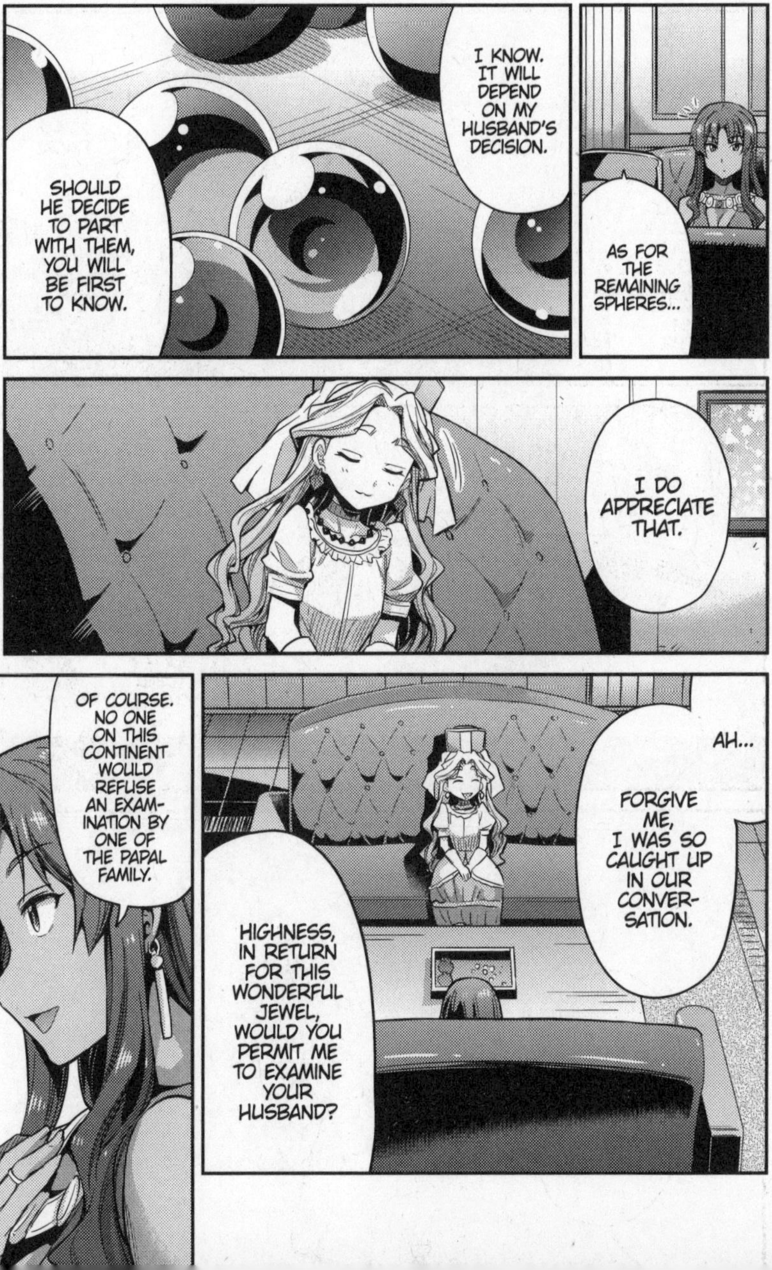
AS FOR THE REMAINING SPHERES...
I KNOW. IT WILL DEPEND ON MY HUSBAND'S DECISION.
SHOULD HE DECIDE TO PART WITH THEM, YOU WILL BE FIRST TO KNOW.
I DO APPRECIATE THAT.
AH...
FORGIVE ME, I WAS SO CAUGHT UP IN OUR CONVER-SATION.
HIGHNESS, IN RETURN FOR THIS WONDERFUL JEWEL, WOULD YOU PERMIT ME TO EXAMINE YOUR HUSBAND?
OF COURSE. NO ONE ON THIS CONTINENT WOULD REFUSE AN EXAM-INATION BY ONE OF THE PAPAL FAMILY.

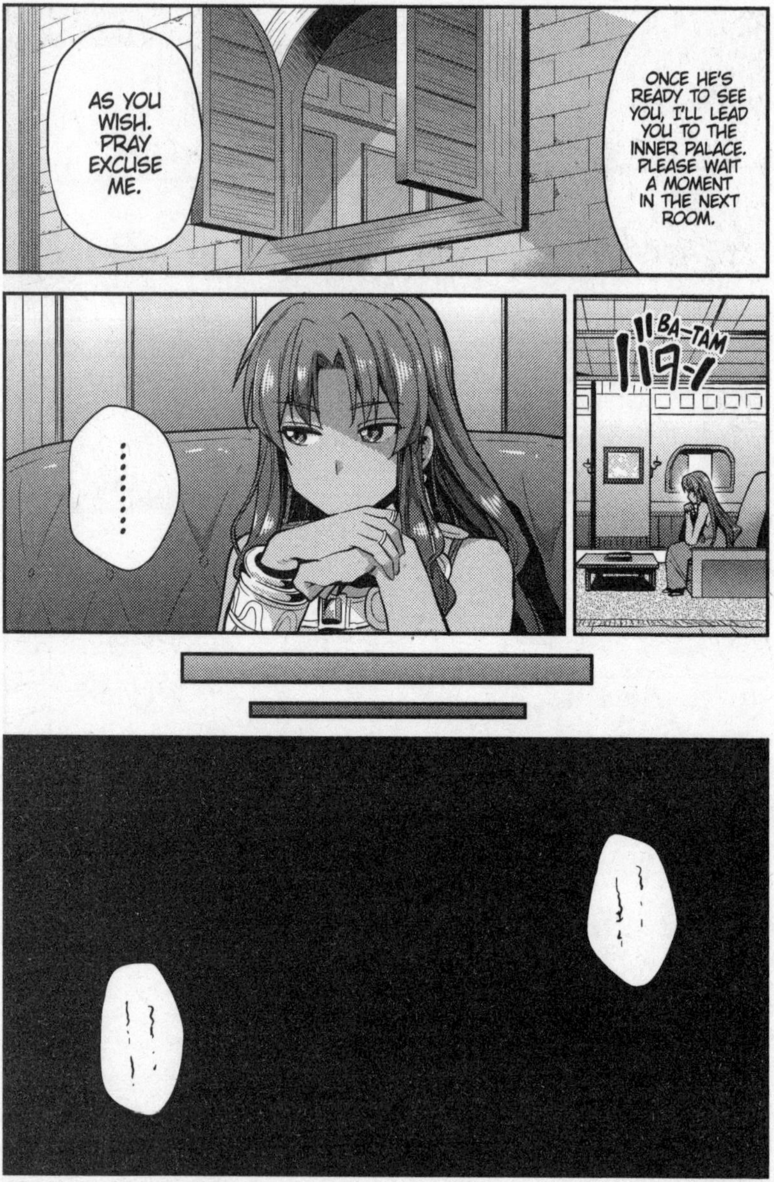
ONCE HE'S READY TO SEE YOU, I'LL LEAD YOU TO THE INNER PALACE. PLEASE WAIT A MOMENT IN THE NEXT ROOM.
AS YOU WISH. PRAY EXCUSE ME.
BA-TAM
......

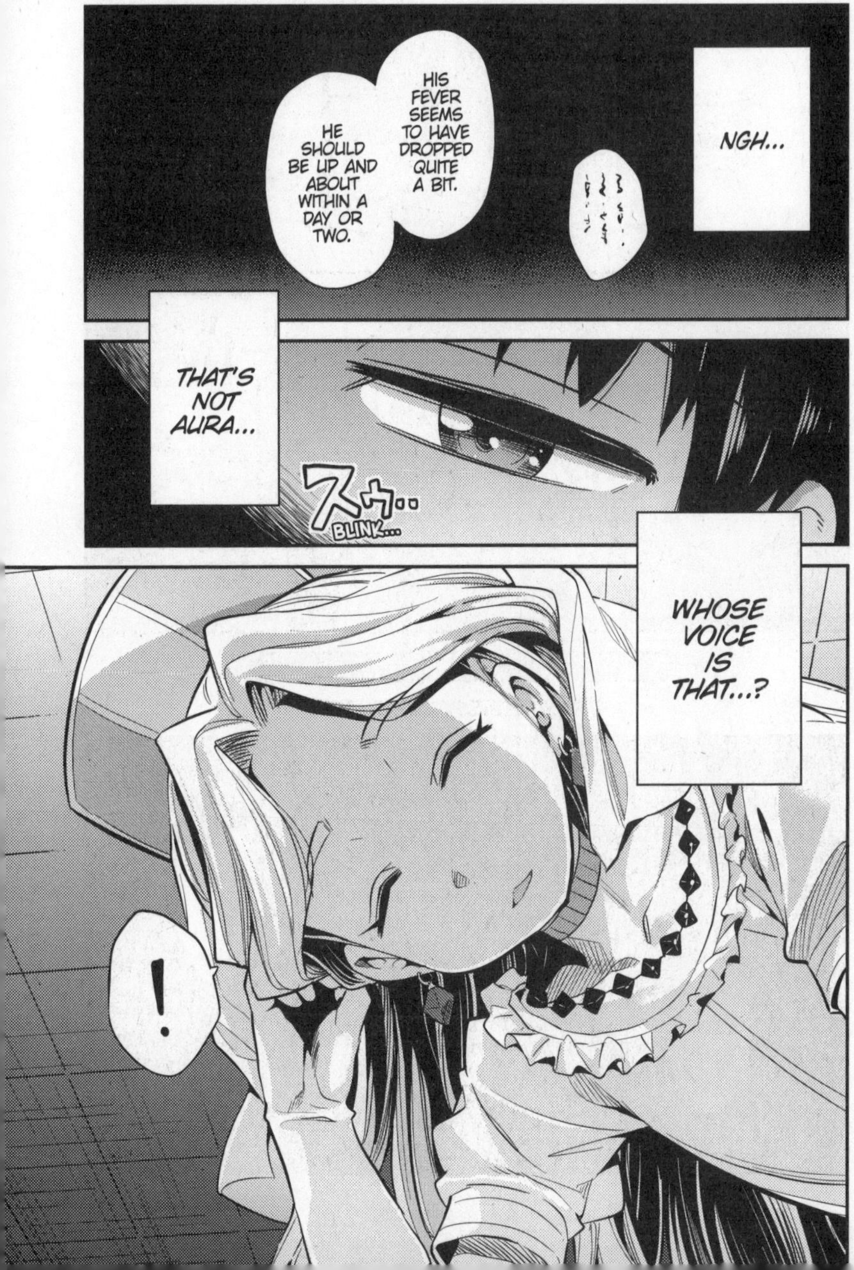
NGH...
HIS FEVER SEEMS TO HAVE DROPPED QUITE A BIT.
HE SHOULD BE UP AND ABOUT WITHIN A DAY OR TWO.
THAT'S NOT AURA...
スゥ..
BLINK...
WHOSE VOICE IS THAT...?
!

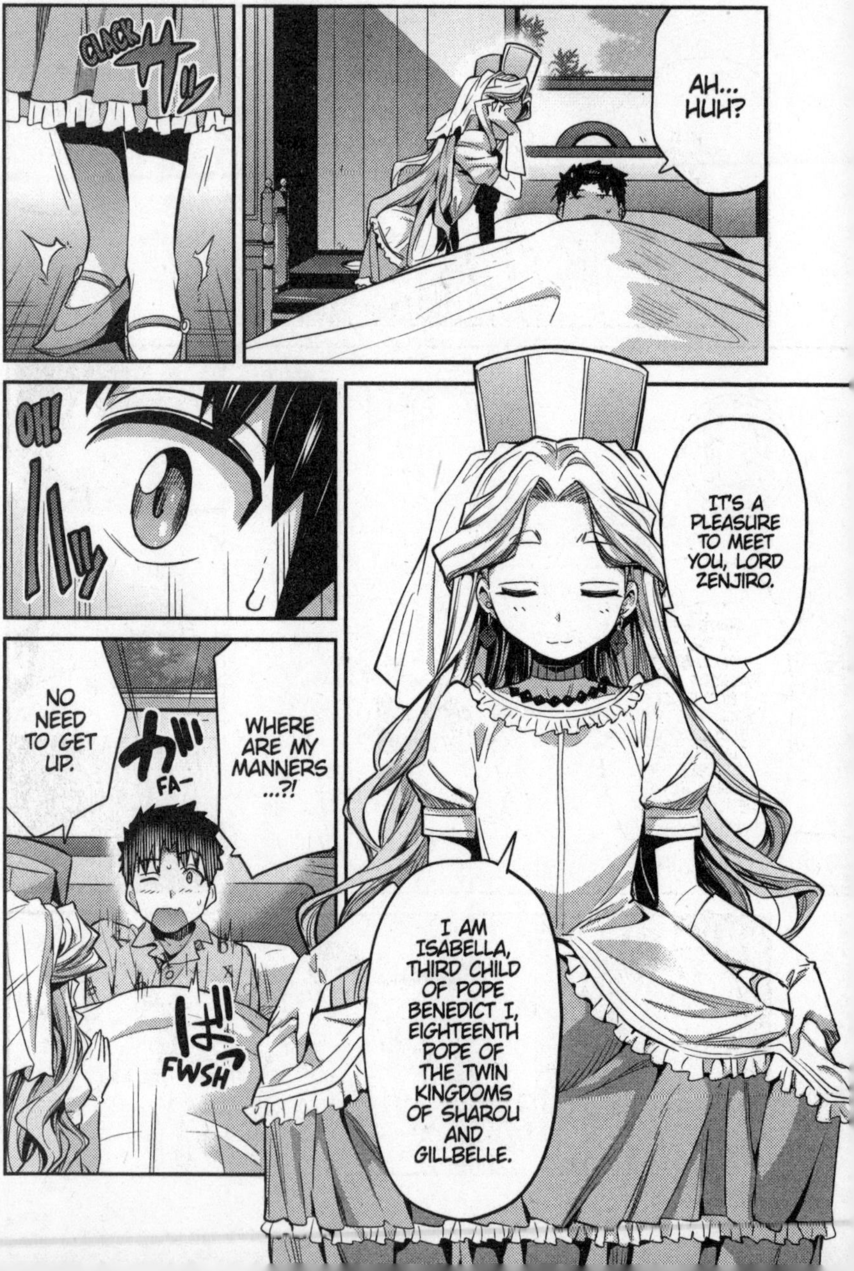
AH... HUH?
CLACK
IT'S A PLEASURE TO MEET YOU, LORD ZENJIRO.
I AM ISABELLA, THIRD CHILD OF POPE BENEDICT I, EIGHTEENTH POPE OF THE TWIN KINGDOMS OF SHAROU AND GILLBELLE.
OH!
WHERE ARE MY MANNERS ...?!
NO NEED TO GET UP.
FA-
FWSH

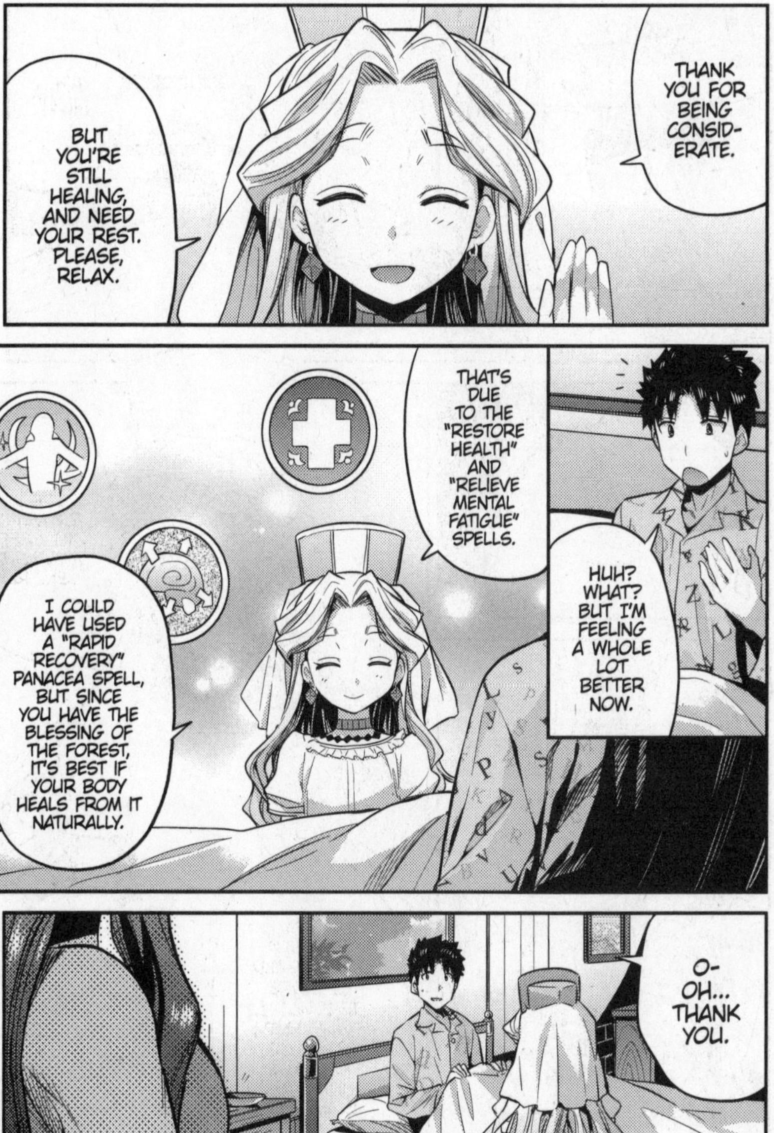
THANK YOU FOR BEING CONSID-ERATE.
BUT YOU'RE STILL HEALING, AND NEED YOUR REST. PLEASE, RELAX.
HUH? WHAT? BUT I'M FEELING A WHOLE LOT BETTER NOW.
THAT'S DUE TO THE "RESTORE HEALTH" AND "RELIEVE MENTAL FATIGUE" SPELLS.
I COULD HAVE USED A "RAPID RECOVERY" PANACEA SPELL, BUT SINCE YOU HAVE THE BLESSING OF THE FOREST, IT'S BEST IF YOUR BODY HEALS FROM IT NATURALLY.
O-OH... THANK YOU.

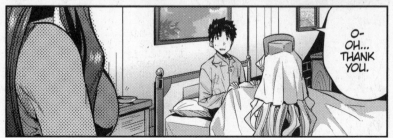

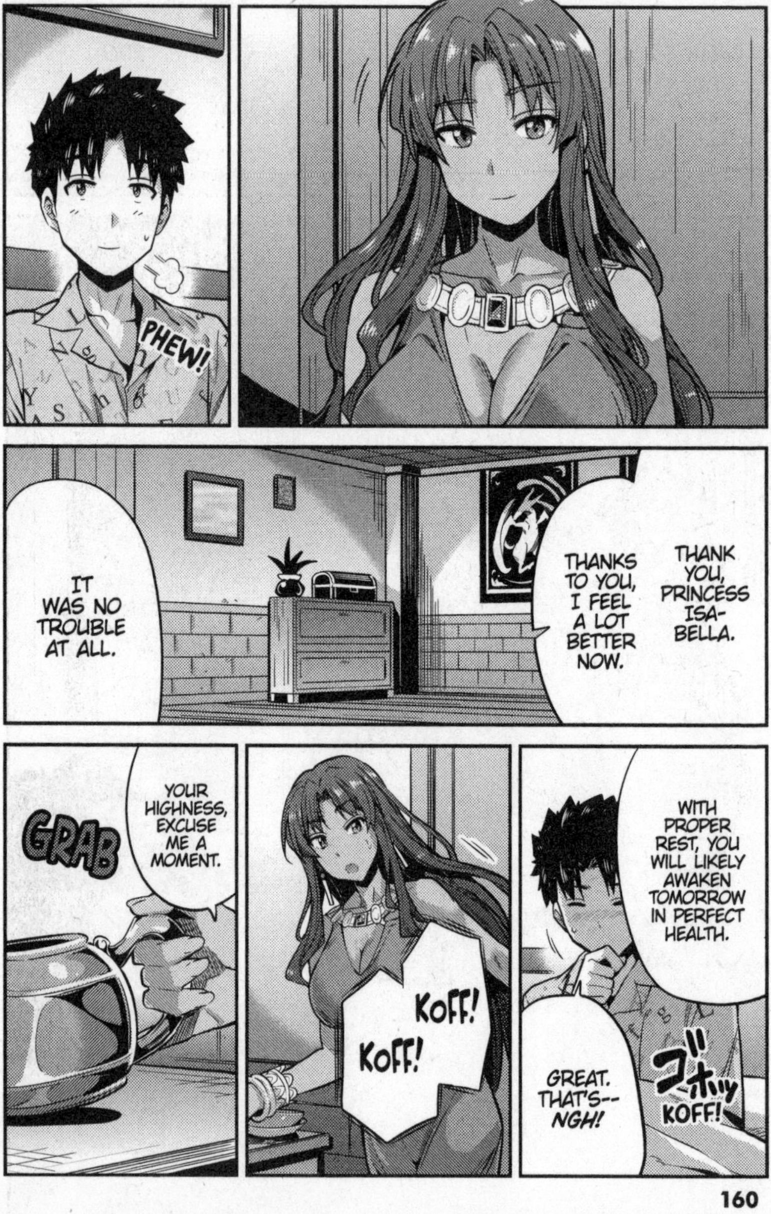
PHEW!
THANK YOU, PRINCESS ISA-BELLA.
THANKS TO YOU, I FEEL A LOT BETTER NOW.
IT WAS NO TROUBLE AT ALL.
WITH PROPER REST, YOU WILL LIKELY AWAKEN TOMORROW IN PERFECT HEALTH.
GREAT. THAT'S--NGH!
ゴホッ
KOFF!
KOFF!
KOFF!
YOUR HIGHNESS, EXCUSE ME A MOMENT.
GRAB

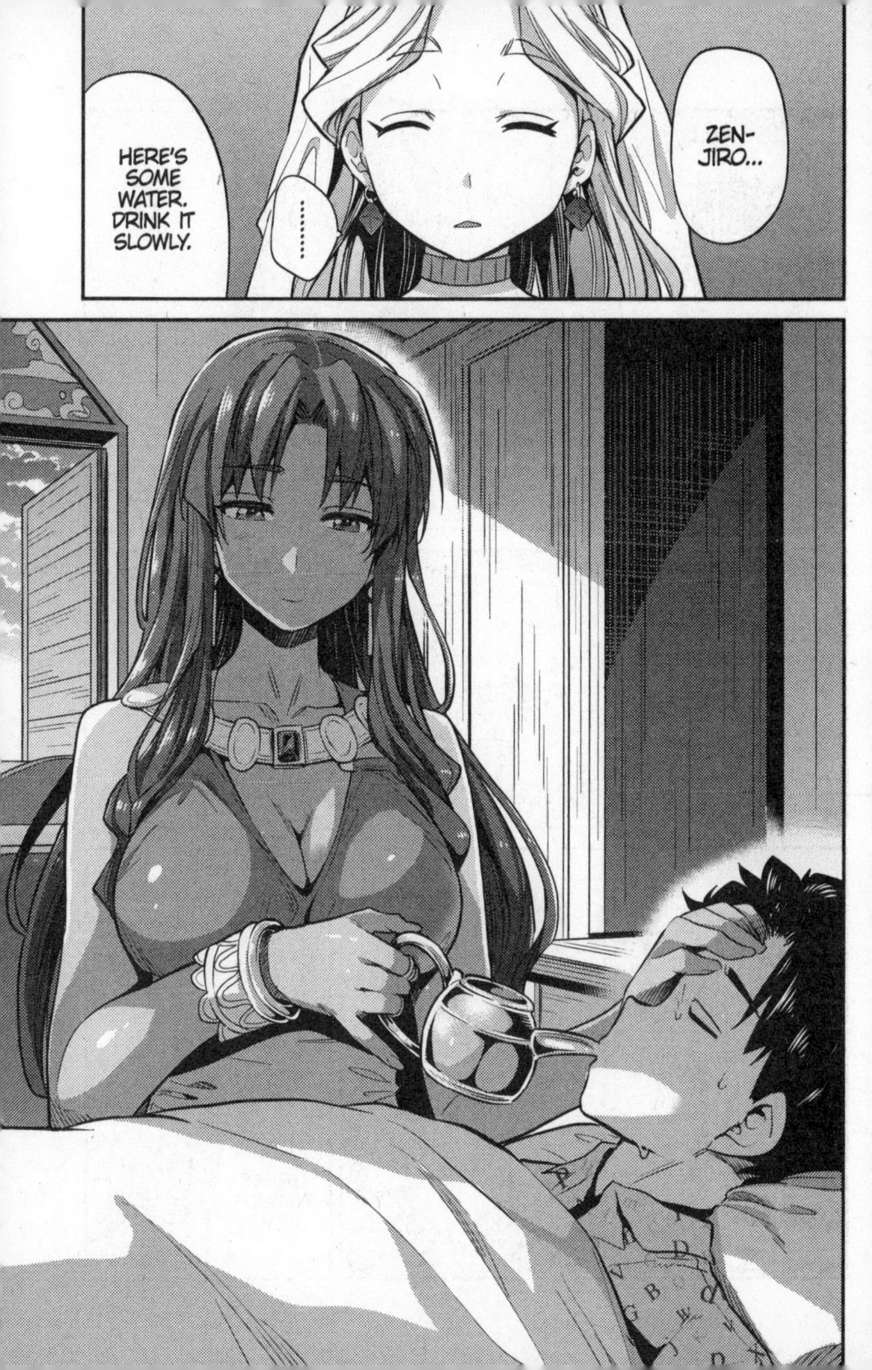
ZEN-JIRO...
......
HERE'S SOME WATER. DRINK IT SLOWLY.

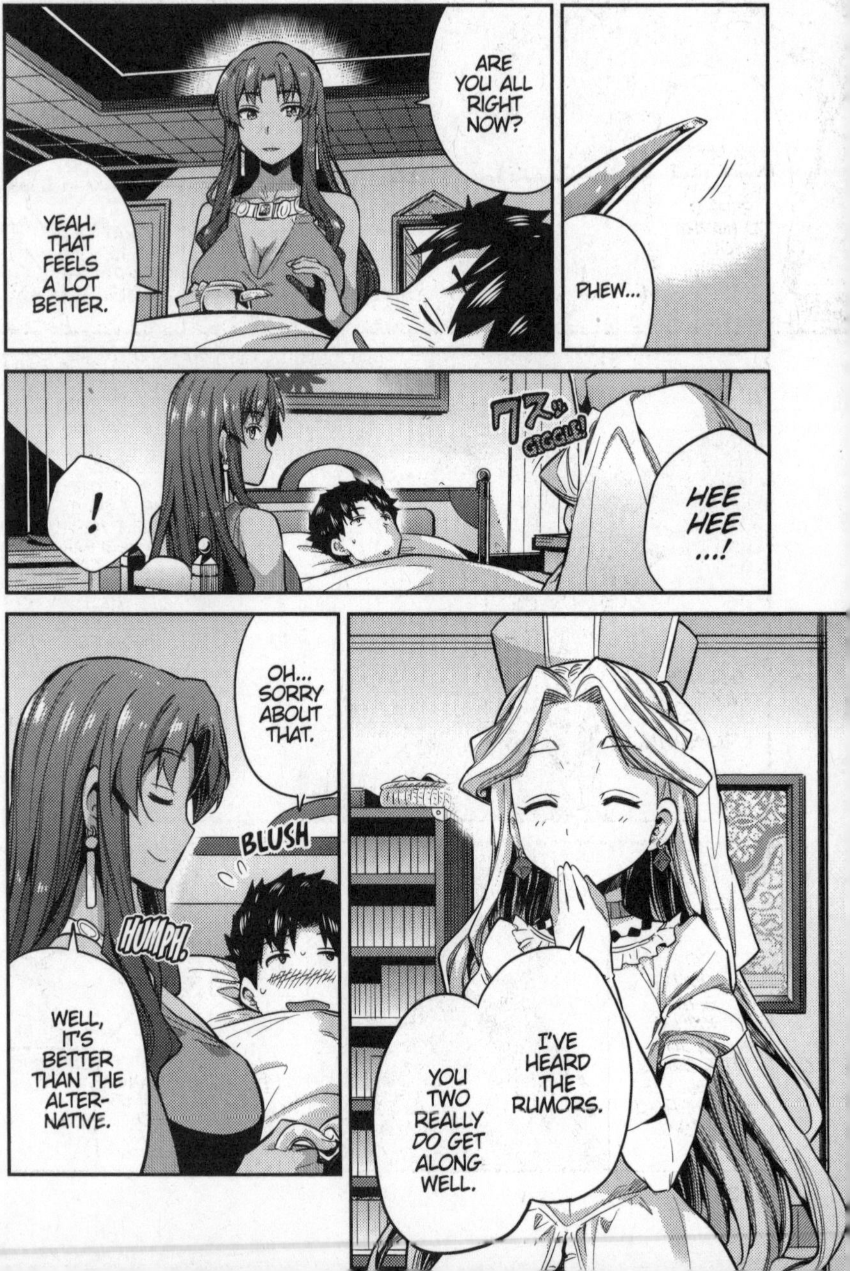
PHEW...
ARE YOU ALL RIGHT NOW?
YEAH. THAT FEELS A LOT BETTER.
クスッ GIGGLE!
HEE HEE ...!
!
I'VE HEARD THE RUMORS.
YOU TWO REALLY DO GET ALONG WELL.
OH... SORRY ABOUT THAT.
BLUSH
HUMPH.
WELL, IT'S BETTER THAN THE ALTER-NATIVE.

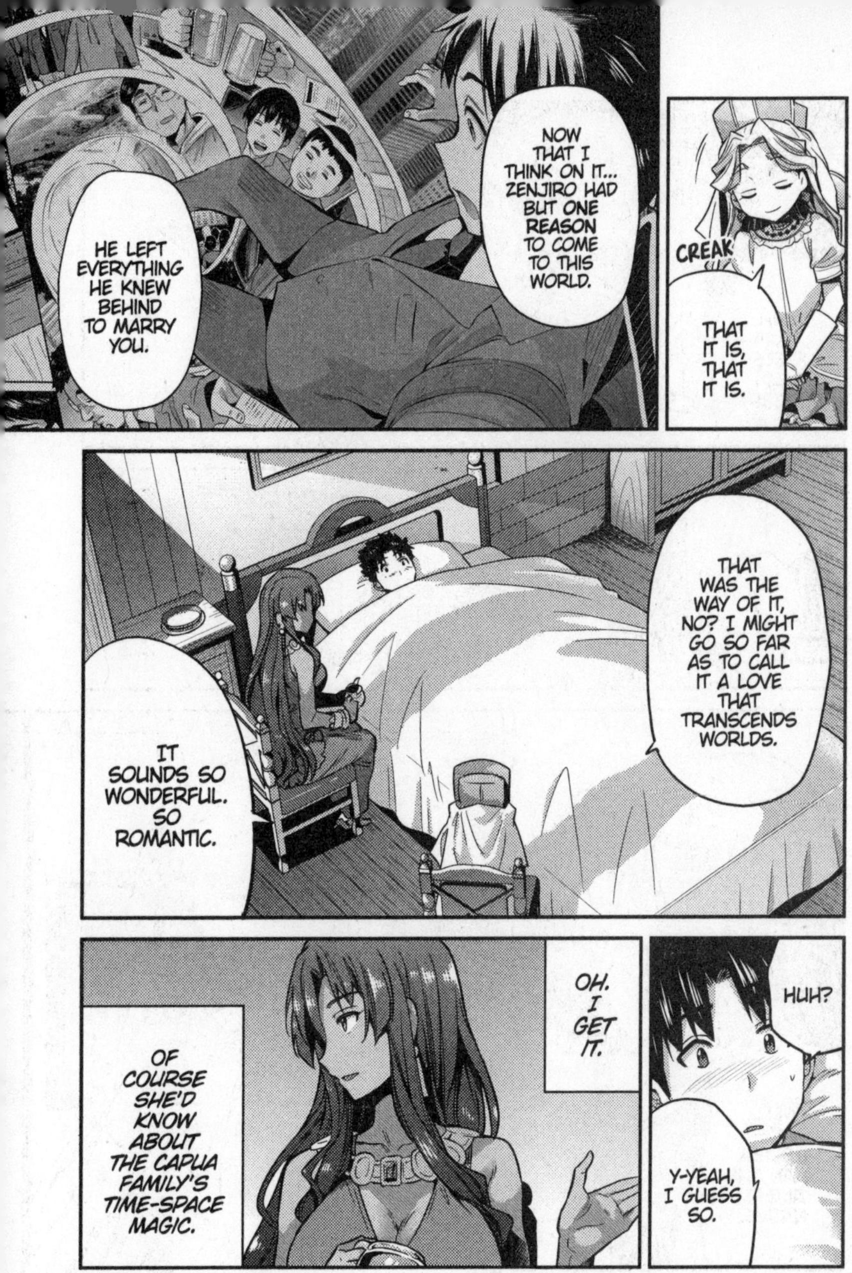
CREAK
THAT IT IS, THAT IT IS.
NOW THAT I THINK ON IT... ZENJIRO HAD BUT ONE REASON TO COME TO THIS WORLD.
HE LEFT EVERYTHING HE KNEW BEHIND TO MARRY YOU.
THAT WAS THE WAY OF IT, NO? I MIGHT GO SO FAR AS TO CALL IT A LOVE THAT TRANSCENDS WORLDS.
IT SOUNDS SO WONDERFUL. SO ROMANTIC.
HUH?
Y-YEAH, I GUESS SO.
OH. I GET IT.
OF COURSE SHE'D KNOW ABOUT THE CAPUA FAMILY'S TIME-SPACE MAGIC.

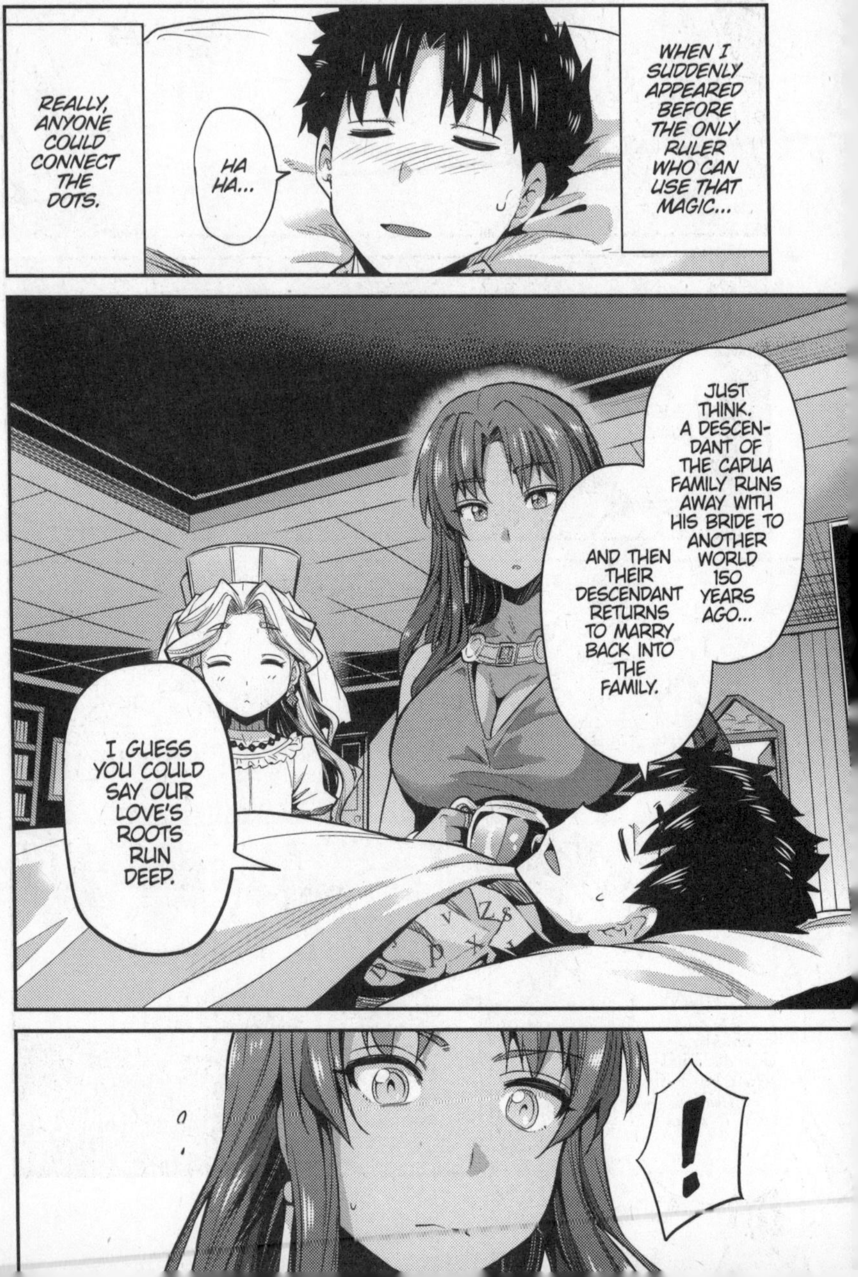
WHEN I SUDDENLY APPEARED BEFORE THE ONLY RULER WHO CAN USE THAT MAGIC...
HA HA...
REALLY, ANYONE COULD CONNECT THE DOTS.
JUST THINK. A DESCEN-DANT OF THE CAPUA FAMILY RUNS AWAY WITH HIS BRIDE TO ANOTHER WORLD 150 YEARS AGO...
AND THEN THEIR DESCENDANT RETURNS TO MARRY BACK INTO THE FAMILY.
I GUESS YOU COULD SAY OUR LOVE'S ROOTS RUN DEEP.
!

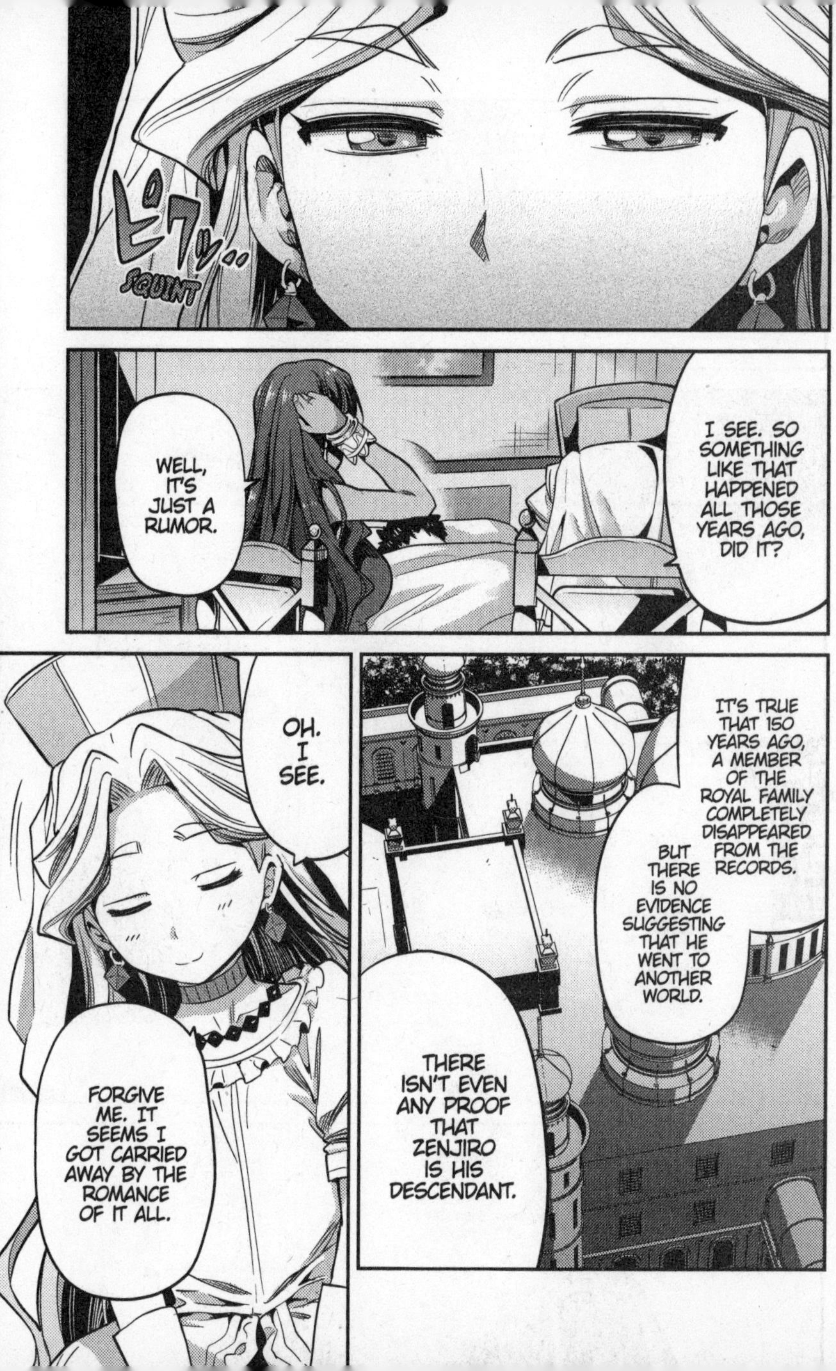
ピクッ..
SQUINT
I SEE. SO SOMETHING LIKE THAT HAPPENED ALL THOSE YEARS AGO, DID IT?
WELL, IT'S JUST A RUMOR.
IT'S TRUE THAT 150 YEARS AGO, A MEMBER OF THE ROYAL FAMILY COMPLETELY DISAPPEARED FROM THE RECORDS.
BUT THERE IS NO EVIDENCE SUGGESTING THAT HE WENT TO ANOTHER WORLD.
THERE ISN'T EVEN ANY PROOF THAT ZENJIRO IS HIS DESCENDANT.
OH. I SEE.
FORGIVE ME. IT SEEMS I GOT CARRIED AWAY BY THE ROMANCE OF IT ALL.

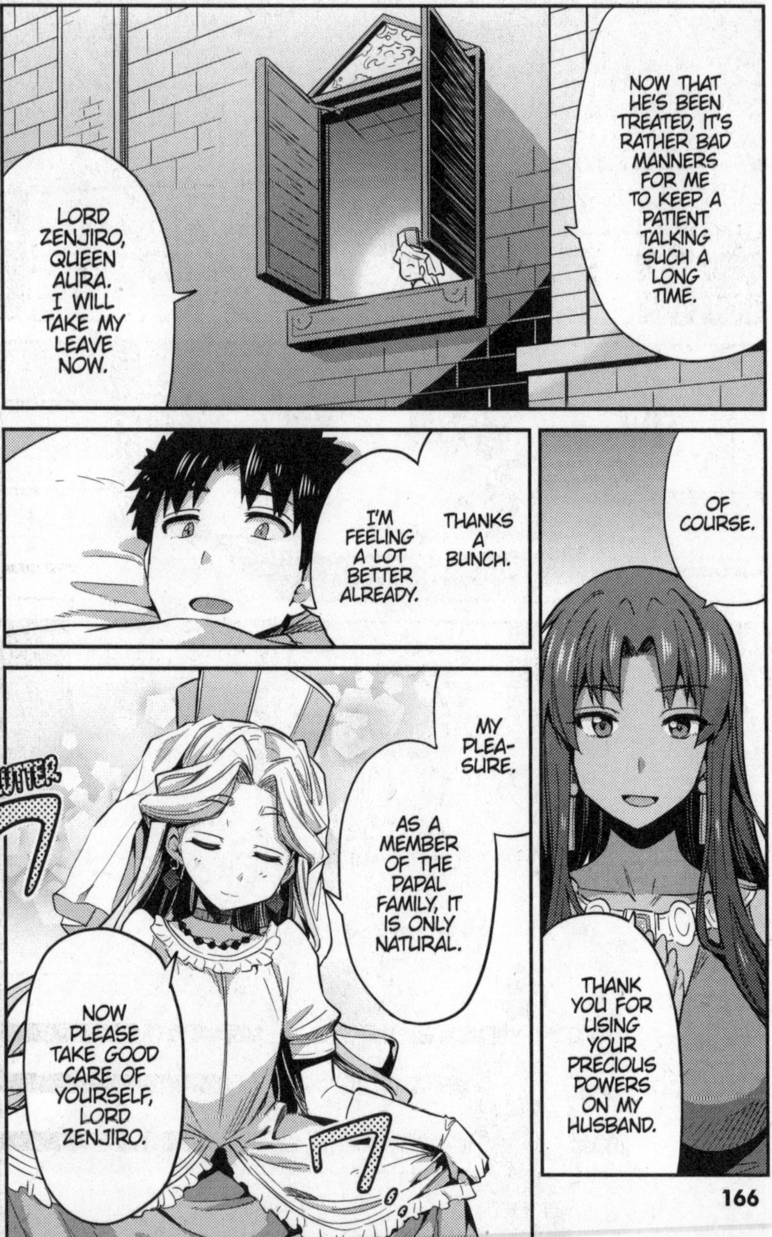
NOW THAT HE'S BEEN TREATED, IT'S RATHER BAD MANNERS FOR ME TO KEEP A PATIENT TALKING SUCH A LONG TIME.
LORD ZENJIRO, QUEEN AURA. I WILL TAKE MY LEAVE NOW.
OF COURSE.
THANK YOU FOR USING YOUR PRECIOUS POWERS ON MY HUSBAND.
THANKS A BUNCH.
I'M FEELING A LOT BETTER ALREADY.
MY PLEA-SURE.
AS A MEMBER OF THE PAPAL FAMILY, IT IS ONLY NATURAL.
FLUTTER
NOW PLEASE TAKE GOOD CARE OF YOURSELF, LORD ZENJIRO.

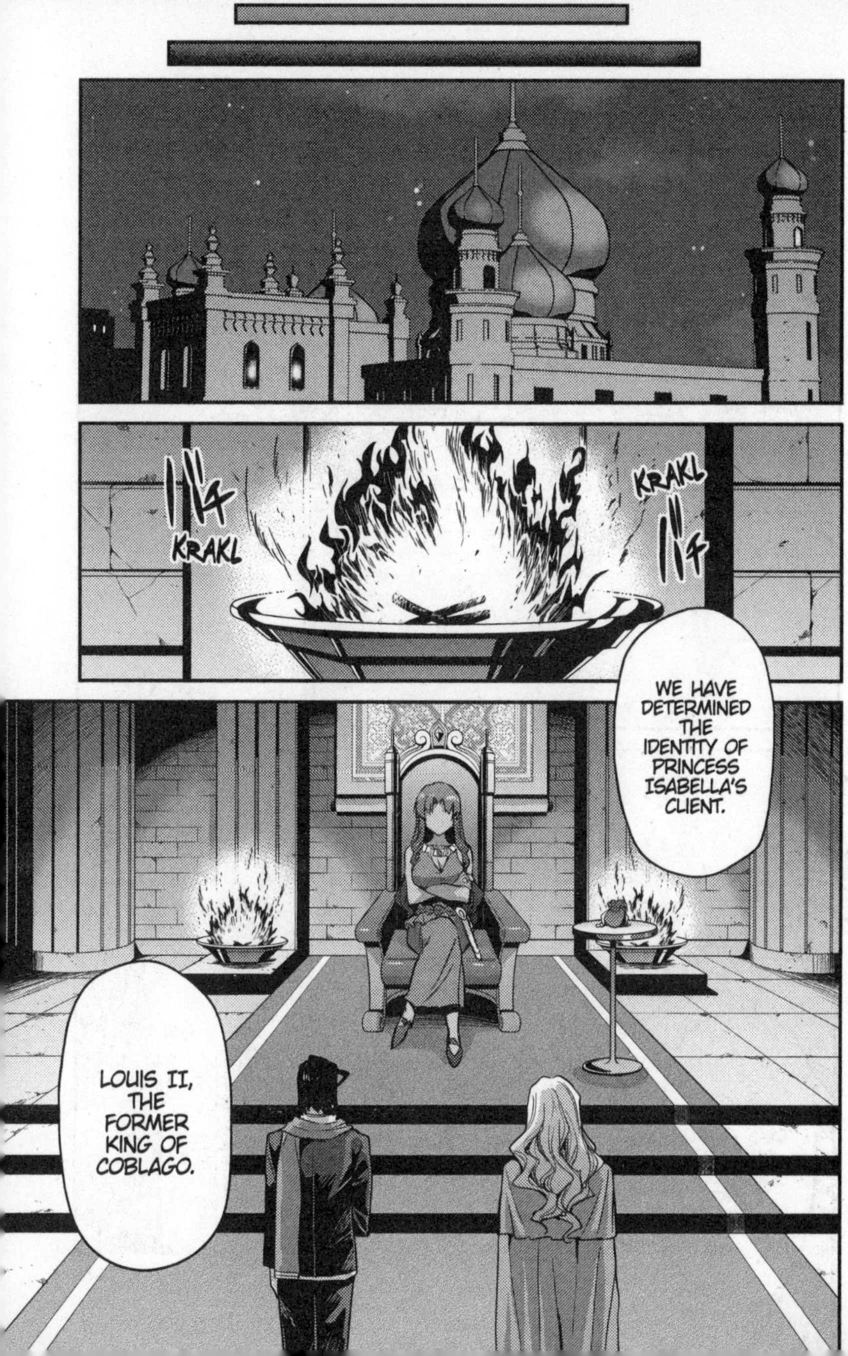
KRAKL
KRAKL
WE HAVE DETERMINED THE IDENTITY OF PRINCESS ISABELLA'S CLIENT.
LOUIS II, THE FORMER KING OF COBLAGO.

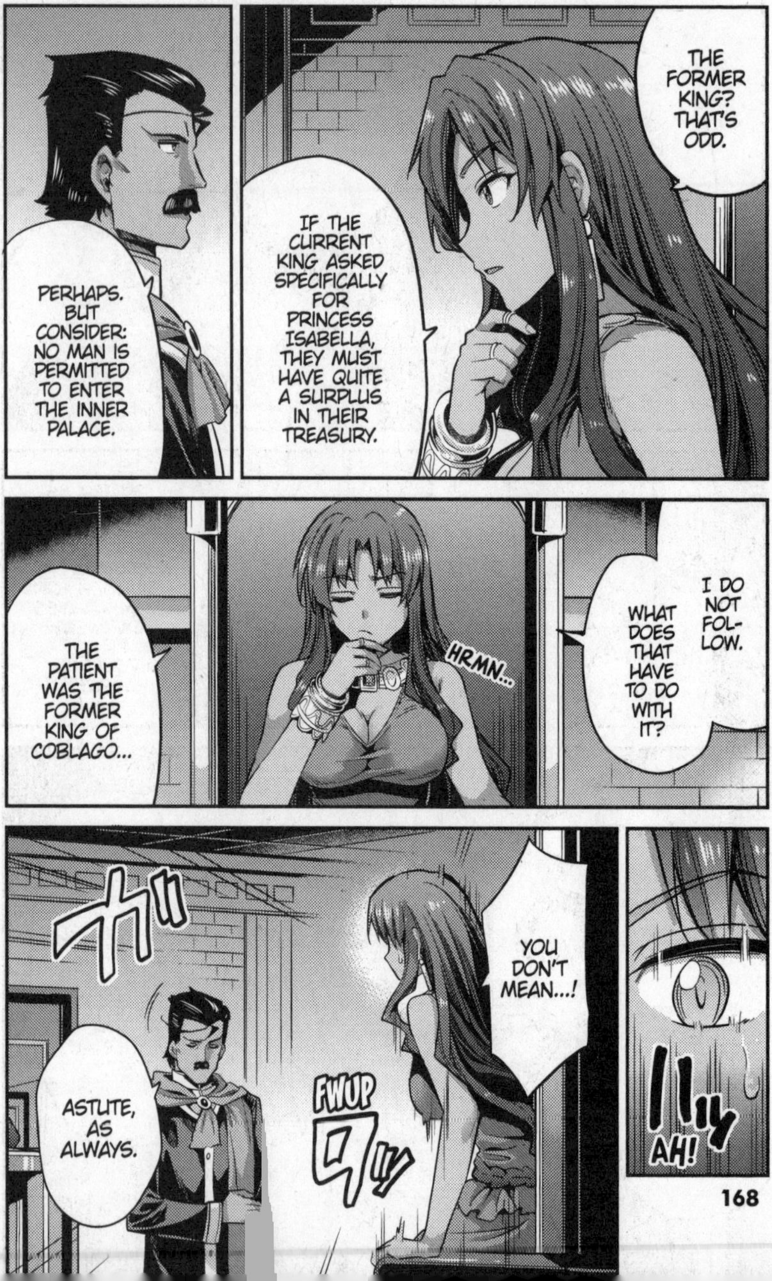
THE FORMER KING? THAT'S ODD.
IF THE CURRENT KING ASKED SPECIFICALLY FOR PRINCESS ISABELLA, THEY MUST HAVE QUITE A SURPLUS IN THEIR TREASURY.
PERHAPS. BUT CONSIDER: NO MAN IS PERMITTED TO ENTER THE INNER PALACE.
I DO NOT FOL-LOW.
WHAT DOES THAT HAVE TO DO WITH IT?
HRMN...
THE PATIENT WAS THE FORMER KING OF COBLAGO...
AH!
YOU DON'T MEAN...!
FWUP
ASTUTE, AS ALWAYS.

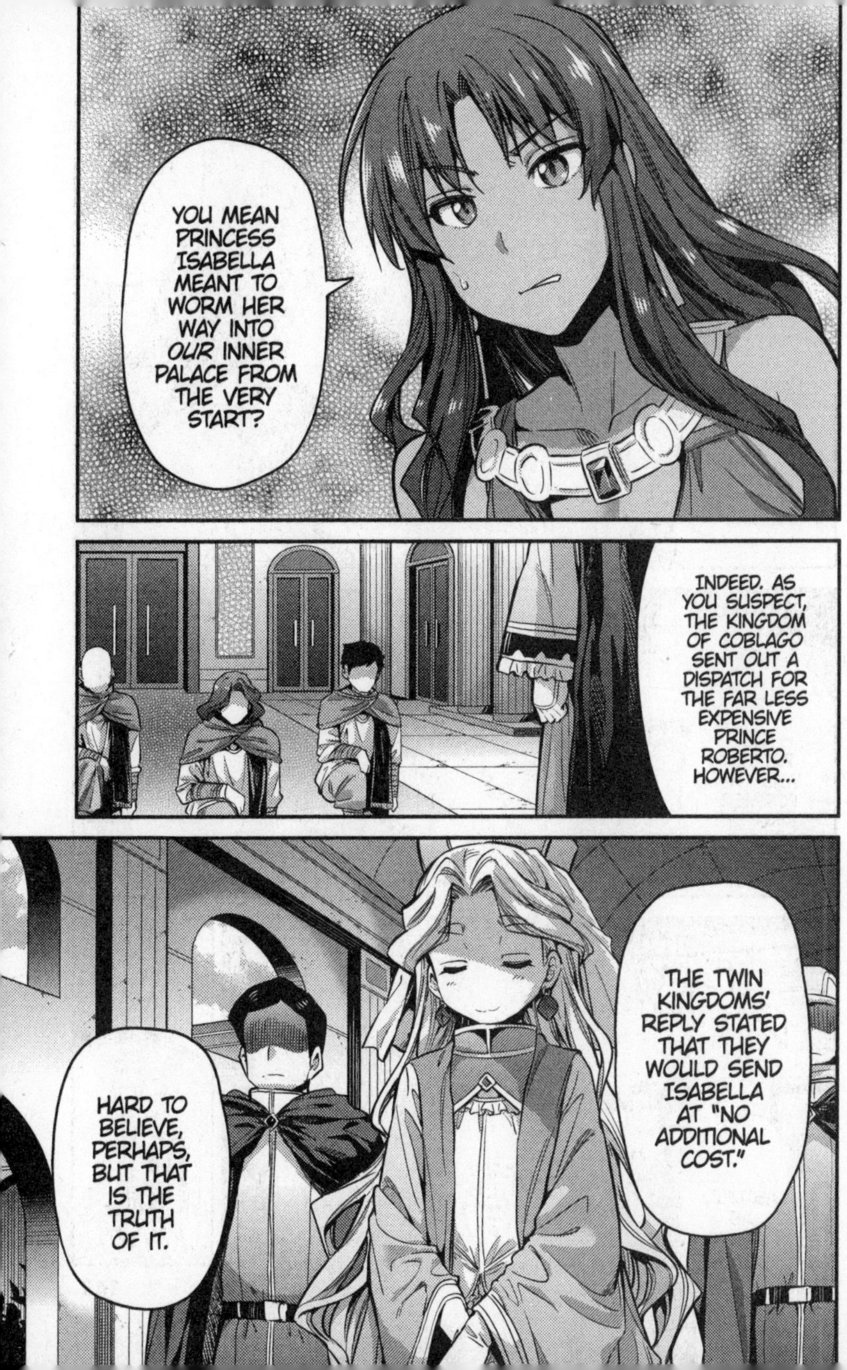
YOU MEAN PRINCESS ISABELLA MEANT TO WORM HER WAY INTO *OUR* INNER PALACE FROM THE VERY START?
INDEED. AS YOU SUSPECT, THE KINGDOM OF COBLAGO SENT OUT A DISPATCH FOR THE FAR LESS EXPENSIVE PRINCE ROBERTO. HOWEVER...
THE TWIN KINGDOMS' REPLY STATED THAT THEY WOULD SEND ISABELLA AT "NO ADDITIONAL COST."
HARD TO BELIEVE, PERHAPS, BUT THAT IS THE TRUTH OF IT.

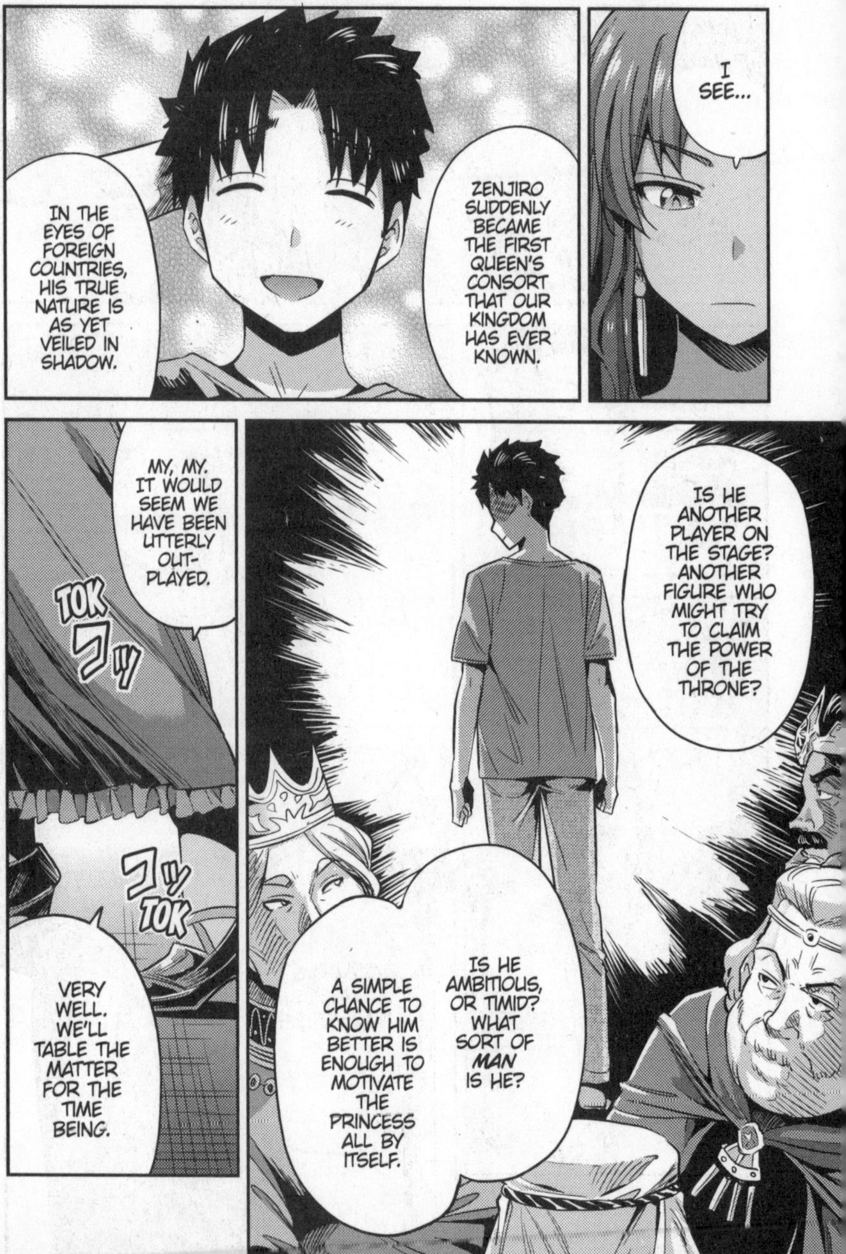
I SEE...
ZENJIRO SUDDENLY BECAME THE FIRST QUEEN'S CONSORT THAT OUR KINGDOM HAS EVER KNOWN.
IN THE EYES OF FOREIGN COUNTRIES, HIS TRUE NATURE IS AS YET VEILED IN SHADOW.
IS HE ANOTHER PLAYER ON THE STAGE? ANOTHER FIGURE WHO MIGHT TRY TO CLAIM THE POWER OF THE THRONE?
IS HE AMBITIOUS, OR TIMID? WHAT SORT OF *MAN* IS HE?
A SIMPLE CHANCE TO KNOW HIM BETTER IS ENOUGH TO MOTIVATE THE PRINCESS ALL BY ITSELF.
MY, MY. IT WOULD SEEM WE HAVE BEEN UTTERLY OUT-PLAYED.
TOK
TOK
VERY WELL. WE'LL TABLE THE MATTER FOR THE TIME BEING.

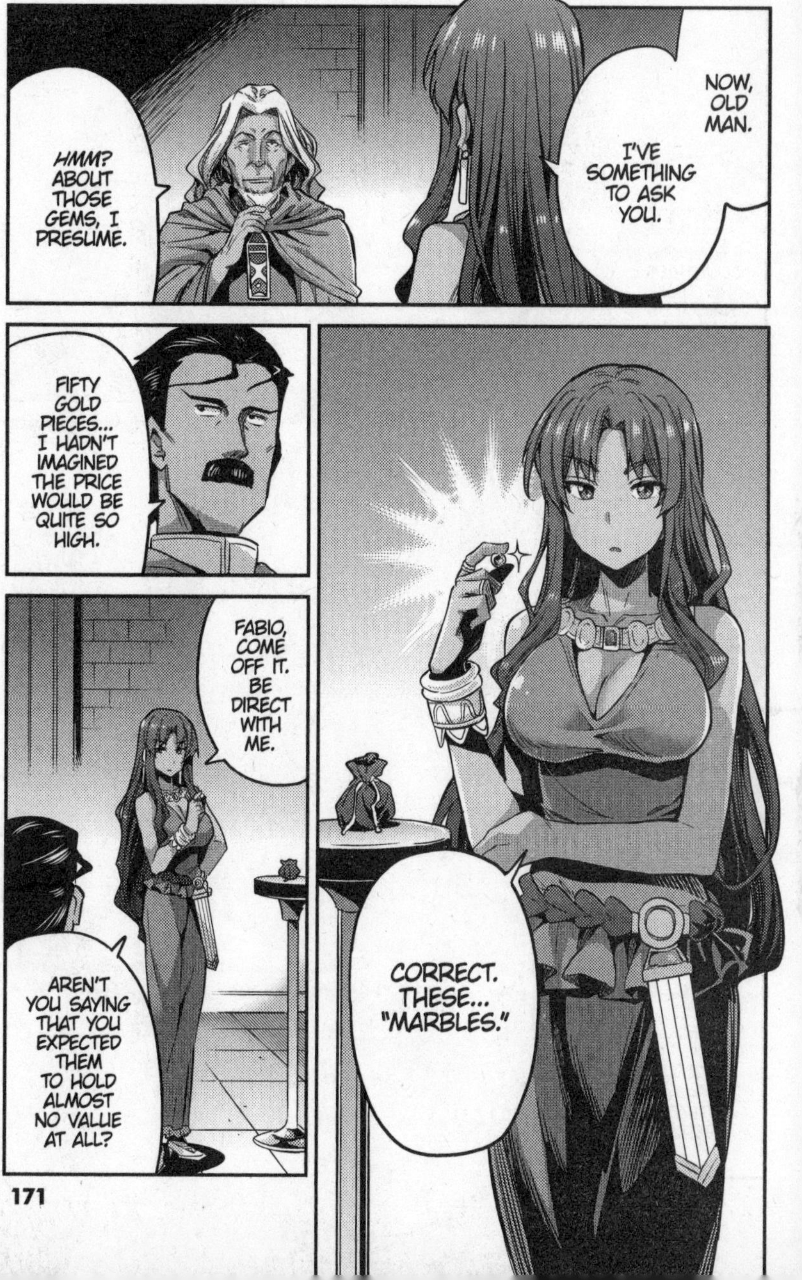
NOW, OLD MAN.
I'VE SOMETHING TO ASK YOU.
HMM? ABOUT THOSE GEMS, I PRESUME.
CORRECT. THESE... "MARBLES."
FIFTY GOLD PIECES... I HADN'T IMAGINED THE PRICE WOULD BE QUITE SO HIGH.
FABIO, COME OFF IT. BE DIRECT WITH ME.
AREN'T YOU SAYING THAT YOU EXPECTED THEM TO HOLD ALMOST NO VALUE AT ALL?

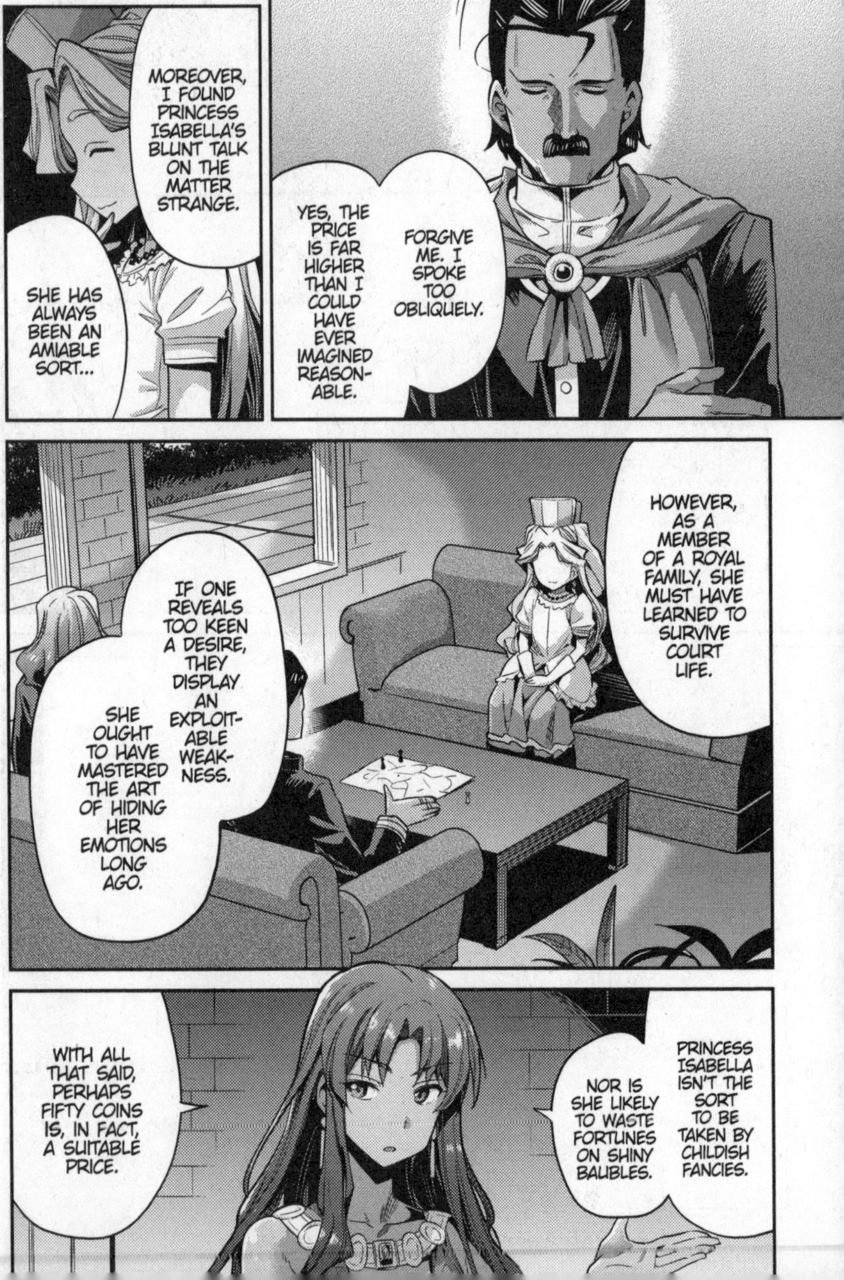
FORGIVE ME. I SPOKE TOO OBLIQUELY.
YES, THE PRICE IS FAR HIGHER THAN I COULD HAVE EVER IMAGINED REASONABLE.
MOREOVER, I FOUND PRINCESS ISABELLA'S BLUNT TALK ON THE MATTER STRANGE.
SHE HAS ALWAYS BEEN AN AMIABLE SORT...
HOWEVER, AS A MEMBER OF A ROYAL FAMILY, SHE MUST HAVE LEARNED TO SURVIVE COURT LIFE.
IF ONE REVEALS TOO KEEN A DESIRE, THEY DISPLAY AN EXPLOITABLE WEAKNESS.
SHE OUGHT TO HAVE MASTERED THE ART OF HIDING HER EMOTIONS LONG AGO.
PRINCESS ISABELLA ISN'T THE SORT TO BE TAKEN BY CHILDISH FANCIES.
NOR IS SHE LIKELY TO WASTE FORTUNES ON SHINY BAUBLES.
WITH ALL THAT SAID, PERHAPS FIFTY COINS IS, IN FACT, A SUITABLE PRICE.

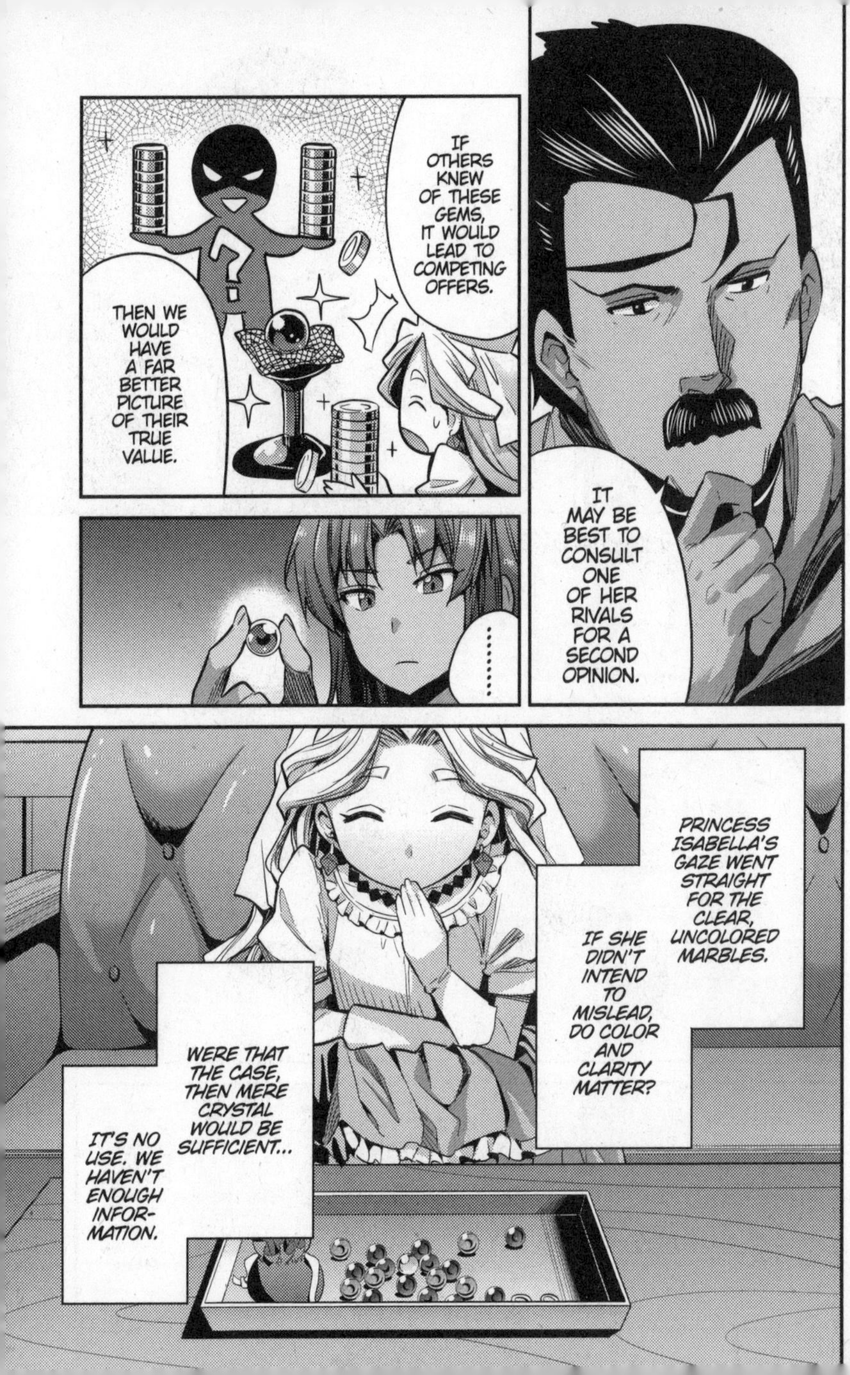
IT MAY BE BEST TO CONSULT ONE OF HER RIVALS FOR A SECOND OPINION.
IF OTHERS KNEW OF THESE GEMS, IT WOULD LEAD TO COMPETING OFFERS.
THEN WE WOULD HAVE A FAR BETTER PICTURE OF THEIR TRUE VALUE.
......
PRINCESS ISABELLA'S GAZE WENT STRAIGHT FOR THE CLEAR, UNCOLORED MARBLES.
IF SHE DIDN'T INTEND TO MISLEAD, DO COLOR AND CLARITY MATTER?
WERE THAT THE CASE, THEN MERE CRYSTAL WOULD BE SUFFICIENT...
IT'S NO USE. WE HAVEN'T ENOUGH INFOR-MATION.

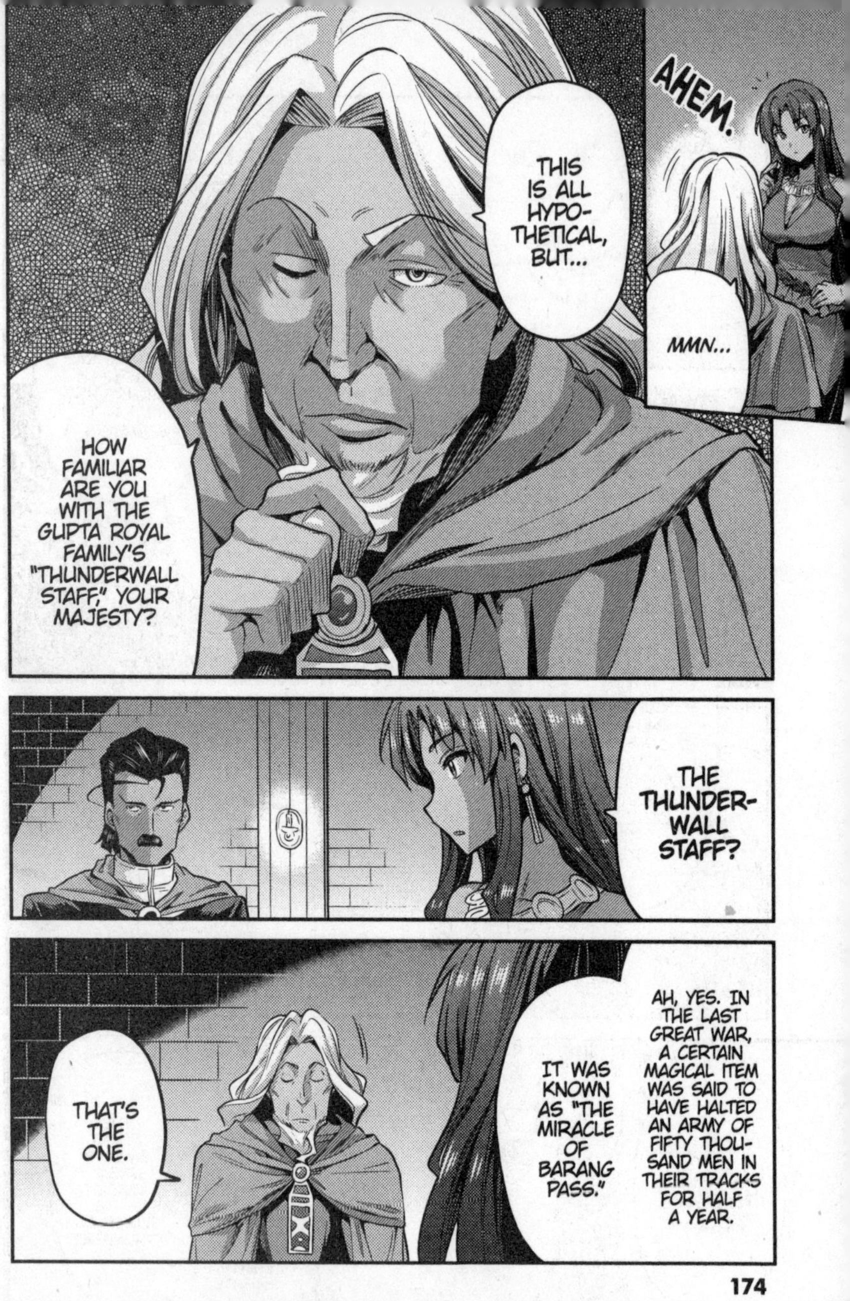
AHEM.
MMN...
THIS IS ALL HYPO-THETICAL, BUT...
HOW FAMILIAR ARE YOU WITH THE GUPTA ROYAL FAMILY'S "THUNDERWALL STAFF," YOUR MAJESTY?
THE THUNDER-WALL STAFF?
AH, YES. IN THE LAST GREAT WAR, A CERTAIN MAGICAL ITEM WAS SAID TO HAVE HALTED AN ARMY OF FIFTY THOU-SAND MEN IN THEIR TRACKS FOR HALF A YEAR.
IT WAS KNOWN AS "THE MIRACLE OF BARANG PASS."
THAT'S THE ONE.

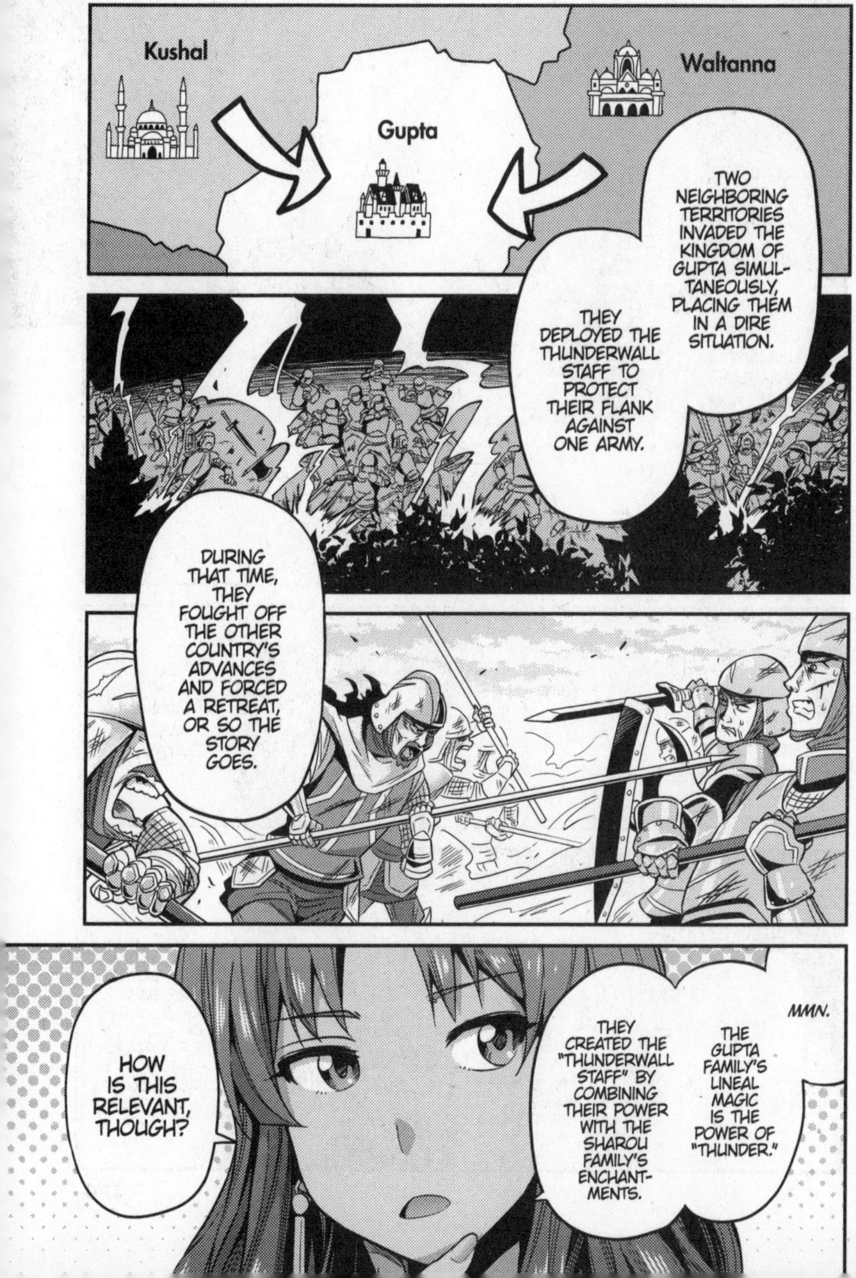

Waltanna
Kushal
Gupta
TWO NEIGHBORING TERRITORIES INVADED THE KINGDOM OF GUPTA SIMUL-TANEOUSLY, PLACING THEM IN A DIRE SITUATION.
THEY DEPLOYED THE THUNDERWALL STAFF TO PROTECT THEIR FLANK AGAINST ONE ARMY.
DURING THAT TIME, THEY FOUGHT OFF THE OTHER COUNTRY'S ADVANCES AND FORCED A RETREAT, OR SO THE STORY GOES.
MMN.
THE GUPTA FAMILY'S LINEAL MAGIC IS THE POWER OF "THUNDER."
THEY CREATED THE "THUNDERWALL STAFF" BY COMBINING THEIR POWER WITH THE SHAROU FAMILY'S ENCHANT-MENTS.
HOW IS THIS RELEVANT, THOUGH?

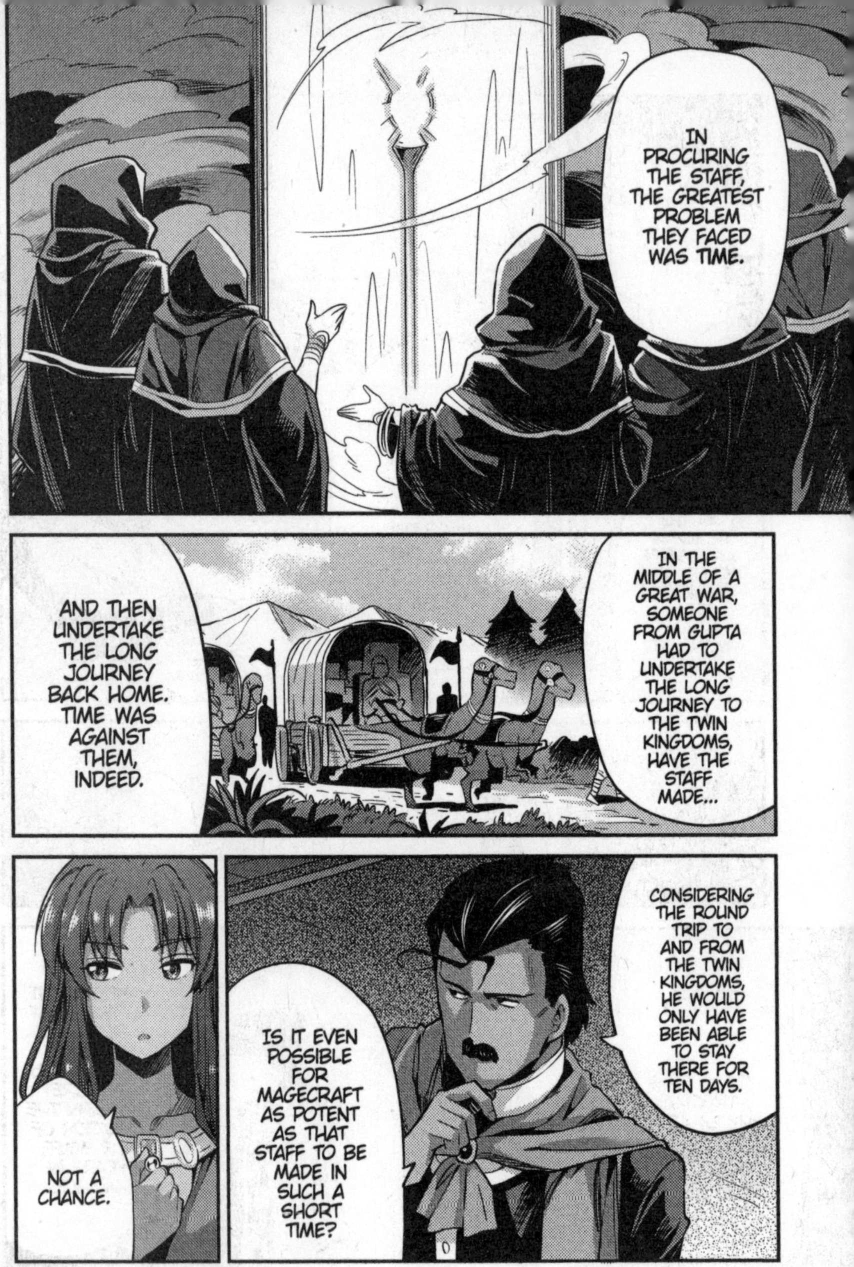
IN PROCURING THE STAFF, THE GREATEST PROBLEM THEY FACED WAS TIME.
IN THE MIDDLE OF A GREAT WAR, SOMEONE FROM GUPTA HAD TO UNDERTAKE THE LONG JOURNEY TO THE TWIN KINGDOMS, HAVE THE STAFF MADE...
AND THEN UNDERTAKE THE LONG JOURNEY BACK HOME. TIME WAS AGAINST THEM, INDEED.
CONSIDERING THE ROUND TRIP TO AND FROM THE TWIN KINGDOMS, HE WOULD ONLY HAVE BEEN ABLE TO STAY THERE FOR TEN DAYS.
IS IT EVEN POSSIBLE FOR MAGECRAFT AS POTENT AS THAT STAFF TO BE MADE IN SUCH A SHORT TIME?
NOT A CHANCE.

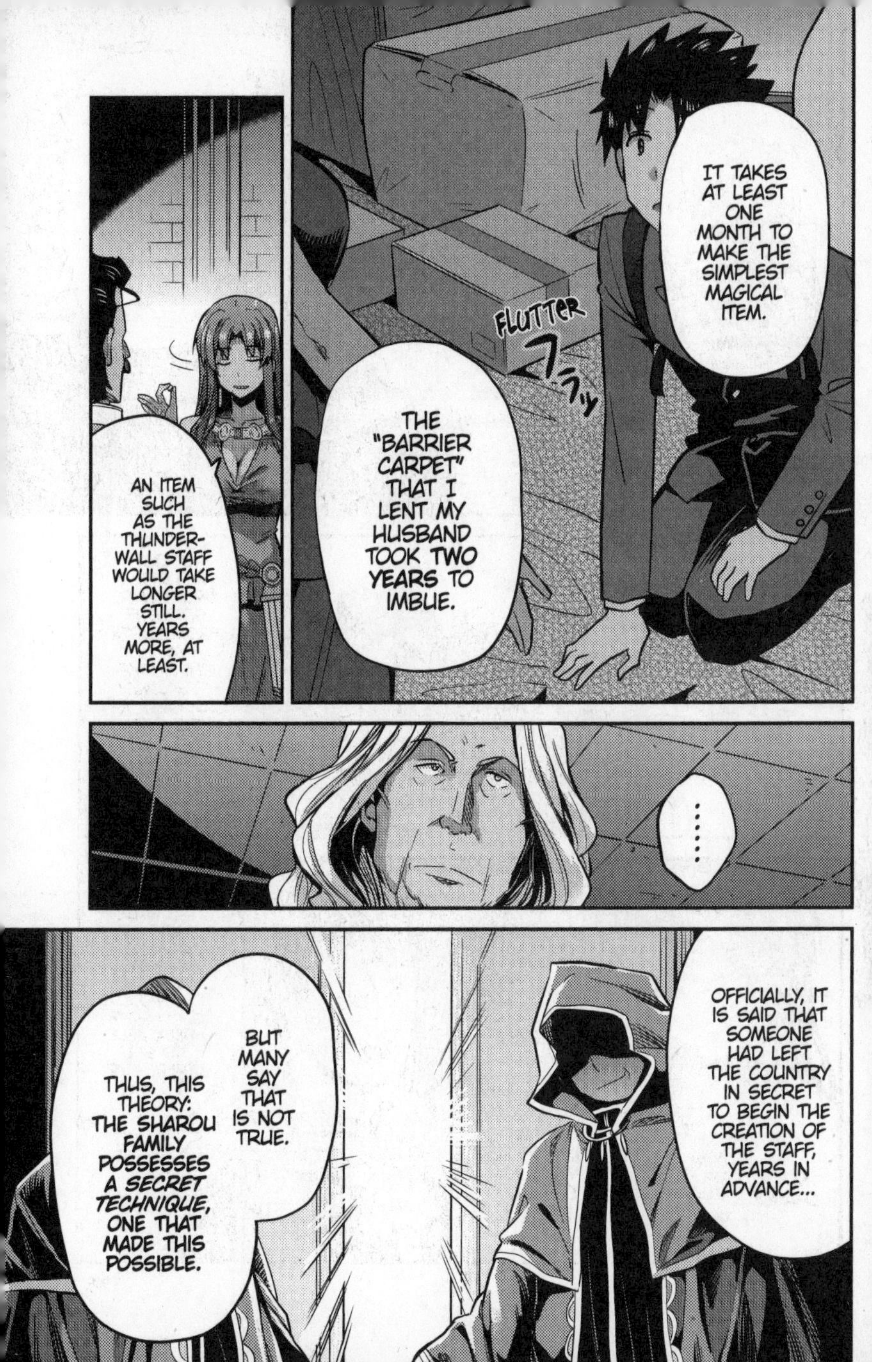
IT TAKES AT LEAST ONE MONTH TO MAKE THE SIMPLEST MAGICAL ITEM.
FLUTTER
THE "BARRIER CARPET" THAT I LENT MY HUSBAND TOOK TWO YEARS TO IMBUE.
AN ITEM SUCH AS THE THUNDER-WALL STAFF WOULD TAKE LONGER STILL. YEARS MORE, AT LEAST.
......
OFFICIALLY, IT IS SAID THAT SOMEONE HAD LEFT THE COUNTRY IN SECRET TO BEGIN THE CREATION OF THE STAFF, YEARS IN ADVANCE...
BUT MANY SAY THAT IS NOT TRUE.
THUS, THIS THEORY: THE SHAROU FAMILY POSSESSES A *SECRET TECHNIQUE*, ONE THAT MADE THIS POSSIBLE.

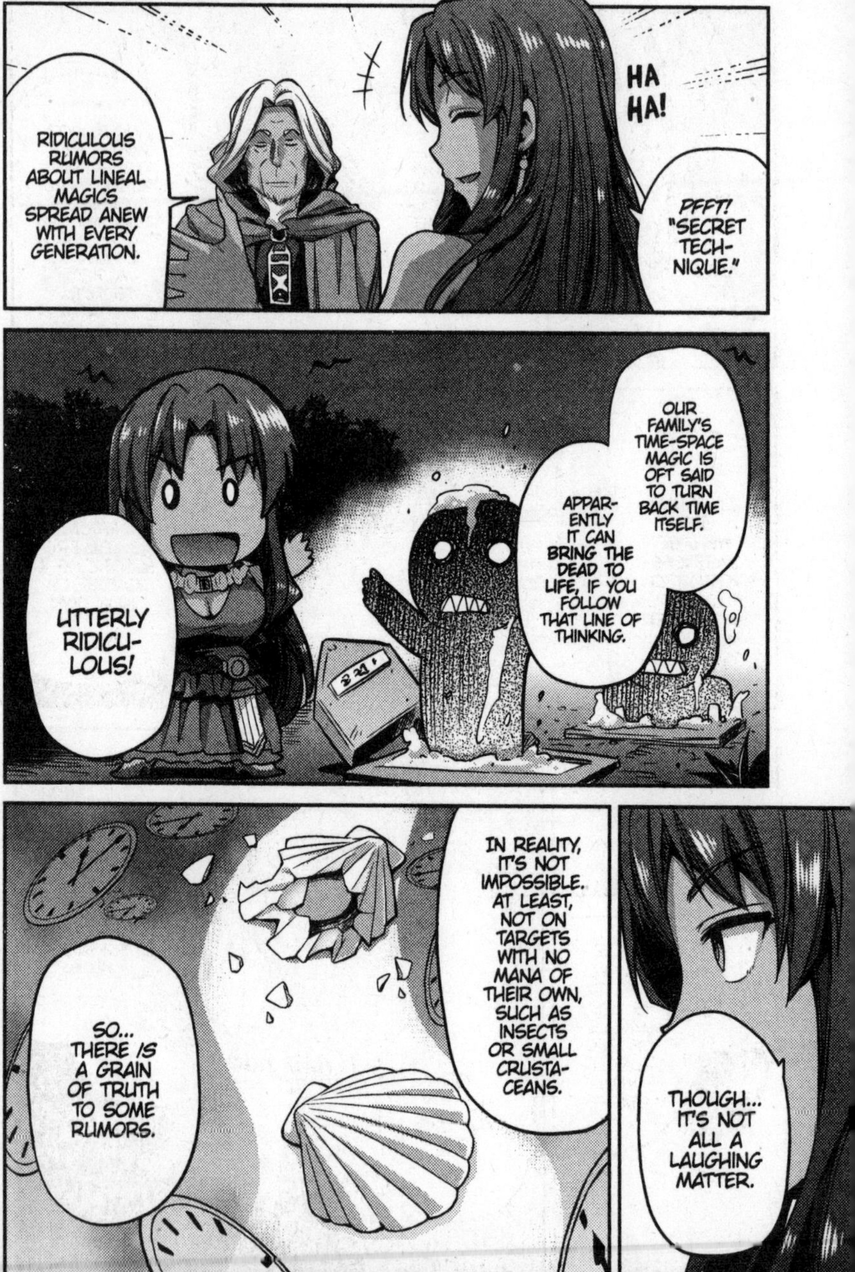
HA HA!
PFFT! "SECRET TECH-NIQUE."
RIDICULOUS RUMORS ABOUT LINEAL MAGICS SPREAD ANEW WITH EVERY GENERATION.
OUR FAMILY'S TIME-SPACE MAGIC IS OFT SAID TO TURN BACK TIME ITSELF.
APPAR-ENTLY IT CAN BRING THE DEAD TO LIFE, IF YOU FOLLOW THAT LINE OF THINKING.
UTTERLY RIDICU-LOUS!
THOUGH... IT'S NOT ALL A LAUGHING MATTER.
IN REALITY, IT'S NOT IMPOSSIBLE. AT LEAST, NOT ON TARGETS WITH NO MANA OF THEIR OWN, SUCH AS INSECTS OR SMALL CRUSTA-CEANS.
SO... THERE *IS* A GRAIN OF TRUTH TO SOME RUMORS.

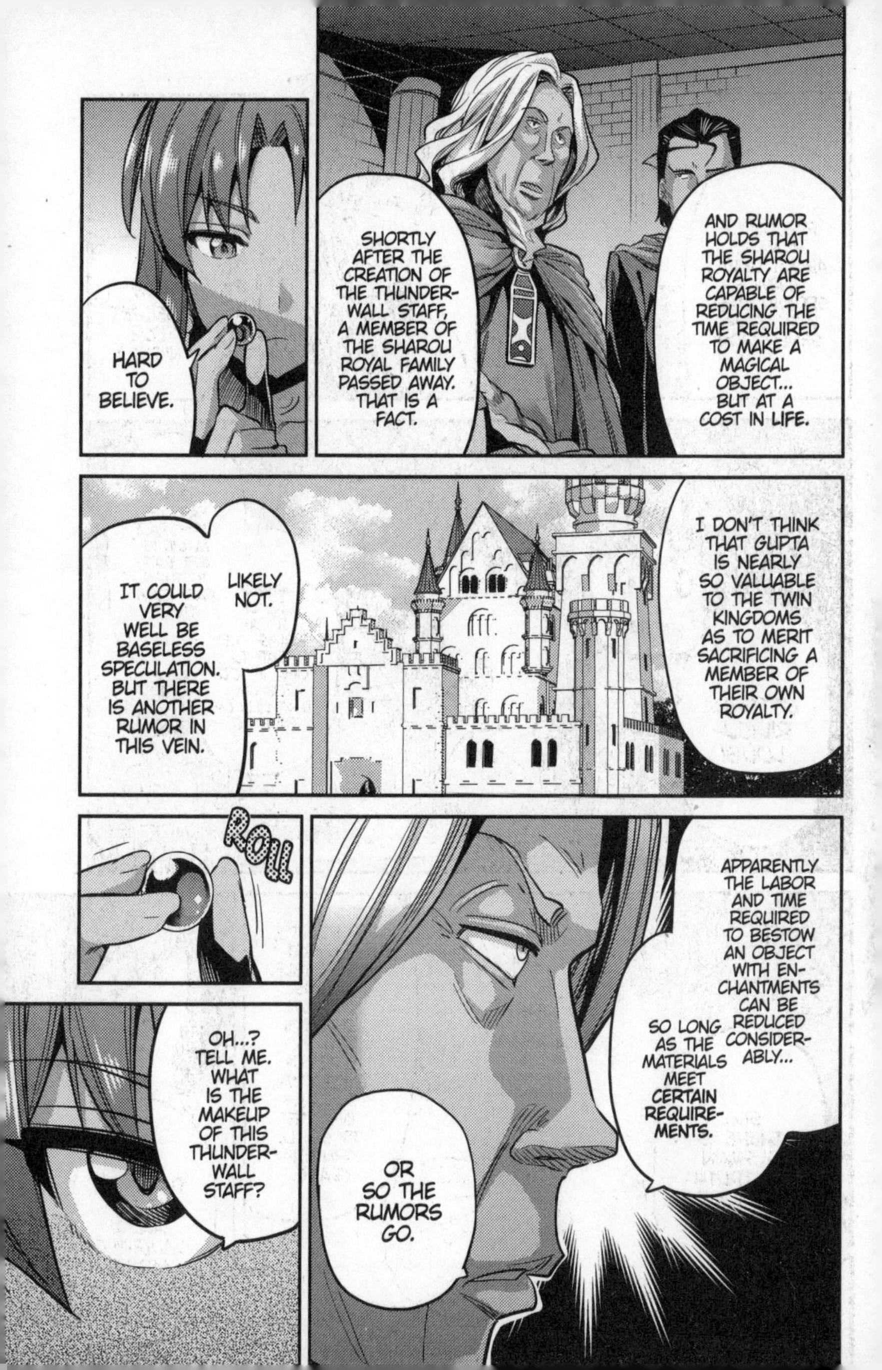
AND RUMOR HOLDS THAT THE SHAROU ROYALTY ARE CAPABLE OF REDUCING THE TIME REQUIRED TO MAKE A MAGICAL OBJECT... BUT AT A COST IN LIFE.
SHORTLY AFTER THE CREATION OF THE THUNDER-WALL STAFF, A MEMBER OF THE SHAROU ROYAL FAMILY PASSED AWAY. THAT IS A FACT.
HARD TO BELIEVE.
I DON'T THINK THAT GUPTA IS NEARLY SO VALUABLE TO THE TWIN KINGDOMS AS TO MERIT SACRIFICING A MEMBER OF THEIR OWN ROYALTY.
LIKELY NOT.
IT COULD VERY WELL BE BASELESS SPECULATION. BUT THERE IS ANOTHER RUMOR IN THIS VEIN.
APPARENTLY THE LABOR AND TIME REQUIRED TO BESTOW AN OBJECT WITH EN-CHANTMENTS CAN BE REDUCED CONSIDER-ABLY...
SO LONG AS THE MATERIALS MEET CERTAIN REQUIRE-MENTS.
OR SO THE RUMORS GO.
ROLL
OH...? TELL ME. WHAT IS THE MAKEUP OF THIS THUNDER-WALL STAFF?

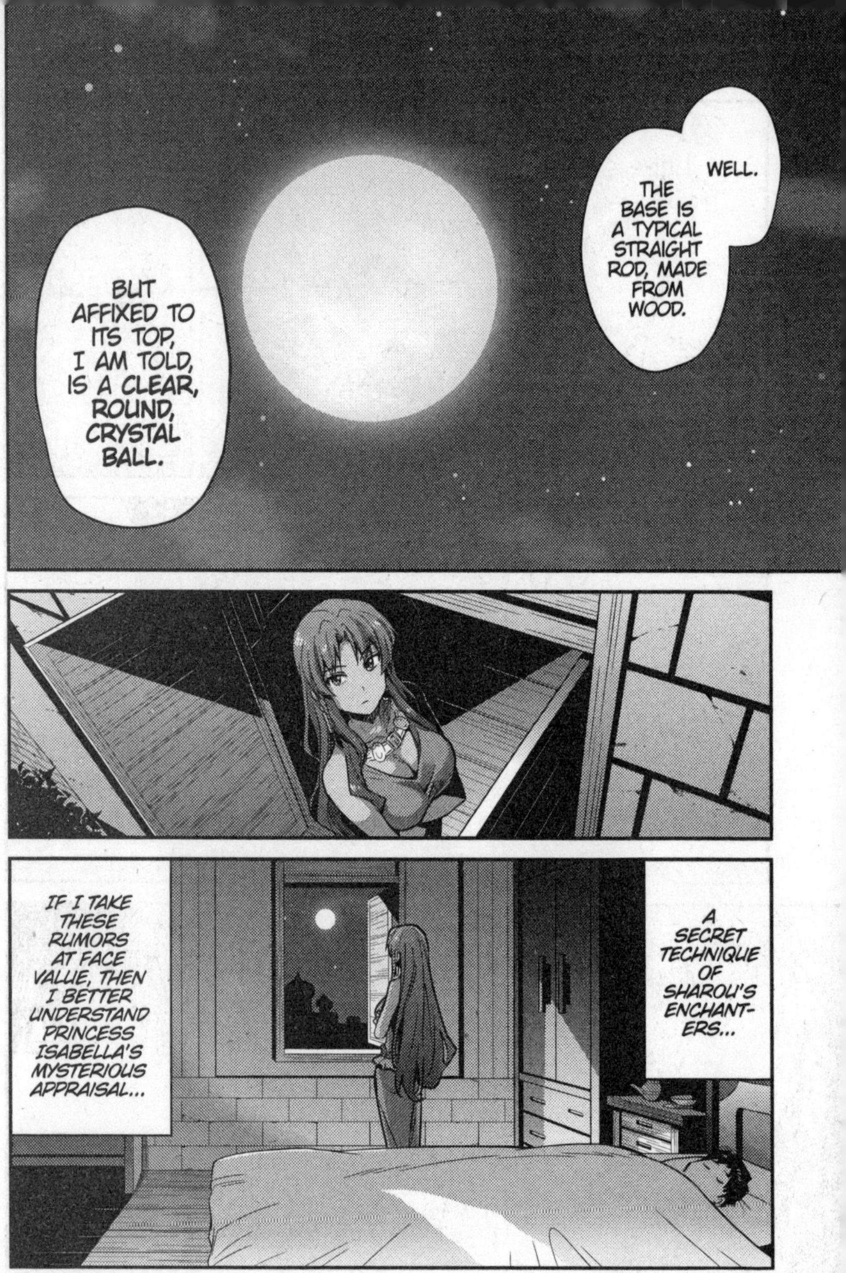
WELL. THE BASE IS A TYPICAL STRAIGHT ROD, MADE FROM WOOD.
BUT AFFIXED TO ITS TOP, I AM TOLD, IS A CLEAR, ROUND, CRYSTAL BALL.
A SECRET TECHNIQUE OF SHAROU'S ENCHANT-ERS...
IF I TAKE THESE RUMORS AT FACE VALUE, THEN I BETTER UNDERSTAND PRINCESS ISABELLA'S MYSTERIOUS APPRAISAL...

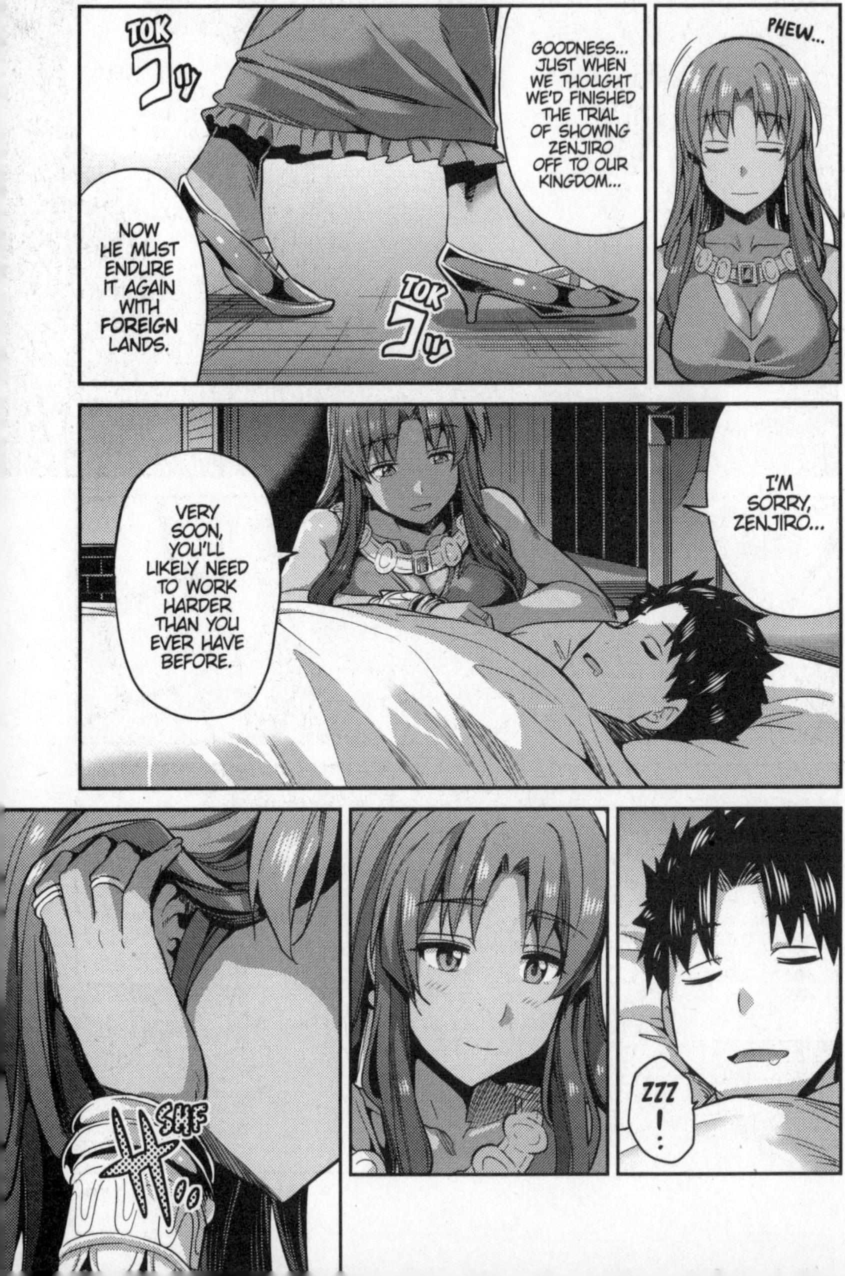
PHEW...
GOODNESS... JUST WHEN WE THOUGHT WE'D FINISHED THE TRIAL OF SHOWING ZENJIRO OFF TO OUR KINGDOM...
NOW HE MUST ENDURE IT AGAIN WITH FOREIGN LANDS.
TOK
フッ
TOK
フッ
I'M SORRY, ZENJIRO...
VERY SOON, YOU'LL LIKELY NEED TO WORK HARDER THAN YOU EVER HAVE BEFORE.
ZZZ
!
SHF

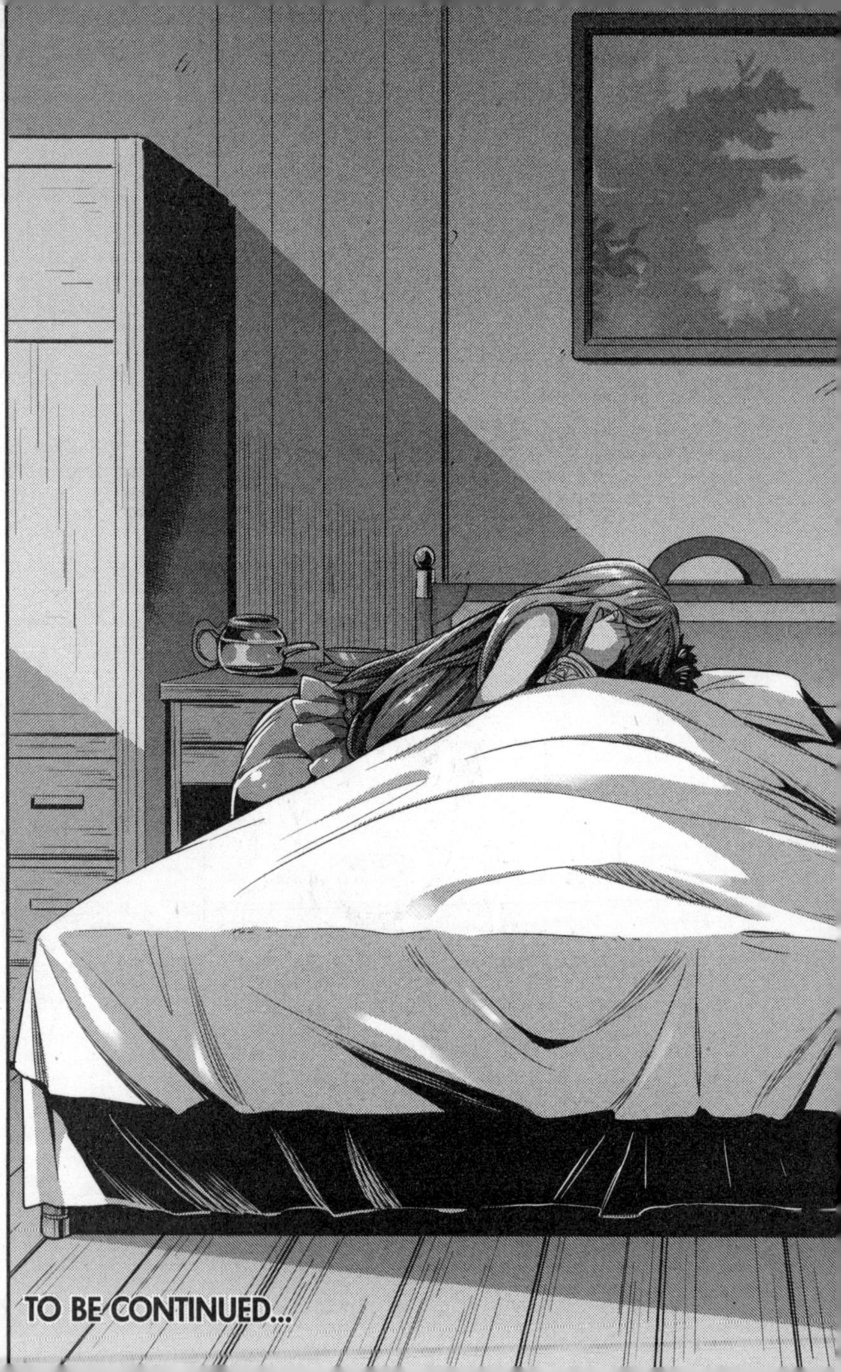
TO BE CONTINUED...

Tsunehiko Watanabe & Neko Hinotsuki
Presents

THE IDEAL SPONGER LIFE

✦ **STAFF** ✦

EMONZU SAKURAI

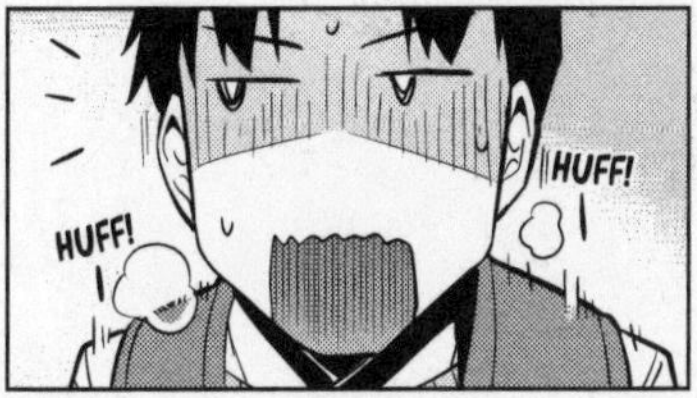
HUFF!
HUFF!

THE IDEAL
SPONGER LIFE

The Girls' After-Party

by: Tsunehiko Watanabe

It was the night of Zenjiro's debut: the party that marked his first appearance in high society.

As prince-consort to Her Highness Queen Aura, ruler of all the country, Zenjiro was the focus of all the night's festivities. After he withdrew, one might assume the party would be over, and that all the nobles would soon disperse.

This was not the case.

Only after Zenjiro's departure would the real event begin—at least for a select few persons privileged enough to be invited. Before long, most of that group was heading to the place where a second party would soon start.

Together, those nobles formed what is known as a political faction.

Now was the perfect time for the leaders of the faction to set the agenda for their party and lay out their plans.

Political factions are—in a word—diverse. Those who create them and those who gather within them are of myriad types and backgrounds.

Throughout the kingdom, there existed numerous such

factions, all vying for political power and influence. Typically, their ranks were bound together by a common interest, such as, say, appreciation of the fine arts.

Fundamentally, political factions made by men tended to be composed of men; those made by women tended to be composed of women. There were factions composed of the entire families of several houses, and by contrast, there were more "domestic" political factions who drew their membership from a single household.

All sorts of factions existed.

Fatima Guillén headed one such faction: The Unmarried Women of the Court.

Soon enough, all the young women of her generation were gathered in a palace chamber for their second party of the night.

"Greetings, everyone! I would like to thank you all for coming tonight. I couldn't prepare anything really special, but I do hope you enjoy yourselves." Speaking from her seat on the sofa, Fatima took a silver goblet full of fruit wine and raised it high.

"Indeed. Thank you for hosting us."

"Thank you for the wine, Lady Fatima."

At the urgings of their leader, the girls sat down and took the silver goblets of wine the maids had prepared for them.

It was late in the evening.

Unlike the main room, lit by dazzling chandeliers, this more intimate chamber was brightened only by five small saucers of oil, set on five tables—one in each corner and one in the center.

The dim light of the oil saucers was just barely enough for those seated to make out each other's faces.

Normally, this was a time where one would be in bed, unable even to see the face of whoever slumbered next to them in the darkness. But gathered here in this room were those who shared the same disposition and the same gender— all of them friends of the same generation.

With so many factors binding them together, it was inevitable that their talk would be bold and direct.

"Say, Lady Fatima… I noticed at the banquet earlier this evening that General Pujol gave you a direct introduction to Lord Zenjiro. Does that mean what I think it means?"

A young lady seated to Fatima's right came right out and slapped that question down. It seemed that everyone in the room had an interest in the topic. Even in the dim light, it felt like all their faces had turned towards Fatima, that all their bodies drew in closer to hear.

Fatima puffed out her thin chest and raised her delicate head.

"Well now… Who knows? After all, I am but a daughter of House Guillén. Everything is up to my brother, the head of our house. If my brother wishes me to marry into the royal family, then I shall. Truthfully, that's all there is to it. My desires are Guillén's desires. I wouldn't have things any other way."

When Fatima finished her straightforward reply, a bright and colorful cheer erupted from all the girls listening. The warmth of their voices seemed to push back the darkness.

"That's our Lady Fatima!"

"You have such wonderful resolve!"

"You need that kind of resolve if you're the young daughter of so great a family as House Guillén."

"I could never be so selfless!"

Now, certainly there were a few self-serving flatterers in there who went a little over the top with their praise, but the girls weren't lying. In that day and age, the act of devoting yourself wholly to your family, as Fatima had, was a virtue that bestowed great honor.

However, all the girls in the room were also well aware that Fatima was obsessed with her brother. A little *too* obsessed. What drove her resolve was a single thought: "I want to be as much help to my beloved brother as I possibly can."

For that reason, though their voices were bright, the stares aimed at Fatima through the darkness were rather lukewarm.

Regardless, since the main topic of the party that evening had been Zenjiro's debut, the conversation naturally gravitated back towards him. Now that he was gone, they could share their candid thoughts.

"For me, it was the first time I've ever seen Lord Zenjiro up close. I was most surprised to see that he was so…petite!"

Once one girl gave her frank opinion, a wave of others followed suit.

"You're right. It's just like he said himself—he hasn't even one drop of a soldier's strength."

"Even if that's true, saying it as publicly as he did seems less than wise. Indeed, anyone assigned to guard or protect him will know they have their work cut out for them."

There was plenty of harsh criticism of Zenjiro that night. The leader of their faction *was* the sister of General Pujol, after all.

"Perhaps he is in poor health—much like King Carlos was?"

"That is a possibility we should consider. If he is sickly, that comes with its own issues. I worry that he and Queen Aura might struggle to conceive a child."

Their comments grew more and more biting. They gave voice to worries and concerns with unladylike bluntness.

"Of course, if he were a normal gentleman, it would be cruel to saddle him with Queen Aura."

"Tell me about it… Her Majesty's personality being what it is. She's good-looking, and she certainly has her charms, but for most men, the thought of accompanying her to bed would be…unpalatable."

"And she's really getting on in years. I know that's unkind to Her Majesty—the reason she put off marriage so long was for the sake of the nation; she was burdened with leadership of the army and government. But to tell the truth…? Something about the whole thing feels *off* to me. I beg your pardons, but the idea of Lord Zenjiro being forced to take on a wife so far beyond marriageable age? I feel a bit sorry for him."

The girls gathered in that room insulted the very Queen to whom they more rightfully owed love and respect.

Of course, no matter how young these girls were, they were still nobles. It's no exaggeration to say that that nobles are always trying to make unsavory rumors bloom.

"Lady Fatima, Lord Zenjiro may indeed be an amateur when it comes to combat, but I think it would be rash to measure his ability by martial prowess alone."

"I agree, Lady Fatima. Pardon my saying so, but in the matter of that gift, General Pujol really got dealt with. When it comes to diplomacy, you shouldn't underestimate Zenjiro."

The ones speaking were the girls seated around Fatima. They were among the most loyal to her position as head of the faction. Just looking at their distance from her in their seating arrangements revealed their loyalty—how closely their views aligned with Fatima's own.

Knowing that they'd always tried to give her the best advice they could, she nodded her head. "You're right. With the way that was handled, everything my brother was trying to accomplish with that plan is now dead and buried. Truth be told, my brother has never been very adept at the nuances of social interactions. But that's precisely why I must follow his lead, no matter what happens."

"That's right, Lady Fatima."

"Ahh, Lady Fatima. You always have such a wonderful way of thinking. I'd expect nothing less."

In truth, Fatima found her brother's lack of social graces exhausting. He made a mountain out of every molehill. Worse, as young as she was, she hadn't enjoyed many opportunities to develop her own diplomatic ability.

Even though she was the daughter of a prominent noble family, she was still just a young girl.

Most of the members of the faction knew how the current topic would play out. The conversation moved on to another area of interest for them. "General Pujol intends to make you Zenjiro's concubine, right? If that's the case, shouldn't you be able to come up with other ways to support the General's intentions?"

"What exactly did you have in mind?"

Seeing her interest, the girls excitedly gave one irresponsible piece of advice after another.

"Well, naturally you should learn about Lord Zenjiro's tastes in things like clothes or jewelry, and learn more about his habits and whatnot."

"Even talking to him seems difficult. Lord Zenjiro said quite clearly that he is not a soldier. Just how are you supposed to talk to a gentleman who thinks like that?"

"It certainly is rare for a nobleman to not be trained in fighting, and Zenjiro isn't even interested in it."

"Perhaps it would be better to think about it as *observing* him, rather than speaking with him?"

"That's right. If you can't talk to him yet, then first, you should study him. Make sure not to take your eyes off him!"

Seeing how the girls of the faction seemed to be amusing themselves at her expense, Fatima shrugged her shoulders and indulged in self-recrimination. "Even if you say I should have clothes and jewelry made, after all, I am how you see me—far too thin."

Tall and slender as she was, Fatima was graced with good looks, and as with most beautiful young women, she had a good sense of style. Fatima took great pride in that. However, at the same time, because of her tall yet petite frame, there were very few clothing options that fit her narrow body.

She had style, but her bosom was lacking. Clothes that accentuated the bust didn't look good on her. Yet at the same time, she was so tall that clothes made to bring out one's cute side seemed a complete mismatch.

It was at this time that a girl without a seat came to Fatima's aid.

"Naturally, it's important to bring out your most beautiful features, Lady Fatima, but if your target is Lord Zenjiro, shouldn't you try to play towards his preferences?"

Seeing Fatima cock her head, like this was some new information of profound importance, the girl elaborated.

"Well, it turns out that Lord Zenjiro took the effort to bring a piece of women's clothing back with him from his hometown. It was a translucent red evening garment."

A translucent evening garment. Upon hearing those words, the tension between the girls grew the strongest it had been all night.

"I heard about it from my brother. He found it among the things Lord Zenjiro brought with him, and tried to hide it somewhere, but Queen Aura saw him and ended up inadvertently showing everyone what was there."

"That means...well...you know...he brought it for Queen Aura to wear, right?"

"I'm sure he did. In that case, if you were to become his concubine, Lady Fatima, you would have to be ready to wear something like that, too, right?"

"..."

"......"

"........."

Suddenly speechless, the girls all focused their gaze upon Fatima.

She was busy imagining herself wearing a translucent red evening gown while standing in front of a man. "M-Me? ...I...I couldn't. Unthinkable! Inconceivable! It is far too shameful!"

She scoffed and turned her face to the side, sticking up her nose.

Despite the way the dim light shrouded her face, you could almost see how her skin turned the deepest, darkest red.

▼▲ ▼▲ ▼▲ ▼▲ ▼▲ ▼▲

This is Tsunehiko Watanabe, the original author.

I was given the opportunity to write a little short story here.

It features Fatima Gullien, the little sister of General Pujol with a big-time brother complex. She is the first character seeking to become Zenjiro's concubine.

Though actually, she's not trying to become his concubine at all; she's being manipulated behind the scenes by her brother. Her ideal man is her brother. Her ideal marriage partner is also her brother.

I hope you enjoy seeing her forbidden feelings come to light. As of this writing, I'm hard at work on the tenth volume of the light novel series. I would be delighted if all the fans of *The Ideal Sponger Life* continue to enjoy the story.

NEXT SPONGER LIFE

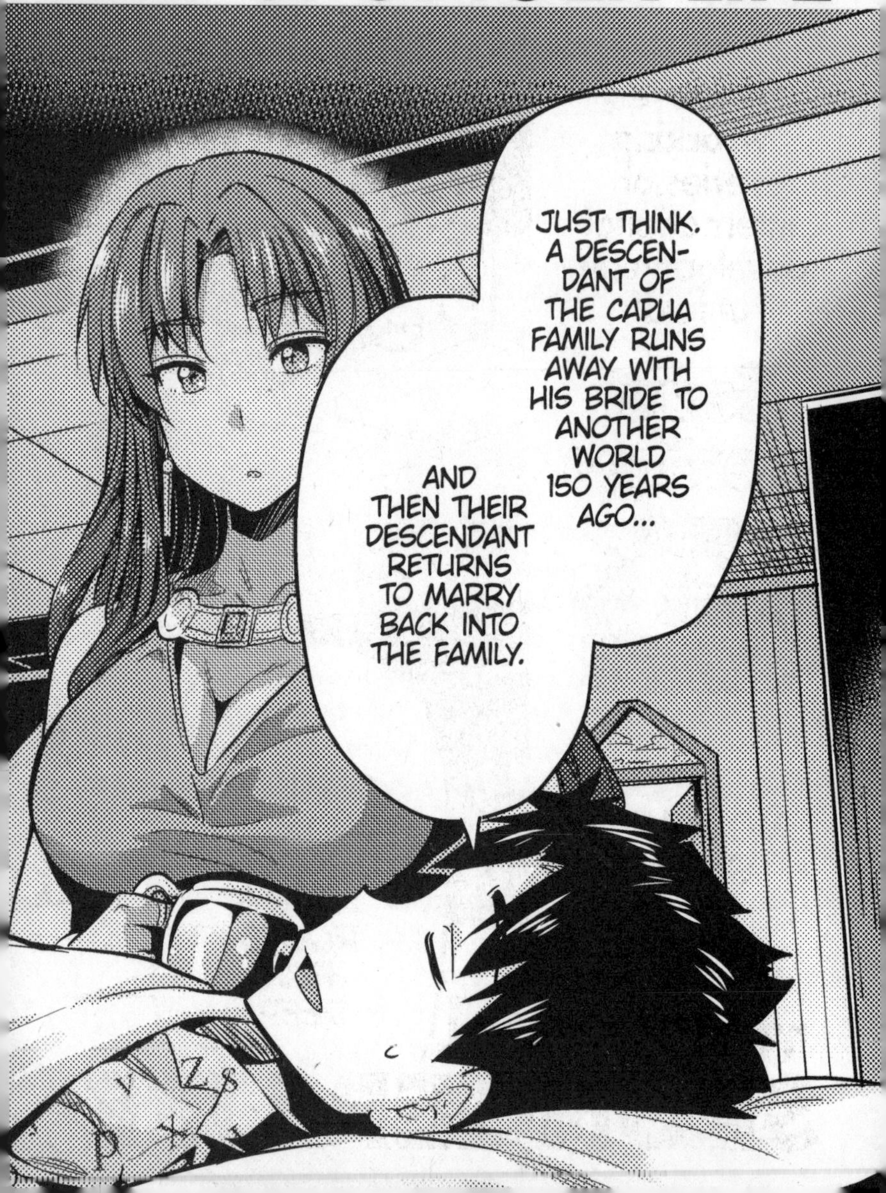
JUST THINK. A DESCEN-DANT OF THE CAPUA FAMILY RUNS AWAY WITH HIS BRIDE TO ANOTHER WORLD 150 YEARS AGO...
AND THEN THEIR DESCENDANT RETURNS TO MARRY BACK INTO THE FAMILY.